Democratic Liberalism in South Africa

Democratic Liberalism in South Africa

Its History and Prospect

Edited by Jeffrey Butler, Richard Elphick, and David Welsh

Wesleyan University Press
Middletown, Connecticut

David Philip, (Pty) Ltd
Cape Town and Johannesburg

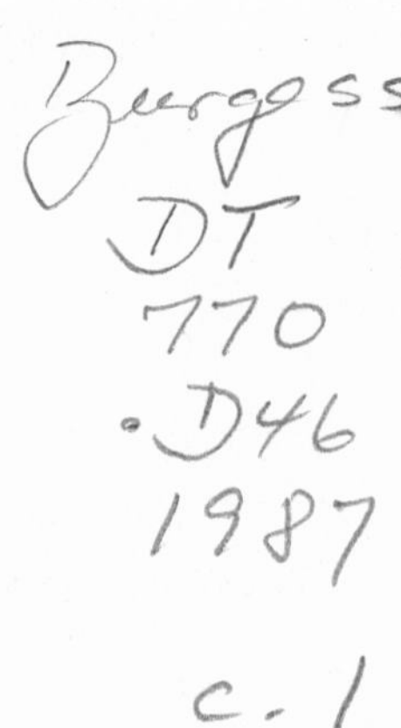

Library of Congress Cataloging-in-Publication Data

Democratic liberalism in South Africa.

Based on a conference held at Houw Hoek, South Africa from June 29 to July 2, 1986.

Includes bibliographies and index.

1. South Africa—Politics and government—Congresses.
2. Liberalism—South Africa—Congresses. I. Butler, Jeffrey. II. Elphick, Richard. III. Welsh, David John.

DT770.D46 1987 320.5'1'0968 87-6071

ISBN 0-8195-5165-1

ISBN 0-8195-6197-5 (pbk.)

ISBN 0-86486-085-4 (pbk.)

All inquiries and permissions requests should be addressed to the Publisher, Wesleyan University Press, 110 Mt. Vernon Street, Middletown, Connecticut 06457.

Published in Southern Africa by David Philip Publisher (Pty) Ltd., 217 Werdmuller Centre, Claremont, 7735, South Africa

Distributed by Harper & Row Publishers, Keystone Industrial Park, Scranton, Pennsylvania 18512.

Manufactured in the United States of America

First Edition

Wesleyan Paperback, 1987

Contents

Preface

In the spring of 1985 we designed the conference on which this book is based and issued invitations to a number of scholars who had recently done sustained research on aspects of the liberal tradition in South Africa. To our great regret we were unable to obtain papers from black scholars.

The conference was funded by the Chairman's Fund of the Anglo-American Corporation; by the Mobil Public Affairs Department; by the Group Public Affairs Department of the Standard Bank Investment Corporation; and by the Public Policy Institute, University of Cape Town. The American Council of Learned Societies and Wesleyan University met the travel expenses of Jeffrey Butler and Richard Elphick.

Colin Campbell, the president of Wesleyan University, and Stuart Saunders, the vice-chancellor of the University of Cape Town, both lent practical and moral support to the conference and were present for some of the proceedings. The Board of Trustees of Wesleyan University lowered the cost of the book through a generous subvention.

Jean Mullins was responsible for supervising all the practical aspects of the project—before, during, and after the conference. Her efficiency reassured the convenors in time of trial and freed them to concentrate on the substance of the conference. She was assisted at the conference by a Wesleyan student, Elizabeth Buss.

The following scholars participated in the conference in addition to those whose papers appear in this book: Colin Bundy, Wilmot James, Merle Lipton, Ian Macdonald, André Odendaal, Michael O'Dowd, and Maynard Swanson. As chairs and critics they immeasurably improved the quality of the conference and hence that of the book. Jane Hofmeyr, who was present at the conference as a critic, agreed to meet unyielding deadlines and wrote a postconference paper that plugs a gap in the proceedings.

The conference placed heavy burdens on the efficient and helpful secretarial staff of the Department of Political Studies at the University of Cape Town, Sue Cassingham, Janet Sandell and Sharol van der Poll. During the preparation of the manuscript for publication, similar burdens fell to the History Department and the College of Social Studies at Wesleyan. Karen Gadomski, Catherine Race-George, Donna Scott, and Frances Warren produced accurate work under enormous pressure. We thank them all.

Finally, all authors of this book (the editors included) are indebted to John Anderson for meticulous copy-editing. Jeannette Hopkins, Director of the Wesleyan University Press, read every chapter, drawing our attention to jargon, obfuscations, and repetitions. The editors are honored to have worked with her.

Jeffrey Butler
Richard Elphick
Middletown, Connecticut

David Welsh
Cape Town

March 4, 1987

Editors and Authors

Editors

Jeffrey Butler	Professor of History, Wesleyan University, Middletown, Connecticut
Richard Elphick	Professor of History, Wesleyan University, Middletown, Connecticut
David Welsh	Professor of Southern African Studies, University of Cape Town

Authors

Heribert Adam	Professor of Sociology and Anthropology, Simon Frazer University, Vancouver, British Columbia
Sean Archer	Senior Lecturer in Economics, University of Cape Town
Norman Bromberger	Senior Lecturer in Economics, University of Natal, Pietermaritzburg
Rodney Davenport	Professor of History, Rhodes University, Grahamstown
Johan Degenaar	Professor of Political Philosophy, University of Stellenbosch
John Dugard	Professor of Law and Director, Centre for Applied Legal Studies, University of the Witwatersrand, Johannesburg
André du Toit	Professor of Political Studies, University of Cape Town
Hermann Giliomee	Professor of Political Studies, University of Cape Town
Jane Hofmeyr	Educational Consultant, Mobil Foundation, Johannesburg

Kenneth Hughes	Senior Lecturer in Mathematics, University of Cape Town
Douglas Irvine	Head of the Department of Political Studies, University of Natal, Pietermaritzburg
Phyllis Lewsen	Former Associate Professor of History, University of the Witwatersrand, Johannesburg
A. S. Mathews	James Scott Wylie Professor of Law, University of Natal, Durban
Jill Nattrass	Professor of Development Studies, University of Natal, Durban
Christopher Saunders	Associate Professor of History, University of Cape Town
Lawrence Schlemmer	Director, Centre for Applied Social Sciences, University of Natal, Durban
Deryck Schreuder	Challis Professor of History, University of Sydney
Gerald Shaw	Associate Editor, *The Cape Times*, Cape Town
Charles Simkins	Senior Lecturer in Economics, University of Cape Town
F. Van Zyl Slabbert	Former leader of the Progressive Federal Party, Political Consultant, Cape Town
David Yudelman	Senior Research Associate, Centre for Resource Studies, Queen's University, Kingston, Ontario

Terminology and Abbreviations

South African terminology is a minefield for the unwary; virtually all terms used to identify groups have caused offense at some time or other. In this book the four "racial" groups legally and conventionally defined in South Africa are normally referred to as "black" or "African"; "white"; "colored"; and "Asian." Today "black" is also frequently used as a synonym for the unacceptable "non white," to refer collectively to Africans, coloreds, and Asians. Some papers follow this usage; the meaning should be clear from the context. In quotations we preserve the terms used by contemporaries.

The South African "reserves" are closely analogous to American Indian reservations. They are areas of occupation and ownership for Africans (formerly "Natives") only. They were defined particularly in the Natives Land Act (1913) and the Native Trust and Land Act (1936), and after the National party victory in 1948, they became known officially as "Bantustans" or "homelands."

The following abbreviations are used in the text:

- ACVV: Afrikaanse Christelike Vroue Vereniging (Afrikaans Women's Christian Union)
- ANC: African National Congress
- APO: African Political Organization
- AZACTU: Azanian Confederation of Trade Unions
- AZAPO: Azanian Peoples Organization
- COSATU: Confederation of South African Trade Unions
- CUSA: Council of Unions of South Africa
- DRC: Dutch Reformed Church
- FOSATU: Federation of South African Trade Unions
- HSRC: Human Sciences Research Council
- NF: National Front
- NP: National Party
- PAC: Pan Africanist Congress
- PFP: Progressive Federal Party

SAAN: South African Associated Newspapers
UDF: United Democratic Front
UP: United Party
UWUSA: United Workers Union of South Africa

Democratic Liberalism in South Africa

Jeffrey Butler, Richard Elphick, and David Welsh

Editors' Introduction

This book is the product of a conference held at Houw Hoek, near Cape Town, South Africa, from 29 June to 2 July 1986. Many participants were active in South African public life and in current debates, on and off campuses, but all were scholars who had done intensive research or analysis on the liberal tradition in South Africa. A newspaper editor and a former politician among them were invited in their capacity as scholars.

As the title of the book indicates, the editors prefer to call the subject of the conference "democratic liberalism" to emphasize how the concept of liberalism has evolved from earlier eras when South African "liberals," for all their courageous denunciation of injustice, often recoiled from a fully democratic South Africa. To be "liberal" in South Africa is to demand limitations on the power of government, holding it to strict adherence to the rule of law and demanding protection of minorities, individuals, and nongovernmental entities like the press. And to be "democratic" is to insist unambiguously on a universal franchise, exercised in free and open elections for the country's rulers, and hence to insist on black preponderance in government. However, no attempt has been made to distinguish systematically between "liberalism" and "democratic liberalism" as used by the various authors. The context should indicate which phase of the tradition is indicated.

Most of the participants, including the editors, would call themselves democratic liberals and hoped that the conference would enhance the long-term chances of a democratic liberal outcome of the South African crisis. They also had three more immediate goals: (1) to clarify the history of liberal institutions and ideas in South Africa, (2) to rethink the liberal tradition in the light of current South African realities, and (3) to reflect on the best strategies for furthering the democratic liberal cause in the present crisis. Though they reached a wide measure of agreement on some issues, they disagreed on others; no resolutions were discussed at the conference, nor votes taken. Other participants, while sharing many of the aspirations of the democratic liberal tradition, would not identify themselves with it; their critical perspectives were invaluable to the conference.

In this introduction the editors highlight a few of the themes found in the following chapters and a few of the propositions that commanded considerable support among many of the conferees. They do not imply that any of their views necessarily represent those of all or even a majority of the conferees. The reader must consider the argument of each chapter on its own.

The first part of the book reflects one of the conference's three themes: the history and character of the liberal tradition in South Africa. For many outside South Africa the tradition hardly exists: few overseas admirers of Alan Paton's novels, or of Helen Suzman's long battle for justice in the South African Parliament, inquire about the origins of their liberalism. Within South Africa, "liberalism" has been a bugbear for many generations, particularly among Afrikaner nationalists, more recently among Marxist critics at English-speaking universities, and also among many black leaders. Because of the widespread suspicion of liberalism in South Africa, the tradition has been largely defined by its enemies, not by its friends. The editors convened the Houw Hoek conference to clarify the record on what liberals had actually done and advocated in South Africa—not to extol a sacrosanct tradition but to acknowledge its deficiencies and to rework it. The characterizations of liberalism which emerged from their discussions frequently diverged from those in the antiliberal literature.

South African liberalism, like liberalism elsewhere, has been centrally concerned with freedom. However, participants generally rejected the notion that liberals in South Africa were concerned solely with the freedom of the individual. While many South African liberals have vigorously defended individuals against unjust laws and abusive administration, they have rarely been animated by an atomistic view of society; nor have they always believed that only individuals have value, and hence rights. Under the influence of Christianity and social humanitarianism, much liberal thinking and action has been concerned with the re-creation of communities shattered by industrialization, urbanization, and apartheid, and with the defense of groups, ethnic and other, that have been objects of discrimination. A valid outgrowth of South African liberalism is, therefore, "affirmative action" (discrimination to compensate for past discriminations), for which a rationale based on John Rawls's *Theory of Justice* is provided in Charles Simkins's chapter in this book. Equally characteristic of South African democratic liberal thinking has been the defense of private institutions threatened by the state. South African liberals have long prized the degree to which the press, business, the judiciary, and more recently the universities have maintained their autonomy from the state. They have been convinced that only a society with multiple centers of power can withstand the pressures for authoritarianism endemic in South African society.

Many members of the conference drew attention to another aspect of South African liberalism that is often obscured by its critics—its strong emphasis on humane values that transcend the usual realm of political ideology. This moral tradition (its critics call it moralistic) is rooted in the close historical ties between South African liberalism and activist Christianity explored in a chapter by Richard Elphick. Religious and humanistic values continue to inspire many South African liberals today and have shaped several distinctive strands of their traditions: a reliance on altruism as a force for social renewal (an altruism which, when practiced by white liberals in relationship to blacks, has often descended into paternalism); an optimism about the regenerative and healing possibilities of history, despite much distressing evidence to the contrary; an emphasis on fair play and ethical behavior in politics; a reluctance to agree that the end can ever justify the means; and a confidence that education and religion based on liberal values can shape a moral, well-informed, and democratically minded citizenry. None of the authors believe that these views and attitudes are held by all liberals, or in equal measure; but most would assert that a definition of South African liberalism that focuses exclusively on political institutions neglects the deeper roots of the tradition—an optimistic assessment of the human condition and its long-term prospects.

Many of the essays deal with a central puzzle in the definition of South African liberalism—its relation to capital and capitalism. In the 1930s, Afrikaner nationalists saw liberalism in race relations as, among other things, a veiled assertion of the greed of "Anglo-Jewish capital." Recent Marxist enemies of South African liberalism have asserted a liberal-capitalist connection, albeit in more sophisticated terms. Martin Legassick, for example, has asserted that "ideologically and institutionally . . . liberals acted to reproduce the particular racially differentiated structures of South African capitalism."[1]

1. Martin Legassick, "Race, Industrialisation and Social Change in South Africa: The

In fact, direct links between liberalism and specific economic or political interests have, for the most part, been tenuous. Merle Lipton has recently noted that South African manufacturing interests, which have long had strong objections to segregation and apartheid, have ordinarily been animated by economic interest, not by liberal sympathies. No significant business group supported the Liberal party when it was formed in 1952.[2] True, in recent times the ties between business and the Progressive (later Progressive Federal) party have been much stronger; there is a substantial body of sentiment in big business that is liberal in a classic economic sense, but also liberal in its commitment to a nonracial democracy. For several authors of the book, such attitudes offer grounds for cautious hope for a democratic liberal outcome in South Africa.

In tracing the origins of South African liberalism in the nineteenth-century Cape Colony, Rodney Davenport also rejects the notion that liberalism was merely a reflection of interest-group politics and shows how it derived its strength from the power of the British Colonial Office and from the widespread prestige of liberal views among various English-speaking and African elites. André du Toit develops the little-known fact that liberalism also enjoyed an efflorescence among Afrikaners influenced by Victorian values of progress and rationalization. But liberals were always a minority and, with the unification of South Africa in 1910, they lacked a power base in the overwhelmingly white electorate both locally and nationally. However, one important group of liberals, the activist Christians, had a substantial institutional base in the humanitarian and educational enterprises they administered. Many liberal-minded reformers were also active on the local level throughout the Union, though with only minimal effect, as illustrated in Jeffrey Butler's study of liberalism in the small town of Cradock. From the 1920s to the election of the present Nationalist government in 1948, a small number of prominent white liberals found a niche in official structures of the Union, as administrators, as elected representatives of Africans, and even in one case as a cabinet minister; here they relied on the moral force of their arguments to mitigate the effects of white domination of Africans—a story told in the chapter by Phyllis Lewsen. During this era probably more Africans than whites were active liberals. In 1952, after the beginning of the apartheid era, a Liberal party was formed with many African members and some African leaders. The

Case of R. F. A. Hoernlé," *African Affairs* 75, 299 (1976), p. 237. Legassick's critique of liberalism has since been broadened and modified, most notably by Paul Rich, *White Power and the Liberal Conscience: Racial Segregation and South African Liberalism* (Johannesburg: Ravan, 1984).

2. Merle Lipton, *Capitalism and Apartheid: South Africa, 1910–84* (Aldershot: Gower/Maurice Temple Smith, 1985), pp. 139, 293.

white electorate, however, never elected a single member of the party to public office. Its activities, generally outside the realm of white parliamentary politics, continued the pre-apartheid tradition of publicizing and protesting injustices, and it cooperated with Africans in forming new strategies of resistance. A short history of the Liberal party is found in the chapter by Douglas Irvine.

Liberalism in South Africa is not a mere extension of the nineteenth-century free-market liberalism of continental Europe. It cannot be understood chiefly in terms of the interests of specific business groups or even in terms of capitalism itself. It is a broad, varied, and pragmatic tradition. An attachment to private ownership in the economy is not a defining value of the tradition, but rather a secondary value rooted in the conviction that private ownership will tend to foster the liberal values of freedom, equality, prosperity, and justice. Most South African liberals have indeed favored free markets and private ownership of much of the economy, or have taken such institutions for granted. But because democratic liberals have been committed primarily to freedom and justice, a number have advocated restraints on capitalism in the South African context. For example, the Liberal party in the early 1960s evolved in a social democratic direction. Such an emphasis resurfaces here in essays by Sean Archer and Jill Nattrass arguing for a mixed economy or participatory capitalism as the best basis for a democratic liberal South Africa.

While the conjunction of the two words "democratic" and "liberal" best explains the aspirations expressed here, this has not always been true of the whole of the South African liberal tradition. In the past, many liberals in South Africa, as in Europe, have shrunk from full democracy out of fear that the majority would subvert liberal values; hence they have defined themselves as reasonable people occupying the middle ground between implacable extremes. This position has resulted in part from the Christian emphasis on peace-making and reconciliation, in part from the fact that many liberals were English-speaking whites with weak connections to the contending forces of Afrikaner and African nationalism, and in part from the comfortable and vulnerable middle-class status of most liberals, blacks included. One outcome of liberals' identification with the middle ground has been their emphasis on compromise and accommodation, and the adoption of stands that seem conservative from today's perspective. There is, as we shall see below, debate among the authors about the wisdom of maintaining the traditional liberal position in the middle. But despite disagreement on this strategic issue, there is no support among the authors for defining liberalism as anything short of democracy based on a universal franchise. Liberalism, if it is to survive in South Africa, must align itself with the democratic aspirations of blacks and with their determination to end several centuries of wrong.

Democracy is in itself an elusive concept; totalitarian regimes of Eastern Europe employ the term as readily as democratic liberals in Europe and America. The word "liberalism" is therefore not dispensable: it affirms the rights of individuals, of minorities, and of institutions against the power of the state; it asserts freedom of speech and assembly; and above all, it affirms the rule of law, the insistence that no governmental official is above the law which is ultimately created and sustained by the people's will.

Parts II and III of the book are concerned with liberal theory of South Africa, past and present. Throughout most of South African history, liberals have had to contend against counterideologies of the right—nationalist, racist, conservative, even fascist. Now, however, the main theoretical and practical challenge comes from the left, and the essays here, while not ignoring Afrikaner nationalism, grapple largely with positions recently advanced by Marxists.

Among the most influential liberals in the twentieth century have been scholars—mostly historians, anthropologists, and economists—whose work has always been critical of the South African status quo. Nonetheless, the Marxist school, which arose in the 1970s, launched a vigorous attack on the liberal corpus, an attack so successful that Marxist characterizations of liberal scholarship are now widely accepted as true, even among scholars whose own values are, broadly speaking, liberal.

The early Marxist critique of liberal scholarship maintained, following Martin Legassick, that liberal writers had blamed the South African racial order on Afrikaner Calvinism, and on the ignorance, isolation, and embattlement of Afrikaners on the frontier. It was also argued that liberals had presented British imperialism as an enlightened counterforce to these influences. While it is true that early liberals were uncritically pro-British, the later liberal writers in, for example, such a major synthetic work as the *Oxford History of South Africa* (1969, 1971) were not. Marxists further characterized liberals as determinists who believed that capitalism and institutionalized racism were incompatible and that economic development would, therefore, inevitably end the irrationalities of apartheid. Such themes were, in fact, minor in the writings of liberals in all eras, as the chapters by Christopher Saunders and by Jeffrey Butler and Deryck Schreuder show. The rare appearance of such determinist views in liberal writings was rooted in a progressive and optimistic view of history, a point of convergence, not of conflict, between liberals and Marxists. Liberals were far more concerned to develop social science models for studying poverty and other South

African social problems (e.g., W. M. Macmillan); to see South Africa in the context of larger historical processes (e.g., C. W. de Kiewiet); and to give voice to African actors in history (as in the "Africanist" liberal work of the 1960s and 1970s pioneered by Leonard Thompson).

In a theoretical characterization of liberal scholarship, Richard Elphick argues that it has lacked a "paradigm" analogous to the Marxist, that it has been pluralist by conviction, and that it has been committed to no causal model and has affirmed no single process as fundamental to South African history. It nonetheless has had a unity resting on common political allegiances, on a critical stance toward the colonial state and its white-dominated successors, and on a thirst for freedom and justice. Several contributors explicitly or implicitly argue that liberals should make a virtue of their theoretical pluralism, using it as a basis for developing new liberal perspectives.

It is not the purpose of this introduction to exaggerate the differences between Marxist and liberal perspectives. However, notwithstanding numerous areas of common aspiration and theoretical agreement, significant differences remain. Part of the power of the Marxist analysis of South Africa derives from its ability to treat all aspects of South African reality within the holistic vision of the political economy. To non-Marxists the danger of the Marxist vision is that one pattern, the "capitalist relations of production" or the class structure, tends constantly to be brought into relief, so that all of the distressing features of South African society—racism, human exploitation, inequality, poverty—are repeatedly attributed to "capitalism." This attribution, more often than not, derives more from the model itself than from argumentation or evidence.

In this volume David Yudelman gives theoretical and empirical grounds for denying that the state (by which he means the administrative bureaucracy as well as the government) should be conceived as subordinate to the dominant, capitalist, class. Rather, he argues that the state and capital form two relatively autonomous spheres each with its own interests, spheres which in South Africa have entered into a long-standing symbiotic relationship.

Two other chapters also begin from a pluralist perspective, in that they assume that capitalism is only one of several forces in South African society; they attempt to assess its import for the development of the racial hierarchy (David Welsh) and for the genesis of poverty or underdevelopment (Norman Bromberger and Kenneth Hughes). Arguing that racism and ethnocentrism are more salient than class interest in most societies, Welsh demonstrates that in South Africa the present racial categories long antedate the development of the class system of modern capitalism. Capitalism did not create South African racism;

rather it adapted to it, and profited from it, fitting a class structure upon a racial hierarchy. Bromberger and Hughes similarly argue against the holist model in assessing the contribution of capitalism to the poverty of South African blacks. Like Yudelman, they stress the role of the state. They distinguish between the direct influence of the capitalist system in the creation of poverty and the indirect role played by capitalists in influencing the state; then they distinguish both from the actions of the state prompted by noncapitalist interests. They conclude that the noncapitalist interests are the most significant. Both Welsh and Bromberger-Hughes rely on comparisons with other capitalist societies in order to avoid the trap of assuming that because South Africa is capitalist, capitalism is therefore chiefly responsible for all features of South Africa. Nonetheless, they, like most authors in the book, have no difficulty in acknowledging that there has been extensive exploitation in South Africa, or that capitalists have profited from the country's pervasive racism.

Not all the conceptual problems of the liberals derive from the Marxist challenge. This book addresses two problems inherent in the liberal emphasis on freedom, problems apparent in Western countries but much intensified in South Africa: the problem of equality (urgently important to blacks and other long exploited groups) and the problem of group rights (which concerns Afrikaners most explicitly, but potentially other South Africans as well). Addressing the first issue, Charles Simkins notes that liberals insist on equal opportunities for all members of society, but not equality in their final attainments and possessions, which would require conformity among individuals and infringements on freedom. But in South Africa, considering the blatant inequalities of opportunity and consequent exploitation that have existed for centuries, does not liberalism require compensation to the victims as, for example, provided by "affirmative action," in the United States? Or would such compensation imperil freedom, above all freedom of property? Simkins expounds two possible liberal positions on this issue, choosing for himself the Rawlsian, or "affirmative action," option.

Liberalism has always been concerned with the rights of minorities. Johan Degenaar tackles the related issue of ethnic rights, obviously of interest in a multicultural society like South Africa, but also highly suspect because of the misuse of the concept by the South African government in the service of white domination. Can a new South Africa enshrine guarantees for ethnic groups (e.g., Afrikaners) and still be a democratic liberal state? Many liberals would deny it, but Degenaar argues that ethnic rights are compatible with a liberal democracy provided certain conditions are fulfilled, principal among them the right freely to associate, or not to associate, with an ethnic group, a freedom denied by the whole theory and practice of the current South African policy of separate development.

The chapters in parts IV and V attempt to clarify the opportunities and perils for liberals in the present South African crisis. South African liberals have been accused of being both strong and weak—as members of the establishment complicit in maintaining apartheid and as peripheral idealists with no political constituency and a long record of failure in producing reform. Both assertions are partly true. At the moment there are relatively few self-defined liberals among Afrikaners and Africans, the two principal contenders for power in South Africa, and hence liberals are likely to remain on the margins of formal political power, as they have always been in South Africa. In this regard, Hermann Giliomee considers reformist (*verligte*) trends among Afrikaner nationalists and concludes that verligtes cannot be regarded as liberals, since they are determined to maintain both Afrikaner dominance and the division of society on racial lines.

Counterbalancing the weakness of liberals in formal politics, however, is their disproportionate presence in powerful and prestigious institutions important both to the present government and to any black-dominated successor. This presence, while laying liberals open to the charge of conservatism, already gives them an influential voice in the management of several sectors of society, a voice which might attain political prominence in negotiations for a new South Africa. These institutions, conduits of liberal values to citizens who would never describe themselves as liberals, attract attention and support from the outside world. Among the Houw Hoek papers are analyses of four sectors of South African society where liberal values are actually or potentially present: the legal profession and judiciary, the press, education, and business. Other areas, not considered here, are the churches and voluntary social organizations.

Two papers on civil liberty and the rule of law (by John Dugard and A. S. Mathews) and one paper on the English-language press (by Gerald Shaw) describe liberal institutions that have long fought rearguard actions against restriction by an authoritarian government. As the conference convened, new restrictions on civil liberties and freedom of the press were being imposed, and many others have followed since. In both cases, however, the authors suggest that (in the long if not the short run) resistance by liberal institutions has had some successes—liberal values have been widely disseminated thereby among the South African public. Groups other than whites now make up a large proportion of the readers of the English press, and blacks, both radicals and "moderates," still look to the courts and to liberal civil-rights organizations for some measure of protection against arbitrary government action. Moreover, Dugard traces unmistakable signs of the growth of rule-of-law notions in the Afrikaner legal establishment, most notably in the strong interest in a bill of rights—a development which he attributes to the dogged advocacy of liberal jurists and legal scholars.

Sadly, and typically of liberal experience, liberals in the law and the press, like scholars in the academic world, having spent decades fighting off encroachments from the right, must now wheel around to face an attack from the left. Leftists argue that the rule of law is a means of preserving the privileges of the dominant classes and that the associated idea of individual and minority rights is designed to protect whites against the full force of democracy under majority rule. Similarly, it is said that the English press is a mouthpiece of the capitalist interests that own it. Mathews and Shaw argue that these charges are fallacious. The rule of law, says Mathews, merely refers to the requirement that government itself is under law and that individuals and other entities have rights over against government; it must be distinguished from the actual content and implementation of law, which in fact is often oppressive, particularly in South Africa. As for the press, editors of English papers have had great independence from interference by owners; but even if there is some general correspondence between the views of owners and editors, a newspaper dependent on profits is more strongly constrained by the views of its readers, who are now largely black. The defense of the formerly free press in South Africa is based on its independence from government, on its demonstrated courage in investigating abuses, and on its capacity to build bridges of understanding among South Africa's citizens.

Chapters on education and business (respectively by Jane Hofmeyr and Heribert Adam) concentrate on the desirability of liberals making common cause with the black majority of South Africans. Liberally inclined missionaries and teachers once dominated the educational system for Africans, but as a result of a government takeover since the 1950s, liberal influence in the primary and secondary educational system (as opposed to the universities) is minimal. Hofmeyr argues that those South African educational ideals and practices that the left denounces as "liberal" are typically conservative; a truly liberal education would be designed to shape a just, non-racial society of self-confident, critically aware, and autonomous citizens. She suggests that such a philosophy converges with strands of radical educational thought; and that liberal bodies and institutions can play an important role in experiments in alternative education so long as liberals are prepared to identify with the black struggle and forgo all attempts to dominate projects initiated by others. Similarly, Adam argues for a convergence of interest between business and both black unions and the African

National Congress, both of which he sees as essentially nationalist rather than Marxist, and as pragmatic and open to alliances.

Business is of course far more powerful than most liberal educational organizations, but it is also less liberal. A strategy designed to save capitalism in South Africa could be rooted in other than liberal aspirations or eventuate in other than liberal solutions. As Adam notes, an alliance between business and the South African government in the interests of stability could have dire consequences both for capitalism and liberal democracy. In this Adam gets indirect support from two economists, Sean Archer and Jill Nattrass, who explore ways in which the survival of capitalism may be compatible with democratic liberal values in general, and with the aspirations of blacks for economic justice in particular. Archer starts with the Freedom Charter, the most revered document of the black struggle, and shows that its aspirations for political freedom and economic justice are most compatible with a mixed economy that maintains a large measure of market pricing and a variety of forms of ownership. Reviewing the economic history of centrally planned, nonmarket economies, he notes that admirable growth rates in early stages of industrialization have been followed by stagnation, inefficiency, and public cynicism.

As noted earlier, most authors here do not regard capitalism as the core of liberalism, but many agree that it would best produce the wealth needed for a just society in South Africa and limit the ability of government to trample on human rights. The essential points of capitalism, on this view, are that market pricing mechanisms not be subordinated to government planning and that government ownership and control of the economy should be balanced by considerable private ownership. However, in a society like South Africa with a massive need to right past wrongs, significant future government intervention to assure redistribution of wealth is unavoidable and desirable. Nattrass suggests in her chapter a number of ways in which government could direct the economy to socially desirable ends without destroying the market or infringing on private ownership, as well as means by which workers and community people could be brought into both the ownership and control of enterprises, to increase democracy at local levels.

These essays imply, then, that liberal values should have considerable appeal among the black majority in South Africa, the collective victims of a highly illiberal society. In making their case, liberals must combat distortions of their values propagated by the left, above all the false notions that laissez-faire capitalism is the central liberal value, and that to insist on the rule of law is to limit democracy or perpetuate injustice. They must, moreover, align themselves firmly with the aspiration for freedom of their black fellow citizens—while retaining the right to argue for distinctively liberal notions—and must articulate liberal positions that balance equality and freedom.

There are obvious tensions within this approach. Liberals have reasonable grounds for fearing that a revolution in South Africa might be catastrophically violent and yet fail to create an effective successor regime; on the other hand, they need to identify with an aggrieved people who have little choice but to take the revolutionary route. Liberals have long played a useful role in mediating between white and black, and now must consider abandoning that role for identification with forces which may repudiate them whatever they do. These problems are reflected in the last two chapters in the book, by Lawrence Schlemmer and F. van Zyl Slabbert. Both papers assess the difficult position of liberals in a polarizing society. And both explicitly or implicitly assert that liberals' allegiance must be to those who demand a fundamental redistribution of power. However, the papers diverge in other respects. Schlemmer assumes that a liberal order will most likely emerge from a process of negotiation, in which one party will be the Nationalist government. He discerns trends in South African society favorable to a liberal outcome and urges liberals to encourage them, by appealing both to the government and to blacks. By implication he assumes that the intermediary role is still available for at least some liberals, and that they should work for nonrevolutionary change in South Africa. By contrast, Slabbert, who once himself practiced similar strategies while leader of the opposition in the South African Parliament, now argues that a fence-sitting role must be abandoned; however unpalatable the choice for drastic and rapid change, liberals must make it.

The conference that led to this book was held during the most serious crisis ever faced by the South African state. Only seventeen days before the conference opened, the government had introduced a state of emergency that ended the tradition of a relatively free press, and severely circumscribed even further the rule of law, freedom of assembly, and judicial review. Never before in South Africa had liberal values seemed more threatened. And never before had the polarization between white and black seemed more severe, or the survival of the middle ground less likely. While black leaders clamored for democracy, some seemed hostile or indifferent to liberal features of democracy designed to forestall tyranny. Whites, by contrast, were coming to appreciate the value of minority safeguards, a bill of rights, and other liberal provisions that might protect them in the future. But they generally resisted democracy, because it would mean a government dominated by blacks.

Consequently the participants were tempted to fear that their project was ill-timed and futile. What possible impact could a group of scholars have when the time for talk and analysis had seemingly passed and when liberals, at that time mostly white, were widely regarded by blacks, and indeed by much of the outside world, as irrelevant? Since the present regime's insistence on racial groups as the basis of politics could easily prompt an equally vehement insistence on ethnic, racial, or class rights by a successor regime, what was the point of liberals insisting on freedom of association and protection of individual rights?

One source of optimism was an ironic by-product of the intractability of the South African crisis. It seemed that the government could never reestablish lasting order among its black subjects, nor could the force of revolution prevail in the immediate future. Yet to some participants it seemed that the present polarization could not be maintained forever; in a prolonged standoff, the contending parties would probably split up, and cross-cutting alliances between blacks, whites, and other groups might form. In such a fragmented and fluid situation, the voice of liberals might yet be influential. Their strong position in academe, business, and the professions meant that they had both expertise and a power base that would be hard to ignore. Moreover, the gradual growth of the middle-class among Afrikaners, Indians, coloreds, and Africans had enlarged the social base that traditionally supports democratic liberal values. Finally, the participants believed that virtually all South Africans had a stake in democratic liberal institutions, since all were potentially members of minorities—not necessarily ethnic minorities, as the present government is fond of saying, but minorities nonetheless. In short, the objective conditions for democratic liberalism were in fact reasonably favorable if one looked at long-term developments. It was the short-term prospects that prompted anxiety: the difficulties of engineering a change of government, of overcoming the polarization between white and black, and of abolishing apartheid without destroying the economy and those liberal institutions already lodged in South African society.

Another source of qualified comfort for democratic liberals was the international context of the South African crisis. While democratic liberal ideals might have relatively few outspoken advocates in South Africa, their prospects elsewhere seemed favorable. The economies and morale of the Western democracies seemed more buoyant than in recent decades; the appeal of communism seemed in decline both in Europe and in most parts of the third world, where a new appreciation of free markets was emerging. Furthermore, political democracy seemed to have widespread support in areas of the world where it had long been absent: in Eastern Europe, in Latin America, the Philippines, and Korea.

In fact, in most regions of the world (Africa being the major exception) the trend seemed to favor democracy, notwithstanding all the economic frustrations of the period, especially in the third world.

Since the early nineteenth century, South African liberals have appealed to the West for political, financial, and moral support. In general, the outside world has given South African liberals enough support to survive, but rarely to prevail. In 1986 it seemed that the commitment of Western churches, unions, universities, and even business to changing South Africa was greater than ever. And the pressures for intervention by governments were mounting to unprecedented heights. Consequently the influence on South Africa of Western values and institutions was not declining, however bleak the prospects appeared to be and however much the government might thumb its nose at its Western enemies. There were two possibilities: The South African government (or its revolutionary successor) could cut itself off increasingly from Western influences, and reaffirm South Africa's distinctively antiliberal traditions. Or South Africans of all political stripes could negotiate a new order, prodded by the economic and political power of the West and inspired by its ideals. The latter possibility enshrined the best hopes for a democratic liberal outcome.

As noted above, the main ideological contender against liberalism is no longer Afrikaner nationalism but Marxism. The massive inequalities in South Africa and the institutionalized exploitation of black labor have made the country amenable to Marxist analysis, and since the First World War, Marxists, including members of the South African Communist party, have been staunch supporters of black liberation. Moreover, many whites and blacks are tempted to espouse Marxism in order to defy the South African government by embracing its favorite source of paranoia. Yet Marxism—whatever its value in analyzing South African history and political economy—does not offer convincing solutions to South African dilemmas. Early in this century, it was understandable that liberal-minded people would turn to Marxism for inspiration, but today, given the record of Marxism in action, it is not. All of the sixteen Marxist-Leninist states in Europe, Asia, and America are one-party states; all have human rights records that range from poor to appalling; all have economies that have been shackled with cumbersome central plans; and none has so far taught us much about the elimination of ethnic prejudice. In Africa, it is true, there are some Marxist-inspired states that are gentler than their Marxist-Leninist counterparts in other parts of the world, but on the whole their economic performance (like that of most but not all capitalist-oriented African states) has not been promising. There is no existing state whose revolution gives plausible grounds for hoping that Marxism has unique insights that will help South Africa realize the goals of freedom, prosperity, and justice enshrined in such documents as the Freedom Charter. Many South Africans of all classes, races, and ethnic affiliations might, given a choice, opt for models of liberal and social democracy taken from the West, rather than totalitarian models from the East or one-party models from Africa. Consequently, it is the job of liberals to argue the advantages of democratic liberalism in season and out.

Thus, if democratic liberals are to have any hope, it must be based on three considerations: the objective interest of all South Africans in a democratic liberal order, the power and prestige of the West, and the failure of authoritarian and Marxist regimes in the third world. This analysis, however, leaves liberals with two daunting tasks. First, South Africans, but particularly Afrikaners and Africans, have to be persuaded that their interests do lie with democratic liberalism rather than with tyrannical shortcuts to their immediate goals. Second, the rest of the world has again to take notice of liberalism in South Africa and stop regarding it as politically irrelevant, as it has in recent years. Perhaps even more crucially, liberals have to recover confidence in themselves and their values in order to communicate these values to their fellow South Africans and the outside world. There is much to be done, and very little time.

The conference—and this book—were conceived in the hopes of advancing the chances of a democratic liberal outcome in South Africa. The editors did not convene the conference because they thought such an outcome certain, or even probable. They did so because they considered the values of freedom and justice worth affirming, even under the most unpromising circumstances; and because they believed in the open and creative possibilities of human history. In the words of Geoffrey Clayton, later the first Archbishop of Cape Town to take a firm stand against the Nationalist government: "When we have done our best, the resources of the universe are not exhausted."[3]

3. Geoffrey Johannesburg to R. F. A. Hoernlé, 25 October 1941, Douglas Smit papers, Albany Museum, Grahamstown.

I

The Liberal Tradition in South African History

Rodney Davenport

1. The Cape Liberal Tradition to 1910

The specific concern of this chapter is to identify the phenomenon of Cape liberalism as it developed before Union in 1910. Liberalism is often thought of as peculiar to the Cape, as distinct from other South African provinces, and therefore by implication indigenous. But our reflections would be badly amiss unless we related it to European liberalism; for Cape liberalism, like Cape Calvinism, was initially an exotic plant. There are European origins of liberal thinking in the four fundamental fields: access to justice in the broadest sense of the term, to freedom of speech, economic freedom, and political rights. One must therefore assess how far Cape thinking and practice in the century or so before 1910 can properly be seen to stem from these older traditions from which liberalism emerged.

Perhaps the deepest of all liberal traditions derives from the legal principles, rooted in classic feudalism, that every person has the rights of access to justice,[1] and of freedom from arrest without speedy trial.[2] This insistence on the legal rights of the individual is summed up in the notion of the "rule of law," which must be seen as an indispensable

1. Magna Carta, cap. 40.

2. See the Roman Dutch interdict *de homine libero exhibendo,* referred to in H. R. Hahlo and E. Kahn, *The Union of South Africa: The Development of Its Laws and Constitution* (Cape Town: Juta, 1960), pp. 137–38, and in C. J. R. Dugard, *Human Rights and the South African Legal Order* (Princeton: Princeton University Press, 1978), p. 351; and the English writ *habeas corpus cum causa,* which was given the force of statute in 1679.

defense against tyranny even though there has been a tendency in left-wing circles to discuss it as a mere "institution of bourgeois society."

The notion of equality before the law was not as deeply rooted as the notion of access to justice, for the inequality of persons was basic both in the Roman law and in Germanic custom, out of which our Western systems grew. Equality before the law was also a particularly hard concept to introduce in societies that had experienced the practice of slave ownership with its built-in inequalities with regard to property, residence, movement, matrimony, and other key areas of life. Furthermore, as critics of the left have pointed out, the formal provision of equality before the law is not in itself sufficient unless distributive justice exists alongside it, assuring that access to justice shall not be much easier for some than it is for others. This is a proposition with which liberals ought to have no difficulty in agreeing, since it firms up rather than weakens the central principle itself.

I have argued elsewhere that the principle of equality before the law did not exist at the Cape during the period of Dutch East India Company rule (1652–1795).[3] The British authorities that first took over in 1795 were clearly aware of the entrenched inequalities at the time of their arrival.[4] But at a time when serious attempts were being made in Britain to humanize the criminal law and reform a brutal penal code, as had begun to happen on the Continent under the Old Regime,[5] a forward movement began in the colonies as well, including the Cape. The slave trade was abolished (1807), and attempts were made to ameliorate the condition of slavery between 1807 and 1834, and to administer the criminal law without respect to personal status.[6] Eventually, serious efforts were made to equalize status as a general principle of law through the abolition of the courts of *landdrost* and *heemraden* (rural courts in effect controlled by local white landholders), through the introduction of jury trials under the Charters of Justice of 1827 and 1832, and through the emancipation of the indigenous Khoikhoi ("Hottentots") under Ordinance 50 of 1828, and with the emancipation of the slaves by imperial legislation between 1833 and 1840.[7]

---

3. *Oxford History of South Africa (OHSA)* 1 (Oxford: Clarendon, 1969), pp. 297–99; but see R. Ross, "The Rule of Law at the Cape of Good Hope in the Eighteenth Century," *Journal of Imperial and Commonwealth History* 9 (1980), pp. 5–16.

4. See G. M. Theal, ed., *Records of the Cape Colony* 9 (Cape Town: Government of Cape Colony, 1901), pp. 143–61.

5. N. Gash, *Mr. Secretary Peel: The Life of Sir Robert Peel to 1830* (London: Longman, 1961), pp. 339–41.

6. I. E. Edwards, *Towards Emancipation* (Cardiff: Gomerian, 1942); J. S. Marais, *The Cape Coloured People* (London: Longman, 1939), pp. 161–78.

7. *OHSA* 1, pp. 300–11.

So much for the legal changes, but what about the practice? It has long been commonly assumed that the emancipation legislation was broadly effective. But doubts have been cast on this assertion. In 1939, J. S. Marais produced evidence to suggest that the legal emancipation of slaves resulted in considerable dislocation and hardship at the Cape, and that this counterbalanced the positive effects of legal freedom once the period of apprenticeship was over. This was a rather different view from that expressed by S. J. du Toit in the early Afrikaans history, *Die Geskiedenis van ons Land,* which asserted that the Good Lord caused it to rain so continuously when apprenticeship ended that most ex-slaves crept meekly back into the service of their erstwhile owners, to the mutual satisfaction of all.[8] We have long been aware of the hostile attitudes of white employers to the free movement of Khoikhoi labor under Ordinance 50 of 1828, but we also need to be reminded of Leslie Duly's evidence that the ordinance was largely inoperable under frontier conditions.[9] Circumstances seem often to have been stronger than legal principle when it came to enforcing equal justice, even though the Cape could boast distinguished administrators of the law like the attorney–general William Porter. The Cape had emerged from the Company period as a society structured upon unequal status groups,[10] and the inequalities lived on in the minds of the dominant and the dominated because they were reinforced in other directions, such as unequal access to land and education.[11]

The Cape Supreme Court was on occasion able to resist the pressures of endemic racialism; two well-known examples are the celebrated "Black Circuit" of 1813, and the judgment of Sir Henry de Villiers in Sigcau's case in 1895. However, they had serious repercussions: the Black Circuit led indirectly to a frontier rebellion.[12] And though de Villiers did administer a heavy rebuke to Cecil Rhodes for detaining Sigcau against the law, and ordered his liberation,[13] after two years the

8. Marais, *Cape Coloured People,* pp. 186–99; S. J. du Toit et al., *Die Geskiedenis van ons Land in die Taal van ons Volk* (Paarl: Paarl Drukkerij, 1877), p. 84.

9. L. C. Duly, "A Revisit with the Cape's Hottentot Ordinance of 1828," in M. Kooy, ed., *Studies in Economics and Economic History: Essays in Honour of H. M. Robertson* (London: Macmillan, 1972), pp. 26–56.

10. R. Elphick and H. Giliomee, eds., *The Shaping of South African Society 1652–1820* (Cape Town: Longman, 1979), pp. 364–65.

11. For the land story, see A. J. Christopher, *The Crown Lands of British South Africa* (Kingston, Ontario: Limestone, 1984), and T. R. H. Davenport and K. S. Hunt, *The Right to the Land* (Cape Town: Philip, 1974), and T. R. H. Davenport, "Some Reflections on the History of Land Tenure in South Africa, seen in the light of attempts by the state to impose political and economic control," *Acta Juridica* (1985): 53–76.

12. E. A. Walker, ed., *The Cambridge History of the British Empire* 8, *South Africa,* 2nd ed. (London: Cambridge University Press, 1963), pp. 217, 290–91.

13. E. A. Walker, *Lord de Villiers and His Times: South Africa 1842–1914* (London: Constable, 1925), pp. 258–60.

Cape Parliament amended the law to regularize such detentions in the Transkei for periods of up to three months.[14]

The real blow came during the Anglo-Boer war, when the creeping paralysis of martial law overcame the judicial institutions of South Africa, including those of Cape Colony. Opinions varied over the extent to which martial law was necessary. The government of William Schreiner was torn apart over it in June 1900, when two members of the cabinet, John X. Merriman and T. N. G. te Water, refused to countenance the disfranchisement of rank-and-file Afrikaner rebels in the colony.[15] James Rose Innes, who at first accepted the need for martial law as attorney general after the fall of the Schreiner ministry, ended by protesting strongly to the military.[16] Arbitrary detentions and restriction orders (including one on Merriman himself), and the summary trials leading in a few cases to summary executions, were a predictable consequence of martial law, which Merriman denounced in the House of Assembly as not really worthy of being called law at all, or at best "the law of Tilly and Wallenstein."[17] It was a moment when white South Africans learned what it was like to be deprived of civil liberties. There were some noteworthy protests, for example those made by the women's movement under the leadership of Olive Schreiner and Marie Koopmans de Wet in 1900.[18] But the experiences were never allowed to become part of the stock-in-trade of public education, and the lessons in that way to become universalized, as they certainly ought to have been; for South African society was later to build its legal system around normative restrictions on movement, resettlement camps, detentions without trial, legislative inequalities of a racial kind, and other practices which the experiences of the Anglo-Boer war ought to have taught the colony to abandon. The spirit and the practice of Cape liberalism had taken hard knocks during the war of 1899–1902, and the introduction of compulsory segregation in the classroom under the School Board Act of 1905 showed how far this tendency had gone.[19]

Access to knowledge, and its necessary extensions, is a liberal principle

14. D. Welsh, "The State President's powers under the Bantu Administration Act," *Acta Juridica* (1968): 84–85.

15. T. R. H. Davenport, *The Afrikaner Bond (1880–1911): The History of a South African Political Party* (Cape Town: Oxford University Press, 1966), pp. 147–48.

16. H. Wright, ed., *Sir James Rose Innes: Selected Correspondence (1884-1902)* (Cape Town: Van Riebeeck Society, 1972), pp. 286–315.

17. *House of Assembly Debates* (1900), pp. 10–13. J. H. Snyman is less harsh in "Rebelle-Verhoor in Kaapland in die Tweede Vryheidsoorlog met spesiale Verwysing na die Militêre Howe," *Archives Year Book for South African History 2* (Pretoria: Government Printer, 1962) chapter 6.

18. Davenport, *Afrikaner Bond,* p. 227.

19. Marais, *Cape Coloured People,* p. 270.

comparable in significance with access to equal justice. It involves the freedom to choose what to read and write, or to hear and say, subject only to the criterion that others should not be wrongfully harmed thereby. It is a reasonably ancient freedom, classically articulated in the second chapter of J. S. Mill's *Essay on Liberty* (1859). The right to express heretical opinions without jeopardy was an indirect gain of the Reformation struggle, though it subsequently had to be won from the protagonists of both sides. It was extended, mainly during the seventeenth, eighteenth, and nineteenth centuries, into the borderland between theology and science, and—as is shown elsewhere in this volume—these issues strongly affected the Cape.[20]

By the late eighteenth century, too, the emergence of periodical journalism on a large scale had cleared the way for the free expression of political opinion in Europe as a whole, though in some parts more than others. In Britain, where freedom of speech had long before been cleared for members of Parliament, the issue of freedom outside Parliament was fought and won in the half-century ending soon after the Napoleonic Wars.[21] A similar battle took place at the Cape at the same time, as a result of the stand taken by George Greig and John Fairbairn against the efforts of Lord Charles Somerset to maintain censorship, and they won their point in 1827 by acquiring the right to publish without a permit, subject only to the law of libel.[22] It would be unhistorical to review the history of the Cape liberal political tradition without mention, at the outset, of this initial clearing of the ground. If it had not happened, the institution of a parliamentary system would not have been possible, for parliamentary government required the continuous communication between legislators and the general public that only a free press can ensure.

Press freedom survived to enliven public life, giving direction and stimulation to the regional conflicts that became a major feature of political life until the 1870s, providing a focus for Afrikaner political and cultural reawakening with the setting up of the Paarl *Drukkerij* (Press) which published *Die Afrikaanse Patriot* from the mid-1870s. Journalism performed the same function for the beginnings of African political activity with the founding of *Imvo Zabantsundu* by Tengo Jabavu in 1884. During the Anglo-Boer war (1899–1902), a number of pro-

20. See pp. 48–63 for André du Toit's discussion of theological controversies at the Cape in the mid-nineteenth century.

21. G. Rudé, *Wilkes and Liberty* (Oxford: Clarendon, 1962); W. H. Wickwar, *The Struggle for the Freedom of the Press, 1819–1832* (London: Allen and Unwin, 1928).

22. *OHSA* 1, pp. 314–17; A. M. L. Robinson, *None Daring to Make Us Afraid: A Study of English Periodical Literature in the Cape Colony from its Beginnings in 1824 to 1835* (Cape Town: Maskew Miller, 1962); H. C. Botha, *John Fairbairn in South Africa* (Cape Town: Historical Publication Society, 1984), pp. 35–62.

Boer newspapers were closed down by the military authorities under the restrictions of martial law; some editors were convicted of seditious libel and imprisoned.[23] War, as already noted, had its own necessities, but public indignation over these actions was enough to suggest that the general concern for the existence of a free press was alive and well. Cape newspapers also successfully resisted two major attempts to limit the powers of representative institutions, one by Governor Sir Philip Wodehouse in the 1860s, the other in 1902 by Sir Alfred Milner (High Commissioner, 1897–1905).[24]

The attitude of liberalism toward economic and political freedom remains to be considered. At the heart of liberal idealism lies a devotion to principles which go beyond, and to some extent are independent of, the simple assertion of rights for their own sake. Liberal thinking carries a deep-seated assumption that a political community is a moral entity—a community, not a mere amalgam of atomistic Hobbesian individuals competing selfishly for rights or power or things. This makes its relationship to political democracy problematic, because it is not easy to balance the "responsible" (community-minded) and the "interested" use of economic or political power. English political tradition insisted that the exercise of power could be made "responsible," in part by insisting that the enfranchised possess qualifications, whether of inherited or acquired expertise, or of an accumulated stake in the system, both of which pulled society in a conservative direction. But increasingly, in Europe from the middle of the eighteenth century, and aided by the power of the stage, the coffee house, and the press, radicals with followings began to appear, like John Wilkes in Britain or the Abbé Sièyes in France, to challenge the established position in the name of democracy. The problem became, as Montesquieu had seen it, essentially one of accommodating the perspectives of the "classes" and the interests of the masses in such a way that the former were not swamped. Against the authoritarian state, dictatorial or democratic, there was a total taboo.

At the level of economic policy, a central feature of the liberal philosophy was the inviolability of the individual's access to a means of livelihood. Even the villein of Magna Carta, it was remembered, had a right to the protection of his wainage (the seed for the next year's crop). But classic liberalism grew up in an age of mercantilist ascendancy and sought to counter the interests of monopoly merchant capital with a plea for freedom of trade which, it asserted, would promote the greatest happiness for the greatest number. The idea came also to be linked with

23. Davenport, *Afrikaner Bond,* pp. 33, 120–21, 231.

24. T. R. H. Davenport, *South Africa: A Modern History,* 3rd ed., (London: Macmillan, 1987), pp. 101, 224.

minimalist government, especially since the state and monopoly capital had commonly worked together in the mercantilist age.

Until shortly before the British finally took over Cape Colony in 1806, it had been run by a mercantilist trading company, but the company's power had been broken shortly before the first British occupation (1795–1803), and a start had been made on the economic emancipation of local merchants in the last years of Dutch rule. To a small extent the job had to be done again by the British authorities, for the English East India Company soon managed to get a foot in the door. British policy at the Cape moved steadily toward economic liberation, which had been as good as achieved by 1860, though not necessarily to the Cape's advantage. The signing of the Cobden Treaty with France in 1860, which lowered a number of duties, especially on wines, actually created new difficulties for Cape exports.[25] This was part of the liberation of Manchester at the Cape's expense through the opening up of colonial markets.

The liberal impact on economic policy at the Cape has been illuminated by Colin Bundy's *Rise and Fall of the South African Peasantry* (1979). Bundy has shown how the African peasant economy expanded in the Cape and elsewhere during the 1870s and after, through a number of means: increased marketing of commodities such as wool, hides, timber, and crops; the purchase or hiring of farmland and its cultivation with the plow; participation in agricultural shows; and the conclusion of business deals with white merchant houses keen to supply a growing variety and volume of trade goods.[26] Broadly speaking, the Cape government between 1860 and 1880 wished to promote black entrepreneurial activity, especially if it was linked with the erosion of precolonial political structures then deemed to endanger the security of the white community. Sir George Grey (governor, 1854–1861) attempted to inculcate bourgeois values among Africans, a policy that made political as well as business sense, though it is becoming increasingly clear that the individualism promoted by Grey was exceptionally rugged and was hardly motivated by thoughts of African welfare in the short term.[27] These considerations help to explain the ease with which the notion of a multiracial, market-oriented political community, hierarchical in structure but not rigidly so, came to be accepted at the Cape,

25. *OHSA* 1, pp. 89–90; M. Arkin, "John Company at the Cape: A History of the Agency under Pringle" *Archives Year Book for South African History 2* (Pretoria: Government Printer, 1960), pp. 177–344.

26. C. Bundy, *The Rise and Fall of the South African Peasantry* (London: Heinemann, 1979), pp. 65–108, especially p. 74.

27. J. B. Peires, "Sir George Grey versus the Kaffir Relief Committee," *Journal of Southern African Studies* 10 (1982): 145–69.

and was hardly questioned during the governorships of Grey, Wodehouse, and Barkly, covering the period 1854–1877. These were the years in which white settlement advanced into the interior, towns were built, and the Cape wool industry established itself in response to the revolution in textile manufacture in Europe.

In his essay on "The 'Friends of the Natives,' " Stanley Trapido went further and sought to endow the link between Cape mercantile interests and black peasant entrepreneurs with a certain electoral logic. In his view, a "great tradition" of liberalism brought the white merchants together with a curious assortment of political administrators, missionaries, lawyers, editors, and "almost invariably the government's opponents of the day" in an advocacy of the rights of the black peasant.[28] His most questionable assertion is the community of objectives between the merchant houses and the missionaries because "the Christianity of free trade hastened the process of creating the market-oriented peasants which had begun with earlier settler conquests and economic expansion."[29] But this assumes an identity of outlook between contrasting groups whose association is surprising enough on ideological grounds to require an explanation. Such an explanation should do justice to the value systems of all parties, not simply those of one. One needs also to ask whether there was a "free trade of Christianity" if the religious (and in this instance the liberal) dynamic is to be adequately appraised.

When Trapido turns to the parallel existence of a "small tradition"[30] of consciously liberal-minded people, he seems to be on firmer ground. This he identifies as "more stable," and to be found "most markedly in the constituencies where a combination of peasant and 'town' voters—mostly those associated with the merchant interest—could hold one of the two seats in the two-member constituencies." McCracken has demonstrated that in certain Eastern Cape constituencies the size of the African electorate in the 1880s was considerable—between 15 and 34 percent of the total in fifteen of forty-one constituencies[31]—and certainly capable of holding the balance where two seats were contested between rival white candidates. Thus the small tradition survived in border regions even where circumstances did change radically over time.

The distinction between the two traditions matters, in Trapido's view, because he goes on to argue that, although the small tradition survived, even to the extent that by the first decade of the twentieth century "the

28. S. Trapido, "The 'Friends of the Natives': Merchants, Peasants and the Political and Ideological Structure of Liberalism at the Cape, 1854–1910," in S. Marks and A. Atmore, eds., *Economy and Society in Pre-Industrial South Africa* (London: Longman, 1980), pp. 251–52.

29. Trapido, "Friends of the Natives," pp. 247–74, especially p. 249.

30. *Ibid.*, p. 259.

31. J. L. McCracken, *The Cape Parliament* (Oxford: Clarendon Press, 1967), p. 80.

liberal ideology had achieved a degree of legitimacy,"[32] the great tradition fell victim to macroeconomic forces. Change in the political economy resulting from the growth of mining and capitalist farming, he argues, destroyed the usefulness of the black as a business associate and therefore as a voter. It also increased his value as a migrant worker—in which case his voting rights were an embarrassment, and the general inclination of whites to support black electoral participation waned significantly. The argument rests on an assumption that there was a real decline in the fortunes of the Cape's black entrepreneurs at the close of the nineteenth century, and on this point the evidence provided by Colin Bundy is strong. His comments on the intensification of antisquatter legislation between 1894 and 1909, and his conclusion that in consequence Cape liberalism had "divested itself of some of its ideological baggage: its spokesmen were by then more cautious, less optimistic,"[33] carry a better nuance than Trapido's great tradition, which seems about as diaphanous as Carroll's Cheshire cat.

But the loss of confidence among liberals was not engendered simply by forces of the market. In the 1890s, liberals were torn between suggesting that liquor should be made available to all races on the ground that to discriminate was wrong, and arguing that access be limited to whites on the ground that others, being "minors," were too vulnerable to abuse; but this was to raise the question of whether "minors" in the matter of alcohol could at the same time be "adults" in the matter of politics.[34] A growing paternalism seemed to be blunting liberal principles.

There was in the nineteenth century a contradiction at the heart of the liberal movement between those elements that were historicist in their reverence for the gains of the past, like the English Whig historians,[35] and those whose political values had come to rest increasingly on latter-day democratic, antihistorical assumptions based on notions of right associated with the American and French revolutions. Constitutions for the latter were no longer unwritten rituals of political behavior dignified by usage, but original written contracts made between contemporary political leaders for the ordering of their immediate public relationships, more after the thinking of Rousseau.[36]

32. Trapido, "Friends of the Natives," p. 257.

33. Bundy, *South African Peasantry,* pp. 109–45. Quotation at p. 137.

34. J. H. Hofmeyr, *The Life of Jan Hendrik Hofmeyr* (*Onze Jan*) (Cape Town: Van de Sandt de Villiers, 1913), pp. 360–69.

35. See, e.g., T. B. Macaulay, *History of England from the Accession of James the Second* III, ed. C. H. Firth (London: Macmillan, 1914), pp. 1304–12.

36. R. R. Palmer, *The Age of the Democratic Revolution* (Princeton: Princeton University Press, 1959) pp. 213–35 (the Enlightenment approach to constitutionalism).

There were no real democratic advances in Britain before 1832, partly on account of the suspicion over the merits of democracy as such in British liberal circles.[37] Nor did a Liberal party under that name emerge until 1868, when Gladstone's great ministry took office.[38] This new Liberal party was a combination of Whigs and Radicals who, despite their generally more conservative disposition than continental liberals, had already achieved a notable record of reform between 1832 and 1867. With the help of some Tories, they sought successfully to alleviate the conditions of slaves, climbing boys, factory workers, and—in modern parlance—other "disadvantaged communities."[39]

Cape liberalism derived its inspiration largely from British evangelical sources. It acquired a reputation for altruism, though not among those whose interests it injured. The Christian humanitarianism of the London Missionary Society, blending with a frontier realism, ensured an influence for John Philip and Andries Stockenström on the Aborigines Committee of the House of Commons in 1836.[40] Simultaneously, we must note the altruism, or respect for the rights of others, of the English-speaking pro-Boer, as represented in the activities of Emily Hobhouse and John X. Merriman during the South African War, and of Olive Schreiner, one of the few who managed to be vehemently pro-Boer and pro-black at the same time.[41] It was a tradition that became increasingly secularized, though never wholly so, and continued into the twentieth century in the stance of leaders such as Edgar Brookes, Z. K. Matthews, and Leo Marquard. One of its features was a much greater concern for justice than for the mechanics of power, and a reliance instead on a moral appeal. For this reason its political relevance was often questioned, but public life would have been poorer without it, as must be clear to anyone who ponders its total range rather than any particular manifestation of it. Cape liberalism did not attach itself to the rights of one particular group, but sought to protect the members of all groups in what it regarded as a common society.

The forces that led to the extension of political rights to the Cape

37. G. de Ruggiero, *European Liberalism,* tr. R. G. Collingwood (London, Oxford University Press, 1927), pp. 187–91.

38. J. Vincent, *The Formation of the Liberal Party* (London: Constable, 1966), p. 38.

39. E. L. Woodward, *The Age of Reform,* 2nd ed. (Oxford: Clarendon, 1962), pp. 444–73.

40. John Philip, *Researches in South Africa* (London: James Duncan, 1828); *Report of the Select Committee on Aborigines (British Settlements, 1836)* (facsimile reprint, Cape Town: C. Struik, 1966).

41. R. van Reenen, *Heldin uit die Vreemde: Emily Hobhouse* (Cape Town: Tafelberg, 1971); P. Lewsen, *John X. Merriman: Paradoxical South African Statesman* (New Haven: Yale University Press, 1982); R. First and A. Scott, *Olive Schreiner: A Biography* (New York: Schocken, 1980).

Colony were complex, and reflected the pragmatic "one-step-at-a-time" approach typical of the Colonial Office during the mid-nineteenth century. The demand for elective self-government was less vociferously made at the Cape than in some other British colonies of settlement, despite the campaign for press freedom during the 1820s. Early requests to British Tory governments for a representative assembly between 1827 and 1842 met with unfavorable responses for various stated reasons: a feared incompatibility between British and other cultural and legal traditions, the unresolved problem of slavery, the smallness and dispersal of the population, and the numerical imbalance between the business elite and a much larger class of people without political experience.[42]

After the return of the Whigs to power in 1846, the Colonial Office under Earl Grey became more responsive to constitutional development in the colonies, and initiated a reform process at the Cape which led to representative government in 1853. The controversy that preceded this event drew in a variety of interests relating to region, ethnicity, and class. What determined the end result, however, was the impact of Cape politicians on successive secretaries of state during a turbulent period of British and Cape history that, in Britain, saw three changes of government and the rise and fall of Chartism, and at the Cape, two frontier wars, the Kat River Khoikhoi rebellion, and a stirring anticonvict agitation in the capital. The accession to power of the Aberdeen coalition in 1853, the replacement of Pakington by Newcastle at the Colonial Office, and the appointment of Charles Darling as lieutenant governor with authority to make key decisions after the recall of Sir Harry Smith in 1851, facilitated an important change in policy. In 1852, the British government decided to grant self-government under the surprisingly low franchise proposals of Fairbairn, Stockenström, and the "popular" party, rather than the stiffer qualifications demanded by Godlonton and the "conservatives." Had the Derby-Disraeli ministry not gone out of office in 1853, it might well have deferred the grant of a constitution, or settled for higher qualifications.[43]

At no point during the preliminary debate about representative government did ethnicity or race feature as an absolute criterion for admission to or exclusion from the franchise, but merely as a factor in the calculations of those who pondered the effects of high or low qualifications.[44] The approach was on a par with that of the Aborigines

42. *OHSA* 1, pp. 319–20.

43. B. A. le Cordeur, *The Politics of Eastern Cape Separatism, 1820–1854* (Cape Town: Oxford University Press, 1981); Botha, *John Fairbairn;* S. Trapido, "The Origins of the Cape Franchise Qualifications of 1853," *Journal of African History* 5 (1964): 37–54.

44. Botha, *John Fairbairn,* p. 278, citing views of C. J. Brand and the *Cape Monitor;* le Cordeur, *Eastern Cape Separatism,* pp. 259–61; Trapido, "Origins," *passim.*

Committee, and in line with the nonracial franchise already adopted with respect to municipal self-government at the Cape in 1836;[45] and furthermore, the contrast is striking with the constitutions adopted by the Afrikaner republics in the interior in the 1850s.[46] Unlike these, the Cape constitution was not the constitution of a besieged white community seeking security in alien surroundings.

Although the economic explanation for the decline of Cape liberalism offered by Bundy and Trapido takes us much of the way, the most easily identifiable explanation of its political decline is that the incorporation into the Colony of large numbers of Africans eroded white support. Whites feared that unless they changed the electoral rules they would one day lose political control of the Cape legislature. The Ciskei, a region of dense African population, was incorporated against the wishes of the Cape Parliament in 1865 and was given two seats with two representatives each, with no color-bar restrictions on franchise or membership. The Transkei was incorporated in 1885, and two years later was given two constituencies with only one member each.

At this point the ministry of Sir Gordon Sprigg dug in its heels, and over the following eight years the Cape Parliament systematically limited black representation. In 1887, without changing the letter of the 1853 constitution, it redefined the rules to exclude property held under communal tenure, having received advice that a hut taken with the adjacent land was worth the £25 minimum qualification. In the Franchise and Ballot Act of 1892, the qualification itself was raised to £75, though the income qualification of £50 was left unaltered. A simple literacy test was also introduced, though its effects were hard to assess. In 1894, the Glen Grey Act, while encouraging Africans to buy land under individual tenure in certain proclaimed areas, excluded such land as qualification for the vote. On top of these laws to restrict black access to the franchise there were concerted efforts to remove black voters from the common roll by challenging their registration and placing the onus on them to reapply.[47] There was also one successful attempt—perhaps one was enough, for there was no repetition—to deter a bid by a person who was not white, a Malay teacher, to gain membership in Parliament by election.[48]

A surge toward racial discrimination was thus apparent in Cape politics following the incorporation of the African areas. This was hardly

45. G. W. Eybers, *Select Constitutional Documents Illustrating South African History, 1795–1910* (London: Routledge, 1918), pp. 78–81; P. Lewsen, "The Cape Liberal Tradition—Myth or Reality?" *Race* 13 (1971): 71.

46. T. R. H. Davenport, *South Africa: A Modern History,* pp. 76–89.

47. Trapido, "Friends of the Natives," p. 261; Davenport, *Afrikaner Bond,* pp. 352–53.

48. J. H. Hofmeyr, *Life of J. H. Hofmeyr,* p. 451; Lewsen, *Merriman,* p. 169.

surprising. What is less commonly noticed is that attempts to destroy the black franchise as such were never sufficiently forceful entirely to succeed. I have tried to explain this elsewhere in terms of the balance of forces in the Cape Parliament, rather than in terms of a color-blind ideology as such.[49] Through the period 1880–1904, when the Afrikaner Bond played a prominent role in Cape politics, the Bond and its opponents fought a series of very close and keenly contested elections. The black electorate, as we have already noted, was able to hold the balance in half a dozen constituencies in the Eastern Cape, as well as some in the west where the colored vote was strong.

But the Bond's opponents, politically less well organized and numerically weaker, knew they had to court black support if they were to compete with the Bond at the hustings. It was not politically expedient for the Bond, therefore, to declare any intention to disfranchise and thus alienate the black voter, however much they may have desired to do so. Nor was it prudent to advocate raising the minimum qualifications across the board, for this would cut out another section of their supporters, the *bywoners* (white tenant farmers) and other poor whites. So the Cape nonracial franchise was locked into position by the necessities of Cape political life. Only after 1908, when the Bond for the first time won a landslide victory as a consequence of the reenfranchisement of the rebels of 1900, was this delicate balance of power shattered. The African voter became expendable in interwhite political conflict.

A sign of this change appeared when at the national convention in 1908–1909 the Cape delegation felt free to forgo the claim that Africans should have the right both to vote for parliamentary candidates and to sit in Parliament. They settled for limitation of the colored and African franchise to the Cape only, under entrenched safeguards, and for limitation of colored and African eligibility to the Cape Provincial Council. Indeed, it is hard to read the debate on Schreiner's motion in the Assembly in March 1909, when almost the entire liberal establishment spoke for the South African bill (the proposed constitution), without receiving the impression that even liberals were more concerned in the final resort to preserve the dignity of the Cape in its relations with other colonies than the rights of blacks.

Cape liberalism in 1910 was not, therefore, the untarnished creed of a confident, perhaps even dominant, minority as it had appeared to be in 1830. Civil liberties had taken a severe knock: unfortunate precedents had been set that undermined equality before the law. Freedom of

49. Davenport, *Afrikaner Bond*, pp. 118–23.

expression, by contrast, appeared safe, though it too had had some anxious moments. Freedom of trade had expanded, and in doing so presented certain new challenges for the Colony; but the real danger to liberalism on the economic front, a danger with ominous political implications, had come through destruction of the African peasantry as an independent economic class. Political freedom, once widespread, had now diminished sharply with the expansion of the Colony to incorporate African territories, together with a de facto, if not explicitly de jure, color bar created in 1887–1894. The Cape Parliament apparently intended to do nothing about it.

A measure of optimism—perhaps naive, certainly humane—kept the spirit of liberalism alive. Lord Brand, secretary to the Transvaal delegation at the national convention in 1908 and 1909, visited the University of Cape Town in the mid-1950s. Replying to a question asked within earshot of the writer as to why the Cape delegation had so easily accepted the shallow entrenchment of black political rights, he said, "We were children then." But even that remark implied a trust in human nature that may be the subtlest contribution liberal-minded individuals can make to public life. Liberal rhetoric is less insulting to political humanity than the opposite tendency of assuming that egocentrism is the only valid key to political behavior.

André du Toit

2. The Cape Afrikaners' Failed Liberal Moment 1850–1870

There is no tradition of Afrikaner liberalism. One could, no doubt, compile a suitably qualified list of individuals who were both Afrikaners and liberals: from W. C. Van Ryneveld, Sir John Truter, and Andries Stockenström through T. F. Burgers, Lord de Villiers, J. W. Sauer, F. S. Malan and Jan Hofmeyr to the F. Van Zyl Slabberts of our own time. It would even be possible to trace various links and continuities in the thought and activities of these and similar individuals. Taken together, however, they do not amount to even a minor tradition. The links are often superficial, the continuities tenuous. Time and again these Afrikaner liberals have rather to be understood in relation to wider social and political forces. Key cultural figures such as Tobie Müller and N. P. Van Wyk Louw were, first and last, liberal *nationalists.* Afrikaner liberalism never even began to emerge as an independent and coherent movement with its own social base and distinct cultural and political objectives, except for one brief moment at the Cape just after the middle of the nineteenth century.

The Cape Afrikaners' liberal moment is a little-known and puzzling

This chapter is a substantially abbreviated version of a research paper that was itself part of a preliminary study. The nature of the present volume precluded fuller documentation and argument. I am indebted to Kathryn Andrews Gerstner and Jean du Plessis for many references to primary sources. Research for this paper was made possible by a grant from the Human Sciences Research Council (HSRC).

phenomenon. For a brief period there were the makings of a definite liberal tendency among Cape Afrikaners. It belongs to one of the most neglected periods of Afrikaner and South African history; it does not seem to fit with the familiar story of trekboer settlement and frontier conflict or the subsequent rise of Afrikaner nationalism; and it is primarily known from the partisan perspectives of its victorious opponents. Launched in the context of the public agitation fomented by the Anti-Convict Association in 1849, it became most pronounced during the subsequent constitutional controversies leading up to the granting of representative government in 1853. However, this liberal discourse was not sustained in the arena of parliamentary politics. Instead, in the following decade, the battle for public opinion shifted to the realms of education and above all the church, culminating in the "liberalism struggle" within the Dutch Reformed Church (DRC) during the 1860s. For a while the liberals seemed to be winning all the main battles, yet when the dust of the synodical disputes, theological controversies, and court actions began to settle after 1870, it became clear that the liberal tendency was a spent force. The real, and lasting, victors were the "orthodox" party, who would henceforth put their stamp on the mainstream of DRC piety and religious culture.

Given the problematic status and the historical fate of Cape liberalism in general, there is probably a greater need to account for the emergence of this liberal tendency among Cape Afrikaners than to account for its eventual failure. The Cape Afrikaners' brief liberal moment does not appear to fit into the standard accounts of the Cape liberal tradition,[1] which emphasize the role of imperial officials, missionaries, financial and commercial interests, and independent black peasantries, and which hardly allow for the possibility of liberal initiatives by colonial Afrikaners, least of all DRC clergy. What, then, was the social base of this anomalous liberal tendency, and what was the ground of its wider, though transient, popular appeal? Given the political origins of the new Afrikaner liberal discourse, why did the church become the main arena of struggle?

Even as these questions are pursued, one must also account for the historical *failure* of this liberal moment. The liberals were confident that they had history on their side, and that their "orthodox" opponents represented the persistence of reactionary traditions and of those "irrational" forces which were bound to be superseded in the modern world. The liberal tendency stood for rationality, progress, and univer-

1. For a careful restatement of Cape liberalism, see, e.g., Phyllis Lewsen, "The Cape Liberal Tradition—Myth or Reality?" *Race* 13 (1971): 65–80; S. Trapido, "The 'Friends of the Natives': Merchants, Peasants and the Political and Ideological Structure of Liberalism at the Cape, 1854–1910," in S. Marks and A. Atmore, eds., *Economy and Society in Pre-Industrial South Africa* (London: Longman, 1980), pp. 247–74.

salist values; it counted on the modernizing forces of free trade, education, and democracy to overcome ignorance, prejudice, and local oligarchies. However, the substantial economic, educational, and political developments of the time did not deliver the results on which the liberals were counting. I will argue that it was the "orthodox" party who proved to be the effective modernizers and cultural entrepreneurs who successfully built on current socioeconomic developments to restructure and transform the entire organizational mode and the religious sensibility of the DRC—and to prepare the ground for the emergence of modern Afrikaner nationalism.

We cannot, in the present context, do more than hint at the structural changes and the social dynamics which made the Cape Afrikaners' liberal moment possible. The 1840s saw the growth and consolidation of a more modern state and of "regular" society in the Cape Colony. The colonial economy was drawn into the dynamic new imperialism of free trade, commercial agriculture was introduced in the eastern districts by the British settlers from the 1820s, and the Commissioners of Inquiry abolished mercantilist institutions and constraints as well as the earlier system of arbitrary autocratic power and patronage.[2] Population increased rapidly: despite the emigration of upwards of 30,000 Afrikaners during and following the Great Trek, the number of whites in the Colony increased from 66,000 in 1832 to 140,000 in 1854; some 80 percent of these were Afrikaners.[3] Major social institutions like the church and the schools began to establish a more effective presence outside the handful of older towns. Small villages or *dorpe* began to develop, usually centered around the Dutch Reformed Church, with a few traders, a school, and sometimes a local bank; by 1850 there were forty-five in the Cape Colony, very few of them with a population of more than a thousand; the number of DRC congregations had increased from fourteen in 1824 to forty-nine in 1854.

Under the energetic John Montagu as colonial secretary (1845–1852), the administrative system of the colonial state was revamped and centralized, colonial finances were put on a sounder footing, and an

2. See, e.g., Jeffrey Peires, " 'Casting off our old skin': The British and the Cape, 1814–1834," in R. Elphick and H. Giliomee, eds., *The Shaping of South African Society,* 2nd ed. (Cape Town: Longman, 1987); Saul Dubow, *Land, Labour and Merchant Capital: the experience of the Graaff-Reinet District in the pre-industrial rural economy of the Cape 1852–1872,* Centre for African Studies, University of Cape Town, Communication No. 6/1982; Alan Mabin, "The Making of Colonial Capitalism: intensification and expansion of the economic geography of the Cape Colony, 1854–1899" (unpublished Ph.D. thesis, Simon Fraser University, 1984).

3. See, e.g., M. H. de Kock, *Selected Subjects in the Economic History of South Africa* (Cape Town: Juta, 1924), p. 136.

ambitious scheme of harbor and road improvement begun. Montagu introduced a more efficient postal service to the interior and, by the construction of a hard road over the sandy wastes of the Cape Flats in 1845, brought Cape Town much closer to its rural surroundings. He opened up the main roads to the interior for more rapid transport.[4] The much improved means of transportation stimulated trade and the development of regional markets and, together with the spread of local banking institutions and easier access to credit, accelerated the change from the former extensive subsistence agriculture to more intensive commercial farming.[5] These developments provided the basis for the rapid growth of the colonial economy in the 1850s, led by the export of wool from the Eastern Cape. From the point of view of the more enterprising colonists, including Afrikaners, the changes flowing from incorporation into the world capitalist economy opened up exciting new prospects of progress and prosperity. The modern world, perhaps best symbolized by the introduction of railways after the 1850s, was on its way.

More specifically, the educational reforms of the 1840s also prepared the way for the liberal groundswell in the decades that followed. With the Bell-Herschell reforms and the appointment of James Rose Innes as the first superintendent-general of education, the colonial school system was finally put on a sounder footing. The number of children at school rapidly increased from fewer than 4,000 in 1842 (with 2,800 whites) to almost 20,000 in 1860 (9,500 whites) and more than 40,000 in 1870 (18,000 whites).[6] With the introduction of state-aided public schools from 1843 there was a rapid move away from the proliferation of small private schools, which had earlier competed with the (English-medium) government "free schools." State control of the school system meant an increasingly secular orientation of education. Of particular importance was the emergence of the first vigorous local institutions to provide secondary and higher education, at first principally in Cape Town. The Zuid-Afrikaansche Athenaeum (later South African College) was launched in 1829. Dr. A. N. E. Changuion, who since 1831 had taught classical languages there, founded his own Institute in 1843. Until mid-century these remained the chief institutions for secondary education, but in the next decade they were followed and complemented

4. J. J. Breitenbach, "The Development of the Secretaryship to the Government at the Cape of Good Hope under John Montagu, 1845–1852," *Archives Year Book for South African History*, 2 (Elsiesrivier: Government Printer, 1960), pp. 223ff., 238ff.

5. See, e.g., Hermann Giliomee, "Processes in Development of the Southern African Frontier," in Howard Lamar and Leonard Thompson, eds., *The Frontier in History: North America and Southern Africa Compared* (New Haven: Yale University Press, 1981), pp. 93ff.

6. E. G. Malherbe, *Education in South Africa (1652–1922)*, (Cape Town: Juta, 1925), pp. 92, 98–99.

by the Diocesan College ("Bishops") in 1849, St. Andrew's in Grahamstown (1856), the Grey Institute in Port Elizabeth (1856), the Graaff-Reinet College (1860), the Gymnasia in Paarl (1857) and in Stellenbosch (1866), and, of course, the Theological Seminary in Stellenbosch (1859). With the establishment of a Board of Examiners in 1858 the first step was taken toward the creation of an examining university.

This takeoff in the number and level of colonial educational facilities at mid-century had a marked impact on the general and political literacy of Cape Afrikaners. A more informed reading public emerged along with the first generation of Afrikaner cultural entrepreneurs. Until mid-century there had been, with a few short-lived exceptions, only one newspaper in Dutch, *De Zuid-Afrikaan,* and only one Dutch journal of any substance, *De Nederlandsch Zuid-Afrikaansche Tijdschrift* (until 1843). After 1850 journalistic activity increased significantly. *Het Volksblad* was established in 1856, *De Volksvriend* in 1862. A number of new English and local newspapers appeared, as well as a growing number of journals in Dutch, including *De Gereformeerde Kerkbode* (1849), *Elpis* (1857), *De Wekker* (1859) and *De Onderzoeker* (1860). There was a substantial increase in the circulation of books and occasional literature, imported from the Netherlands and from England, but also produced locally at printing works such as that of B. J. van de Sandt de Villiers, N. H. Marais and the Zuid-Afrikaansche Christelijke Boekvereeniging (1854). By the 1850s there existed, therefore, for the first time, a more substantial public audience among Cape Afrikaners capable of participating in public debates and controversies. We also find at this time the first generation of locally educated Afrikaner journalists and clergymen prepared to engage in public affairs and to reach out to a wider audience.

This marked a major watershed in the development of Afrikaner intellectual history and political thinking. For almost two hundred years the Afrikaners had lacked an indigenous intellectual class. The tiny professional and cultural elite, mainly concentrated in Cape Town itself, had throughout its colonial history been heavily dependent on recruitment from "outside" for its small number of clergymen, teachers, lawyers, and journalists.[7] Now, local institutions of secondary education began to produce increasing numbers of well-trained Cape men. For the time being, all who wanted further university education or professional training still had to proceed to Europe, but even so there were significant differences. Before the 1840s only a few isolated individuals, drawn mainly from the tiny group of Cape Town gentry, studied in Europe; now the numbers of Cape Afrikaners studying in Utrecht and

7. André du Toit and Hermann Giliomee, *Afrikaner Political Thought: Analysis and Documents,* Vol. I: *1780–1850* (Cape Town: Philip, 1983), pp. xxiv–xxv.

Leiden grew to become recognizable and cohesive groups; and they included not a few born and bred in Paarl, Stellenbosch, Graaff-Reinet, and even farther afield.

Particularly important to the cultural and political formation of these first generations of indigenous Afrikaner intellectuals was Changuion's Institute. By 1847 it had an enrollment of 85, and throughout the 1850s it maintained an enrollment of well over 100 students, of which 40 or more were in the senior classes.[8] Almost all of the principal protagonists on both sides in the "liberalism struggle" of the following decades came from these graduates. Even apart from Changuion's considerable personal influence, the general ambience of the Institute had a pronouncedly liberal character and, in the words of a student, "a peculiarly political atmosphere."[9] Young Afrikaners, therefore, did not need to go to universities in the Netherlands in order to be exposed to liberal and progressive ideas. The general orientation of their education at Changuion's Institute and at the older and renowned elementary school *Tot Nut van 't Algemeen,* whose influence was even more pervasive, was liberal in outlook. The social and cultural conditions at the Cape at mid-century thus generated both young intellectuals with a liberal orientation as well as a wider public of Cape Afrikaners interested in social progress and democracy.

A pronouncedly liberal discourse first emerged among Cape Afrikaners during the events leading up to the granting of representative government in 1853. While the European revolutions of 1848 did not quite reach southern Africa, the local political climate during the following few years was one of popular agitation and pervasive crisis. The colony had not yet recovered from the "War of the Axe" of 1846–47, which saw serious tensions developing between the burgher force and the British military command,[10] when the eastern frontier was once again engulfed by a major frontier war in 1851, this time compounded by the rebellion of Khoikhoi or coloreds at the Kat River. On the other side of the Orange River, Andries Pretorius had led a campaign openly challenging British forces. At the Cape the major catalyst was the anticonvict agitation of 1849. Adamantly resisting the plan of the imperial authorities in London to settle convicts at the Cape, the "Anti-Convict Association" mounted a boycott, successfully mobilizing its supporters through a

8. J. Olivier, "Die Opvoedkundige Werksaamhede van dr. A.N.E. Changuion: 'n Histories-kritiese Evalueering" (unpublished M.Ed. thesis, University of South Africa, 1973), p. 101.

9. D. P. Faure, *My Life and Times* (Cape Town: Juta, 1907), p. 15.

10. T. Kirk, "Self-government and self-defence in South Africa: the interplay between British and Cape politics (1846–1854)," (unpublished D. Phil. thesis, Oxford, 1972).

public "pledge" to ostracize anyone found supplying or aiding the government, until it backed down from the imminent convict settlement. The agitation forged important new intergroup alliances: Afrikaner leaders from Cape Town and elsewhere joined English liberals such as John Fairbairn in a united stand against the imperial authorities. Those involved tended to regard the anticonvict agitation as their own version of the Boston Tea Party, and compared it to the events leading up to the American War of Independence.[11]

Although the anticonvict agitation was a passing episode, it served, at a time when the 1848 revolutions were very much on everyone's mind, to impart a new and unprecedented urgency to the colonists' long-standing, but previously more timid, aspirations for self-government. By 1848 the Legislative Council, with its minority of appointed unofficial members, no longer had much legitimacy in the colony. The imperial authorities, for their part, were not unsympathetic to the idea of self-government for the Cape, which well suited the new imperial free-trade policies.[12] However, the constitutional proposals, first initiated in 1848, became bogged down in lengthy deliberations in which the "popular" members of the Legislative Council, Andries Stockenström, Christoffel Brand, F. W. Reitz, and John Fairbairn, found themselves in open confrontation with officials like Montagu and the nominated representative and spokesman of the Eastern Cape merchant interests, Robert Godlonton.[13]

In this context of a semirevolutionary political climate and against the wider background of frontier wars and general upheaval, a distinct Afrikaner liberal discourse first began to take shape at the Cape between 1849 and 1853. Some of the earliest articulations of the new radical rhetoric appeared in the writings of F. S. Watermeyr, a brilliant young lawyer who had founded and edited *The Cape of Good Hope Observer* to give support to the anticonvict movement. As early as May 1849, he was harnessing the anticonvict agitation to the constitutional cause of self-government and preparing the case for a "right of resistance."[14] By

11. See, e.g., S. Trapido, "Origins of the Cape franchise qualifications of 1853," *Journal of African History* 5 (1964).

12. J. Gallagher and R. Robinson, "The Imperialism of Free Trade," *The Economic History Review* 6 (1953); A. Atmore and S. Marks, "The Imperial Factor in South Africa in the Nineteenth Century: Towards a Reassessment," *Journal of Imperial and Commonwealth History* 3 (1974).

13. See, e.g., A. H. Duminy, "The Role of Sir Andries Stockenström in Cape Politics, 1848–1856," *Archives Year Book for South African History,* 2 (Elsiesriver: Government Printer, 1960). Unofficial members of the Legislative Council were appointed to represent the public; in order to consider the proposed new constitution in 1850, they were chosen from nominations by the municipalities and road boards, the only elected bodies which then existed.

14. *The Cape of Good Hope Observer,* 15 May 1849.

July he had cast all caution aside in articulating the demands for sovereignty of an aroused populist movement; deliberately playing up the links with revolutionary developments in Europe he wrote:

> Be it known that the revolutionary genius of the age has reached even unto the Cape: . . . The people . . . do not choose longer to have others rule them. They will not that the heel of power shall longer be upon their necks. They now demand that there shall be established in their country, forthwith, a free and liberal constitution. . . . Not again with prayers or petitions do [the people] approach the government. . . . Their object is not to *pray* for a dissolution of the Legislative Council: but as a people, possessing a people's power, and desirous of enforcing a people's authority, they resolve upon its instant destruction.[15]

Similarly, in September 1849, Changuion gave one of his regular public speeches, but instead of offering his accustomed civilized discourse or mild homily on some cultural or educational topic, he now invoked a liberal rhetoric of rights in arguing the need for public education:

> The land of our birth and residence is not an independent state but a colony. . . . As English subjects, we do have obligations, but also rights and privileges; in meeting the former, we will also fight with tooth and nail any encroachment upon the latter. . . . From now on we will not be fooled by appearances. We will allow ourselves to be shorn, but not to be skinned. Or, to put it bluntly, we refuse to be oppressed.

He went on to stress the importance of an informed and active public opinion for a genuinely democratic political culture as well as the need to forget ethnic divisions in the struggle for general political rights:

> In England popular sentiment has ascended the throne. All high officials are publicly accountable, while the free press serves as the lever by which unpopular Ministers are ousted from their seats. This is what we must strive for here as well. . . . Our youth must be acquainted with all that happens in this country, as well as everything that is concocted for us in England. No official in the colony should be able to put a foot wrong without a hundred reprimanding hands lifting in unison. No speaker in Parliament should be allowed to say anything that is potentially harmful to us, without fifty pens being dipped into ink to indicate to the Honourable Gentleman that we do not accept everything. Thus the spirit of the coming generation must be directed towards concern with public affairs. It must be moulded into national awareness.[16]

In the following years the editorial columns of *De Zuid-Afrikaan,* to which Changuion was a regular contributor, would increasingly reflect this political vocabulary by insisting on the colonists' aspirations as a matter of rights.[17]

When the "popular" members appointed to the Legislative Council

15. Ibid., 15 July 1849.
16. *De Zuid-Afrikaan,* 2 September 1849 (translated from the Dutch).
17. See, e.g., *De Zuid-Afrikaan,* 21 February 1850.

clashed there with the executive officials, led by Montagu and supported by Godlonton, they explicitly took their stand on the historical ground of ancient English liberties. Christoffel Brand, who not many years before had been the spokesman for Dutch slaveholders against unwarranted imperial interference with their property rights, now pictured the colonial struggle as being in the same historical tradition as Magna Carta; he claimed that his legitimacy as a representative derived not from his formal appointment by the governor, but from the implied and basic contract with the people who had elected him.[18]

A similar liberal discourse informed an "Address" to the public on 21 September 1850 by the four "popular" members, Brand, Stockenström, Reitz, and Fairbairn, in which they enlarged on their reasons for resigning from the Legislative Council; it also informed the subsequent correspondence of Stockenström and Fairbairn, pressing, as "popular" delegates to London, for constitutional reforms and casting themselves as champions of liberty against the entire colonial "system" of patronage and despotism.[19]

The real test for these rather abstract and rhetorical liberal sentiments lay in the specific issue of the precise qualification of the franchise. The "popular" members claimed in their address that "we have helped to prepare the way for the establishment of an elective franchise which shall embrace the whole of the community;—that is, every man who has the least stake in the country,—or rather, who is not a mere vagrant, a pauper, or a criminal."[20] During the discussions of the Legislative Council in September 1850, officials like Montagu and Porter and the four "popular" members initially agreed on a surprisingly low £25 occupation franchise (i.e., owning or occupying property to the value of £25) for the Representative Assembly (much lower than the franchise in the United Kingdom or any of its colonies at the time). Effectively this would have been to the advantage of the larger but poorer Afrikaner group (predominantly in the Western Cape) as against the smaller number of more prosperous English-speaking colonists (mainly in the Eastern Cape), and of the farming community as against the strong merchant interests based in Cape Town and Port Elizabeth. It also meant that the franchise would be given to substantial numbers of the colored community.

In the subsequent deliberations it was the officials and the merchant

18. Report of the proceedings of the Legislative Council on 20 September 1850, in *The Cape Town Mail,* 28 September 1850.

19. Letter from Stockenström to the Cape Town Municipality, 12 September 1851, in C.W. Hutton, ed., *The Autobiography of Sir Andries Stockenström* 2 (Cape Town: Juta, 1887), pp. 337–48.

20. Address of 21 September 1850 in *The Cape Town Mail,* 28 September 1850.

nominees who increasingly resisted such a popular franchise. Following the resignation of the "popular" members on 21 September 1850, the Legislative Council proposed that the occupation qualification be increased to £50. Montagu explained that a £25 franchise was too low because it would give power to "a body of ignorant coloured persons whose numbers would swamp the wealthy and educated portion of the community."[21] The "popular" members, by contrast, consistently strove for a widely based nonracial electorate to be obtained by a low property qualification. They did so in full cognizance of the implications for the enfranchisement of colored voters. Thus Christoffel Brand in a speech at a public meeting in Cape Town, held following the publication of the draft ordinances in December 1851, declared:

> . . . And, gentlemen, why should [people of color] not be entitled to vote? Here, in this municipality they enjoy the same privileges that we do, and what inconvenience has ever arisen? . . . These people pay their share of the taxes, and why should they not have a voice in the appropriation of their own money? . . . Shall we withhold from them the same liberties we ourselves enjoy? If we had the slightest idea of such a thing, we would be unworthy of having a free constitution.[22]

These sentiments were echoed in other speeches at the same meeting by Stockenström and by J. H. Wicht, and at a further public meeting on 1 March 1852 in speeches by J. de Wet and again by Wicht. Wicht's speech at the December meeting is of particular interest for his development of the "safety valve" argument associated with the attorney general, William Porter. In a famous speech during the debates in the Legislative Council, Porter had argued that the only way to learn political responsibility was by being granted the opportunity to exercise such responsibility. To those who warned of the dangers of giving the vote to disaffected coloreds, Porter replied that common political participation was preferable to violent confrontation: "I would rather meet the Hottentot at the hustings voting for his representative, than meet the Hottentot in the wilds with his gun upon his shoulder."[23] On similar lines Wicht argued that the Kat River Rebellion and other indications of colored grievances were no reason for withholding the franchise from them; on the contrary, as recent European experience had shown, a constitutional safety valve was all the more needed if the "fatal results" and "terrible explosions" incurred by attempts to smother popular grievances were to be avoided.[24]

21. "Further Papers Relative to the Establishment of a Representative Assembly," *British Parliamentary Papers,* Vol. 24, No. 1427 of 1852, p. 159.
22. *The Cape Town Mail,* 6 December 1851.
23. Legislative Council Debates, in "Further Papers," pp. 218–19.
24. *The Cape Town Mail,* 6 December 1851.

Significantly, the liberal discourse of Afrikaner leaders like Brand and Stockenström was adopted by supporters even from remote areas. Thus a delegation from Clanwilliam prepared an address to the governor in the following liberal and explicitly nonracial terms:

> We are unwilling to conceal . . . that we shudder at the idea of the distinction made in the present Legislative Council between rich and poor, white and coloured, contrary to Her Majesty's decision, as contained in the draft constitution ordinance. We wish earnestly to impress . . . that the abolition of the £25 franchise, and the introduction of a £2000 qualification for the Legislative Council will affect the same civil right which the coloured are as much entitled to enjoy as we, and would only give to the rich the whole influence in the Legislature. . . .[25]

At the time both Stockenström and Porter acknowledged that these were remarkable sentiments to emanate from Cape Afrikaner circles. In the Western Cape, relations between Afrikaners and coloreds were still very much in the shadow of the emancipation of the slaves little more than a decade earlier, which had been followed by agitation against "vagrancy" among the colored population. It may be thought that Afrikaner farmers implicitly counted on their practical hold over their laborers and tenants, but if so, that confidence contrasted markedly with their earlier behavior when the prospect of emancipation unleashed the most extravagant fears of social revolution. Only the previous year, rumors of a conspiracy aimed at inciting a general rising of colored farm laborers against their masters had caused widespread alarm in the so-called "Swartland Panic." Rural Afrikaners did, however, have an immediate stake in a low franchise, just as English mercantile and propertied interests had a stake in a restrictive one. However, the strength of traditional popular prejudices is notorious, and the political implications of enfranchising coloreds could be calculated in different ways, as appears from Porter's comments: "The English minority affecting to be afraid of Dutch preponderance, and whose strength might lie in the support of the Coloured population, are found depriving the Coloured population of those privileges which our liberal-hearted Dutchman holds forth with a free hand. I cannot comprehend this. It seems to me suicide."[26]

If these developments exasperated Porter, they evidently gave great satisfaction to Stockenström. Long isolated from his fellow Afrikaners by his uncompromising liberal stands, Stockenström now seemed vindicated. As he spelled out in his reply to the address of the Clanwilliam deputation:

> As your countryman, and as a boer like yourselves, I am proud of South Africa,—

25. Ibid., 1 April 1852.

26. "Further Papers," pp. 18, 247.

as it has stood forward in the matter of the constitution, and particularly in the noble generosity with which the interests of the weaker and coloured classes have been upheld and cherished by the great body of the community. . . . It is, above all, a subject of triumphant exaltation to see so glorious and christian a course pursued by the very men who were suspected and accused of a desire to crush and enslave the weaker portion of their fellow-subjects, especially to see them do so in defiance of the machinations and intrigues of those who have always boasted of their superior education, liberality, and philanthropy.[27]

The Cape Afrikaners did not confine such statements of their newfound liberal willingness to share equal political rights with colored people to petitions and addresses aimed at London only. According to contemporary newspaper reports, there were coloreds present at the public meetings held in Cape Town. And on at least one occasion Reitz, one of the four "popular members" and a prominent farmer from Swellendam, addressed a meeting at the Zuurbraak Missionary Institution in his district:

Believe me, . . . it is deception to speak of opposite interests of black and white. . . . Judge for yourselves. The Attorney-General has rightly said, that the simplest farmer and the simplest Hottentot is well able to judge who is the man in whom he can confide. He can thus, although incompetent perhaps to make laws himself, easily tell who will make the most righteous laws for him. Let no enmity between your race and mine exist. It would be unnatural if anyone did not more cleave to his own family than to a stranger. It would be unnatural if I was not more bound to my own race: and even so it is with you. But nothing need hinder us to be just to all—to do rightly between kinsman and stranger; and nothing need prevent us from living together in peace with one another, and to become more closely united to each other in the bonds of christian love. . . .[28]

Once it was decided that the Cape Colony would have representative government, and once the low nonracial franchise was written into the new constitution, the political controversies began to wane; by 1853 they were a thing of the past. The new Cape Afrikaner liberal discourse of the previous few years also became distinctly less pronounced. In October 1853 *De Zuid-Afrikaan* still looked forward to the effects of the coming era of representative government in very much the same liberal terms: "the perfect equality of political privileges" would tend to diminish "the fictitious inequality of wealth," and in the long run the new order would also "obliterate the odious distinction between English and Dutch."[29] But barely six months later, in editorial comments on the first elections for the new legislative assembly, the newspaper took a much more jaundiced view of political equality in practice. It contrasted "the *people*" with "the *rabble*," who "look upon their votes as so much

27. *The Cape Town Mail*, 1 April 1852.
28. Ibid., 6 April 1852.
29. *De Zuid-Afrikaan*, 6 October 1853.

ready money for which they can purchase the means of indulging their degrading appetites."[30] It now saw elections as a "demoralising disease," thus anticipating the cynical realism that would later, particularly from 1880 on, become the dominant mode in Cape Afrikaner discourse on constitutional politics.

The liberal discourse so prominent in the early 1850s did not simply disappear. On the contrary, in the following years we continue to find individual Afrikaner spokesmen and politicians employing a distinctly liberal idiom in a variety of contexts. Take, for example, a speech in 1861 by F. S. Watermeyr as a member of the Legislative Assembly in which he grounded his opposition to separation of the Eastern Cape on the suspicion that the real objective of the separationists was to curtail the equal rights of blacks, i.e., Africans and coloreds, under the constitution. He held it a matter of political "*duty*" to see that the rights of blacks were protected under the constitution and that the proper and liberal objectives of parliamentary government be maintained. Watermeyr, who was of German extraction, made a point of associating his liberal convictions specifically with an "Afrikaner" cause:

> I may cherish the hope that those who live hundreds of years hence, when the people of this colony, who may then be a nation of some importance, look back upon the records of the country, that they may see the names of some of us who desire to be remembered as Africanders and as Cape men. And I trust that when they do look they will see our names always associated with the idea of duty. . . .[31]

In the following decades the principal mouthpiece for such liberal views among Cape Afrikaners was the newspaper *Het Volksblad*, which had been founded in the heady days of the anticonvict agitation in 1849 and later, in 1856, revived by B. J. van de Sandt de Villiers, publisher and printer and a key figure in the liberal tendency. In an editorial from 1865, *Het Volksblad* recapitulated the classic "safety valve" arguments in defense of a liberal constitution: though certainly not enthusiastic about the prospect of having coloreds in Parliament, the editorial held that "it would still be better for Parliament to listen now and again to a little native eloquence, than it would be for us to have to quieten Hottentot mutiny or Malay commotions from time to time."[32] Compared to the confident and high-minded rhetoric of the earlier liberal discourse, these remarks were more defensive and qualified. At least in the political arena, any liberal discourse from Cape Afrikaners after 1854 tended to be incidental, muted, and sporadic.

30. Ibid., 15 May 1854.
31. *The Cape Separation Debates* (Cape Town: Saul Solomon, 1861), 8 June 1861.
32. *Het Volksblad*, 19 January 1865 (translated from the Dutch).

There are a number of possible reasons for this demise of a distinctive liberal Afrikaner stand in Cape politics. Success in the constitutional struggle had perhaps been gained too easily and quickly. Had the granting of representative government been postponed, a prolonged and arduous constitutional struggle might have brought about a further and more durable radicalization of incipient liberal views. Also, certain leading figures in the constitutional struggle soon disappeared from active politics: Stockenström was at the end of his long career; Brand became speaker of the new legislative assembly. In general, the numerically stronger Afrikaner group made little organized effort to capitalize on the potential advantages to them of the low franchise, a relative lack of politicization in the parliamentary arena that may be attributed to their inexperience as well as to the effects of the economic boom of the 1850s.

However, the liberal discourse which disappeared from the political arena was to some extent diverted to a different context. In the following decades the groundswell of a more enlightened public opinion among Cape Afrikaners channeled its energies into the different arena of religious and theological controversy.

The "liberalism struggle" in the Dutch Reformed Church came to a head during the dramatic synod of 1862 with the attempted moves against two young clergymen, J. J. Kotzé and T. F. Burgers, because of their alleged doctrinal heterodoxy. Kotzé and Burgers challenged the propriety of these synodical actions in the secular courts; a protracted series of legal battles began, with appeals reaching even the Privy Council in London. At the same time, an extensive theological controversy developed as the "orthodox" spokesmen, such as Andrew Murray, Jr., and N. J. Hofmeyr, professor of theology at Stellenbosch, debated their liberal opponents and critics, Kotzé, Burgers, and D. P. Faure in particular, in lecture series and theological treatises. Yet the liberalism struggle was not exclusively, or even primarily, a doctrinal and theological conflict even though this is the way in which it is generally presented in the literature, based on the standard account by T. N. Hanekom.[33] The social and historical roots of the liberalism struggle in the DRC went back a long way, and its ramifications involved a complex configuration of overlapping and interrelated social, political, legal, cultural, and religious issues.

The first indications of where the battle lines would be drawn appeared

33. T. N. Hanekom, *Die Liberale Rigting in Suid-Afrika: n Kerk-historiese Studie* (Stellenbosch: C.S.V.-Uitgewers, 1951).

even before any of the major controversial issues had emerged. By 1850, when the church was about to enter a crucial period of expansion and growth, at least two fault lines began to appear in the ranks of the DRC. The first polarity arose between the conservative sway of G. W. A. van der Lingen, the formidable pastor of the congregation at Paarl, and the more liberal stance of the Cape Town church council, which included Changuion and other progressive figures of the local gentry. From his strong base in the rural congregation of Paarl, van der Lingen was able to mobilize considerable local resources in defense of what he regarded as the traditional order in church and society. A man of considerable though somewhat eccentric learning, he was much disturbed by the 1848 revolutions in Europe—which he viewed in explicitly eschatological terms—and by their echoes at the Cape in the "constitutional and democratic mania" of the anticonvict agitation, which he saw as a potentially revolutionary subversion of authority.[34] He warned against the dangers to religion of the spread of "European enlightenment and civilisation" in colonial society; he published diatribes against the subversive influence of the secular press; and he was the moving spirit in founding the Paarl Gymnasium to counter the threats of secular education, as well as in organizing the later boycott of Sunday trains in 1862.[35] Van der Lingen was setting himself against precisely those social forces which Changuion and the liberal Afrikaners of Cape Town welcomed. On 24 October 1853, Changuion was appointed as elder to the church council of Cape Town, and throughout the 1850s such liberals as Christoffel Brand, P. J. Kotzé (the father of J. J. Kotzé and later mayor of Cape Town), J. de Wet, P. E. de Roubaix, and others played an active part in the Cape Town congregation.

It is not difficult to see the strategic importance of the church as a social institution at this time. In the relatively undeveloped and undiversified colonial society, the Dutch Reformed Church was one of the few, it not the only, major institution which, in principle, encompassed the majority of the population. Along with the spread of functioning congregations by mid-century throughout the Cape interior came increasing opportunities for social communication and control. Church councils, which had control of much of the few available resources,

34. See, e.g., M. de Villiers, *Herinnering aan het leven en de Werkzaamheden van de Wel-Eerw. Zeer Geleerde Heer Gotl. Wilh, Ant. van der Lingen, in Leven Herder en Leeraar der Nederd. Geref. Gemeente aan de Paarl* (Cape Town: Smuts and Hofmeyr, 1874), pp. 92–95.

35. See, e.g., M. C. Kitshoff, *Gottlieb Willem Antony van der Lingen: Kaapse Predikant uit die Negentiende Eeu* (Groningen: VRB-Offset Drukkerij, 1972); G. W. A. van der Lingen, *Iet, doch niet al wat er te zeggen is op de Oordeelvelling van den Papieren "Zuid-Afrikaan"* (Cape Town: N. H. Marais, 1853).

also played a key role in the founding of new dorpe (towns), which coincided with the setting up of new congregations.[36] Moreover, the DRC was still a single church: there was no tradition of fission as in the Anglo-Saxon world, where divisive issues almost always led to secession. The church thus provided a kind of protonational institution, a strategic prize to capture especially in times of rapid social change and development. But if the Afrikaner liberals of Cape Town sensed something of what was at stake in gaining more influence in the church, conservatives like van der Lingen were outraged. He saw Changuion's appointment to the Cape Town church council as nothing less than a "declaration of apostasy" endangering the whole church; he attempted, without success, to get the synodical commission to meet in order to annul Changuion's election.[37]

Meanwhile, a second rift within the church had opened, this one in the ranks of the Afrikaner theological students in the Netherlands, whose numbers had begun to increase substantially during the 1840s. Most of those in the first generation of the mid-1840s and early 1850s, which included the Murrays, Hofmeyrs, and Neethlings, tended to insulate themselves from secular and liberal influences at the Dutch universities, where the "modernist" theology of such men as J. H. Scholten, professor of dogmatics at Leiden University, was beginning to gain the ascendancy. Instead they became active members of the society "Secor Dabar" (Remember the Word), which was influenced by the revivalist Réveil movement with its stress on conversion, personal piety, and evangelical mission work.[38] They also founded their own society of students from the Cape, "Elpis agape en chariti" (Good Hope and Grace), a tightly knit group of friends and compatriots who worked and lived together.[39] The members of Elpis would later form the core and provide most of the dynamism of the "orthodox" party in its battles with the liberal tendency in the DRC. But not all the Afrikaans theological students in the Netherlands joined Secor Dabar and Elpis. The majority of the next generation, who arrived in the Netherlands from the early 1850s, were much more open to the intellectual and cultural influences of their new environment. This progression was monitored with growing alarm by the former Elpiste as well as by such members of the old guard as van der Lingen and William Robertson, a

36. Jean P. du Plessis, "The Politics of Marginalisation" (forthcoming M.A. thesis, University of Stellenbosch).

37. Kitshoff, *G. W. A. van der Lingen*, pp. 214–15.

38. See, e.g., J. du Plessis, *The Life of Andrew Murray of South Africa* (London: Marshall, 1919), pp. 58–65.

39. S. du Toit, "Professor N. J. Hofmeyr, 1827–1909: Predikant in die Lesinglokaal" (unpublished D.Th. thesis, University of Stellenbosch, 1984), pp. 35f.

senior member of the DRC moderature.[40] As the new generation began to return to the Cape, these rifts reinforced the existing polarities in the DRC, and underlying factional conflicts in local churches and communities came into the open in relation to a range of controversial issues.

After 1853, a number of controversies began to develop in and around the DRC. Together they constituted the public agenda on which the liberalism struggle was waged for a decade and more. The first main issue to lead to a public controversy concerned the proposed founding of a local theological seminary for the DRC. This had long been a fond project in the church, and in 1852 the synod decided to call professors from the Netherlands and to involve all church councils in fund raising for the seminary. At this late stage, Changuion began to wage a public campaign against the whole project. Much of his argument concerned the feasibility and financial viability of such an institution, but much was also polemical and partisan, revealing his fear that the seminary would become a training ground for conservative clergy.[41] Changuion's objections provoked a spirited public response, especially from the younger ministers such as J. H. Neethling and N. J. Hofmeyr, who had only recently returned from the Netherlands.[42] Although Changuion did not continue with his campaign against the seminary with the same intensity after 1853, significant opposition to it remained. At the synod of 1857, where the final moves were made to launch the seminary, eighteen delegates, including Changuion and many of the later "liberals," persisted to the end with their objections.

A second issue concerned the separation of church and state, or the "voluntary principle," i.e., that the church should not depend on state support but solely on the voluntary contributions of its own members. During its first two centuries the DRC had been closely linked to the state; then, under Batavian and subsequently under British rule, it lost its position as a state church although the DRC still received its "charter" from the state in the form of Ordinance 7 of 1843. This ordinance made the church subservient to the civil courts and gave the governor a say in the nomination of members of church councils, the appointment of ministers to congregations supported by state funds, and the deposing of ministers.[43] The state continued to provide financial support to the

40. Hanekom, *Die Liberale Rigting*, pp. 281–82.

41. A. N. E. Changuion, *Bezwaren tegen het oprigten eener Theologisch Kweekschool in deze Volksplanting* (Cape Town: W. F. van der Vliet, 1853).

42. N. J. Hofmeyr, J. H. Neethling, and J. M. Brink, *Bezwaren tegen bezware, of dr. A.N.E. Changuion weerlegd* (Cape Town: Marais, 1854).

43. See, e.g., P. B. van der Watt, *Die Loedolff-saak en die Nederduitse Gereformeerde Kerk 1862–1962* (Cape Town: Tafelberg, 1973), pp. 38–40.

DRC, though not as a matter of right, and this had now to be shared with other denominations. Such close ties to the state had significant consequences for the character of the church. Ministers were primarily dependent, not on their local congregations, but on the colonial authorities who appointed them and paid their salaries. Accordingly the church tended to align itself with the colonial authorities rather than with its own membership on controversial issues such as the Great Trek. During the first session of the new colonial parliament on 7 August 1854, Saul Solomon introduced a motion to stop state funding for the church. The motion stood over until the next year, when it was reintroduced; it appeared almost every year until 1875 when it finally became law.

The "voluntary principle" increasingly became a central issue in colonial politics and church affairs. At first the DRC reacted almost unanimously in alarm at what it saw as a major threat to its own interests, and this included Changuion and the prominent liberal members of the Cape Town congregation.[44] In the course of the next few years, however, this consensus broke down. The conservative or "orthodox" party remained vehemently opposed to the voluntary principle, even though it could be argued that it was more in line with the reformed doctrinal principles they professed than was the de facto situation. But more and more Afrikaner liberals began to support the voluntary principle, including Reitz, P. J. Kotzé, and J. J. Meintjies of Graaff-Reinet.[45] As the conflicts of the "liberalism struggle" intensified during the 1860s, views on the voluntary principle polarized as well. Liberals such as S. P. Naudé hammered home the anomaly that the same orthodox party that protested any authority of the civil courts over the church demanded state funding for it.[46] And Burgers, in an open letter to Andrew Murray, claimed that "never has there been a more anomalous claim than this demand for state support but without state control. . . . You want to serve one Lord, but receive wages from two."[47]

By 1869 the voluntary principle had become a dominant issue in the parliamentary elections, and candidates were openly canvassing as pro- or anti-Voluntarists. With responsible government imminent in 1872, the issue became even more politicized as the conservatives in the DRC threw their weight behind the "anti-Voluntarist" candidates and also

44. See the report of the protest meeting of August 1854 in *De Gereformeerde Kerkbode,* 5 and 19 August 1854, pp. 267–74, and Changuion's speech at the 1857 synod as reported in *Elpis* 2 (1858), pp. 87–95.

45. See, e.g., F. W. Reitz, *Moet de Regering zich met Kerkelyke Zaken inlaten?: Eene Voorlezing over het Vrywillig Stelsel* (Cape Town: Solomon, 1861); and the editorial (by Changuion?) in *De Zuid-Afrikaan,* 22 January 1858.

46. *Het Volksblad,* 18 October 1866.

47. *De Onderzoeker,* 25 January 1868.

began to oppose responsible government as such. The liberal quest for the separation of church and state was thus associated with the broader political movement for democratic self-determination. One of the underlying issues in the church's campaign for continuing state support had been the fear that, without it, ministers would become dependent on their local congregations and ordinary members would thus gain a more direct say in the affairs of the church.[48] The liberal tendency in the church did in fact derive much of its popular support precisely from such a groundswell in favor of a democratization of the church, as also appears from the issue of free elections.

In the 1850s the issue of "free elections" became a third point of contention. Although it was a reformed principle that the congregation should have a say in the election of office-bearers, the DRC in practice had developed marked oligarchic features. Ordinary members of the congregation had no say in the election of the church council or in the calling of ministers. Church councils were quite small, and new members were elected on a co-optive basis; councils thus tended to reproduce themselves as tiny cliques drawn from a few families only. As late as 1870 the church council of Paarl was still said to be "in the hands of only thirteen people."[49] In addition, the prominent role of the Murray clan in the church hierarchy accentuated oligarchic control. With the key role of the church in the growth of a more settled and organized society in the Cape Colony toward the mid-nineteenth century, this oligarchic structure became a matter of wider significance; it gave rise to increasing controversy. At the same time, the spread of organized education and the rise of a local press meant that the church had to contend with new pressures and rival interest groups. Local opponents of these self-perpetuating church councils were thus added to those who argued for free elections as the key to greater liberal influence in the church.

In the early stages, though, free elections still received support from senior figures like the then moderator P. E. Faure.[50] However, Faure's motion for free elections was rejected at the synod of 1857 despite support expressed in popular petitions and from prominent conservatives as well as liberals. In particular it was the elders from the rural congregations who rallied against "this dangerous and pernicious innovation." As *De Zuid-Afrikaan* commented, the decision was clearly

48. See, e.g., *De Gereformeerde Kerkbode,* 5 August 1854, pp. 254–55.

49. Letter from "Een lid der Ned. Geref. Kerk," *Het Volksblad,* 13 October 1870; see also the statistics on the lopsided composition of the Cape Town congregation cited in *De Volksvriend,* 30 July 1862.

50. See, e.g., P. E. Faure, "Iets omtrent den vorm van het bestier der Gereformeerder Kerk van Zuid-Afrika," *De Gereformeerde Kerkbode,* 28 February 1857.

self-interested: "The synod is not the proper body to decide such a question. The elders who, under the present system, have obtained the distinction of a seat in their consistories, are not sure that they would be returned by their congregations."[51] During the next few years the issue of free elections became increasingly entangled in the growing controversies involving the liberal tendency. More and more frequently, members alleged that church councils were, or would be, manipulated to deny positions to some of the young ministers returning from their theological studies in the Netherlands, who were, rightly or wrongly, suspected of liberal leanings. From 1860 the issue of free elections appeared on the agenda of almost every church meeting, usually proposed by liberals. These calls for free elections in the church evidently also tied in with the spread of democratic ideas in society and politics at large: "We want representative institutions both in the Church and in the State," wrote *Het Volksblad* in an editorial on "Church Reform."[52]

This connection, as well as the idea that the synod itself was incapable of bringing about the needed reforms, probably accounted for the peculiar turn of events through which the issue of free elections in the church appeared on the agenda of Parliament in 1861. On 23 May 1861, P. E. de Roubaix, in close association with other Afrikaner liberals in the Cape Town congregation, proposed a motion in Parliament to prepare the way for free elections in the church. De Roubaix's motion, and the ensuing parliamentary debates, caused a tremendous public stir.[53] Even those who were not in favor of a complete separation of state and church tended to see this as an intolerable interference in the internal affairs of the church. The use of Parliament provided the opportunity for conservatives to counter that the rights of the church itself were endangered. Thus N. J. Hofmeyr, in an open letter to de Roubaix, claimed that his motion would in effect "destroy the liberty which the church has enjoyed for many years."[54] Protest meetings were organized in Cape Town and elsewhere, and petitions were circulated in the country districts. Although de Roubaix's motion in the council, and a similar proposal by Haupt in the legislative assembly, easily gained majorities in Parliament, the governor declined to promulgate these as law.

The issue of free elections in the church had now been thoroughly politicized. To conservative opponents, democratization held out a threat to the character of the church as a religious institution: many pro forma members of somewhat suspect piety could not be trusted with a direct

51. *De Zuid-Afrikaan*, 5 November 1857. 52. *Het Volksblad*, 28 May 1861.

53. Cf. *Het parlement en de Vrije Verkiezingen* (Cape Town: W. F. Mathew, 1861); see also the correspondence columns of *Het Volksblad* for May–June 1861.

54. *Het Volksblad*, 6 July 1861.

say in church affairs. They also saw that free elections might pave the way for the more progressive groups and commercial interests allied to the liberals.[55] Meanwhile, the liberals utilized the defects and abuses of the existing arrangements to publicize their own cause. In anticipation of the 1862 synod, the liberal mouthpiece, *De Onderzoeker,* published one long article after another in favor of free elections.[56] The synod, despite determined efforts by the liberals, nevertheless once again decided to retain the status quo. The liberals appeared powerless to overcome oligarchic control within the church either constitutionally or in practice. This failure to reform the church from within may in part explain why they availed themselves of other recourses, such as the civil courts, in their doctrinal battles with the ruling "orthodox" faction.

The last two principal issues in the "liberalism struggle," the ones around which the battle came to a head in the 1860s, concerned on the one hand the problematic relation between the church and the civil courts, and on the other the conflicts regarding the alleged doctrinal heresies of leading liberals such as J. J. Kotzé and T. F. Burgers. These issues were closely interlinked, since Kotzé and Burgers appealed to the civil courts against the decisions of the synod to remove them from their offices for doctrinal deviations; the years of court battles that followed paralleled the theological controversies. Nor was the liberals' recourse to the civil courts in church matters a fortuitous strategy: the relation of the church to the civil courts had become a highly contentious issue well before the doctrinal conflicts came into the open at the synod of 1862. The roots of this issue lay in the peculiarly close relation between church and state. With the DRC traditionally virtually a state church, some of its members had come to regard baptism and confirmation as a matter of political right without test of their personal piety.[57] Ecclesiastical censure also had important social and civil consequences well beyond the confines of the church itself. Thus some individuals were prepared to contest censure in the civil courts. The best known of such cases was that of *Weber v. Van der Spuy* in 1854.[58] There was a growing tendency for individuals to appeal against the decisions of church councils to the civil courts.

By 1857 this had become such a widespread practice that a motion for such civil appeals to be made censurable was put before the synod.[59] At this same synod a controversy arose about the territorial jurisdiction

55. See, e.g., *Het Volksblad,* 29 June 1861: letter from "Predikant."

56. Cf., e.g., the articles by "A.B.C." and "H." in *De Onderzoeker,* 15 September 1862.

57. This had been the cause of a bitter conflict around the dominee, Robert Shand, in Tulbagh from 1830 for more than a decade. A. Moorrees, *Die Nederduitse Gereformeerde Kerk in Suid-Afrika, 1652–1873* (Cape Town: S.A. Bybelvereniging, 1937), pp. 677–90.

58. Ibid., pp. 670–76.

59. *De Zuid-Afrikaan,* 22 October 1857.

of the DRC. It soon grew into a major confrontation with the courts. In 1862 the civil court's decision in this case, brought by an elder, H. H. Loedolff, necessitated the suspension of synodical business to await a counterappeal just as the doctrinal conflicts were coming to a climax. Loedolff's move was interpreted by the conservatives as a strategy aimed at undercutting their substantial support in congregations outside the boundaries of the Cape Colony.[60] It was thus in line with this wider pattern that Kotzé and Burgers decided they should have recourse against the synod in the civil courts. In their view, this was necessary to ensure that the church would go about its business in accordance with its regular laws and procedures and would not be dictated to by the power of the majority, and particularly that of the "orthodox" faction, who were usurping the functions of the church in general for their sectional aims. For their part, the "orthodox" party considered the intervention of the civil courts to be a direct challenge to the spiritual authority of the church.[61]

The doctrinal differences between the liberals and the "orthodox" party had been evident for a considerable time.[62] In the early 1850s, even before the advent of such outspoken young liberal ministers as J. J. Kotzé and Burgers, the Hofmeyrs and Murrays were publishing series of articles in *De Gereformeerde Kerkbode* warning against the dangers of the "modernist" theology and of liberalism in general.[63] For their part, liberals such as P. J. Kotzé, the father of J. J. Kotzé, made efforts to publicize the work of the leading liberal Dutch theologian, J. H. Scholten, at the Cape, and from 1860 the journal *De Onderzoeker*, with Leopoldt Marquardt as editor, provided a sustained forum for more liberal theological views.[64] In general, the liberals reflected a more humanist outlook, a greater trust in human reason, and a readiness to allow some scope for critical reflection on scriptural truths and traditional doctrines. Their underlying trust in social progress and in the perfectibility of humanity evidently brought them into conflict with such traditional

60. For a vivid contemporary account of the dramatic events at the 1862 Synod, see F. Lion Cachet, *Vyftien jaar in Zuid-Afrika* (Leeuwarden: Bokma, 1875), pp. 174–95.

61. See N. J. Hofmeyr, *De Kerk en de Regtbank* (Cape Town: Marais, 1865).

62. It is quite another matter how "orthodox" the conservatives actually were in strict theological terms. See, e.g., the polemic between Kotzé and Murray regarding the latter's orthodoxy on such basic Calvinist tenets as the doctrine of predestination in *De Onderzoeker* of 1871.

63. "J.M." (N. J. Hofmeyr), "Het Hedendaagsche Liberalisme in de Gereformeerde Kerk in Holland," *De Gereformeerde Kerkbode*, 2 September–11 November 1854; idem, "Liberalen en Orthodoxen," ibid., 29 April 1854.

64. P. J. Kotzé published a sermon by Scholten in Cape Town in 1858: J. H. Scholten, *De Aard, de Bestemming, de Toekomst van het Christendom* (Cape Town: Van de Sandt de Villiers, 1858). For Changuion's depiction of the different tendencies within the Dutch Reformed Church, see his letters in *De Zuid-Afrikaan*, 21, 24, and 31 May and 4 June 1860.

doctrines as original sin, and it was indeed against the teaching of the catechism that "man is at all times inclined to all evil" that J. J. Kotzé took his "heretical" stand in the synod of 1862.[65] While the appeals and counterappeals in the Kotzé and Burgers cases proceeded through the various civil courts in Cape Colony and even to the Privy Council in London, the conservative and liberal spokesmen pursued their theological and doctrinal disputes in sermons, public lecture series, pamphlets, and theological treatises.[66] No doubt these theological controversies formed the intellectual culmination of the entire "liberalism struggle"; they aroused public interest and concern to a degree unknown in Cape intellectual life before (or since).[67]

The theological controversies ended inconclusively. The "liberalism struggle" was decided, or so it seemed at first, by the courts who found in favor of both Kotzé and Burgers. When Kotzé and Burgers had to be reinstated at the synod of 1870, some conservatives saw this as such a defeat that they seriously considered resigning from the church.[68] The liberals quietly celebrated.[69] In retrospect, though, it would appear that both parties had misjudged the actual course of events. After 1870, interest in theological matters waned along with the demise of the church struggle: the liberals' moment had gone; the decisive battles had been lost long before, outside either the courts or the theological forum, and in ways not well understood at the time or since.

Apart from Burgers' controversial and abortive presidency of the Transvaal and D. P. Faure's small (Unitarian) Free Protestant Church in Cape Town, these liberal Afrikaners made no further impact on public life after 1870. Yet there had been, between 1850 and 1870, a liberal

65. See, e.g., "Een Lid der Synode," *Geen Leervrijheid: De Zaak van ds. J. J. Kotzé voor de Synode van 1862 en 1863* (Cape Town: Van de Sandt de Villiers, 1863). On Burgers's case, cf. *Report of the Case of the Rev. Thomas François Burgers versus the Synodical Commission of the Dutch Reformed Church in the Supreme Court* (Cape Town: Juta, 1865), and C. F. Le R. Stodart, "Die Nederduitse Gereformeerde Ring van Graaff-Reinet: 'n Tipering en Beskrywing van sy Werksaamhede 1824–1928" (unpublished D.Th. dissertation, University of Stellenbosch, 1983), pp. 200–24.

66. D. P. Faure, *De Moderne Theologie* (Cape Town: Juta 1868); Andrew Murray, *Het Moderne Ongeloof* (Cape Town: Hofmeijr, 1868); J. J. Kotzé and T. F. Burgers, *Wederlegging van dr. A. Murray's Boek 'Het Moderne Ongeloof'* (Cape Town: Van de Sandt de Villiers, 1878); other contributions to the theological controversies included N. J. Hofmeyr, *Eene Getuigenis tegen de Hedendaagsche Dwaling* (Cape Town: Marais, 1860); idem, *Mijne Bezwaren tegen het Hedendaagsche Liberalisme* (Cape Town: Van de Sandt de Villiers, 1862); idem., *De Moderne theologie* (Swellendam: Pike and Byles, 1863); J. J. Kotzé, D. P. Faure, and L. Marquardt, *Hoe de Orthodoxie Strijd Voert* (Cape Town: Juta, 1868).

67. D. P. Faure, *The Past and the Present* (Cape Town: Van de Sandt de Villiers, 1887), pp. 1–6.

68. *De Onderzoeker*, 31 October 1870; S. du Toit, *N. J. Hofmeyr*, pp. 237–38.

69. *Verslag van de Zevenden Algemeene Jaarlijksche Vergadering van het Kerkverdedigings Genootschap* (Cape Town: Van de Sandt de Villiers, 1870).

moment, and we have to account for both its emergence and its failure. A larger question is whether the failure of the Cape Afrikaners' liberal moment can help us understand *why* there is no continuing tradition of Afrikaner liberalism and, more generally, why liberalism in South Africa is so weak today.

The key to a better historical understanding is to see the earlier political discourse and the subsequent church struggle as complementary aspects of the Cape Afrikaners' liberal moment. The political rhetoric of the initial Afrikaner liberal discourse around 1850 no longer seems such an inexplicable (or opportunist?) historical aberration once we begin to trace its later articulation in the arena of the church struggles. The grand themes of liberal rights and equal freedoms did not remain mere abstractions but found application, as we have seen, in a more secular orientation of education, growing support for the separation of church and state, popular challenges to the oligarchic authority structures in local congregations as well as in the church at large, increasing use of appeals to the secular courts and to the rule of law, a growing interest in public debates on controversial matters in newspapers, journals, conferences, and lecture series, and, in general, a more positive orientation toward whatever was perceived as introducing progress, enlightenment, and the modern world to South Africa.

Conversely, the abstruse doctrinal conflicts between the proponents of a "liberal theology" and the stalwart defenders of theological orthodoxy also begin to become more comprehensible if we do not view them solely as a clash of abstract theological doctrines. The doctrinal conflicts should be viewed rather as part and parcel of the whole set of controversies, including those around the voluntary principle, free elections, and recourse to the secular courts, all being fought out in the arena of church affairs but embedded in wider social, economic, and political changes taking place in colonial society. Only in this way does the evident popular interest in the "liberalism struggle" in the church—not only among the colonial elite in Cape Town but in rural communities as far afield as Graaff-Reinet, Hanover, Darling, Bredasdorp, and other places—begin to make sense. In the minds of these Cape Afrikaners there were implicit links between a more liberal approach to religion on the one hand and the general spread of education and enlightenment, the coming of modern means of communication and the railways, the opening up of markets, and the increase of trade and prosperity on the other. We must look to those traders, townsmen, and farmers who responded positively to these forces of "modernization" for the social base of the liberal tendency among Cape Afrikaners; the educationists, journalists, and DRC clergy who produced this Afrikaner liberal discourse at mid-century spoke for and to this specific social grouping.

The "orthodox" party actually was of two minds. For the old guard, with van der Lingen as its preeminent representative, it was indeed the traditional order in church and society that was at stake; it needed to be defended against the diverse threatening incursions of the "modern" world. Van der Lingen was deeply concerned about the spread of the democratic notions of the 1848 revolutions, about the increase in social mobility, the subversive influence of the secular press, the dangers of secular education, the coming of the railways and, of course, the heresies of liberal theology. The nature of the traditional order in church and society he was defending, and the specific objectives of his traditionalist project, remain a challenging historical puzzle.

In part this mystery is precisely because van der Lingen's peculiar project has been so thoroughly obscured by the successes of the younger members of the "orthodox" grouping, the Hofmeyrs, Murrays, and Neethlings. For even if the two factions joined forces in a long series of synodical and court battles against the liberals, decisive differences existed between the old guard and the young activists in the "orthodox" party. These well-educated young men were not rooted in traditional rural communities or restricted to localized resources; they were highly mobile, skilled organizers and enthusiastic conference-goers, trying to reach a wider audience. Compared to the laborious and sometimes obscurantist sermons and speeches of a van der Lingen, the Hofmeyrs, Murrays, and Neethlings were proficient publicists, making fluent and effective use of newspapers, journals, and pamphlets and generating new forums as they went along. Though they styled themselves "orthodox" in their theological and doctrinal positions, this younger generation was thoroughly of the modern world in its organizational mode, its means of communication, and its methods of popular mobilization. Certainly any assessment of the nature and objectives of the "orthodox" project will have to take account of its effects, and these were to transform the traditional patterns of DRC church practices and religious sensibility almost beyond recognition.

In many ways the synod of 1857 marked the changing of the guard in the "orthodox" party. It was during this synod that the young activists began to take over from van der Lingen and the Scottish old guard. The results were quickly evident. The founding of the Theological Seminary, so long on the drawing boards, was finally realized, though not at Paarl with van der Lingen in charge, but at Stellenbosch with John Murray and N. J. Hofmeyr as the first professors.[70] In the synodical commission on mission work—long a special concern of his, though

70. See, e.g., P. B. van der Watt, *John Murray 1826–1882: Die Eerste Stellenbosse Professor* (Pretoria: N.G. Kerkboekhandel, 1979), 99ff., and *passim*.

with little success—van der Lingen made way for Hofmeyr and the Murrays, and despite his skepticism about their ambitious plans, this change at the helm would indeed prove to be a major turning point in the DRC's missionary endeavors.[71] In this connection it is of some significance that whereas such "orthodox" stalwarts as van der Lingen and Robertson had always been firm protagonists of the official church policy that white and colored members should be accommodated within common services in a single congregation, it was Hofmeyr who was the prime mover at the 1857 synod behind the fateful decision to allow separate services and facilities "because of the weakness of some."

After 1857 the pace quickened. During the next few years these younger men took the lead in providing the "orthodox" church party with its own press organs: they founded *Elpis,* a substantial quarterly with international ecumenical connections; *De Wekker,* a more popular monthly; and even a full-fledged newspaper in *De Volksvriend,* with the young J. H. Hofmeyr (the later "Onze Jan") as editor. In 1860 an interdenominational Christian conference, the first of its kind, was organized in Worcester, where Andrew Murray had just been confirmed as minister. The conference was used as a rallying point for the "orthodox" forces and had such an impact that within a few years it was followed by half a dozen other conferences. At the same time, the younger generation was introducing a whole range of innovations in church activities and religious practice: their preaching had an unwonted evangelical urgency and pietist emphasis on personal conversion; they introduced special sermons and services for children; they founded numerous Sunday schools, and actively sponsored and produced a wide range of religious publications aimed at the youth and a more popular audience; they encouraged regular prayer meetings actively involving more members of the congregation; and they organized women's working groups and even children's working groups to raise funds for mission projects.[72] No wonder the liberals became alarmed at this organizational energy and popular mobilization.

As the "liberalism struggle" built up toward open conflict and confrontation at the 1862 synod, there were two contextual developments which in different ways had a major impact on the eventual success of the "orthodox" project and the corresponding failure of the liberal tendency. The first was the occurrence, from 1861, of an extraordinary revivalist movement, the first and most dramatic of its

71. See, e.g., G. E. Hugo, "Die Voorgeskiedenis van die Godsdienstige Herlewing op Worcester in 1860–61," (unpublished B.D. thesis, University of Stellenbosch, 1952), pp. 68ff.

72. See, e.g., Hugo, "Voorgeskiedenis," pp. 5, 28ff.; van der Watt, *John Murray,* pp. 128ff., 144ff., and *passim.*

kind in the history of the DRC. The second was an economic crisis, brought on by a severe drought, by the final withdrawal of imperial preferences for wine exports, and by a collapse in credit, all leading, after 1862, to severe depression. Of the two, the impact of the economic crisis was probably the more decisive, though it still remains an elusive factor. The ambitious visions of general progress and prosperity that had been engendered by the boom conditions of the 1850s collapsed, and this failure in the economic sphere undoubtedly debilitated the social and cultural confidence on which the liberal tendency fed. It would require a major study to trace this in any detailed way, if it can be done at all.

The great DRC revival of the early 1860s also has not been properly studied, and like any religious movement of this kind it poses special problems for historical interpretation and social explanation. Still, in outline its course and effects are more readily apparent. A prominent feature of the DRC revival was the way in which expectations had been aroused and the ground prepared. Contemporary accounts and later studies both saw a direct connection between the Worcester conference of 1860 and the emergence of the first popular religious awakenings in Montagu, Calvinia, and many other places the next year.[73] It would go too far to suggest that in any literal or serious sense the revival had been "organized." The significance of the way in which the revival had been prepared and anticipated and subsequently endorsed by these churchmen is rather to be found in the basic shift in the attitude of the official church toward such religious practices.

In the course of the eighteenth and early nineteenth centuries there are indications that some submerged currents and pockets of more pietist and popular evangelical traditions existed among lay members of the DRC. But the official church, which was Calvinist in the specific sense that issues of discipline and control always tended to be more salient than personal piety, doctrine, or liturgy, made it its business to act firmly against any such unauthorized practices, as were performed, for example, by men such as Van Dyk and Willem Raassel around 1750.[74] The Murrays, Hofmeyrs, and Neethlings, who had been profoundly influenced in their student days by the more evangelical and pietist orientation of circles like the revivalist society Secor Dabar, were much more sympathetic to these evangelical tendencies. After some

73. N. J. Hofmeyr, *A brief account of the present revival of religion in some parts of this colony* (Cape Town: Robertson and Marais, 1860); du Plessis, *Andrew Murray,* pp. 193–203; du Toit, *N. J. Hofmeyr,* pp. 164–69.

74. See, e.g., H. D. A. du Toit, "Predikers en hul prediking in die Nederduitse Gereformeerde Kerk van Suid-Afrika: 'n Histories-homiletiese studie" (unpublished D.D. thesis, University of Pretoria, 1947).

initial hesitation engendered by populist "excesses" at certain revival meetings, they decided to endorse the revival, to incorporate its fruits into regular church practice, and not to oppose it with disciplinary measures as had been the predominant response to smaller but similar practices in the past.

The result was a historic watershed in the development of the DRC. In many ways, the characteristic traditions of DRC piety and religious sensibility can be traced to this time.[75] The incorporation of the revival movement into regular church practice unleashed a vital source of emotional and spiritual energy; it was to prove a decisive factor in the recruitment of candidates for the theological seminary and for mission work at home and abroad. Prepared to risk a certain kind of democratization of the church in terms of allowing more scope for individual and popular piety, this group of modernizing clergy succeeded in blunting and diverting that groundswell of resistance to oligarchic structures on which the liberals depended.

More generally we can see here a twofold historical irony. These fervid opponents of the liberal tendency had a conservative self-conception which was at variance with the modernizing means and effects of their orthodox project. But the liberals also failed to grasp what had happened to them and why they had failed in their historical mission. Nowhere is this better encapsulated than in the *Valedictory Address* Changuion delivered during a tour of country towns in 1865 before his return to Europe. Reflecting on the failure of his Institute, which he had to close for financial reasons in spite of all its achievements, he suggested that the liberating project of rational enlightenment and its universalist values of progress and civilization had not yet managed to overcome the inertia of irrational prejudices and insular perspectives. Changuion prescribed, as a cure for the colonial ills which had proved too much for his efforts, simply more of the same medicine, namely, education as a means to modernization.[76] The irony that escaped him was that it had been precisely the products of his own educational

75. So much did the activists of the "orthodox" party (with the aid of the Great Revival) put their stamp on the character of the DRC that the historical memory of earlier religious traditions and practices has been largely obscured. To the extent that it can be recovered from primary sources and later studies, cf. J. D. Kestell, *Het Leven van Professor N.J. Hofmeyr* (Cape Town: Hollandsche Afrikaansche Uitgewer-Maatskappij, 1911), pp. 4, 10, 36 ff.; *Leven en Preken van J. R. Albertyn* (New York: Longmans, 1922), pp. 24-28; Hugo, "Voorgeskiedenis," pp. 39–44, 71ff.; W. Brown, "Ds Johannes Henoch Neethling" (unpublished M.Th. thesis, University of Stellenbosch, 1981), pp. 33f., 47f. The religious sensibility and practices in the DRC before the 1850s differ in a number of fundamental ways from the later traditions, but this requires a major historical investigation.

76. A. N. E. Changuion, *Valedictory Address Delivered at Various Country Towns and Villages* (Cape Town: Van der Sandt de Villiers, 1865), pp. 1–2; cf. *De Zuid-Afrikaan*, 26 January 1865; Hanekom, *Die Liberale Rigting*, pp. 417ff.

efforts, the Hofmeyrs and Neethlings, who had defeated him by using these very modern educational skills and intellectual resources for purposes more realizable in the colonial context. The trajectory of progress and modernization did not, as the liberals had supposed, inevitably lead to a single goal, with the forces of enlightenment finally winning out over the obstacles of ignorance and prejudice. Instead, the very dynamics of modernization produced both the cultural entrepreneurs and the new social constituencies on which these entrepreneurs could set to work to much greater effect precisely because of their command of the new organizational resources and media of communication.

In the long term and in the larger context of South African history, the failure of the Cape Afrikaner liberal moment and the restructuring and transformation of the DRC tradition are significant for what they prefigured. The DRC tradition itself remained limited to its own Afrikaner and church context, but it was the rise of Afrikaner nationalism as a major political force that would expose the innocence and powerlessness of liberal aspirations in our time. Here it is not too difficult to see the analogies between the Hofmeyrs, the Murrays, and the Neethlings, with their "orthodox" project in the church, and the political and cultural projects of later Afrikaner cultural entrepreneurs in the Afrikaans language movement and the Afrikaner Broederbond, the secret body coordinating nationalist projects in the 1930s and 1940s. Indeed, in some ways the historical continuities are quite direct: S. J. du Toit, prime mover of the first Afrikaans language movement and, with "Onze Jan" Hofmeyr, founder of the first Afrikaner-dominated political party, the Afrikaner Bond, was the spiritual heir of van der Lingen in his Paarl congregation and a first-generation product of the Stellenbosch Theological Seminary. There is a close connection, still to be adequately explored, between the "orthodox" project of the 1860s and the first emergence of Afrikaner nationalism in the next decade. But the supreme irony is that the man with perhaps the best title to being the first articulate Afrikaner nationalist in the early 1870s was none other than T. F. Burgers, president of the Transvaal, 1872–1877, one of the main protagonists of the liberal tendency in the church struggles of the 1860s. The underlying connections and interactions between liberalism and nationalism may be even more complex than has been suggested here, and could well be explored by a study of Burgers' project in the Transvaal, which proved to be a tragic failure both in terms of his liberal and his nationalist objectives.

Richard Elphick

3. Mission Christianity and Interwar Liberalism

Neo-Calvinists and other Afrikaner nationalists have long attacked liberalism as an offspring of the Enlightenment and the French Revolution. In 1940 the leading Afrikaner nationalist thinker, L. J. du Plessis, argued that many aspects of contemporary South African society—forced labor, the reserve system, rising African wages, miscegenation, and so forth—had a fundamental unity and that unity was "liberal individualism." Du Plessis identified liberalism as the modern South African offspring of the "heathen humanism of antiquity." Liberal thought, according to du Plessis, began with "the civilized or rational person as the measure and sovereign of all things." At every point this human-centered philosophy was bound to conflict with (Reformed) Christianity, which began, not with humanity, but with God, his revealed Word, and the orders of creation he had laid down.[1] Such nationalist critiques of liberalism did not falter before the fact that many South African liberals have been practicing Christians. Nationalists have found many ways around this fact; among the most common is to trace the liberal tradition back to J. T. Van der Kemp and John Philip of the London Missionary Society and to show how their Christianity had been contaminated by Rousseau and French Revolutionary ideals.[2]

I wrote this chapter while a fellow at the Center for the Humanities, Wesleyan University. I am grateful to Eugene Klaaren for helpful comments.

1. L. J. du Plessis, "Liberalistiese en Calvinistiese Naturelle-Politiek," *Koers in die Krisis* II (Stellenbosch: Pro-Ecclesia Drukkery, 1940), p. 222.

2. C. E. G. Schutte, "Dr. John Philip's Observations regarding the Hottentots of South

Can we say, then, that Christianity and liberalism are in some sort of necessary tension? If liberalism is a celebration of human freedom over tradition and authority, and if Christianity is an affirmation of a transcendent authority over all human institutions and actions, then there is clear conflict between them. A conflict along these lines surfaced in the Enlightenment and is still embodied in the politics of those European states where liberal parties are tinged with skepticism and anticlericalism. For example, the neo-Calvinism of du Plessis was a product of the Netherlands in the nineteenth century, where its enemy from first to last was liberalism.

On the other hand, it has often been asserted that Christianity, and especially Puritanism, was highly influential in shaping and maintaining the liberal tradition in Anglo-Saxon societies. For example, Michael Walzer, writing of seventeenth-century England, has asserted that Puritanism was a necessary precondition to the rise of liberalism.[3] Without the self-discipline that Puritanism had imprinted on the English character, the liberals' optimistic assessment of human potential would have been impossible. Other thinkers have seen in North American society a "liberal-Puritan synthesis" that endures to this day. The Canadian philosopher George Grant calls this synthesis an "intimate and yet ambiguous co-penetration between contractual liberalism and Protestantism in the minds of generations of our people." He lists numerous points of contact: a common preoccupation with freedom and with the responsibility of the individual; a similarity between Christian millenarianism and a secular progressive view of history; and a common egalitarian tradition.[4]

The question of Christian links to liberalism is central to understanding the liberal tradition in South Africa. The problem covers two centuries of history and is of immense complexity. This chapter offers preliminary comments on liberalism in a specific period—between the two World Wars—when it was common for liberals to argue, as Alfred Hoernlé did in 1939, that they stood in a tradition begun by the Christian missionaries of the nineteenth century.[5] But the link was not merely

---

Africa," *Archives Yearbook of South African History* 3 (1940), p. 134 cited with approval in G. D. Scholtz, *Die Bedreiging van die Liberalisme* (Pretoria: Voortrekkerpers, 1965), pp. 30–31.

3. Michael Walzer, "Puritanism as a Revolutionary Ideology," *History and Theory* 3 (1963): 65–66.

4. George Parkin Grant, *English-Speaking Justice* (Notre Dame, Ind.: University of Notre Dame Press, [1974], 1985), pp. 58–59.

5. Hoernlé affirmed the link in 1939: "The old historic quarrel between 'colonist' and 'missionary' continues to be fought, though in a much more complex setting and with ampler arguments": *South African Native Policy and the Liberal Spirit* (Johannesburg: Witwatersrand University Press, 1945), p. 43. See also W. M. Macmillan, *The Cape Colour*

historical: in the interwar years an extraordinarily high proportion of so-called liberals were intimately related to churches and missions. This was also true, of course, of African "moderates," who can also be called liberals. This chapter concentrates, however, on whites.

There is a problem in deciding who was a "liberal" in that time because the term was not as widely used as in earlier and later periods. There was no liberal party between the wars, not even a parliamentary faction as in the nineteenth-century Cape Colony. Martin Legassick and Paul Rich[6] have tended to label as liberals all whites (Communists excepted) who saw themselves as "friends of the native" and who advocated policies toward Africans more generous than those of mainstream white South Africans. I will follow the precedent of Legassick and Rich, but I do not prejudge the question of whether the ideology of these "liberals" was compatible with liberalism as it is known in broader contexts.

Interwar liberals concentrated on improving the social conditions of Africans, on encouraging dialogue between white and black, and on trying to influence "Native Policy" through an appeal to enlightened whites, both in the civil service and in the general public. The characteristic liberal institutions of this period were the five European-Bantu Conferences (1923, 1924, 1927, 1929, 1933) and many other conferences on specific topics; the ongoing joint councils in cities and towns throughout the Union; and the South African Institute of Race Relations, founded in 1929. These institutions were dominated by a small number of men and women, mostly white but with a substantial number of blacks. The same names recur in all of their membership lists; the liberal community was very small, though dedicated and well-organized and of considerable social standing.

The considerable overlap between the liberals and a group I shall call the Mission Christians[7] is illustrated by the European-Bantu conferences convened to break down misunderstandings between whites and blacks. Two of these (in 1923 and 1927) were convened by the Dutch Reformed

Question: A Historical Survey (Cape Town: Balkema, [1927] 1968) and *Bantu, Boer and Briton: The Making of the South African Native Problem* (Oxford: Clarendon Press [1929] 1963).

6. Martin Legassick, "The Rise of Modern South African Liberalism: Its Assumptions and Its Social Base" (unpublished paper, Institute of Commonwealth Studies, University of London, 1972); Paul B. Rich, *White Power and the Liberal Conscience: Racial Segregation and South African Liberalism 1921–60* (Johannesburg: Ravan, 1984).

7. I use this term to refer not only to the personnel of mission stations but to all Christians anxious to realize social goals by working through religious organizations. The broader term "mission" has virtually replaced "missions" in the mainline Protestant churches of our own time. It was slowly coming into use in the twenties.

Church and were quite naturally dominated by activist Christians. But the same was true of the other conferences; that of 1929, for example, called by the joint councils, represented the moderately reformist tendency in white and African society. Of the 112 delegates, 43 were clergymen or wives of clergymen; moreover, at least 13 can immediately be identified as lay people with strong ties to the church or to missions; careful research would probably uncover even more. In the same year, a committee of eight distinguished South Africans met at the home of an American missionary, Ray Phillips, to found the South African Institute of Race Relations. Of these, six—J. D. Rheinallt Jones, Howard Pim, Edgar Brookes, J. du Plessis, D. D. T. Jabavu, and C. T. Loram—all worked closely with missionaries and church people, all wrote on mission topics, and almost all were men of deep personal piety. Du Plessis was the professor of missions at Stellenbosch, shortly to become the victim of a heresy trial.[8]

Thus the small network of persons we are labeling liberals was intertwined with the network of Mission Christians (i.e., missionaries, their white associates, and their African converts). The intertwining was particularly prominent at the top, though also present at the local level.[9] One must not confuse the two networks. The mission network consisted of people centrally concerned with converting Africans to Christianity. By the 1920s, however, many Mission Christians had come to believe that the missions should also manifest a far greater concern for the education, health, and social welfare of African converts than had been the case in the nineteenth century. At this point the activities of Mission Christians overlapped with those of liberals. Still, for almost all Mission Christians, personal conversion remained the core of the enterprise.

The mission network was fragmented along denominational lines, but at the top there was much ecumenical cooperation. One tie that bound these people together was their subscription to the *Christian Express*, published at the Lovedale mission. Another was the series of General Missionary Conferences (eight between 1904 and 1932), where the most prominent Mission Christians debated many of the same social and political issues that preoccupied the joint councils and other liberal bodies. These South African debates were, in turn, interlocked with a vast international movement in which the purposes of missions were being rethought against the backdrop of twentieth-century nationalism, Western secularism, racism, etc. Much of this discussion took place in books widely read in South Africa and at global conferences attended

8. Edgar H. Brookes, *A South African Pilgrimage* (Johannesburg: Ravan, 1977), p. 39
9. See Jeffrey Butler, "Interwar Liberalism and Local Activism," pp. 95–97.

by many from South Africa, particularly the conferences at Edinburgh (1910); Le Zoute, Belgium (1926); Jerusalem (1928); and Tambaram, South India (1938). Much of South African liberalism in this period derived from these international mission discussions, rather than from political sources in Europe or America.

To understand the Mission Christians of the interwar years, we must modify the image of a missionary preaching the gospel under a gum tree. A survey of 1928 found that forty-eight mission organizations in South Africa employed a total of 1,007 non-African[10] ministers and 189 non-African women evangelists. The same missions employed 3,855 African clergy (ordained and unordained) and 19,625 African lay preachers. These figures exclude African Independent churches. Thus, even in churches dominated by non-Africans it was Africans who undertook the bulk of evangelistic and pastoral work, in large part because they could do it more effectively than the most talented outsiders. The predominance of Africans over non-Africans was greatest in the mission societies that had been longest in South Africa: ratios of black to white clergy[11] were 19.5 to 1 in the London Missionary Society, 45.6 to 1 in the United Free Church of Scotland Mission, and 46.5 to 1 in the American Board.

Striking as they are, these figures probably overstate the role of non-Africans in the traditional functions of a mission or church. Many listed as pastors in fact spent much of their time in supervising black clergy, inspecting schools, and sitting on numerous committees concerned with religious and civil matters. Moreover, in addition to the 1,007 ministers and 189 women evangelists (a total of 1,196 non-Africans), 721 other non-Africans working in missions were specialists of other sorts. These broke down as follows: 34 doctors, 115 nurses, 293 teachers, 57 industrial teachers (i.e., teachers of crafts and other marketable skills), 121 social workers, and 115 other specialists. Whites vastly outnumbered blacks in all of these specialized, nonclergy roles, with the exception of education. There were 7,721 black teachers in mission institutions, most of them in primary day schools, but only 23 black nurses and no black doctors or other specialists at all. Thus there was a clear division of labor along racial lines: Africans preached and taught in primary schools; non-Africans supervised Africans and managed what we can fairly call an enormous benevolent empire.

It is hard to get firm statistics on the scope of this empire, but the

10. One cannot say "white" because American blacks were among their number.

11. Counting women evangelists as clergy, and "Coloured" clergy as "black." Figures in this and subsequent paragraphs include some statistics from Southern Rhodesia, Basutoland, Bechuanaland, and Swaziland.

following will be suggestive. In 1928 there were 377,640 African pupils in mission-run day schools, 3,900 in night schools for adults, and 7,107 in "institutions," i.e., schools with a secondary component. These comprised the vast majority of African pupils in southern Africa. In addition, the only institute of higher education for Africans, the South African Native College at Fort Hare, had three missions represented on its council and was profoundly mission-oriented. In 1938 there were 45 mission hospitals in the Union, and another 37 sanitoria, dispensaries, clinics, and health centers. In social work, the missionaries also took the lead; in 1938 there were 16 mission-run orphanages and homes for destitute "non-European" children and 28 homes and hostels run for Africans, coloreds, and Indians.[12] Several social centers were modeled loosely on the YMCA, of which the best known was the Bantu Men's Social Center in Johannesburg, with the American missionary Ray Phillips at its head. Phillips also founded the first school for training African social workers, the Jan Hofmeyr School for Social Work in Johannesburg.

As in the nineteenth century, missionaries continued to be important as investigators of African cultures and languages. During the interwar years, university-based scholars were beginning to enter these fields, but some of them, most notably Monica Hunter Wilson, were themselves products of a mission upbringing. Also, the missions continued to dominate the field of publishing in African languages, particularly at the Lovedale Press and at the Paris Evangelical Mission Society Press at Morija, Basutoland.

To understand the liberalism of the twenties and thirties one must situate the small group of liberals in relation to the vast network of religious and social institutions that constituted the benevolent empire. A large number of liberals were leaders in this empire; others, like Loram and Rheinallt Jones, relied on it heavily and were highly sympathetic to its goals. Others were products of Christian homes (W. M. Macmillan's father was a minister, Hoernlé's a missionary in India); they associated closely with Christian activists and could speak their language, even if, as in the case of Hoernlé, they were not themselves Christians.

Of the two parts of the interlocking network—the liberal and the Christian—the Christian was by far the larger, the better funded, and the more firmly established. It is possible that liberalism drew significantly

12. J. Dexter Taylor, *Christianity and the Natives of South Africa: A Year-Book of South African Missions* (Lovedale: General Missionary Conference of South Africa, 1928), chart after p. 500; and *The Christian Handbook of South Africa: Die Suid-Afrikaanse Kristen-Handboek* (Lovedale: Christian Council of South Africa, 1938), pp. 121–26, 113–15.

from Christian sources, and hence that the characteristic weaknesses and strengths of liberalism in this period are partially explicable in terms of the religious ethos of the day.

There is a contradiction, more apparent than real, in standard judgments on liberalism in the period between the wars. On the one hand it is said that liberals were part of the "system" oppressing blacks; on the other, that they were marginal and powerless, lacking a solid political base. The degree to which these statements are true and false can be seen in the relationship of liberals to the network of Christian humanitarianism. This network was quite distinct from the "system" as generally understood, i.e., the South African state as servant of the white electorate. Much of the network's funding, it is true, came from the state—for example, for the running of schools. But much of it also came from independent sources like mission-minded Christians in Europe and America, overseas philanthropic foundations, the churches in South Africa, and the revenues of mission-owned farmlands. Many of the most prominent members of the humanitarian elite were expatriates; their pensions would be paid and their children would be educated regardless of what the white public thought of their work. Nor was their quasi-autonomy from South African society merely material. Often their families, their superiors, and their role models lived overseas; they participated in an intellectual discourse whose center of gravity lay in America, England, and Scotland. Their vision was not bounded by the horizons of white South Africa; nor was their freedom of action entirely dependent on its goodwill.

The benevolent empire drew further strength from its intermediary role between whites and blacks. White Mission Christians had access to the small but influential group of "moderate" Christian Africans; moreover, through the African clergy, they also had some contact with the mass of Africans in both city and countryside. In the view of many politicians, the Mission Christians were "experts" on "Native affairs"; they were important witnesses whose advice was sought, if seldom heeded, by commissions, members of Parliament, and administrators. They were in constant demand as speakers on the "Native Question."

The social and political impact of missions apparently peaked in the twenties and thirties. An unusual combination of circumstances heightened their importance in this era. The mass conversion of Africans, which generally did not begin until the 1890s, had by now produced considerable communities of people Christianized to various degrees. More important, a black Christian elite had formed throughout the country. The social power of Christianity had seemingly been demonstrated. For those whites who fretted about the decay of "tribal" bonds and the rapid urbanization of Africans, missions seemed to offer the only way to regain social control over their black compatriots.

Many whites, however, continued to regard the benevolent empire as a threat. They perceived it as dominated by alien personnel and ideas; in their view it corrupted Africans with a bookish education, raised their expectations unrealistically high, and encouraged both laziness and rebellion. Other whites, however, were glad that missions provided low-cost services to blacks which the newly formed South African state was only beginning to provide to whites. Those who thought this way were the "enlightened" whites. It was an article of faith with Mission Christians (a faith which liberals took over) that the higher one went in the state bureaucracy (and the further away from parliamentary demagogues), the more likely one was to encounter officials who held enlightened views. This uneasy goodwill between sections of the bureaucracy and the mission establishment allowed the latter to flourish until such time as the Union government took over the social welfare (and social control) of its black citizens. The twenties and thirties were an ephemeral time of influence for missionaries, not only in South Africa but throughout British Africa and in other parts of the colonized world as well.

Though the rulers of the benevolent empire were hardly marginal or powerless, their empire rested on a shaky foundation, and they knew it. In South Africa the security of the mission enterprise (and the liberal extension of it) rested on keeping some important whites and some important blacks reasonably happy. In particular, the Mission Christians relied on the goodwill of those whites in administration, politics, and business who interpreted administration of Africans as "trusteeship"; and on those blacks (particularly clergy and teachers) without whose cooperation the Mission Christians would lose all claim to influence among blacks. In retrospect we are aware most vividly of the danger from whites: the mounting demands for government intervention in labor relations, education, urbanization, job reservation—all to guarantee white survival and white advantage in the new multiracial South African state. But the threat from the black side was just as pressing. The extension of traditional missions into the realm of social service had largely coincided with the greatest tremor ever to shake the missionary enterprise in South Africa: the revolt of black clergy after the 1890s and the founding of Independent churches. By the mid-twenties it was clear, however, that the missions and white-dominated churches would not totally disintegrate. Many black clergy, among them the most talented and most schooled, had decided to stay with the mission churches. But the aspirations of black clergy had not vanished, and in each denomination there was an undercurrent of tension between non-African missionaries, who clung to their administrative roles, and African clergy, who demanded more authority and independence. White leadership and authority survived, in part because whites could tap into foreign funds and exploit contacts in government and white society. Thus, the benevolent empire justified the continuation of the white missionary enterprise in an era when the traditional roles of evangelist and pastor had largely been taken over by black Christians.

Thus, many interwar liberals were prominent rulers of the benevolent empire and many others were dependent upon it for contacts, support, and ideas. Against this background their endemic caution can be better understood. Few were natural politicians: they had few demagogic skills, and little taste for conflict. They were organizers, administrators, publicists, fund-raisers—closer in spirit to Rotarians than to revolutionaries. They formed committees, corresponded with like-minded people, wrote letters to newspapers, studied problems, held conferences, issued policy statements, and made discreet representations to congenial persons in power. The detached, benign tone of their discourse was not due to the handful of academics in their midst but to the traditions of the benevolent empire, whose very existence depended on the maintenance of precisely that tone. Modern activist clergy would dismiss these Christians as insufficiently "prophetic," as indeed they were. But in the twenties and thirties, Mission Christians and liberals were trying to preserve vulnerable institutions whose capacity for good seemed beyond question. They had readier access to centers of power than modern clergy, however powerless they were in influencing electoral politics, and they enjoyed greater public prestige. In short, they formed a professional elite of experts, at once truly altruistic and profoundly self-protective. From such material, prophets are rarely made.

The justification, indeed the existence, of the Mission Christians' enterprise depended on breaking down barriers between black and white. Not surprisingly, many of their characteristic activities were designed with this end in view: the joint councils, the European-Bantu conferences, the Gamma Sigma Club in Johannesburg, where blacks were addressed by eminent white businessmen, scholars, and officials. Similarly, much of their intellectual effort was devoted to proving that if blacks gained, whites would not lose; or at the very least that reasonable compromises were possible between conflicting interests. If blacks could understand the pressures felt by responsible whites, they would be more patient; if whites could understand the sorrows and indignities suffered by blacks, they would be more fair in devising and implementing policy. The liberals, like the Mission Christians, put great store, not so much in reason, as in *reasonableness.* "We were anxious," recalled Edgar Brookes, "to appear as co-operative and reasonable South

Africans, putting a good case reasonably to our fellow-citizens. . . . I fear that, like many liberals in many countries, we were over-optimistic about the reasonableness of our fellow-men."[13]

Like nineteenth-century missionaries, twentieth-century liberals were sometimes persuaded to become officials of the regime. When the government created the Native Affairs Commission in 1920 to advise on the interests of blacks, two of the three seats were taken by persons in the mission orbit, C. T. Loram and Dr. A. W. Roberts, a teacher at Lovedale. (Roberts also sat on the Native Economic Commission which reported in 1933).[14] Some also played a legislative role: after the abolition of the Cape franchise for Africans in 1936, liberals like Rheinallt Jones and Brookes were elected as senators to represent African interests. Brookes later recalled that between 1937 and 1948 he and his colleagues were dealing with governments "uncertain in their friendliness" but not "hostile." They worked mostly behind the scenes in getting sympathetic politicians and civil servants to reword legislation before it reached the floor of the House. Their African constituents could know little of their achievements:

> . . . if they read that the government had doubled the appropriation for African education or purchased pedigree bulls for the Xhosa Agricultural Colleges, or lifted a burdensome restriction on the gathering of fuel in government forests, they found nothing to show that their representatives were in any way responsible for these concessions . . . .[15]

Against this background, the failure of most liberals in this period to mount a sustained critique of the South African political order can be understood. Rarely did their thinking begin with abstract principles and proceed to a critique of existing or proposed policy. Much more typically, they began with a problem—declining productivity on the reserves, crime in the cities, drunkenness, abusive police, or inadequate housing—and proceeded to debate its solution; or they began with a piece of legislation proposed by the government and began to spell out its likely effects. More like social workers than social analysts, they began from the ground up, and rarely (until Hoernlé's lectures in 1939) did they subject the society or themselves to a systematic critique. In this they merely reflected the cautious vantage point of Mission Christianity, which comprised a semiautonomous but vulnerable establishment with roots in the most troubled sectors of South African society.

Mission Christians were often nonetheless the first whites to publicize

13. Brookes, *South African Pilgrimage*, p. 78.

14. Robert H. W. Shepherd, *Lovedale, South Africa: The Story of a Century, 1841–1941* (Lovedale: Lovedale Press, 1940), pp. 362, 392.

15. Brookes, *South African Pilgrimage*, pp. 79–81; quotation on pp. 80–81.

new ills in South African society, and they often launched into complex debates among themselves, and with other experts, about what should be done about them. In this sense they were an articulate intelligentsia. Yet, unlike that of more conventional intelligentsias, their knowledge, reflecting the ethos of the mission enterprise, was concrete, pragmatic, experimental; in general it was not systematic or theoretical. Like the pioneering missionaries of the nineteenth century, they had to be gifted generalists.

If the characteristic activity of interwar liberals is best understood against the backdrop of mission Christianity and the benevolent empire, can the same be said of their ideology? This is a central question in the history of South African liberalism. To my knowledge it has never been asked, much less answered; my own attempts to answer it must therefore be provisional.

South African Mission Christians were profoundly deferential to European and American thinkers in the field of "race relations." Many of these were Christians who advocated a Christian campaign to remake the world order after the First World War. The theology of these Christians was generally called "liberal," which meant a rejection of Biblical literalism, dogmatism, and narrow denominationalism. Although South African liberal theology rarely entailed an explicit denial of traditional Protestant doctrines, it did imply comparative indifference to doctrinal questions, an eager ecumenism, a modest openness to the values of non-Christian cultures, and a thoroughgoing engagement with the problems of the "world." At this point theological liberalism shaded into the Social Gospel, a largely American product which had wide repercussions in South Africa. The key principles of Social Gospel preaching were that society, not just individuals, stood under God's judgment and that Christians were obligated to act directly on the social order to effect its reconstruction. In the United States the Social Gospel often took radical or socialist forms.[16] However, in South Africa, liberal Christians ordinarily took their ideas from the most cautious wing of the Social Gospel movement. For example, conservative American ideas on race relations, rooted in the views of Booker T. Washington, were brought to South Africa by figures such as Dr. J. E. K. Aggrey of the Gold Coast, the Welsh American Dr. Thomas Jesse Jones, and the South African educator C. T. Loram.[17] They also came to South Africa via the

16. See, e.g., Paul A. Carter, *The Decline and Revival of the Social Gospel: Social and Political Liberalism in American Protestant Churches, 1920–1940* (Hamden, Conn.: Archon, [1954], 1971).

17. Some information on this school can be found scattered in Rich, *White Power and the Liberal Conscience.* A thorough study of its impact on East Africa is Kenneth James

international missionary movement, evolving in the interwar years into what is today called the ecumenical movement. Particularly important was the birth of the International Missionary Council (IMC) in 1921 and the effort to redirect the YMCA and the World Student Christian Federation more into social concerns. These organizations had British as well as American leaders; the Britons tended to advocate "trusteeship" in the governance of "native races," an aspiration congenial to some South African ears. The missionary thinker who probably had the greatest influence in this respect in South Africa was J. H. Oldham, a secretary of the IMC. His *Christianity and the Race Problem,*[18] published in 1924, had enormous impact, especially on Edgar Brookes and J. H. Hofmeyr, virtually the only liberal who was also an important politician. Hofmeyr quoted extensively from it in his Hoernlé lectures of 1945.

A central slogan of the Social Gospel and liberal Christianity was the Fatherhood of God and the brotherhood of man. As expressed by Hofmeyr:

> The central truth, which we cannot escape, try as we may, is that of the Fatherhood of God, carrying with it the implication of the brotherhood of man, irrespective of race, creed, or colour, and the concept of a world-wide family, all the members of which stand in the same relationship to the Head.[19]

This passage well illustrates how a traditional missionary doctrine (that all people can be saved) continued to serve as a critique of racism and exclusivist nationalism; note, however, that the idea had been secularized to include all people, not just all Christians; and that the problems of South Africa now found their answer in a *global* solution. Oldham had argued that European colonialism had created a world economy but without a spiritual or moral unity to match. Everywhere in the world "racial antagonism" was manifest in the racism of white settlers, in the nationalism of colonized peoples, and in problems caused by immigration and interracial marriage. For him the supreme task lay in "establishing harmonious relations between the different peoples of the world and of providing a moral basis for the Great Society."[20] He argued that this could be done through Christianity. His book was offered as an explicit antidote to the pessimism and anarchism which had swept Europe after the First World War.

Oldham's analysis proceeded as follows: There were divisions everywhere; people failed to rise above their own interests; each group was

---

King, *Pan-Africanism and Education: A Study of Race Philanthropy and Education in the Southern States of America and East Africa* (Oxford: Clarendon Press, 1971).

18. London: Student Christian Movement, 1924.

19. Jan H. Hofmeyr, *Christian Principles and Race Problems* (Johannesburg: S.A. Institute of Race Relations, 1945), p. 13.

20. Oldham, *Race Problem,* p. 6.

ignorant of the other; each had ill-founded prejudices against the other. Against this stood Christianity's declaration that all "men" had one Father and hence that all were brothers. But precisely what was the value of this ideal? For Oldham, Christian theology showed that altruistic yearnings for brotherhood were "not simply our ideals but the purpose of God." The notion of the future Kingdom of God (a favorite Social Gospel teaching) provided Christians with a goal beyond earthly relativities and stirred them to heroic action. And, more practically, it supplied humanity here and now with "an outlook, a temper, a spirit which more than anything else is capable of bringing harmony into the relations of men with one another."[21] Theological affirmation assured one of the ontological reality (and historical possibility) of the brotherhood which otherwise seemed so elusive. "The universal community of the loyal is a possibility and actuality because it draws its life from God and leads to God, in Whom is man's eternal home."[22]

South African Mission Christians and liberals often experienced the reality of this brotherhood at formative times in their lives. A notable experience for many young South Africans was the Bantu-European Student Christian Conference, held at Fort Hare in 1930. A total of 183 students (53 white and 130 African), 156 adults (87 white and 69 African), and five overseas visitors gathered for a week of prayer, conversation, and lectures on Christianity and race relations. The mingling of white and black caused consternation in the Nationalist press, but for those who were present the interracial fellowship, "the getting together, was really the main and most memorable thing. . . . We swung together, precariously suspended on the foot-bridge over the Tyumie; we strolled in eager conversation across ground once steeped in the blood of our predecessors engaged in mortal conflict; we pitted our speed and our strength against each other in the sports field . . . in a word, in every imaginable way we demonstrated and revelled in our common humanity together. And we found it good and true."[23]

The Mission Christians realized that their brotherhood was only one of several that could appeal to modern youth. At the Fort Hare conference the president of the World Student Christian Federation identified the two main competitors of Christian brotherhood: Communism and nationalism.[24] In the 1930s the Mission Christians were much clearer on their objections to "Bolshevism" (which among other things threat-

21. Ibid., pp. 21, 22.

22. Ibid., pp. 253, 265.

23. Oswin Bull, "The Conference," in *Christian Students and Modern South Africa. A Report of the Bantu-European Student Christian Conference, Fort Hare, June 27th–July 3rd, 1930* (Fort Hare: Student Christian Association, Christian Union, 1930), pp. 45, 47.

24. Francis P. Miller, "Present Day Life and Thought Among Students," in *Christian Students*, pp. 95–96.

ened their influence with blacks) than to nationalism, which they still understood as the liberal constitutional nationalism of the prime minister, J. B. M. Hertzog. Edgar Brookes listed the faults of Communism: its materialism, godlessness, ruthlessness, emphasis on violence and conflict. But perhaps most offensive to Brookes was "the exclusive character of its brotherhood."[25]

In the South African context the Mission Christian approach to race relations had competitors besides Communism and nationalism: other forms of "liberalism," loosely defined. In his Phelps-Stokes lectures of 1933, Brookes identified two of these as the "economic approach" of the historian W. M. Macmillan and the "anthropological approach" of university departments of "Bantu Studies." Charitable to a fault, and short of allies, Brookes found more to praise than blame in these alternatives. Economic analysis brought "into the discussion of race relations a scientific accuracy and a respect for facts too often alien to such controversies. . . . It has drawn our attention to the points of unity of interests between White and Black . . . and given South Africa a set of incontrovertible arguments for Native progress which are exempt from all taint of sentimentality." As for the anthropologists, they had "taught us the importance of knowing the Native, the dangers of attempting to interfere with his way of life if we are ignorant or scornful of his past." But the failings of each were also clear: the economic approach neglected the psychological and irrational sources of injustice; the anthropological had encouraged conservative segregationist thinking. The Christian approach avoided both these problems, and moreover, it had much more power than either. It was not only "the greatest conscious force for change operating upon Bantu life," but it also commanded far greater loyalty from whites than "is usually found in twentieth century communities."[26]

Perhaps here we have a clue why the language of Kingdom and brotherhood, which seems so anemic in light of subsequent events, was taken seriously by many clearheaded analysts of South African society. Christianity *had* had revolutionary social influence among Africans; could it not have the same among whites? The "economic school" saw South African society in terms of production, acquisition, and exploitation; the anthropologists saw a "contact situation" between two discrete cultures. The Mission Christian, by contrast, saw that "behind anthropological, cultural, political—yes, even behind economic—forces,

25. Edgar Brookes, "The Racial Question and Christian Teaching," in *Christian Students*, p. 186.

26. Edgar Brookes, *The Colour Problems of South Africa: Being the Phelps-Stokes Lectures, 1933, Delivered at the University of Cape Town* (Lovedale: Lovedale Press, 1934), pp. 128, 133, 137, 141, 145, 153.

there stands the world of moral values, by which in the last resort South Africa, White and Black, must inevitably be judged."[27] Brookes presented a list of moral failings which would long be the stock-in-trade of the more moralistic strain of South African liberalism. The whites of South Africa were dishonest in failing to face facts and in advocating a policy (segregation) which led to manifest absurdities and injustices. They were guilty of timidity: knowing the right, they failed to do it. Above all they lacked faith: "The grinding fear which the White man has for the future of his race is utterly incompatible with a belief in the sovereignty and love of God."[28] Christianity offered white South Africa what it had long offered black South Africa: conversion. Or, as liberals of a later generation would put it, "a change of heart."

The various themes we have been considering—brotherhood, Kingdom, morality, conversion—came together in the relationship between the individual and God. True, Mission Christians and liberal Christians had rejected a Christianity which *ended* with the individual's salvation. They had adopted the modern mode of thinking of human "problems" in the collective. But when it came to answers, they had only the most pragmatic of notions (more money for African education, more doctors, better laws), or they had the spiritual answer of conversion and character building, a process which, like their Protestant missionary forbears, they conceived in rigorously personal and individual terms. It was the value of the individual which made racism hateful. It was the individual who, in the presence of God, would acquire the vision, the efficacious love to break down barriers. It was as individuals that Christians entered voluntarily into powerful friendships with fellow Christians of another race. And it was the individual whose stalwart character would form the basis of a new South Africa as it drew closer to the Kingdom of God. This conception of the value of the individual sustained the Mission Christians in their hopeless battle; and this more than anything else makes it possible—with all due reservation—to call them "liberals" in the widely accepted international sense. But it failed to appeal to white South Africans who were steadily developing segregationist policies that made groups, not individuals, the bedrock of social analysis.

To us who live fifty years onward in a frightening South African crisis, the prescriptions and the faith of the interwar liberals seem pallid and embarrassing; indeed, their views seem shot through with the evasiveness, timidity, and fear which they themselves condemned in white South Africans. Even in the context of their own time they were rather outmoded. In Europe the optimism of liberal Christianity had been

27. Ibid., p. 166.

28. Ibid., pp. 166–68.

shaken by the First World War and powerfully rejected in the crisis theology of Karl Barth. Perhaps more pertinently, in America the Social Gospel was being reworked into a new ironic vision of history in the "Christian realism" of Reinhold Niebuhr. The impact of Barth on the Mission Christians seems to have been slight: Brookes understood him only to be calling for a renewed personal experience of God, and one rarely encounters a reference to Niebuhr in the South African literature of the period.

Christian liberalism was strong on practical projects and on personal dedication, weak in its understanding of society and on Christian teachings about sin and judgment. The greatest liberal analysis of the era, Hoernlé's *South African Native Policy and the Liberal Spirit* of 1939, drew sad reviews from Christians who suspected that the author had lost hope for South Africa and faith in the usefulness of the liberal enterprise. It was not Hoernlé who should have been on the defensive, but the Christians. Without naming names, Hoernlé had argued that liberals had no clear conception of the kind of society they wanted, no clear ground from which they could assail white domination. His own attempt to provide this analysis had led him to the brink of despair. It was not only Hoernlé's agnosticism that made him a pessimist, as Archbishop Geoffrey Clayton implied.[29] It was also his intimate knowledge of events in Europe and of Afrikaans political thought. This, after all, was the era of Hitler and Mussolini, the coming of age of architects of apartheid like Hendrik Verwoerd. To be hopeful in such a time was possibly a virtue, but it was no substitute for rigorous thought.

Consequently, much of the liberalism of Christian liberals seems rather pale. They fought for good liberal values: freedom from tyranny, equality of all before the law, the dignity of the individual, limitation of the power of the state. But in many cases these notions originated in the commonplaces of Anglo-American thinking and were not the products of hard thought about South Africa. In the seventeenth century, says Walzer, liberalism was dependent on a preexisting Christianity; here it was the reverse. Here Christian thought assumed the reasonable human being of liberalism, assumed the capitalistic order, assumed the continuing validity of British legal traditions in South Africa. Christian liberals were not aware that liberal institutions needed to be imagined, planted, and nurtured in South Africa as exotic plants; their survivability outside the greenhouse was far from assured.

The liberal-Christian synthesis in South Africa was not entirely impotent; and it was not at all disreputable. Quite the contrary, it

29. Geoffrey Johannesburg to R. F. A. Hoernlé, 21 October 1941, Douglas Smit Papers, Albany Museum, Grahamstown.

inspired men and women of admirable character and dedication and left a record of sheer decency amidst sorrow which future generations may honor more wholeheartedly than we are able to do. But, as I have suggested, its confidence and vigor were rooted in the solid presence of the benevolent empire, and in the missionary tradition of a practical Christianity, whose social power had been amply demonstrated. The former was to succumb very soon to an unholy and ironic alliance of Afrikaans nationalism and the universal forces of secularization; the latter proved to be a feeble trumpet against the high walls of white exclusivism and supremacy. As in Europe, and in China, forces were gathering with power beyond the imagining of liberal Mission Christians. Soon the hope of a reasonable Christian order would fade, almost beyond recall.

Jeffrey Butler

4. Interwar Liberalism and Local Activism

Modern liberalism has had a difficult enough time of it in the relatively homogeneous societies of Western Europe where it was born and nurtured. Where political power was so manifestly skewed in favor of a racially defined group, as in South Africa, or in the American South until recent times, liberalism was an exotic import in a hardly congenial environment.[1] Anyone who challenged the racial order, as the liberals did, was likely to give the term "liberal" a bad name: it became synonymous with "pro-Native," or, pejoratively, with "kaffer-boetie," South Africa's version of "nigger lover." Supporters of the racial order lumped all opponents of racism together, thereby failing to distinguish between a paternalist humanitarianism on the one hand and a genuine democratic liberalism on the other. In the period discussed in this paper, most liberals also failed to make that distinction or to define their liberalism clearly.

Liberalism has never been a dominant force in South Africa, or even the core of the program of a major political party, but it did exist in a limited form in certain institutions and practices of the Cape Colony before 1910. There was, for example, a nonracial but qualified franchise, which was for some a kind of "safety valve," and substantial equality

I thank members of the Southern African Research Program seminar, New Haven, and of the History Department's faculty seminar at Wesleyan University for comments on this paper.

1. R.F.A. Hoernlé, *South African Native Policy and the Liberal Spirit* (Johannesburg: Witwatersrand University Press, 1945), p. viii.

was available in many areas of law.[2] But even as a philosophy of government it was in decline before 1910, and between 1910 and 1948 South African liberals fought a losing rearguard action as the new South African state consolidated its law and practice, virtually always at the expense of the Cape tradition. In this context, there occurred among liberals a steady depoliticization of view and strategy. They were a tiny minority of the enfranchised, and they concentrated on questions of welfare rather than on those of power, on influencing the existing masters of South Africa rather than on trying to supersede them.[3] It is on that period that this paper focuses, before the new Afrikaner regime after 1948 set about dismantling what was left of the liberal tradition.

Among the largely disfranchised majority of Africans, coloreds, and Asians, there were great limitations on education and therefore on occupational mobility—the overwhelming proportion of employed African men and women were laborers and domestic servants; coloreds and Asians were in an intermediate position but still far from equal with whites.[4] For the small minority who had had access to education, the interest in equality was clear: many became members of an articulate if dispersed group, expressing their desire for an inclusive state, a more egalitarian society. Their position was relatively unambiguous, but for the small number of privileged whites who wanted to help them, the dilemma between a paternalist humanitarianism and a more political and egalitarian liberalism remained, at both the national and the local level.

Rather then define "liberal" precisely and then search the record for actors who fit the definition, we shall examine the origins and activities of a multiracial group in a small town, Cradock, in the eastern Cape Province between 1920 and 1940. The members of the group shared a minimal belief in the necessity of joint action to mitigate the consequences for Africans, Asians, and coloreds of pervasive discrimination in favor of whites. With a record of their activity before us, we can see what kind of liberals they were, and then place them in a wider context.

In 1921 the town of Cradock had a population of 6,807, made up of 3,275 whites, 1,759 Africans, 1,659 coloreds, and 114 Asians.[5] It was

2. L. M. Thompson, *The Unification of South Africa 1902–1910* (Oxford: Clarendon, 1960), pp. 108–26; see p. 118 for use of "safety valve" by John X. Merriman, a defender of Cape liberalism.

3. Paul Rich, *White Power and the Liberal Conscience* (Manchester: Manchester University Press, 1984), pp. 114–22.

4. Leonard Thompson and Andrew Prior, *South African Politics* (New Haven: Yale University Press, 1982), pp. 43–44.

5. Union of South Africa, Office of Census and Statistics, *Third Census of the Population of the Union of South Africa enumerated May 3, 1921,* Part I, Population, p. 6, Table V.

a sheep and irrigation farmers' service center on the main railway from Port Elizabeth to Johannesburg, with minor commerce for the needs of a farming population but no industry. The town's development, stimulated by mining to the north in the seventies and by the coming of the railway in 1882, had largely come to an end, and the growth rates of all population groups were well below national averages.[6]

The groups identified in the census were not systematically segregated from each other. Under Cape law there had been few *legal* restrictions on the ownership and occupation of land: there was a "location" next to the town where sites were reserved for the use of colored people and Africans on payment of rent to the municipality, but there was no law requiring all members of those groups to live there. So the urban population was spread between "municipal area" and location, both of them racially and ethnically mixed: in the location, Africans (Xhosa- and Sesuto-speaking), coloreds, but no Asians or whites; in the municipal area, whites, all Asians, a few Africans, and many coloreds, occupying and frequently owning property.[7] Within these broad categories there was, in spite of spatial intermixture, much "spontaneous" segregation: of English-speaking and Afrikaans-speaking whites from each other, of Africans from colored people, of Asians from everybody else. There were few crosscutting associations and friendships, and virtually no crosscutting institutions. All the churches were divided racially and ethnically, but those hands that stretched across the many gulfs were, as we shall see, mostly those of the clergy, not the laity.

National politics was an activity for whites. This was an area of Afrikaner preponderance where white English-speakers had always had to find Afrikaner allies. Before the unification of South Africa in 1910, politics in Cradock had been dominated by the Afrikaner Bond, which selected the local M.P. and provided the Union with its second minister of agriculture, H. C. van Heerden.[8] After the founding in 1913 of the Afrikaner National party (NP), there was a steady but fluctuating drift of Afrikaners from the South African party (SAP) toward the NP. The parliamentary seat went Nationalist in 1920, SAP in 1924, NP in 1929. From 1934 to 1939 both parliamentary and provincial seats were held by the new United party (UP) formed from fusion of the SAP and NP, but became Nationalist upon the schism in the UP in 1939, and have remained so ever since.[9]

6. Jeffrey Butler, "Introduction: Land and People." This paper, and other papers of mine cited, are part of a larger study in preparation: "South African Small Town: Cradock, 1926–1960."

7. Ibid.

8. *Dictionary of South African Biography* 3 (Cape Town: HSRC, 1977): p. 807.

9. R. Bouch, "Farming and Politics in the Karoo and Eastern Cape, 1910–1924," *South African Historical Journal* 12 (1980): 60–64.

Within these parties there was no formal representation of colored and African voters and no hint of a liberalism interested in a further redistribution of power improving the position of African, Asian, or colored people. White women began increasingly to demand the vote, and simultaneously to demand action on issues close to the home: the control of liquor, education and school feeding, public health, and public order.[10] Like their white working-class predecessors on the Witwatersrand, most saw these issues in white terms: few looked across the racial divide in order to bridge it, and none in Cradock pressed the extension of the franchise to African and colored women. Nor did organized Africans and colored people press publicly for such incorporation, and their role in petitioning public bodies was limited. Both the African Political Organization (APO) for colored people and the Cape African Congress for Africans were represented locally, but invariably they acted separately, and on occasion disagreed with each other, as we shall see. Asians played no political role at all.[11] Cradock was, all in all, to adapt Clem Goodfellow's phrase, "stiff clay for liberal potters."[12]

Local organizations interested in political issues were all affected by the increasing activity of white women. Here English-speaking women, goaded by the example of their United Kingdom and United States equivalents a generation earlier, played a major role, linked as they were to national bodies like the Women's Enfranchisement Association of the Union and thereby to international ones.[13] Their Afrikaner equivalents in Cradock preferred to work through the Afrikaanse Christelike Vroue Vereniging, the Afrikaans Christian Women's Association (ACVV), a relentlessly ethnic organization interested in preservation of the church, *volk,* and language.[14]

In the twenties, in the aftermath of the influenza pandemic from 1918, white women began to take up issues like public health, housing, education, and liquor, the latter subject to a major debate because of national legislation—the Natives (Urban Areas) Act of 1923, and the Liquor Act of 1928. Out of this interest in public issues, the Women's Civic Association was founded in Cradock in 1924, led by English-

10. For women in Cradock, see Jeffrey Butler, "Public Health in a Small South African Town: Cradock, Cape Province 1924–1937" and idem, "Afrikaner Women, Social Welfare, and Education in a Small South African Town, 1920–1939."

11. At one time the British Indian Association owned property in Cradock, but it was defunct by the mid-twenties.

12. C. F. Goodfellow, *Great Britain and South African Confederation, 1870–1881* (Cape Town: Oxford University Press, 1966), p. v.

13. Cheryl Walker, *The Women's Suffrage Movement in South Africa* (Cape Town: Center for African Studies, University of Cape Town, 1979), pp. 75–88.

14. Butler, "Afrikaner Women," pp. 19–26. "*Volk,*" meaning, roughly, "people," is not easily translatable into English.

speakers but Anglo-Afrikaner in membership, which took up a range of local issues, concentrating on public health, the appointment of a resident nurse, and the building of a dispensary to cater to all of the poor.[15] The movement soon ran into trouble because of the impossibility of treating the poor in Cradock as a single group, so the Association's project, aided by a crucial anonymous donation from a local English-speaking lawyer, Alfred Metcalf, became one for African and colored people. The ACVV stuck to its major concern, the uplift, or *opheffing*, of the Afrikaner poor by education, school feeding, and segregated housing.[16]

Some of the members of the Association were interested in more than the location dispensary, public nuisances, and proper segregation at the public market.[17] The dispensary soon began to develop a life of its own under the leadership of Mary Butler, a trained nurse who had been appointed by the town council and the Association in preference to colored and African applicants.[18] She was the daughter of James Butler (1854–1923), the Quaker editor of *The Midland News,* the local daily paper, and a longtime champion of education for women. Mary Butler retained close ties with Quakers in Britain, especially with an uncle, Joseph Butler, an active member of the British Labour party, who visited Cradock in 1933.[19] In the Association, she was supported by the president, Mrs. Brown, the wife of a commercial traveler and sister of J. D. Rheinallt Jones, the national "Advisor" to the Institute of Race Relations in Johannesburg, founded in 1929.[20]

The dispensary was controlled by a multiracial committee from its start in January 1927, and Mary Butler reported to it regularly, but in 1929 it changed itself into a "Joint Council of Europeans and Non-Europeans," affiliated to the Institute of Race Relations. The continuity of membership and function is shown in the minute book of the dispensary committee, which became that of the joint council.[21] The

15. Butler, "Public Health," pp. 22–34.

16. Ibid., pp. 44–45.

17. The Cradock municipal records are in the Cape Archives (CA), general reference 3/CDK. There is a file marked "Women's Civic Association," but the material stops abruptly in April 1934. CA 3/CDK 4/1/105.

18. Butler, "Public Health," pp. 42, 48.

19. For James Butler, see Guy Butler, *Karoo Morning* (Cape Town: David Philip, 1977), pp. 14–24; for Joseph Butler, see ibid., pp. 177–80; for Mary Butler, see ibid., pp. 161–63. James Butler is my grandfather, Mary Butler an aunt, and Guy Butler an elder brother.

20. Rich, *White Power,* p. 30; Ellen Hellman, ed., *Handbook of Race Relations in South Africa* (Cape Town, London and New York: Oxford University Press, 1949), pp. 653–54.

21. For a brief sketch of the Grahamstown Joint Council, see T. R. H. Davenport, *Black Grahamstown* (Johannesburg: Institute of Race Relations, 1980), pp. 5–8. The major sources for this paper are *The Midland News;* Mary Butler's Papers (MBP) and especially a minute book "Joint Council April 1927–May 1934" in author's possession; and file

Association continued to give support to the location dispensary and to press the town council for better amenities in the location. It did so, however, frequently independently of the new joint council, and otherwise raised issues of interest to whites only.[22]

The joint council had a life of eleven years before a combination of factors dispersed its crucial figures. In addition to Mary Butler, it depended on a few individuals, chief of whom were Charles Gould, the Anglican minister;[23] James Calata, a young Xhosa Anglican priest;[24] and F. P. Evans, the local Methodist minister. P. C. Goodman, a colored schoolteacher active in the APO, had been a leader in the creation of the dispensary—he claimed that the APO had "started the idea"—but he left Cradock soon after participating in the founding of the council on 6 December 1928.[25] Among active members were three businessmen: Charles Tapp, a pharmacist; W. W. Lidbetter, a Quaker, the local photographer; and E. B. Philips, an accountant. At the beginning of the council, the name of D. J. Schoombee, the Afrikaner manager of a chain clothing store, Hepworth's, appears twice in the minutes but he never attended a meeting; he went on to become a major leader in Afrikaner cultural affairs in Cradock. No *dominee* of the Dutch Reformed Church attended.[26] Two farmers, Owen and Richard Walters, recent settlers from England and active Anglicans, joined the council, but it failed to expand its membership among farmers.

The structure of the organization was closely modeled on joint councils elsewhere. It set out to have a racially balanced membership, but no strict racial quota was applied. There were two vice presidents, one white, one usually colored; two secretaries, one white (Mary Butler), one black (James Calata). There were to be three committees, suggested by Calata—health and child welfare, social and economic, and education and recreation—expanded in July 1929 to four by the addition of justice, but then contracted on 28 January 1930 to two: (1) social, economic, and justice, and (2) health, child welfare, and recreation.[27]

"Cradock Joint Council," Institute of Race Relations Papers (IRRP) in University of Witwatersrand Library, Johannesburg.

22. CA 3/CDK 4/1/105

23. Charles James Baines Gould, b. 1882; BA (Cantab.) 1902; ordained priest 1910; to South Africa 1911; rector of Cradock 1928–1937; author: *Grahamstown Cathedral* (Grahamstown: the Cathedral Chapter, 1924).

24. For biographical details on Calata, see note 47.

25. For Goodman's claim see MBP Minute Book, 21 November 1927. Goodman last attended the joint council on 3 December 1929; MBP Minute Book.

26. On 6 December 1928 and 25 February 1929 Schoombee sent apologies for absence; on 16 July 1929 the name of Rev. C. J. Olivier, one of the two *dominees* of the Dutch Reformed Church, appears as a new member, but neither played any part. MBP Minute Book.

27. MBP Minute Book, 16 July 1929.

The committees were expected to engage in their own activities, to have their own officers, and to report to the full council, which aimed to meet at least quarterly, with an annual meeting, usually in December.

Organizationally, the council was closely linked to its equivalents elsewhere, particularly the Johannesburg joint council which regularly circulated its minutes. With the founding of the Institute of Race Relations, Rheinallt Jones became an occasional visitor, staying in Cradock for long weekends in 1930 and 1931.[28] The council sent Calata as a delegate to participate in the European/Bantu Conference in Cape Town in February 1929, and Michael Curry, a colored teacher, to a European/Coloured one, also in Cape Town, in June 1933.[29] It received and circulated material, in English and in Afrikaans, from the Institute. It was, however, too poor to raise the £10 required for an affiliation fee, and tried to share the cost in a "regional membership" with councils in Grahamstown and Port Elizabeth.[30] Its resources were tiny, expenditures in the first year amounting to 6/3, income to 18/0, less than $5.00 at that time.[31]

There were no regular contacts with either of the white political parties, much less any formal ties.[32] Nor were there any links with the APO or the Cape African Congress: Calata, on his way to becoming a major figure in the national body, the African National Congress, kept his political activities clearly separate from his joint council ones. The council rarely passed resolutions to send to political bodies, though on one occasion it contacted the Cradock Ratepayers' Association, to the resentment of the town council; in May 1930 it telegraphed the members of Parliament for Cradock and Somerset East to protest a Riotous Assemblies bill before parliament.[33]

The joint council's activities were premised on a belief that the dominant whites were substantially ignorant of the lives of "Non-Europeans," and that there existed no institutions within which the virtually disfranchised groups could be heard.[34] The names used reflected some confusion of purpose and a search for an appropriate, inoffensive terminology. The origins of the movement in Cradock in interest in welfare questions can be seen in the first typed draft of the constitution of the "Cradock Welfare Council." Councils elsewhere were described

28. *Midland News,* 3 December 1930, and MBP Minute Book, 2 February 1931.

29. *Midland News,* 26 February 1929; MBP Minute Book, 15 June, 1933.

30. MBP Minute Book, 21 November 1932 and 7 February 1933.

31. *Midland News,* 4 December 1929.

32. MBP Minute Book. However, on 21 November 1927 P. J. J. Coetzee, the SAP member of the provincial council, attended a meeting of the dispensary committee.

33. Ibid., 2 May 1930. Lidbetter paid for the telegrams.

34. *Midland News,* 23 November 1928. Address by Rev. Allen Lea: "The Joint Council Movement."

as those of "Europeans and Non-Europeans," "Europeans and Natives" (East London), "European and Bantu," depending, presumably, on the makeup of the populations being served—East London, for example, had few colored inhabitants.[35] Given the size of the colored population in Cradock, roughly equal to that of the African, the new joint council *either* referred to "Non-Europeans" *or* avoided the issue of terminology by referring to itself as simply the joint council, which was, however, "subject to the regulations of, and affiliated to the Central Joint Council of Europeans and Bantu."[36]

Given the prejudices of the dominant white society, most of whose members, English- and Afrikaans-speaking, deplored *any* contact with other races outside the work place, the movement was a mildly challenging one. With the exception of the South African Communist party, there were few, if any, other associations in South Africa based on the notion of regular meetings between members of different "races," setting up committees and sharing offices, deliberately seeking an unarticulated racial balance—"16 Europeans, 12 Bantu and 8 Coloured (approximately)"—and even accepting a nonwhite majority in membership, all members having equal voting rights. But it was also paternalist in tone. When Mary Butler, on 20 November 1928, proposed that the "Non-European Health Society" should be superseded, she argued that it had succeeded in establishing "a point of contact between the European, Native, and Coloured people where the interests of the latter two can be freely discussed." According to the constitution, finally passed in 1929, the council was to "promote harmonious relations between the various races," to "secure . . . just and fair treatment for them," and "to help towards the development of the Non-European races." The inequalities of the South African order were implicitly acknowledged, as well as the necessity of whites to help bring the "Non-European races" forward.[37]

Cradock's joint council was, then, a collection of local citizens with public spirit which was linked to like bodies in South Africa. It depended crucially on a few leaders. The Reverend Charles Gould, the first president, read widely in current historical scholarship, and could communicate some of its conclusions. He was born in England, trained in history at Cambridge, a man of wide reading, and with a capacity to look at a situation from outside. On 6 December 1928, he drew attention to Eric Walker's *History of South Africa* (1928), to W. M. Macmillan's *Cape Coloured Question* (1927) and *Bantu, Boer and Briton* (1929), to J. Agar-Hamilton's *Native Policy of the Voortrekkers* (1928), to Sarah

35. Ibid.
36. Constitution of Cradock Joint Council, passed 3 December 1929.
37. Ibid.

Gertrude Millin's *South Africans* (1926), and to Edgar Brookes's *History of Native Policy in South Africa* (1927).[38] He was not only aware of recent scholarship, but he kept up with new work, alluding to Macmillan's *Complex South Africa* (1930), Leonard Barnes's *Caliban in Africa* (1930), both eloquent and polemical works, on 18 November 1930.[39]

As president, Gould introduced annual meetings with well-designed addresses on South African history and society, drawing on all the classic liberal themes. First, he expressed faith in reason and respect for fact: the "Native" was not a "question" or a "problem" but a "fact"; the "forces of knowledge and goodwill" should be mobilized to overcome the weaker ones such as "ignorance, malice, and racial prejudice."[40] Second, South Africa was a unit and no one section had an exclusive claim on patriotism; "the only people whose thoughts are worth following are those who think of South Africa as a unit"; hence, he said later, it was absurd to conduct a "whites only" census in 1931.[41] Third, he resisted the notion of local expertise: people like himself and W. M. Carter, the Archbishop of Cape Town, with years of experience in South Africa, were entitled to opinions on its national issues.[42] Fourth, he pointed to the poverty of South Africa, a place of low output per person in agriculture, high wages in industry, and low wages for unskilled labor.[43]

Gould was, however, no radical; he confined himself largely to general historical and economic themes. He did not address political issues like the distribution of power, or take the lead in protesting the Riotous Assemblies Bill of 1930 which drastically limited freedom of speech and assembly, or take up local issues with force and conviction. At one point he referred rather obliquely to politics: "Touching briefly on the present controversy [the *swart gevaar* or black peril theme in the 1929 election] Mr. Gould said that it would probably be found that the political contacts were not the most important—it was a much wider problem than that."[44] Taken with his frequent reference to "contact" between "the races" as the major problem, it is probable that he was himself uneasy about contact. In minimizing the political he agreed with Rheinallt Jones who, a year later, argued that the joint councils were not places for the "airing of grievances"; they were for "cooperation

38. *Midland News*, 7 December 1929.

39. *Midland News*, 8 December 1928; for reference to Barnes see *Midland News*, 22 November 1930.

40. Ibid.

41. On patriotism, *Midland News*, 7 December 1929; on South Africa as a unit, ibid., 3 December 1930; on the "whites only" census, ibid., 26 December 1931.

42. *Midland News*, 4 December 1929, and MBP Minute Book, 18 November 1930.

43. MBP Minute Book, 18 November 1930; *Midland News*, 22 November 1930.

44. Ibid., 26 February 1929.

not conflict," which would do more "than any number of wild speeches on Market Squares or anywhere else."[45] After serving as president until December 1931, Gould was ineligible for reelection, and by 1933 he had allowed his membership to lapse.[46] He had been, however, virtually alone in appealing to scholarship or any kind of coherent body of ideas to support his positions.

Gould had a remarkable colleague in James Calata, rector of St. James Church. Born on 22 June 1895 near Kingwilliamstown, and educated and trained at St. Matthew's, a major Anglican seminary in the Ciskei, Calata came from a family of ministers in the Independent Presbyterian Church, and early developed a wide interest in theology and church music, throughout his life adapting hymns and liturgy for Africans—his papers contain many musical scores.[47] In addition, he showed himself to be a formidable fund-raiser and organizer, establishing "out-stations" and churches in the district, including St. Barnabas on land provided by the Walters brothers at Mortimer.[48] After service in Port Elizabeth and in Somerset East he came to Cradock. He was a delicate man and suffered from tuberculosis, hence his settling in Cradock to benefit from its dry climate, where he remained until his retirement in 1968 and death in 1984. Already while in Port Elizabeth he had shown both his capacity to organize young people into choirs, and to run afoul of J. Cowan, his "priest in charge."[49] Throughout his career, especially when active in African National Congress matters in the forties and fifties, he was involved in disputes with his ecclesiastical superiors, but he apparently never came near to a breach with them—he was not a potential founder of an African Independent church.[50] From the time he arrived in Cradock, he was both liberal and conservative, demanding by his stances that the Cape liberal tradition be protected and expanded, and at the same time insisting on a consistent Christian position, which brought him into conflict throughout his political career with the Communist allies of the ANC.[51] However, he rarely articulated in general

45. Ibid., 3 December 1930.

46. MBP Minute Book, 22 December 1931 and 7 February 1933.

47. For biographical detail, see "Life History of James Arthur Calata" (typescript), made available to author by Patrick Mali, Cradock, 2 June 1984, author unknown; James A. Calata papers (JACP), University of the Witwatersrand, especially a summary by Karen Shapiro, the original sorter of the papers.

48. "Brief History of Churches and Schools at Cradock" by J. A. Calata. This account spans 1883–1970. JACP, folder 23.

49. Cowan to Calata, 16 July 1923, rebuking him for exceeding his authority as deacon; Calata replied on 20 July, respectfully but unrepentantly; both in JACP, folder 60.

50. See, e.g., A. Cullen (Bishop of Grahamstown) to Calata, 20 September 1945.

51. Gail M. Gerhart, *Black Power in South Africa* (Berkeley: University of California Press, 1978), p. 99.

terms the bases of his positions by reference to any body of scholarship, doctrine, or scripture.

As to other members of the council, Mary Butler might also be singled out as something of an intellectual. She sought her inspiration in her religious affiliations, the Methodist church and the local Quaker meeting, reading regularly in the Quaker journal *The Friend*, published in England, drawing on secular pacifist literature and on Gandhian writing as well.[52] The rest of the members, apart from the other ministers, seemed to have been unintellectual humanitarians, seldom contributing to debate in council, concentrating rather on practical local welfare issues, sometimes with emphases that led to deep internal divisions.

The Cradock joint council had begun as an extension of a local welfare body, dealing with the local consequences of policy rather than the making of policies themselves, in a wide range of activities. There were school feeding schemes during the depression, and a great deal of worrying about "morality," especially by Calata, about the effect of town life on the morals of girls.[53] Most of the issues were municipal ones—provision of water, housing, sanitary facilities—but also the conduct of the police in raids searching for "kaffir" beer illegally brewed by African women in the township. On all these matters the joint council achieved limited successes, gaining the sympathetic ear of the Afrikaner Nationalist mayor, M. J. Hattingh, who explicitly acknowledged his special responsibility to people without the vote.[54]

The joint council did, however, become involved in highly sensitive issues in a way that showed how wary all of its members were. First, Calata seems to have organized a "company of natives" who wished to buy land in the Fish River valley to be settled by the families of peripatetic and seasonal workers like sheep shearers.[55] Calata's group had approached a farmer near Mortimer, an area of irrigation farms seventeen miles south of Cradock, and the farmer had agreed to sell them some land.[56] Soon after, outraged farmers attacked the scheme at a meeting of the Mortimer Farmers' Association and elected a committee to "interview the parties concerned"; as a result of the interview, *The Midland News* reported "there is no further cause for concern in this

52. The MBP contain many extracts from *The Friend;* personal reminiscence; her brother Ernest subscribed to the Left Book Club.

53. On his typed draft of a constitution for the joint council, Calata added in his hand: "They [the Social and Economic Committee] should also promote better morals and discipline among the young people in the Location." MBP Minute Book, 6 December 1928.

54. Ibid., 4 February 1930.

55. Ibid., 20 June 1929.

56. *Midland News*, 15 July 1929.

matter."[57] There is no record of what other members of the joint council felt about the project—Calata merely mentioned it in passing at a council meeting.[58] The council seems also to have accepted implicitly the official doctrine that African influx into the towns had to be controlled. These limits were later explicitly accepted by F. P. Evans, the Methodist minister who succeeded Gould as council president in 1932.[59]

More directly political was the joint council's reaction to the breakaway from the Cape African Congress of the Independent African Congress led by Elliot Tonjeni, who had begun his activities in the western Cape. The authorities had closed certain districts to him, so he turned to the eastern Cape in June 1931 and mounted comprehensive verbal attacks on the whole order at well-attended meetings in locations, and particularly at Cradock.[60] Calata, supported by the council, urged the authorities to exclude Tonjeni, but even after Tonjeni was arrested and sentenced to jail in 1931 the activity continued, outside the location boundaries.[61] In response, the council mounted a program of lectures to instruct the African and colored population on a variety of issues dear to liberals—thrift, self-help, housing, and education.[62] But Calata also called for the granting of executive powers to the Advisory Boards, the only representative body available to location residents, on the grounds that "agitators" got nowhere if Natives were given "responsibility."[63] The council did not take up the suggestion, and it later turned down a proposal (origin unclear) for a "poor man's lawyer" because it "is being supported by people who are known to be not working in the best interests of the Natives."[64]

A third issue was that of access to liquor by Africans and coloreds. The Natives (Urban Areas) Act of 1923 had provided for municipalities to choose between total prohibition for Africans, a municipal monopoly of production and distribution, and toleration of domestic brewing; coloreds were given greater but still limited access to wine and commercially produced beer.[65] The municipality wanted to continue with a

57. Ibid.

58. MBP Minute Book, 6 August 1929.

59. Ibid., 8 February 1932; *The Midland News*, 26 April 1926, accepted the doctrine that Africans were "guests" in towns.

60. Peter Walshe, *The Rise of African Nationalism in South Africa* (Berkeley: University of California Press, 1970), pp.181–83, 221; Willie Hofmeyr, "Agricultural Crisis and Rural Organisation in the Cape: 1929–1933" (unpublished M.A. thesis, University of Cape Town, March 1985), chapter 7.

61. *Midland News*, 15 June, 19 June, and 3 July 1931; MBP Minute Book, 22 December 1931.

62. See ibid., 4 August 1931, for the setting up of the lectures.

63. Ibid., 25 November 1931.

64. Ibid., 16 March 1933. Calata was absent.

65. T. R. H. Davenport, "The Triumph of Colonel Stallard," *South African Historical Journal* 2 (1970): 78-79.

ban on brewing, but Africans, according to a typed statement by the "Vigilance Committee of the Location of Cradock," virtually certainly led by Calata, wanted a system of controlled domestic brewing. The committee suggested a subdivision of the location into three wards, which would each have turns at brewing. The wards would be headed by "wardens," who would take over policing functions far larger than simply overseeing the production of beer by permit—"rents, overcrowding, infectious diseases, etc." The wardens would be paid £60, £40, and £40 (clearly per annum), and their appointment would make possible the dismissal of the "European assistant at the [Location] Office." To achieve all this, the Committee suggested that the joint council convene a round-table conference of interested public and private bodies.[66]

The ministers on the council, black and white, were hopelessly divided on the issue along denominational lines. Methodists, Baptists, and Quakers, but not Anglicans, were principled teetotalers and opposed to municipal or domestic brewing. Mary Butler was caught in the middle between a powerful personal teetotalism, a belief in the nutritional value of the traditional African beer, and a desire to meet African wishes.[67] On 6 May 1930, the council met with the mayor, the magistrate, and the commandant of police as invited guests and voted 12 to 2 in favor of domestic brewing.[68] Another meeting was called and the Methodist minister, Evans, moved that the motion be rescinded, but he failed by 10 votes to 9, with colored members voting against domestic brewing, African members for it.[69] The municipality, however, stuck to prohibition; it established municipal brewing in 1940, ten years later.

Fourth, the close political limits within which the council operated were shown in an incident involving Mary Butler, *The Midland News* (managed by her brother Ernest), and the magistrate. As the depression deepened and infant mortality in the location increased, Mary Butler turned for help to the family newspaper. She had for long been an author in a small way on religious and social issues,[70] and now sought to dramatize the starvation issue by writing little vignettes of children dying of hunger and disease. The paper was willing to publish these, but when in the same article she tried to include comparative figures on whites, Ernest Butler demurred and consulted a member of the joint

66. MBP Minute Book, 2 December 1930.

67. Personal reminiscence.

68. MBP Minute Book.

69. *Midland News*, 20 June 1930; MBP Minute Book. The votes were: against (i.e., for domestic brewing): European 4, "Natives" 5, colored 1; for: European 4, "Native" 1, colored 4.

70. MBP, "Location Sketches," all published in *The Midland News*, 1927–1935. She published two pieces, both entitled "Observations at a Location Clinic" in *The Nursing Record*, September and October 1928 respectively, using the unlikely nom de plume "Socrates."

council and the magistrate, A. G. Oakes. Both doubted whether such comparison would "improve race relations." So to her chagrin, the article was published without making the point that, even with a high local level of unemployment and poverty among whites, whites were still much better off than blacks.[71]

Finally, there was an administrative issue that developed into a political one, the recruitment of African or colored nurses for the location. When the location dispensary was originally started in 1927, the Women's Civic Association had advertised for black or colored nurses, offering £7 a month. There was at least one applicant, but she was turned down in favor of Butler, originally at £14 a month, later at £17 when a provincial subsidy was secured.[72] In the mid-thirties the issue of black nurses appeared once more, leading finally to Mary Butler's resignation. The hiring of colored and African nurses in the local hospital entirely as additional staff was an issue in the town council in 1931, and also for the dispensary.[73] An African nurse was hired after the opening of a new, considerably larger, "Metcalf Clinic" in 1936.[74] She and Butler did not "get on." She soon became pregnant and her appointment was terminated. Things were not much better with her successor, and in late 1936, Butler, handling a difficult delivery, called in a doctor too late and the mother and baby died. The local branch of the Cape African Congress led by Calata took up the issue, arguing among other things that had the nurse been African, the outcome would have been better.[75] To the annoyance of the town council, which was clearly prepared to back her even if she were proved culpable in this particular case, Mary Butler resigned, insisting that if Africans wanted African nurses, they ought to have them.[76] Regrettably, the minutes of the joint council after 1934 are missing, so we have no record of the development of these issues there. It seems clear, however, that the council did not play a role in conciliating two of its most important members, Butler and Calata, and with Butler's departure, it soon stopped functioning altogether. "If the Natives are not going to use it," wrote the president, "it might as well die."[77]

71. Mary Butler to J. Rheinallt Jones, 15 February 1931, enclosing a proof of her article as first submitted, and the final version as published in *The Midland News*, 14 February 1931: "Do you think the censors were right?" Ernest Butler was my father.

72. Butler, "Public Health," pp. 42, 48.

73. Ibid., 7 June 1932, 16 March 1933.

74. Butler, "Public Health," p. 47.

75. Ibid., p. 48.

76. Town Council Minutes, Location Committee, 15 March, 1 April, 3 May, and 17 May 1937.

77. Owen Walters to J. Rheinallt Jones, 24 June 1937, reporting Butler's resignation; on 10 December 1940, Lynn Saffery, secretary of the Institute of Race Relations, wrote to Charles Butler, mayor of Cradock, an uncle of Mary Butler: "Is the Joint Council dead?"; both in IRRP, Cradock Joint Council.

* * *

What was the impact of all this activity by joint councils on racial attitudes and political alignments? The councils played no substantial role in the major conflicts among whites on the question of relationships to the British Commonwealth, and of Afrikaners and British to each other. Locally, they seem to have had no effect on the racial attitudes of the dominant whites toward Africans, Asians, and colored people. Moreover, they had no effect on relations between Africans and colored people, who seem to have been moving apart from each other politically on issues such as liquor, and never seemed to approach forming an alliance of the "nonwhite" poor; some colored leaders looked sympathetically at proposals to segregate the housing of African and colored people from each other.[78] While the joint councils did not affect the structure of politics, locally or nationally, they did achieve some limited success in local issues—in Cradock, in delaying a lodgers' tax; in obtaining better water supply, and a soup kitchen; and in opening a Carnegie Library. And they put in a great deal of time preparing material on wages and welfare for a major national commission, the Native Economic Commission of 1931.[79]

If we look at the whites in this joint council more closely, we can note a possible explanation for the limited successes and the demise of this small group of public-spirited men and women. They were almost entirely English-born, or with recent experience of England: Mary Butler alone was born in South Africa, but she went to school in England and remained in touch with English Quakers. Most of the young people recruited by Butler left Cradock, and so far as the joint council depended on recruiting whites in Cradock, its position was worse in 1940 than it had been in, say, 1930. The white council members had shallow roots in the white community, so their capacity for influence was limited. For in secular terms most political forces were against them: whites were not demanding changes in the structure of power in favor of the majority—rather the reverse. There was no equivalent of those middle-class liberals who in mid-nineteenth-century Britain demanded political change to extend political rights to those below them in the social scale.

They were also a largely Christian group, active, not nominal, Christians: two Quakers and the Anglican, Methodist, and Baptist ministers—each responsible for white congregations—but no Catholics

78. MBP Minute Book, 8 February 1932.

79. See MBP Minute Book for lodgers' tax, 4 February 1930; for water, 7 June 1932; for soup kitchen, 22 November 1931 and 8 February 1932; for the Carnegie Library, see Minutes of Executive of Cradock Joint Council, 27 November 1936, IRRP, Cradock Joint Council; their evidence for the Commission was ready at the meeting of 14 April 1931, MBP Minute Book.

or members of the Dutch Reformed Church, either its white or colored branches.[80] They regularly opened their proceedings with silence (a Quaker influence) and closed with the benediction, which offended no one. However, they were part of a deeply divided Christian community, in which religion was not a major force for the creation of a humane order for all God's creatures. Even in the joint council there were seldom references or appeals to a common faith. As Elphick has shown, much South African Christianity seems pallid, dependent on liberalism rather than the other way around.[81]

The limited impact of the council's activities on whites is paralleled by its failure to produce changes that would have retained the support of Africans like Calata. For Calata the disillusionment with the council was part of a disillusionment with English-speaking South Africans generally. Two events were crucial in producing it: first, the racist structuring of the Boy Scout movement in 1935 offended him deeply, leading him to plead with its leaders that the "parallelism" be temporary: ". . . let it be definitely said that it is only the policy for the time being."[82] This was a particularly important issue for him: the Pathfinders and Wayfarers, African Boy Scouts and Girl Guides respectively, were critical parts of his activities in Cradock.[83] Calata received no such assurance, and the 1936 legislation, which eliminated the last political remnant of the Cape liberal tradition for Africans, might well have been a final exasperation. Second, in 1937 he became Secretary-General of the ANC, and in 1938 he said, "I do not believe we can any longer look to the South African Britishers for our champion. . . ."[84] His grasping at the African-nurse issue in 1936 may well have been an attempt to restore his political position locally, which might have been damaged by his resolute refusal to side with "agitators" like Tonjeni. Yet he remained a liberal to the end, resisting the Communist allies of the ANC, remaining a loyal son of the Anglican church, and demanding a redistribution of power from whites to other groups.

This is, then, the story of a few public-spirited whites, coloreds, and Africans. They were liberals in trying to further regular, nonhierarchical

80. There were two Dutch Reformed Churches: the *Moederkerk* was the mother church, with an all-white congregation; the *Zendingkerk* was the mission church for colored people.

81. See pp. 78–80.

82. Calata to Rheinallt Jones, 9 November 1935. IRRP.

83. Institute of Race Relations Papers (IRRP) Series RR17. These folders contain lengthy correspondence between Rheinallt Jones, who was the national Commissioner of the Pathfinder movement, and Calata, who became commissioner for the eastern Cape.

84. Thomas Karis and Gwendolen Carter, eds., *From Protest to Challenge: A Documentary History of African Politics in South Africa 1882–1964*, Vol. 2, Thomas Karis (ed.), *Hope and Challenge 1935–52* (Palo Alto: Hoover Institution Press, 1975), p. 136.

relations between white and "nonwhite" and in their hope of changing the attitudes of the dominant; but they were also paternalist humanitarians working for betterment of the daily lives of the African and colored poor. To what extent were they really supporters of segregation, instruments of "social control," as has recently been suggested?[85] Their fears of "agitators" can easily be made to appear as an attempt at social control, their meliorative activity a kind of "opium of the masses." In fact, however, their moderation was largely resistance to uncontrollably rapid and violent change. They were not supporters of the economic and social status quo—they would hardly have joined the council if they had been. But theirs was an embattled, defensive stance, not a confident, crusading one; they were essentially cautious, trying to conserve what little liberalism existed. Hence they adopted what were essentially administrative strategies, a line of action parallel to that followed by South African liberals at the national level in the interwar period. Like them, the Cradock joint council was unable to transform a body of ideas into practice, because they could not appeal to the perceived interests of a sufficient number of the enfranchised.

85. Rich, "White Power," pp. 10–18.

Phyllis Lewsen

5. Liberals in Politics and Administration, 1936-1948

Segregation was the first officially proclaimed "Native policy" of the South African government. The policy began in 1936–1937, when the prime minister, J. B. M. Hertzog, persuaded Parliament to pass his segregation acts, and it lasted until 1948, when the National party gained power. It called for the "development of the Natives on their own lines in their own areas" under white (Christian) trusteeship, and for the maintenance of white civilization (based on genetic, or on divinely determined, white superiority). As a policy it was paradoxical and contradictory. A third of the Africans continued to be clamped on white-owned farms by penally enforced pass laws. The African reserves, as before, emitted streams of migrant labor indispensable to the white economy. The mines adjusted their wages to the supposed earnings from the reserves. Within the towns, the small proportion of Africans accepted in them were housed in segregated "locations" or townships. An enormous and growing "surplus" of urban Africans, on whom burgeoning industry had earlier depended, were deemed "temporary" and superfluous, and were due to be returned to their homes in the reserves. Color bars, customary and legal, blocked access to skills. A huge, incompetent, and bureaucratic Department of Native Affairs tried to manage this agglomeration, and had the power to issue restrictive,

I thank Mary Lucas and Marian Lacey for research material; and R. M. de Villiers, R. J. P. Jordan, and Miriam Basner for the information noted. The Human Sciences Research Council funded my work on the manuscript collections listed, to whose curators and librarians I am grateful.

punitive, and discriminatory proclamations and regulations. This, broadly, was the pattern of segregation as it had evolved over decades and was in 1936–1937 declared definitive. Its underlying assumptions were shared by English- and Afrikaans-speaking whites alike, though with varying degrees of intensity.

Hertzog had first attempted his "solution" of the "Native problem" in 1926, when he was South Africa's first Nationalist prime minister. A discomforting relic of the old Cape color-blind qualified franchise obstructed him. The "non-European" Cape vote had been specially protected in the constitution by the requirement of a two-thirds majority to change it. J. C. Smuts, Hertzog's predecessor as prime minister and now leader of the opposition, approved of segregation and trusteeship, but had qualms about interfering with a historic constitutional right. The result was a nine-years' delay. Only after the merging in 1934 of Hertzog's Nationalists and Smuts's South African party into the United party (a broad alliance of English-speakers and Afrikaners) did Smuts succumb and accept the "compromise" of a separate communal roll to elect three white members of Parliament to represent all the Cape Africans in the House of Assembly. (The Cape colored vote, already diminished in power by the adoption of whites-only female suffrage in 1931, was retained.) Smuts's chief lieutenant, J. H. Hofmeyr, made a brilliant speech opposing any curtailment of the voting right cherished by Africans,[1] who had hoped for its extension and felt grievously betrayed. He attacked the destruction of a "vested right," and asked pertinently if trusteeship was meant to continue indefinitely. However, he optimistically foresaw "a rising tide of liberalism" among younger white South Africans. The struggle over the Cape African vote was a pointer to two divergent directions: one ultimately to the completion of segregation as apartheid; the other to the upheavals of today.

Another feature of Hertzog's system for African representation was that four whites were to be elected (by a complex system of indirect election) to represent Africans throughout the Union in the Senate. Moreover, a partly nominated advisory African body, the Native Representative Council, was created, with five white magistrates added and the secretary of Native affairs presiding. The Council's comments and suggestions were so insultingly ignored that it moved in eight years from moderation to what most whites deemed an outrageous demand for the end of all discrimination and for total equality. Meanwhile, the existing (white) Native Affairs Commission grew in power and influ-

1. *Parliamentary Debates, House of Assembly (H of Ass.),* special session, (1936), cols. 1089–91.

ence.[2] The only change in favor of Africans was the addition of two liberals, but they were regularly outvoted. Despite the valid demands of the Native Representative Council that the old Commission be abolished, it continued as a powerful competitor.

The 1936 Native Trust and Land Act was the second major segregation measure. The land set aside in 1913 under the hated Natives' Land Act was increased to the meager total of about 14 percent, with the Native Trust handling purchase and distribution. But the excited hopes of the landless were disappointed. All purchases were stopped during the Second World War. The land already bought (adjoining the Reserves) was found to be densely settled, and when legal rights of occupation were granted in this "released land," the allotments were too small for subsistence, the rents were high, and the network of regulations to check erosion and overstocking were deemed by occupants to be a new tyranny. In short, Africans judged the 1936 act a fraud, and there was serious unrest in the northern Transvaal over the small size of allotments.[3]

The third measure, the 1937 Native Laws Amendment Act, was meant to tighten the already harsh constraints of the 1923 Urban Areas Act and to check the influx of Africans into towns and cities. The purchase of land and property by Africans in urban areas was forbidden. A biennial census was ordered in each town; estimates of the number of workers needed, and lists of redundant Africans, were to be provided, and the latter were supposed to be returned to the reserves. Yet it was desperate overcrowding that had squeezed them out of the reserves in the first place. Meanwhile, industry demanded cheap African labor. Despite the lack of houses and home life in town, despite the malnutrition,[4] the police raids for technical offenses, and the color prejudices encountered in the workplace, no town laborer would willingly work on the farms; urban life, however hazardous, chaotic, and unstable, was better than starvation in the reserves.

These policies provoked a reaction among philanthropic whites. The Institute of Race Relations (founded in 1929) expanded its efforts to collect facts and alter attitudes; by 1936 it included a large spectrum of

2. Margaret Ballinger, *From Union to Apartheid* (Cape Town, Johannesburg and Wynberg: Juta, 1969): on NRC, pp. 141–203; on NAC, pp. 30–34, 36, 152, 180. In this chapter "Ballinger" refers only to Margaret, not to her husband, William.

3. Ballinger, *To Apartheid*, pp. 27–34; H. Basner, "The Black Price of Gold from 1870–1960," University of the Witwatersrand, A 1740, chapter 27.

4. See *Report of the Inter-departmental Committee on the Social, Health and Economic Conditions of Urban Africans* (Smit Report), Molteno Papers University of Cape Town (MP), Bc 279 D1.28.

welfare activity and promotion.[5] This role was an important stimulus to the new liberalism. Though not politically aligned, the Institute was broadly liberal in its quest for individual freedoms and social advancement. Radical historians have strongly attacked it as both capitalist and segregationist. Both charges are exaggerated. The rather prosy Institute organizer, researcher, and welfare activist, J. D. Rheinallt Jones, was often conservative in outlook, but he was a dedicated practical reformer; and it is absurd, on the basis of issues taken out of context, to refer to R. F. A. Hoernlé, a lucid thinker and inspiring liberal, as a segregationist and forerunner of apartheid: though he gave serious attention to the abstract merits of total segregation, he judged it utterly impracticable.[6] Members of the Institute had a Fabian belief that accurate information can change attitudes. They soon found that it seldom does. But they continued their practical tasks and wider investigations, and made some converts—at least to compassion.

In 1937 the Africans' white parliamentary representatives were elected, and they took their seats in 1938. In the House of Assembly, Margaret Ballinger, previously an economic historian at the University of the Witwatersrand with a long record of work for African causes, combined an exceptional gift for factual presentation with an eloquence that astonished the House;[7] her maiden speech, on the topic of underpaid African railway workers, was cheered. She and Donald Molteno, another representative of Africans, shared the same views on the need for basic structural economic and legal reforms. Molteno was a young Cape Town advocate with a family liberal tradition, a compassionate sense of justice, and a lucid, wide-ranging intellect. He had an endless capacity for work and organization; but it was Ballinger, through force of personality, who from 1941 was asked to lead the tiny team. The third Native representative, Gordon Hemming, a Transkeian lawyer, was also a fine parliamentarian and an expert on his Transkeian constituency. Conditions which before had been taken for granted gained sudden illumination. In Ballinger's aphorism, it was soon evident that "all South African politics are Native affairs."[8]

5. South African Institute of Race Relations, *Race Relations Journal* (RR) 1943, 14th Annual Report, SAIRR, pp. 44–45.

6. Paul Rich, *White Power and the Liberal Conscience* (Johannesburg: Ravan, 1934), pp. 48–85; D. L. Smit Papers (SP), Albany Museum, Grahamstown, 25/41, Hoernlé to Smit, 27 November 1942; Martin Legassick's interesting interpretation of Hoernlé's equivocal liberal stance, as he sees it, which has gained wide currency among radical historians, is in his article "Race, Industrialization and Social Change in South Africa, the Case of R. F. A. Hoernlé," *African Affairs,* 75 (1976): 224–37.

7. For Ballinger, a personal friend, I consulted R. M. de Villiers and current political biographies.

8. *Umteteli wa Bantu,* 15 April 1939.

The senators elected to represent Africans were likewise an outstanding group, and in the less contentious smaller house they had a great impact. Some of their amendments passed. Rheinallt Jones, who had unequaled knowledge of African social conditions, rural and urban, funneled Institute reports into the Senate. Senator Edgar Brookes could hold the Senate enthralled. He was appointed to important bodies such as the Social and Economic Planning Council, the Advisory Council for Native Education, as well as the Native Affairs Commission. At the start he was less critical of government policy than Molteno and Ballinger. But his liberalism steadily advanced, and by 1947 he was arguing for a common-roll, though qualified, franchise for Africans at all levels, municipal, provincial, and parliamentary.[9]

The term "racialism" in 1937 still referred principally to rivalries and hostilities among whites. The chief debate of the session was on the national anthem.[10] The same year that the "Native" representatives entered Parliament, 1938, was the centenary celebration of the Great Trek. The symbolic ox-wagon trek and the concluding ceremony on what became the hallowed "Day of the Covenant" transformed an already potent mythology into a sacred history of the suffering and national survival of the Afrikaner.[11] The whole milieu was changing, and a distinctive "organic" Afrikaner nationalism was spreading. Young intellectuals who had studied in Holland and Germany were infused with current ideologies of neo-Calvinism and romantic nationalism. Coordinated by the secret and elitist Afrikaner Broederbond, and working through journalism, economic and cultural projects, and labor organizations, they reshaped Afrikaner nationalism to the preoccupations of a new era.[12] Anti-Semitism became prominent, even in Parliament among the purified National party, whose leading members attacked the Jews as alien capitalists, depriving Afrikaners of their birthright in the commercial sphere, or as Communist agitators. In this context, the outbreak of war in 1939 provoked a major realignment of Afrikaners in politics. The United party, the party of Anglo-Afrikaner conciliation, split, and a Reunited National party denounced the "imperialist" British war against Germany. But Smuts gained a narrow pro-war majority in Parliament, helped by the "Native" representatives, who saw Nazism as a threat they were bound to oppose.

9. *The Forum*, 3 August 1947, pp. 15–26.

10. *H of Ass.*, vol. 32 (1937), col. 356; Ballinger, *To Apartheid*, pp. 69–74.

11. Leonard Thompson, *The Political Mythology of Apartheid* (New Haven and London: Yale University Press, 1985), chapter 5.

12. Dan O'Meara, *Volkskapitalisme* (Johannesburg: Ravan, 1983), pp. 61–62 (Broederbond); see also pp. 64, 85, 110.

The Society of Jews and Christians had been founded in 1936 in Johannesburg to fight such racist and Nazi trends.[13] Its small, esoteric membership overlapped with white members of the joint councils (established in the twenties to make contact with African leaders), the Institute of Race Relations, and liberal intellectuals at the University of the Witwatersrand. Molteno later contributed brilliant reports on Parliament to the Society's journal, *Common Sense.* He also promoted the Libertas and Civil Rights Leagues, and William and Margaret Ballinger created the "Friends of Africa" in 1940.[14] All these societies were, however, further examples of liberals talking largely to each other.

Among Afrikaners, herrenvolk concepts buttressed existing antiblack attitudes. With the growth of urbanization, the hatred of blacks became obsessional among many whites, English-speaking as well as Afrikaans-speaking, and any physical contact or proximity was abhorred as contamination. For example, the Nationalists inveighed against conditions in the clothing industry, where young Afrikaner women were forced to mingle with other races at work and even joined trade unions.[15] In this emotionally charged milieu the liberals fought for wage increases and welfare grants for Africans; exposed inroads on civil rights; and gained one important change in 1943 when Hofmeyr in his budget made a small grant to Native education from general revenues. (Previously it had been financed from African taxation sources only).[16] They also raised fundamental issues; for example, in 1938 Molteno attacked the poll tax paid only by African males, and later Ballinger called for the immediate alignment of "Native policy" with African needs and aspirations as marked in the principles of the Atlantic Charter. Over and over again the liberals explained how hunger and poverty in the reserves, along with job opportunities in town, fostered migration of blacks into urban areas. They argued for a settled population of black farmers and urban workers and the abolition of migrant labor and the pass laws. In 1947 Margaret Ballinger again asked for reconsideration of the whole of Native policy,[17] while Brookes pleaded for the full

13. *Common Sense,* vol. 1. Hoernlé was on the panel of editors. *Common Sense* published several of Nadine Gordimer's early short stories.

14. Winifred Holtby organized "The Friends of Africa" in 1934 in London after a visit to South Africa; William Ballinger reorganized it locally in 1940. Alan Paton, *Hofmeyr* (London, Toronto and Cape Town: Oxford University Press, 1954), on the Libertas League, pp. 303–4; also MP, Bc579 El.25, El.26 and El.3.

15. The exclusion of Africans from the Industrial Conciliation Act did not extend to women. The skilled trade unionist Solly Sachs exercised a strong influence in overcoming color prejudice among Afrikaner women in the Garment Workers Union. See E. S. (Solly) Sachs, *Rebels' Daughters* (London: MacGibbon and Kee, 1957).

16. Paton, *Hofmeyr,* p. 380.

17. Ballinger, *To Apartheid,* p. 131; *H of Ass.,* vol. 61 (1947), cols. 1158–59.

acceptance of Africans as citizens and the eschewing of all "black peril" election propaganda.[18]

Not only the Reunited Nationalists but the ruling United party (UP) and its allies (the Dominion and the Labour parties) had a horror of social equality. The fear of losing "the purity of the white race" was felt by the great majority of whites. Even liberals objected to social intermixture, with rare exceptions; and at times Molteno, Ballinger, Brookes, and the truculent radical Hymie Basner were evasive in a way that today would be deemed racist. To liberals of today it is puzzling and shocking to find Hofmeyr, in a speech to students in 1932, pronouncing that white South Africans "are revolted in particular by the notion of social equality, with its corollary, as it seems to us, of intermarriage and miscegenation."[19] Friendly personal relations across the color line were rare, though meetings were fostered by official occasions, and letters were exchanged. Awareness of color, an unfortunate product of the times, rendered much liberal activity ambivalent in its effects, but this should be seen in context. Understandably, this liberal ambivalence raised, and still raises, questions as to liberals' commitment to fundamental change.

How effective were the liberals in representing black interests in Parliament? Through hard work and persistence, and through Ballinger's oratory, they won the respect of the UP majority, but the opposition, the Nationalists, resented their presence and demanded their removal from Parliament. Ballinger, after the first grueling years, was still optimistic, however. Prime Minister Smuts admired her, and with the war going badly and an inflamed Afrikaner opinion, he hoped to soothe African hostility. In late 1939 he told her privately to talk to the new minister of railways, F. C. Sturrock;[20] the result was a small rise in wages for African workers and a housing and pension scheme.[21] The government made larger grants to education and social welfare; most promising of all, Smuts agreed to extend legal recognition to African trade unions. In *Umteteli wa Bantu*, a newspaper founded by the Chamber of Mines in 1920 to counter the influence of the African National Congress, (ANC), she wrote trenchantly on many issues, in spite of the capitalist support of the paper.[22] She was optimistic at this time, in 1941, and saw "the possibility of getting valuable concessions for the

18. *Parliamentary Debates, Senate Debates* (*Senate*), (1947), cols. 1158–59.

19. *Rand Daily Mail,* 6 August 1932.

20. Ballinger, *To Apartheid,* pp. 113, 124.

21. M. V. Ballinger and W. G. Ballinger Papers (BP), University of the Witwatersrand, A410/B2.8.15.

22. See also Tim Couzens, *The New African, A Study of the Life and Work of H. I. E. Dhlomo* (Johannesburg: Ravan, 1985), pp. 90–92.

African people within the limits of our present Native Policy, if the government has the will and courage to propose them."[23]

On 21 January 1942, Smuts gave his famous address to a public meeting in Cape Town organized by the Institute of Race Relations. Many people felt that at last a government was about to change policy. One sentence, "Isolation has gone and segregation has fallen on evil days," seized the headlines. He added that segregation had failed to stop the urbanization of Africans—"You might as well try to sweep the ocean back with a broom." Smuts described the responsibility for trusteeship, this "sacred trust of civilization," as an "ethical" and almost "religious" duty. His practical proposals did not go beyond welfare services, such as the duties of providing housing, nutrition, education, and transport. "There are helpless people on our doorstep. . . . It will be an evil day for us if ever the day comes when in the testing hour there is alienation, distrust and hatred."[24] The speech brimmed over with goodwill, but Smuts's envisaged social benefits were within the framework of the systematic oppression of the Land and Urban Areas Acts and the system of migrant labor.

Yet the speech pleased liberals, blacks and whites—even Ballinger thought a "definitive new phase" had begun. On the other hand, it dismayed UP traditionalists and infuriated the Nationalist opposition. In Parliament Ballinger was encouraged in 1942 to ask for the minimum wage for African employees of the government, which would set an example for private business not to lag behind; and she also called for the abolition of the pass laws.[25] Smuts replied that the government was moving forward—"we have almost outpaced public opinion . . . we shall do more and more until substantial justice is done" and he hoped she "would not despair and accuse us as mere reactionaries."[26] More positively, the minister of Native affairs, Denys Reitz, made a sweeping attack on the pass laws in the Senate. He said that nothing was so conducive to creating bad feelings and disturbing race relations; in the Transvaal alone, pass offenses between 1939 and 1941 had totaled 270,790, which meant that more than a million Africans in South Africa had been accosted and their passes demanded. He promised to discuss abolition with the prime minister and cabinet.[27]

The result was that the police were instructed to ask for passes only

23. *Umteteli,* 7 June 1941.

24. Jean van der Poel, ed., *Selections from the Smuts Papers* 6, (London: Cambridge University Press, 1973), pp. 331–43.

25. Ballinger, *To Apartheid,* on the dilemma of her position, pp. 101, 110. For Molteno, see *H of Ass.*, vol. 46 (1942), col. 1642.

26. Ibid., vol. 46 (1942), col. 3370.

27. *Senate,* (1942), cols. 1582–88.

if an intention to commit a crime was suspected. Unfortunately, a "crime wave" followed. Justice F. E. T. Krause took the lead as reformer, after his address on "Crime and Punishment" in 1939 had shown the effects of imprisonment on poll tax and pass offenders. The Institute of Race Relations set up a Penal Reform League; a special committee in 1942 showed that Africans did not predominate in crime, and that half of their offenses were against special laws. Meanwhile, the crime wave continued; it was still an argument against ameliorating the pass laws in 1946. The "abominable pass laws," as the African leader J. L. Dube had described them, remained a hated persecution. (President P. W. Botha said in January 1986 that they were seen as "an affront to human dignity" and would be scrapped.[28]) Molteno, who saw politics as "the struggle against tyranny and poverty," wrote in his election manifesto for 1943 that despite "prejudice, ignorance . . . and overwhelming opposition we have gained many improvements for the people." He stressed the trend to higher wages after official wage board investigations, and said that major gains would follow with legalized trade unions. But the latter promise was not fulfilled by 1948, despite many reminders.

Molteno was persistent and comprehensive:

> No one realises more than I do . . . how much remains to be done. There is the struggle against the poll tax . . . against the pass laws (these have been relaxed but not yet abolished); for more land, greater economic opportunities, the extension of democratic rights of Africans in the Northern Provinces and the complete defeat of the policy of segregation. In respect of all these things we have fought and will continue to fight.
>
> Apart from the larger national question above referred to, I have daily been dealing with the countless cases of individuals . . . who have come to see me for advice and help and have constantly been making representation to employers, local authorities and Government departments on their behalf. The same applies to the numerous groups, such as advisory boards [for town "locations"], vigilance associations, school committees, church societies and tribes whose representatives have likewise approached me either in person or by letter. The volume of this work has been immense and has extended throughout the enormous area of my constituency. If I may mention an example of the services I have rendered in this connection, the stopping of the objectionable use of the pick-up van in Langa was due to my representations.[29]

Molteno was so pertinacious that he won redress for the affronts to many constituents. He replied to all letters in his courteous style, and the throng in the corridors outside his chambers was so large that his

28. *Umteteli*, 3 October 1942; E. Hellmann, ed., *Handbook on Race Relations in South Africa* (Cape Town, London and New York: Oxford University Press, 1949), p. 103; U.G. 47-1947; Ballinger, *To Apartheid*, p. 166 on J. L. Dube; for Botha, see *The Star*, editorial, 5 February 1986.

29. Manifesto drafted in 1942, copy in the MP, Bc 579 A 54.31; see also draft article, MP, "The Tyranny of the Pass Laws," Bc 579 D1.28.

barrister colleagues protested.[30] He was quick to detect new political trends among the Africans. "I found the people seething in every place," he wrote to Ballinger after touring his constituency in 1945. "Unless the government changes its attitude there may be ugly trouble soon."[31] By contrast she believed she could mediate between the Native Representative Council and Smuts in 1947.[32] She did not realize that the rejection of its "toy telephone" role—as one councillor described it—was not a spontaneous outburst due to frustration, but had been carefully planned with the ANC, which in turn had been radicalized by its youth league.[33]

Though she, and perhaps Molteno, did not know it, the time for deferential consultation with "Native representatives" was passed. Only Basner had connections with African leaders at the grass roots. His contemptuous anger and unbridled vocabulary of abuse against injustice were intended as a goad. Reitz's successor, Piet van der Bijl, called Basner an aggressive, arrogant exhibitionist, and compared his manner with Brookes's "blend of fearless criticism and restraint." But Basner did not believe that he could shift policy—he could only expose it. "Don't shout," the UP Senator Hartog, who detested him, once heckled. Basner retorted, "I know it is easy for the Senators in the House to keep cool. They do not have to live on 27s 6d [almost 28s] a week, when the cost of living is at least £.3.15s [75s]. They do not see their children eat grass. I am not going to keep cool."[34]

Nationalists angrily attacked the Cape "Native representatives" and the "Native" senators for including colored and Indian discrimination in their domain. The liberals opposed the constant demands for separate coaches for all Asians, Africans, and coloreds on Cape suburban trains, and for enforced residential separation in the new colored townships the government was planning. Even more inflammatory, and crossing all party lines, was the issue of Indian "penetration" into "white areas." The liberals fought, clause by clause, the preliminary "pegging" measures, which tried to freeze property holding by Asians until the Commission had reported.[35] Molteno in 1943 summed up their attitude in an article for *Bantu World*.

30. Information from R. J. P. Jordan. 31. *BP,* A4.01/B2.8.15.

32. Ballinger, *To Apartheid,* pp. 200–1.

33. T. Lodge, *Black Politics in South Africa since 1945,* (Johannesburg: Ravan, 1983), pp. 11–26; Paton, *Hofmeyr,* pp. 142ff., 244; personal discussions, especially with Hugh Macmillan (son of W. M. Macmillan) and Mrs. M. Macmillan.

34. *Senate,* (1943), cols. 1330, 1335 (van der Bijl); ibid., (1946), cols. 49–50, 70 (Basner).

35. Segregation was legal in the Transvaal but not in Natal, where Indian penetration into "white areas" caused intense disapproval. S. Bhana and P. Pachai, *A Documentary History of Indian South Africans* (Cape Town: Philip, 1984), pp. 153–61, 176–82.

We regard unjust, discriminatory legislation against any racial component of South Africa's population, by which their rights to improve their economic position by use of their natural abilities are impaired, as against the interest of the whole community, irrespective of the racial character of the groups comprising it. . . . The more racial discrimination in general there is in South Africa, the harder will it be for the African people to free themselves from it.[36]

In 1946, under strong Natal pressure, Smuts put through his notorious "Ghetto Act," which drastically restricted Indian residential and trading rights, and as compensation granted communal representation of Indians by whites in Parliament. The latter provision was very unpopular with Smuts' UP; the Labour party split; the Natal Dominion and the National party voted together in the longest debate in Union history; and the Indians rejected the communal vote as an insult.[37]

The sequel was fought at the United Nations in New York, where Smuts was requested to bring South African policy on Asians into conformity with the principles and purposes of the United Nations Charter (whose preamble he himself had composed). Smuts replied that this was a domestic matter, beyond the competence of the United Nations—but he lost the moral battle.[38] Second, his request for South Africa to annex the mandated territory of South West Africa, with UN consent, was rejected.[39] Already in 1940 Molteno had written that South Africa had to make democracy a "local reality" and not merely "a sentimental appeal to the historic achievements of the British people in Britain, the values of which are flatly contradicted by South African practice." And he wrote in *Common Sense* in November 1947:

South Africa stands alone—entirely alone—in upholding such racial discrimination as a desirable and meritorious thing in itself. Yet we live in an ever more integrated world. We shall continue to ignore the vital forces that are abroad in that world at our mortal peril.[40]

In retrospect, 1942 was the last hopeful year for liberalism. An election was due in 1943, and Smuts was worried and took no risks. Reitz, who was ailing (and, as Smuts thought, too liberal for current opinion) was sent to London as high commissioner. Smuts then appointed the conservative, ill-informed Piet van der Bijl, a staunch segregationist, as minister of Native affairs. "Smuts' choice of me was not a good one and I had no qualifications for the job," van der Bijl confessed in his memoirs, adding that at least six persons were better qualified.[41] His

36. Paton, *Hofmeyr,* pp. 423–24.

37. Bhana and Pachai, *Indian South Africans,* pp. 182, 191; *Umteteli,* 27 April 1946.

38. W. K. Hancock, *Smuts,* Vol. 2, The Fields of Force, 1919–1950 (London: Cambridge, 1968), pp. 467–71.

39. Hancock, *Smuts* 2, pp. 467–68.

40. MP, Bc 579 D1.15.

41. P. van der Bijl, *From Top-Hat to Veldskoen* (Cape Town: Timmins, 1972), pp. 213ff.

appointment was just a further illustration of the low prestige among white politicians of the portfolio of Native affairs. After the war, Smuts became preoccupied with the growth of Russian power and the Indian imbroglio, and consequently was inattentive to domestic affairs. He spoke benevolently but would only act pragmatically; the small list of social reforms did nothing to appease the rising African discontent.

The limited achievement of reform was a consequence both of the pressure of the "Native representatives" and of the planning and initiative of the most famous of the liberals, Hofmeyr. He could master any cabinet portfolio, and had handled five from 1933 to 1938 under Hertzog, who made allowances for his sensitive but intermittent liberal conscience. In 1937 he was so disturbed at threats by the UP against coloreds that he wanted to resign. Smuts wrote to an English friend:

> If he were to leave the Government it will be a great loss and a distinct blow to me, as he is one of my most promising young men and the reactionaries don't like him. He is a good liberal with a fine human outlook. Unfortunately he is also somewhat academic and exaggerates things and aspects of no real importance. . . . Politics is the art of the possible and the practicable, and one has to give in on small things in order to carry the bigger things. But it is just in this comparative valuation that the snag lies.[42]

Hertzog, still prime minister in 1937, pulled back on the colored issue, but a few months later a more divisive one arose. Hertzog appointed his personal friend A. P. J. Fourie to a Senate vacancy as a person "thoroughly acquainted" with Native affairs, as required by the constitution.[43] Hofmeyr was outraged at the choice and resigned from the cabinet. In 1939 he was expelled from the caucus for opposing an Indian "pegging" bill for the Transvaal.[44] A varied group of liberals asked him to lead a Liberal party. His personal loyalty to Smuts, who was now prime minister, was too strong, and he had distinct limitations of temperament. He could not easily have held together disparate liberals who did not all share his basic principle of "Christian trusteeship." On the one hand, Hoernlé and Ballinger had differed with him. On the other hand, Molteno admired him greatly and the economist Herbert Frankel would have followed him gladly; so, though he was closest to Brookes in his Christian dedication and motivation, he could draw to himself people with very different values.

Too much has been made of the intramural ideological tensions among this small group of liberals. Some rivalries over personal status

42. Van der Poel, *Smuts Papers* 6, p. 67.
43. Ibid., Smuts to M. C. Gillett, 28 July 1938, p. 40.
44. Paton, *Hofmeyr,* pp. 284–99.

and position did exist, particularly in academia. The only battle of enduring importance was between the competing claims of an anthropological and a trade-union and economic focus—chiefly the Hoernlés (Alfred and Winifred) vs. the Ballingers (Margaret and William). This was related to a conflict between William Ballinger, who wanted to emphasize trade-union activity, and Rheinallt Jones, who adopted the more general "race relations" approach. There were also divisions over tactics, between the vehement, explosive Basner with his all-or-nothing attitude and the diplomatic Brookes. It should be remembered that powerless minorities are often quarrelsome and feud-ridden. When one thinks of Karl Marx and his associates, the South African liberals score fairly well on the factious-minority scale.

When the schism in white politics arose over the war, Hofmeyr returned to office under Smuts, as minister of finance and education. He remained in charge of finance and a shifting roster of additional departments until 1947, when for health reasons his load was lightened. He was acting prime minister five times and deputy prime minister—and heir apparent—in 1947. The result was that this brilliant man could never stretch his whole mind and attention to the great priorities of the "color problem." Unlike Margaret Ballinger and Molteno, who knew that class conflict was entwined with color discrimination, Hofmeyr was conventional in his affirmations and often contradictory. For example, his attitude to the succession of Indian Acts was ambivalent. He could speak one way and vote another. His inability to challenge Smuts was a further impediment to consistent progress. Near the end of his life, Hofmeyr felt overburdened and wanted to resign.[45]

The few "liberals" in the UP, such as B. Friedman, M. Kentridge, and J. R. Stratford, made good speeches but were not always publicly in the liberal camp when it mattered.[46] The large majority of party members were conservative segregationists, and Hofmeyr was frustrated by his own isolation and growing unpopularity. By 1946 he was ready to withdraw as potential leader and prime minister, but Brookes dissuaded him. By then Hofmeyr's liberalism had expanded: he had moved to the conviction that blacks should be directly represented and not through whites. Brookes agreed: "We Europeans who represent Africans in Parliament have always felt that to legislate ourselves out of existence would be our supreme victory,"[47] he wrote, and with Ballinger and Molteno he openly favored a common-roll vote for all, on a qualified franchise. Ballinger wrote in 1946, "Only those who do not believe in this communal type of representation can work it," and added that it

45. See Paton, *Hofmeyr,* chapter 10, for a full and subtle discussion of this relationship.
46. Ibid., p. 285.
47. Brookes, *The Forum,* 30 August 1947, pp. 25–26.

should not be seen as permanent. But liberals as a group seemed to be decreasing. Although commercial and industrial leaders now opposed migrant labor and favored stable urbanization, Brookes felt that "[the liberal] stands, as it were, on a shrinking isthmus, with the oceans of European passion encroaching on it from day to day"; if a black wished to cooperate with white liberals he "was bitterly attacked" by his own people.[48]

Hofmeyr's concrete but limited achievement was the sevenfold increase of expenditure on African education and postwar welfare grants. The charge was to the general revenue, not, as previously, to a fixed proportion of African taxation. The change was an important admission of a common citizenship, although segregation was still the official policy. However, Hofmeyr blundered badly in 1946 when faced by an intransigent Native Representative Council, whom he wholly antagonized.[49] And Smuts was contradictory and cryptic. He said in Parliament in February 1948:

> We have to keep an eye on world opinion, but the facts in regard to the position are that we have developed a White Community here and I can visualise no future government, which will ever dare to touch the basis on which White South Africa has been developed. . . . We are busy on something new. We are not being understood by the UNO and many other countries cannot understand the position here, but we are following a new course and we are going to maintain that course in the years before us.[50]

It is no wonder that Hofmeyr, amidst all these crosscurrents, had lost his ambition before he was made the scapegoat for the defeat of the government in the election of 1948.[51] The irony was that in the campaign he and Smuts were linked together as enemies of the white race, and Smuts genuinely believed that Hofmeyr was too liberal for the people.[52] Hofmeyr indeed was, but he shared the inadequacies of liberals that Hoernlé analyzed in 1943 in a letter to Douglas Smit, secretary of Native affairs. Hoernlé dismissed.

> the illusion that it is possible at once to be a beneficiary of the racial-caste society, and to realize liberal principles. . . . We are to pretend that our cupboard is full, but that the time is not yet ripe to share the treasures with the public. Actually, I suggest, our cupboard is bare: there is nothing in it. Why not? Because we, ourselves, do not know what we want to put into it.[53]

Like other liberals, Hofmeyr failed to rise to Hoernlé's challenge that

48. Brookes, idem.; M. Ballinger, *Forward,* 5 April 1946.

49. Paton, *Hofmeyr,* pp. 459–74. The usual pension was £60 a year for whites, £36 a year for Asians and coloreds, £24 for Africans.

50. *H of Ass.,* vol. 62 (1948), cols. 1007–8.

51. Paton, *Hofmeyr,* pp. 459–74.

52. Hancock, *Smuts,* Vol. 2, p. 505.

53. SP, 35/41.

they think out the principles and blueprint for a liberal order. Hofmeyr's intellectual and political contribution was fragmentary, yet when he died Molteno mourned the loss "to those of us who adhere to the liberal faith; who irrespective of party alignments, regarded Hofmeyr as our leader and our hope."[54]

One way in which liberals did contribute, though marginally, to drawing up blueprints was their assistance to the government commissions that were so prolific in this period. ("Do you think the government really intends to *do* anything as a result of all these enquiries?" Molteno wrote skeptically in 1941 to Margaret Ballinger.[55]) In 1926 the Economic and Wage Commission had drawn attention to the dangers of "restricting the opportunities of low paid Non-European workers."[56] In 1932 the Native Economic Commission continued in the same vein, predicting "an appalling problem of Native poverty" in the reserves; and in 1936 a White Paper on land policy confirmed that view: " . . . it is notorious that the existing Native locations and Reserves are congested, denuded, overstocked, eroded. . . . " As with the British Beveridge Report, the war gave an impetus to replanning society for the benefit of all; and in 1940 General Smuts appointed the able H. J. van Eck chairman of a commission to investigate the South African industrial and agricultural requirements. Its report stressed the growing industrialization that it, like the other commissions of the era, relied on for greater productivity. The van Eck report eventually fathered thirteen detailed reports on a wide range of subjects. Had they been carried out they would have made South Africa a welfare state, within the limits of a capitalism reinforced by the expansion of markets made possible by improved conditions for Africans. The reports thus had liberal implications but were not explicitly liberal documents.[57]

The Social and Economic Planning Council recommended that the Urban Areas legislation should at once be overhauled, and to advise on this issue the government appointed the "Fagan" (Native Laws) Commission of Enquiry, 1946–1948.[58] The Fagan Report was accepted as UP policy, but came too late to influence the election campaign of 1948; if anything, it was used against the government by the opposition. Its main conclusions were that the trend toward urbanization was "irreversible" and could only be regulated and guided; "total segregation" was utterly impracticable. The pass laws should be modified and migrant

54. *Common Sense,* January 1949. 55. BP, A410/B2.8.15.

56. Union of South Africa (UG) 14-1946, paras. 79, 92.

57. UG 32-1939, paras. 49, 62, 69, 84; UG 40-1941, paras. 8, 25, 28, 44, 49, 54, 62, 83–4, 86; UG 32-1946, paras. 7, 25, 28, 49, 62, 83, 84, 66.

58. UG 28-1948.

labor gradually phased out: "We have seen no sign in the country of a readiness to dispense with Native labour," and trade unions should be legalized. "South Africa," it concluded, "is passing through a period of disturbed equilibrium."

The commissions on social security and on national health set up by the Council between 1942 and 1945 included all groups in the benefits they proposed, though on different scales, and admitted common citizenship rights as Hofmeyr had done in his education reform. Their recommendations would have been improvements in a liberal direction but, unfortunately, were far too expensive to apply. The liberals, while thinking the advocated structural changes incomplete, on the whole were very pleased with these reports,[59] but they had a curious consequence. Very few MPs troubled to read them. Much of the evidence came from liberal sources, which made their mark on the reports, memoranda, and speeches. In the eyes of the white electorate the influence of liberalism was thus exaggerated, but there were no practical results.

In 1942 an interdepartmental committee, headed by Smit, secretary of Native affairs, published its immensely important report. The committee had been instructed "to explore possible ways, other than merely increasing wages, of improving the economic, social and health conditions of Natives in urban areas," and it reported that it had been "impressed above all by the poverty of the Native community and by the all pervading ill effects of poverty throughout their social life."[60] The range of topics covered was impressive: it dealt with the results of migrant labor; "the maladjustment arising from broken homes"; the "disgracefully deficient diet"; tuberculosis; deficiencies in hospitals, dental services, housing, and transport; and low wages, especially the fact that unskilled workers, on average, earned £5 2s 11d [almost 103s] a week but needed £7 14s 6d [almost 155s] to support a family of five, i.e., they earned only two-thirds of their needs:

> . . . the Committee considers that it is still not sufficiently recognized that Natives possess a dignity and self-respect which is necessary to the proper relationship between them and the European community. A progressive policy at this stage is not only justified . . . but will unquestionably ease the problems of racial adjustment which the Union will have to face in an increasing degree in the future.[61]

59. *Senate,* (1946), col. 574.

60. *Smit Report,* Appendix 2, p. 29, with summary of recommendations. M. M. S. Bell, "The Politics of Administration: A Study of the Career of Dr. D. L. Smit with Special Reference to His Work in the Department of Native Affairs" (unpublished MA thesis, Rhodes University, 1978), especially pp. 1–34, 81ff.

61. In 1942, the South African (and British) pound was worth approximately U.S. $4.00, so £5 2s 11d was about $20.60, £7 14s 6d about $31.00.

But Smit's advice was ignored, and with appalling consequences. Housing and transport were municipal responsibilities, but the tasks were too large for local governments, and the lack of action by any public body led directly to bus boycotts by Africans and to sprawling shanty towns in every large urban area.

Despite his wide powers to issue repressive regulations, to control meetings, and to arrest offenders, Smit could do little positive. Personally he was a "paternalist liberal." He spoke out against the pass laws and segregation, helped to establish schools, and increased the training of African doctors at the universities of Cape Town and the Witwatersrand. On the other hand, he did not help the Native Representative Council gain more authority. Nor could he always overrule the lower cadres of his Native Affairs Department, which deserved their reputation for bullying and incompetence.

The pressure of liberal paternalists in the Native Affairs Department and in government generally did little to soften the impact of segregation laws on Africans. Complaints about railway and post office officials were common. Africans were kept waiting at counters until all whites were served. Wrong tickets were sold with no redress, and white officials refused to serve behind the same counter as Africans, which would have helped with language difficulties.[62] But worst of all were the grievances against the police. To quote Edwin Mofutsanyana in 1943: "[White] police, recruited from rural areas, are called upon to administer oppressive laws." Small fines instead of prison sentences had been suggested for pass offenders. "But small fines for what?" Mofutsayana asked. "For crimes for which no other nation can be penalised? If so, the Minister must be asked to request the Government to abolish these technical laws, which have made Africans into criminals." Police brutality was particularly resented: "Africans regard police as a foe and not as a protector."[63] Margaret Ballinger drew attention to unprovoked attacks by whites on Africans and the staggeringly light sentences—fines or a few months' imprisonment—for assaults causing death. The Institute of Race Relations in its 1945 report noted

> with profound concern that, notwithstanding many advances in good will and understanding among the European public, there is a growing tendency among younger people in all the Non-European groups to despair of conciliatory methods and to believe that only hatred, employing the method of direct action and, if need be, culminating in revolution, can bring about the fundamental changes in status which we desire.[64]

62. MP, Bc 579 A24.190, and other letters in this file.

63. BP, microfilm A 1335/C3.6.D4, See "Conference on Relations between Africans and the Police": especially the evidence of Edwin Mofutsanyana.

64. Report, RR 1936, no. 16; MP, BC 579 A24.43 on police misconduct.

* * *

As the era of segregation drew to its end, Brookes wrote that it was wrong to say that nothing had been done. He cited the sevenfold increase in expenditure on Africans, the awareness of health needs, and the dropping of fiscal separation. "On the other hand, the pass laws remain after a decade of agitation and protest"; the housing shortage was disastrous:

> Most of all the general status of the African remains virtually unaltered. Politically he is debarred from representing his people in Parliament. In three provinces he has no provincial or municipal franchise. In the public service, even in the Native Affairs Department, the higher and more responsible posts are closed to him. In many directions he meets the intense frustration of barriers depending on race and colour alone, from which there seems to be no escape. It is this frustration which has led to the present deep dissatisfaction with the system of 1936. That system itself is based on presuppositions which, if they were ever correct, have become obsolete.[65]

The objective was not necessarily tied to the attainment of a welfare state, nor, as radical historians claim, was it primarily functional to capitalism. Ballinger and Molteno saw themselves as socialists, but they believed in using existing opportunities for reform—accepting a kind of Fabian realism, and showing an interest in practical welfare issues, not in tackling ultimates that were clearly beyond hope of attainment. Even when they accepted with apparent enthusiasm the small welfare reforms and grants, they did not shirk the big issues the resolution of which would have restructured much of society. Even Basner, who was a Marxist but not a Communist, was prepared to forgo final aims if a worthwhile reform, in immediate terms, was offered. On the other hand, Brookes and Rheinallt Jones expected the result of their reform to be a reinvigorated capitalism. But the advance of capitalism was not their ruling motive, which was to obtain liberal rights—in the context of the times—for oppressed and exploited and suffering people. To define the liberals' attitudes to capitalism more precisely would be pedantic.

Did the liberals succeed? No: their marginal reforms were wiped out after 1948. But with clarity and coherence they held up ideals and objectives that comprehended the franchise-centered ideal of the old Cape liberalism, which, however, would have postponed political equality until a redistribution of income and wealth could be achieved. But liberals of the interwar period went far beyond the old liberalism, recognizing the necessity of rapid change toward a more equal and more humane order. Those aims are still alive today.

65. Brookes, *The Forum,* 3 August 1947, pp. 15–26.

Douglas Irvine

6. The Liberal Party, 1953-1968

Nonracialism was the Liberal party's guiding principle. It was its great strength, in the end its only remaining strength. Before the party's foundation in 1953, only one other political organization had operated on a fully nonracial basis in South Africa, the Communist party. Outlawed in 1950, that party stressed a working-class unity transcending race. The Liberal party based itself on the possibility of an even broader unity, or at any rate insisted that no division is so profound that people of goodwill and good sense cannot find some way of bridging the abyss.

In the 1950s the United party (UP), since 1948 the official opposition to the ruling National party, still stood for the preservation of principles associated with the Western liberal tradition, reinforced by the myths and realities of the war years: the rule of law, constitutionalism, the independence of the judiciary, and opposition to governmental interference with the established rights of individuals. But despite the strand of opinion which had been represented in the UP cabinet by J. H. Hofmeyr until 1948, these principles were not generally construed in nonracial terms. For example, the Torch Commando, a white ex-servicemen's movement which opposed the Nationalist assault on the constitution to remove coloreds from the common voters' roll, was itself incapable of accepting nonracial membership. There was a lingering hope that the UP could be converted to a liberal view on the race issue, but by 1952 a significant number of white liberals were convinced that a more vigorous alternative ought to be posed. They favored a movement, an association, a party committed directly to extending political rights to all South Africans.

The development of this liberal movement and the Liberal party in the 1950s has not been studied comprehensively. This essay, by a liberal sympathizer (and former member of the party), makes use of unpublished material from the collections of some party activists. Briefly, it sets out the ways in which liberals tried to become an effective political force, inside and outside Parliament, and how they failed in the face of resistance to their ideas among the enfranchised whites of South Africa, and the determined response of the government which by statute made their continued existence impossible if they were to remain a multiracial party.

During 1952 liberal groups had been formed in the Cape, Natal, and Johannesburg in response both to apartheid policies and a growing militancy among blacks. The Defiance Campaign of 1952, in its program of nonviolent noncooperation with the authorities, gave expression to the hardening of attitudes among the disfranchised, but especially among Africans.[1] Early in 1953, representatives from these liberal groups met in Cape Town and formally established the Liberal Association. It soon attracted more than a thousand members. When the Nationalists were returned to power in the general election of April there were urgent reconsiderations. The Liberal party was launched. Its first national congress took place in July of 1953.

The Liberal party's primary emphasis was on the protection and extension of civil and political rights, in effect an emphasis on procedural rather than substantive rights. Suffrage was to be nonracial and on a common roll. That was clear from the outset. Whether the vote should be qualified, and if so, what the nature of that qualification might be, was bitterly contested. It was finally resolved in 1960 in favor of universal adult suffrage. In its early days, however, the party aimed primarily at the white electorate,[2] with policies that in many ways resembled those adopted later by the Progressive party, formed in 1959. The Progressive party, while it could present itself as a "moderate" alternative to the Liberal party, undoubtedly benefited from what the latter had done to put nonracialism on the political agenda.

It is not unfair to say that nineteenth-century English Liberals would have found little to quarrel with in the view on economic policy that prevailed initially among South African Liberals. Within a decade,

1. Leo Kuper, *Passive Resistance in South Africa* (London: Jonathan Cape, 1956).

2. Peter Brown, "The Liberal Party. A Chronology with Comment" (unpublished typescript, Liberal Party Workshop, Rhodes University, Grahamstown, Institute of Social and Economic Research, 17–19 July 1985), p. 8.

however, many members came to see that their conception of rights needed amplification. The Liberal party began to move strongly toward social democracy, but, under the repressive onslaught by the government in the 1960s, analysis and the development of principles yielded to the more urgent business of mere survival.[3] The social democratic option still remains to be fully articulated in South African politics.

More immediately in 1953, liberals faced the problems of means, and of finding allies, in their quest for the desired end. They opted for "democratic and constitutional means," while rejecting "communism" together with "all forms of totalitarianism." For years both decisions were to threaten the party's coherence as well as its political connections, especially with the African National Congress, but these decisions exemplified the link between means and ends on which the party laid so much stress.

Official relations with the African National Congress were always problematical, though at a personal level there were close ties between various figures in the two organizations, perhaps most notably between Alan Paton and Chief Albert Luthuli, who became national president of the ANC in 1952. Within the ANC there was an understandable tendency to resent white liberals' initial concern in the 1950s with "civilization" as a criterion for voting rights, and impatience as well with what often seemed too great a regard for respectability and legality. Congress's Youth League, founded in 1944, had fostered a new nationalism and a new militancy among Africans.

Another source of tension was the anticommunism so evident among many liberals. While this must be understood in the context of liberal values and the intellectual and political history of the times, and against the background of the Cold War, it was fertile ground for suspicion and unease in dealings between Liberal party members and the ANC. The relationship with communists and the Communist party was also a matter for controversy within the ANC itself.[4] There had been a considerable degree of interrelationship historically, and communists had established certain credentials, enhanced, if anything, when their party was outlawed by the Suppression of Communism Act of 1950. Matters were complicated further by the establishment in 1953 of an all-white organization, parallel to the ANC, the South African Congress of Democrats, which included many former communists in its small following. Its members were to play an influential part in the Congress

3. Brown, "Liberal Party," pp. 52–54.

4. Tom Lodge, *Black Politics in South Africa since 1945* (Johannesburg: Ravan Press, 1983), pp. 1–30.

movement, (an alliance of the ANC, the South African Indian Congress, and the Congress of Democrats). It is not difficult to understand the rivalry and hostility which so frequently characterized relations between the white Congress of Democrats and the Liberal party.

Ironically, a mutual suspicion of communists provided common ground for the Africanist tendency in the ANC and certain liberals (notably Patrick Duncan) that fostered close contacts between the Liberal party and the Pan-Africanist Congress (PAC) when it broke with the ANC in 1959. Nevertheless the complex nature of the relationships between the Liberal party, the PAC, and the ANC can be clearly illustrated by the fact that late in that same year, 1959, a leading figure in the ANC, Oliver Tambo, told an audience in Alexandra township that "Europeans in South Africa should, as soon as possible, follow the policy of the Liberal Party before the Africans reach a point of no return."[5]

As a multiracial organization the Liberal party stood in sharp contrast to the racially defined structures of the Congress alliance.[6] Paid-up membership in the party was never large, about 5,000 in 1961, at its height. Racial head-counting was, needless to say, contrary to the spirit of the Liberal party. Still, it was apparent that Africans comprised a large proportion of the membership, with considerable support not only in the cities but also in certain rural areas, such as Rustenburg, Northern Natal, and the Transkei. In July 1961 the majority of delegates to the party's national congress were African. People of all races served on the national committee, although whites always predominated there numerically and constituted something like 70 percent of the committee's total membership between 1953 and 1968. Still, the presence of Africans such as H. J. Bhengu (national vice president), Julius Malie (Transvaal organizer), Elliot Mngadi (national treasurer), Selby Msimang (a founder of the ANC), and Jordan Ngubane (national vice president) certainly could never be mistaken for tokenism. These were not men to be patronized.

The party was rich in vivid and forceful personalities. Outstanding even among these were Alan Paton, an acerbic and passionate orator, elected the party's national chairman in 1956 and two years later its president, and Peter Brown, who succeeded Paton as chairman, and

5. Janet Robertson, *Liberalism in South Africa, 1948–1963* (Oxford: Clarendon, 1971), p. 199.

6. The Liberal party was included among *white* opposition groups in a misleading pamphlet produced by the National Union of South African Students, *Dissension in the Ranks: White Opposition in South Africa* (Cape Town: NUSAS, 1981).

exercised a profound influence through his good humor, his sanity, and his dedication. Different as these two men were from each other, they had in common integrity and commitment.

The broad principles seemed clear enough, but there was little self-reflective analysis about the meaning of liberalism. Liberals in South Africa are often accused of innocence—that is, when more sinister motives are not being imputed to them. It has been said that they do not understand the dynamics of history, the imperatives of economics, or the strategic devices of power. Liberals have tended to reply that the first are obscure, the second debatable, and the third are often morally dubious. Both the attack and the defense may be cogent, but the fact is that in the 1950s neither the Liberal party nor the Congress alliance fully appreciated that the white electorate would prove so obdurate, the government so ruthless, and the state's apparatus of coercion so strong.

Even in the 1950s, political developments caused the Liberal party to reconsider the question of nonparliamentary political activity ever more urgently. While the party continued to insist on nonviolent means as its official policy, it broadened its strategies to include collaboration in boycotts and other forms of pressure as it became apparent that the prospect of parliamentary leverage was remote and liberals therefore lacked effective means of bringing about fundamental change. The possibilities of the nonviolent option in South African politics were never to be fully explored, however, given the banning of the ANC and the PAC and the destruction of the Liberal party during the 1960s.

In 1960, Alan Paton had called liberalism a "third force" in South Africa, a nonracial and nonviolent counterbalance.

> As I see it we are entering a phase where the struggle between Afrikaner Nationalism and African Nationalism will be intensified. We ourselves have prophesied that the excesses of Afrikaner Nationalism will provoke a strong counternationalism, and I do not think that we should ever delude ourselves into believing that this struggle at this stage could be converted into a struggle between Nationalism and Liberalism. . . . I fully expect violence to be a feature of this struggle. What do we do? Is our role alternately to respond to and reject appeals for help made by other organisations? I am sure that it is not. But that is what we shall be reduced to if we have no positive contribution to make.
>
> What is that contribution to be? I am sure that there will be millions of people of all races who shrink from the prospect of an unnatural and violent life. Some will be resolutely violent, and what can people like ourselves oppose to resolute violence but resolute non-violence? The only other course seems to me to withdraw from the struggle, either by leaving the country, or by accepting a withdrawn role here. This latter will be one of silent non-acceptance, accompanied by apparent acquiescence, and probably inner suffering of a painful but useless kind. . . . I do not think I could live like that. . . .
>
> I should like to acquaint myself more closely with the instruments of non-

violence. If I decided to use any of them, I should not do so in the name of the Party unless of course the Party wished me to do so. I am sure that there are many, many thousands of people in South Africa who hate and fear violence, who do not wish to play a purely passive role in its presence, but would like if they could to present a spiritual and good and active alternative to what is evil, violent and destructive. In a clash of opposing Nationalisms, both of them always trembling on the brink of violence, we might call this alternative *the third force.* It would, in my opinion, be this *third force,* which, if it were not able to prevent the clash of irreconcilable forces, would be there always present as a factor to be reckoned with and an alternative to them both.[7]

Violence from within its own ranks was soon to be a traumatic experience for the party. In the period of upheaval triggered by the Sharpeville massacre of 1960 there was an undercurrent of unrest and impatience among some of its younger members. They felt—mistakenly, tragically—that the situation was ripe for a chain reaction of change if only it could be triggered off; and they were not prepared to leave the initiative to others, perhaps especially not to the communists. A sabotage organization was born, the African Resistance Movement. Various incidents of sabotage were followed by the Johannesburg station bombing in 1964. Among those involved, and arrested, were several young liberals. At its conference that year the party expelled all members who had taken part in those activities. Officially, the matter was settled. But the challenge to liberalism was, and is, unresolved.

The Liberal party, not alone among opposition and resistance groups in South Africa, was unable to solve the problem of finding adequate means to the ends it had in view. At the outset its founders conceived of its role in the conventional context of Parliament and the party system—essentially, that is, within "white" politics. (Although black members were present at the first party congress, office holders elected were all white, and only in the following year did an important infusion of black membership come into the party's national committee.) In the next five years it was to become evident that the party could not hope for electoral success among white voters.

The Liberal party's only parliamentary spokesmen were those elected as Native representatives.[8] It inherited some representation through the Ballingers; then, in 1955 Walter Stanford joined Margaret Ballinger in the House of Assembly, and Leslie Rubin, a Cape Town lawyer, joined

7. Speech by Alan Paton at the Liberal party national congress, May 1960. Dr. A. S. Paton Papers (PP) (Johannesburg: University of the Witwatersrand, William Cullen Library), AD 1169, D4.

8. "Native representatives" were whites representing African constituents in terms of the 1936 Representation of Natives Act, which abolished even the limited participation of Africans in the common roll in Cape Province.

William Ballinger in the Senate. Together with Labour party members and other Native representatives, they played a part in public life far beyond what their numbers might have suggested. Under the terms of the Promotion of Bantu Self-Government Act of 1959, however, their seats were abolished, and "the four Liberal thorns in the Nationalist flesh were removed from the legislature in 1960."[9]

With the benefit of thirty years' hindsight we can see that the Liberal hope of an effective appeal to the white electorate was clearly a delusion. The hope was not held equally strongly by all members of the party even then, but a significant group believed that the left wing of the UP would eventually find its way into the Liberal party, and were therefore intent that the party should be kept "respectable" and acceptable to the hoped-for recruits. As late as 1957 the Cape leadership illustrated these aspirations in reacting angrily to certain "extra-parliamentary" activities of party members. These included the arrest of the national organizer Patrick Duncan for attending an ANC conference in the Queenstown African township without a permit; while in Pietermaritzburg, Violaine Junod of the national committee, the national secretary June Somers, and several other party members were arrested for taking part in a women's march against the pass laws. In 1956, 156 individuals were charged with treason, and the party became involved from the beginning in setting up the Treason Trial Defense Fund. At the inaugural meeting in Durban, Alan Paton and Leo Kuper, chairman and vice chairman of the party, were on the platform; they were subsequently charged under a bylaw for addressing a "meeting of natives." This was too much for the Cape leadership, and at the national party congress in January 1957, they put forward a resolution stating that extraparliamentary activities should be "purely ancillary and secondary" to conventional electoral activity. A compromise was arrived at and the resolution was withdrawn; extraparliamentary activity was to be "complementary" to electoral work.

The general election of 1958 made it clear, however, that the party's future did not lie with the white electorate as the three liberal candidates were heavily defeated while the National party captured 103 seats to the UP's 53. When Peter Brown became national chairman in that year, he asserted that the main thrust of the party's activities should be extraparliamentary, adding, for good measure, that it might be necessary to defy Government Notice 526, which had banned all meetings of more than ten Africans in the face of the call by the ANC for a three-day stay-away over the election period.[10] In the event the party did not

9. Robertson, *Liberalism*, p. 162.

10. Brown, "Liberal Party," p. 27.

find it necessary to defy the notice, since it was lifted piecemeal by the end of the year.

Over the years the Liberal party contested various elections at the national, provincial, and municipal levels, but no official party candidate was ever elected by whites. The candidates on occasion might nevertheless have been reasonably pleased with their votes. For example, in 1953 the Liberal party gained up to 30 percent of the vote in some Johannesburg municipal constituencies; in the 1958 general election the party's candidate in the Cape Town constituency of Sea Point polled 1,642 votes against the 7,267 for the UP, though candidates in Orange Grove (Johannesburg) and Pietermaritzburg lost their deposits; and in 1959 the party's candidates in the provincial elections averaged about 1,500 votes each in Houghton (Johannesburg), Sea Point, and Pretoria East. In the 1961 general election the party's candidate in Hillbrow (Johannesburg), polled 1,346 votes against the UP's 5,564, even though she had found it impossible to hire a multiracial hall in her constituency, and as a result most of her meetings were held in an open space with the audience attracted by a bullhorn and a penny-whistle band.

More important than the votes, perhaps, was the fact of multiracial canvassing, the multiracial election meetings, and the multiracial protest meetings, as the various measures of the apartheid state came onto the public agenda. It was an example of the curiously oscillating nature of the relations between the Liberal party and the ANC that, when Chief Luthuli was banned for the second time in May 1959, two of the largest protest meetings were organized by the Liberal party with ANC support—2,000 people in the Pietermaritzburg city hall and 2,500 on the Johannesburg city hall steps. By 1961, as white attitudes hardened, the meetings on the city hall steps which had become such a feature of life in Johannesburg were being broken up by white thugs. It is of course impossible to assess the significance or impact of those multiracial meetings, but their formative influence on participants and observers may still be bearing fruit.

The Liberal party's failure to attract white support is much less surprising than the extent to which it appealed to other groups, particularly Africans. For many Africans, whether they became members or not, the Liberal party undoubtedly proved its credentials by its direct engagement with their problems, which Afrikaner Nationalist legislators were compounding so assiduously. When the party was first established, Jordan Ngubane had emphasized the need for "taking liberalism to the man in the location."[11] Attention to individual and local concerns

11. Robertson, *Liberalism,* p. 177.

became a feature of the party's activities, most notably in Natal and the Transvaal, ranging from immediate welfare work to assistance in various forms of opposition and resistance. These included fighting the activities of the police and the Western Areas Resettlement Board, part of the machinery set up by the government to destroy Sophiatown, the black freehold suburb in Johannesburg. There was also active support for those involved in the 1957 bus boycotts in the African township of Alexandra (Johannesburg) and Lady Selborne (Pretoria). After the Sharpeville massacre in 1960, members of the party's Transvaal division became extremely active, with lawyers taking statements from the injured at Baragwanath hospital until their own arrest, while others saw to relief food supplies and support for dependents.

Other important instances of local work involved opposition to the government's removal of "black spots," that is, lands held in freehold by Africans outside the reserves established by the 1913 Natives' Land Act and the 1936 Native Trust and Land Act. These black spots were intolerable to the ideology of apartheid and to the perceived demands of the South African political economy in the 1950s. The Liberal party became deeply involved in opposition to these removals from 1954 onwards, in the case of Charlestown[12] and in the extraordinarily energetic activities of Elliot Mngadi in the Ladysmith area scheduled for "removal." Mngadi organized the Land Owners' Association under the joint auspices of the ANC and the Liberal party, with the latter paying his salary.[13] The example of his work over the years in the "black spots" campaign brought in a flood of applications from Northern Natal for membership in the party. This kind of concern persists today in organizations such as the Association for Rural Advancement initiated during the 1970s by former members of the Liberal party in Natal.

The party's credentials among South Africans of all colors—except whites—were also undoubtedly enhanced by the solicitous attentions it began to receive from the state (in the abstract) and the security police (in the flesh). Most dramatically, there was the State of Emergency in 1960 when a considerable number of Liberals were among those who disappeared into detention, including Peter Brown, the national chairman. A little later, the bannings began, ironically under the Suppression of Communism Act. What the ANC had first endured during the 1950s, the Liberal party was to suffer in the 1960s. In 1961 banning orders were served on Patrick Duncan and Joe Nkatlo, the first Liberals to be banned since Jock Isacowitz in Johannesburg in 1954, at the time of the Western Areas removal campaign. Liberals were to become only too

12. Alan Paton, *The Charlestown Story* (Pietermaritzburg: Liberal Party of South Africa, n.d.).

13. Brown, "Liberal Party," p. 18.

familiar with magisterial warnings to individuals to desist from their activities, bannings, and other intimidatory attentions, devices used freely and cynically to destroy the party. All this took the Liberal party's experience far from the domain of parliamentary politics that had so largely occupied its attention less than ten years previously.

With its background of parliamentary aspirations, it was obviously more problematical for the Liberal party to embark on extraparliamentary action than for an organization such as the ANC. Even so, it is worth recalling that it was not until December 1949 that the ANC endorsed the Programme of Action of 1944, approving strategies such as boycotts, strikes, and other forms of civil disobedience, thus making possible the Defiance Campaign. Subsequently, in 1955, when the ANC launched campaigns against the Western Areas removals and the Bantu Education Act, inadequacies in these campaigns revealed the importance of organization, and of not underestimating the state's coercive strength, the will and ingenuity of the government, nor the appeal to particular interests which it might muster. If all of this has a contemporary ring, so too has the fact that the ANC itself then embarked on illiberal attempts to enforce the boycotts it had launched by intimidation of its own. Against this background, it cannot be supposed that the Liberal party's leadership cherished many naive expectations about the strategic difficulties they would have to face in opting for extraparliamentary activity in 1958. Relinquishing the parliamentary arena certainly released them from bondage to the white voters; but they still retained an insistence on nonviolence, and there was also the obvious demand that the extraparliamentary option should be seen by potential supporters to be more effective than the parliamentary one.

The party now endorsed boycott as a legitimate means of pressure, a hotly contested issue inside, and even more hotly outside it. In their *Statement on the Overseas Boycott* (1958), Paton and Brown argued that white supremacy would never yield "to mere verbal persuasion." Passive resistance and boycott were condoned as "the only two kinds of (non-violent) weapons left to non-white people who resist Apartheid."[14] In this they were largely influenced by African members of the party, who scornfully rejected the argument against boycotts that they would be the first to suffer. Janet Robertson, writing in 1970, remarked that "here, as the ANC had done, the Liberals underestimated the degree of conservatism which poverty and fear could breed among non-whites."[15] In the Liberal party there was certainly an awareness from the outset of some of the practical difficulties involved in the boycott strategy. In

14. Robertson, *Liberalism*, p. 196.

15. Ibid., p. 197.

the first half of 1959 the party's Transvaal Executive met with ANC representatives, led by Oliver Tambo, who were anxious to secure the party's support for a boycott they were launching as part of an anti-pass campaign. Potatoes, and goods held to be manufactured by "Nationalist" firms, were to be boycotted. Liberal party representatives expressed grave reservations about both the theory and the practicalities of the boycott, in particular questioning the ANC's organizational ability and strength to secure the necessary support from consumers. The fairly heated meeting did not improve relations between the Transvaal Liberals and the ANC, which, at the time, were in some ways worse there than elsewhere in the country. The Liberal party, in the end, did not cooperate in this campaign,[16] but later that year it did agree to support the ANC-sponsored Boycott Movement, initiated in Britain. At the time, Patrick van Rensburg, organizing secretary of the party in the Transvaal, was visiting London; he was asked to run the boycott, and did so with Peter Brown's consent. This caused considerable unhappiness in the party, where many opposed both boycott and too close an association with the ANC, and it precipitated some resignations. Members of the party were also active in developing plans for the sports and cultural boycotts that were beginning to crystallize in these years.

One highly significant area of extraparliamentary pressure to which the Liberal party devoted insufficient attention was trade unionism. As specific applications of the party's nonracial principles were developed during the 1950s, it had come out strongly against job reservation, the whites-only makeup of official trade unions, and the inadequate education and training available to black apprentices. It was not until 1961, however, that the party's national congress decided to step up its interest in trade unions. Ernie Wentzel, who had been allocated the trade union portfolio in the party's new organizational structure, saw the party's immediate aim as improving working conditions but its ultimate objective as the use of an organized labor force in bringing down apartheid.[17] The party recognized, however, that its growing interest in trade unionism would elicit hostility not only from the government, on the right, but also on the left, where the South African Congress of Trade Unions was unlikely to welcome this development. In January 1961, *New Age* (the voice of the Congress alliance, and strongly influenced by communists) accused the party—as well as the Pan-Africanist Federation of Free Trade Unions—of trying to split the labor

16. Ernest Wentzel Papers. Unsorted manuscript notes, n.d. (Private possession, Mrs. J. Wentzel, Johannesburg).

17. Peter Brown, untitled. Unpublished typescript. (Private possession, Peter Brown, Pietermaritzburg), pp. 255–56.

movement.[18] The basis for its attack was the successful assistance given by the party's Durban office to a group of disgruntled dockworkers. This kind of attack persisted; but the party's attitude remained that, as so many workers were still unorganized, there was plenty of scope in this field for all contenders. In practice, however, the party was unable to carry its activities very far.

In 1962 Wentzel again urged the party national congress to enter the trade union field more actively. "We have," he said, "recruited into the Liberal Party large numbers of working class Africans and our membership is much more working-class in character than the more 'white collar' membership which the now banned ANC had. The working class African holds a key position in the future."[19] Wentzel therefore recommended the appointment of a commission to investigate the role of the Liberal party in labor relations, and its connections with local and international organizations. As a result of his recommendations a move was set afoot to arrange a conference of all nonapartheid trade union organizations in 1963, with the assistance of the International Confederation of Free Trade Unions. This proved impossible, and in the end the government's growing onslaught on the Liberal party and its members thwarted its expansion into the field of trade unionism. Here, as elsewhere, the party raised issues it was unable to resolve, certainly in practice and possibly not even in theory. It was characteristic of the liberals that Wentzel's recommendation went on to say that "we should not see ourselves as being necessarily in conflict with the employer, and if harmonious relations can be cultivated, so much the better."[20]

Another aspect of the Liberal party's extraparliamentary activities was its various connections with plans for a national convention. Its most notorious step was its refusal to participate officially in the Congress of the People at Kliptown in 1955. This was a controversial decision within the party itself, and in retrospect clearly a mistake, all the more so because of the heroic mythology generated by that dramatic gathering, which adopted the Freedom Charter.[21] Initially, the party had been prepared to join in sponsoring a Congress of the People called by the ANC together with other bodies in the Congress alliance. A number of individual members of the party were associated with the preparations in various ways; but the party found itself excluded from effective participation in the planning stages. There were also serious misgivings about organizational inadequacies, the prominent role of the Commu-

18. Brown, "Liberal Party," p. 54; also Brown, untitled, p. 256; *New Age* 7: 13.

19. Brown, untitled, p. 282.

20. Ibid., p. 283.

21. Raymond Suttner and Jeremy Cronin, *30 Years of the Freedom Charter* (Johannesburg: Ravan Press, 1986).

nist-influenced Congress of Democrats, and the imperfect democracy of the procedures. Eventually, the party's national committee decided to withdraw its unconditional sponsorship, while offering to participate in the final assembly. After a prolonged silence, in which the party heard nothing further about the plans, its Transvaal division was suddenly asked—in the second week of June 1955—to send a message and observers to the Congress of the People on June 26. This request was rejected by the party's national executive. The Transvaal division was infuriated by the decision and threatened rebellion, but in the end appeals for party unity prevailed.[22]

The party made decidedly more positive contributions in 1957 to help breathe life into a multiracial conference proposed by the Interdenominational African Ministers' Federation. The conference, called in response to the apartheid blueprint, the Tomlinson Commission's report on development of African reserves, met at the University of the Witwatersrand on the theme of "Human Relationships in a Multi-Racial Society." Three hundred delegates and two hundred observers heard papers by representatives of all shades of opinion to the left of the United party. The wide area of agreement which was reached astonished observers and participants alike.[23] The conference adopted a resolution, without dissent, to publicize its findings and recommendations as widely as possible, a familiar kind of resolution, with as little impact in practice as other resolutions of this kind were to have down the years.

Recommendations that were to prove equally ineffectual, while reflecting a similar and indeed astonishing degree of agreement among diverse groups, were adopted by the Natal Convention in Pietermaritzburg in April 1961, a direct initiative of the Liberal party as part of its campaign against the declaration of a republic and on behalf of a new national convention.[24] Among the 220 participants in the Pietermaritzburg meeting, representing some 70 organizations, the only significant absentees were the Nationalists and official UP representatives—also a familiar story.

At the same time, in March 1961, the "All-In African Conference" met in Edendale (Pietermaritzburg). The ANC and the PAC had both been banned in the previous year, and the conference was planned to counteract the silencing of these organizations and to reassert an African voice in political affairs. The conference called—unrealistically—for a new national convention before the declaration of the republic on May 31, failing which there would be demonstrations and a stay-away. Leading Liberals had participated in the preparations for this conference

22. Brown, "Liberal Party," pp. 13–17; Lodge, *Black Politics*, pp. 69–74.

23. Brown, "Liberal Party," p. 24.

24. Brown, "Liberal Party," p. 40.

but had felt themselves outmaneuvered in ways that illustrate some of the tensions in their relationship with the ANC.[25] In the previous year the Liberal party had sent to Luthuli some draft principles as a suggested basis for a new organization comprising Liberals, the ANC, the Congress of Democrats, the South African Indian Congress, the PAC, and the Progressives, who in 1959 had split from the UP. There was no direct response. Instead the ANC sent out invitations to an African Leaders' Consultative Conference at Orlando on December 16. After some pressure, the Liberals got themselves included in these invitations, and Jordan Ngubane was elected chairman of the conference's continuation committee, with Hyacinth Bhengu and Julius Malie as other members.

Ngubane, living at Inanda near Durban, failed to take a firm grip on the continuation committee: pamphlets were distributed from Johannesburg without his knowledge; invitations to the follow-up conference were sent to a large number of people, not only to leaders, as had been agreed, but with significant omissions. In February, Z. B. Molete of the PAC said that the conference was being used by "others," meaning the ANC, "to build their own political movements," and he withdrew. Ngubane pressed for a postponement, hoping to get the PAC back; but the ANC opposed him. Ngubane and Duma Nokwe of the ANC were delegated to see Luthuli and other sponsors to discuss the matter: Nokwe passed through Durban without contacting Ngubane and went to see Luthuli on his own. At the Liberal party's national committee meeting in March, Patrick Duncan and Peter Hjul argued vigorously that the movement had been taken over by communists, even threatening to resign from the party's executive unless the conference were repudiated. Ngubane and Bhengu themselves had resigned from the continuation committee a few days previously. At this stage the entire continuation committee was arrested, as were Ngubane and Bhengu. Despite the arrests, the conference took place on March 25–26. Only a handful of Liberals (from the Springs branch in the Transvaal) were present; northern Natal Liberals, certainly the best organized body of African political opinion in that part of the country, had simply never been invited. It was readily apparent that the overwhelming majority of the 1,500 or so people present had been drawn from ANC-oriented groups.

The main speaker at the Edendale conference was Nelson Mandela. Fortuitously his own banning order had expired a few days previously, and he now emerged, for the first time, as a figure of truly national significance. His fiery speech stressed the vital need for African unity if freedom was to be won. No doubt the call was genuine, but the failure

25. Ibid., pp. 38–39.

of the continuation committee to preserve its own unity meant that Mandela was speaking almost exclusively to ANC supporters. The immediate purpose of the conference (it seemed to some observers) had been to issue a rallying cry—emanating from the banned ANC—for a nationwide stay-away on May 31.[26] That call for "non-cooperation and non-collaboration" unless a national convention was summoned before the declaration of the republic was to be thwarted rapidly: a new law was passed providing for twelve-day detention without trial; detentions, raids, a ban on meetings, and the mobilization of the police and army all combined effectively to frustrate the stay-away.

Enough has been said to indicate something of the convoluted and fluctuating relationship between the Liberal party, the Congress alliance, and the PAC, which varied over time and in different parts of the country. Much depended on particular personalities and just as there were divergent views within the party about the desirability of collaboration with the Congresses, so too were there sharply differing opinions about the PAC. Some Liberals, both in the Transvaal and Natal, strongly critical of the PAC, refused to believe that one could ride the road to nonracialism on the back of the tiger of racialism. Other Liberals (especially in the Cape) were openly on the side of the PAC. Jordan Ngubane was closely associated with its leadership, as was Patrick Duncan.[27]

Contact (Duncan's paper) was widely accused of campaigning against the ANC. The role played by *Contact* in general in the late 1950s and early 1960s had subtleties some critics took (or mistook) for deliberate chicanery. *Contact* was not a Liberal party mouthpiece despite the column "The Long View," written by Paton and Brown. It was privately owned, and largely followed whatever point of view Duncan happened to favor at a particular time, though there was always the sanction of Paton's wrath and the threat of withdrawing his column when *Contact* became, as it sometimes did, too much for even a very tolerant party to take.

The government's crackdown on the Liberal party in the 1960s was of course part of the wider pattern of repression, of hardening white attitudes, and a determination to eradicate not only resistance but even mere dissent. The hostility to the Liberal party was given a particular edge, however, by the fact that it decided to challenge the state in a crucial area of apartheid policy—"bantustan" independence—and perhaps came closer to success here than at any other point.

Early in 1962 the prime minister, H. F. Verwoerd, announced his

26. Brown, untitled, pp. 194–202, 211–14.

27. For Duncan's role in the party see C. J. Driver, *Patrick Duncan, 1918–1967* (London: Heinemann, 1980).

intention to move the Transkei toward independence. The chairman of the Transkei Territorial Assembly, Chief Kaiser Matanzima, enjoyed the government's patronage as a result of his support for its Bantu Authorities. With the aid of officials from Pretoria, he presented a fully worked-out apartheid constitution to the relevant committee, appointed by the Transkei Territorial Authority, a committee in which Matanzima had appropriated the chairmanship. An alternative nonracial constitution, submitted by Paramount Chief Sabata Dalindyebo, was ruled out of order. Signs of a coherent opposition had nevertheless begun to emerge, and through contact with Tembu members of the party in Cape Town, the Liberal party moved energetically to assist this opposition. This assistance elicited remarkable enthusiasm among Transkeian groups opposed to Matanzima, but from Matanzima and the government it also elicited hostility and on the part of the government, repression of growing severity.[28]

Toward the end of 1962 there were various violent incidents associated with Poqo, the insurrectionary wing of the banned PAC. In Paarl, in the Cape, two whites and five blacks died in Poqo attacks. Early the next year five whites were killed at Bashee River in the Transkei. From Maseru, his place of exile in Lesotho, Potlako Leballo announced that Poqo was the PAC underground and that these incidents were precursors of a general uprising. In Parliament B. J. Vorster, the minister of justice, accused the Liberals and communists of creating Poqo. In his interim report on Paarl, Judge J. H. Snyman did a remarkable hatchet job through innuendo and association, that implicated Liberals with Poqo.[29] Randolph Vigne and Peter Hjul, two Liberals who had been especially active in the Transkei, were banned. Despite this, the Liberal party members from Cape Town and Grahamstown worked vigorously with others to shape an effective and coherent opposition to Matanzima in the 1963 elections. The magistrate in Umtata responded by banning all Liberal party meetings, the police raided the party's Umtata office regularly, and party members were deported, banned, given magisterial "warnings."

The price for Liberals was high, but worthwhile paying: in the elections, candidates opposed to Matanzima won all the elected seats except in Matanzima's own Emigrant Tembuland and the Umzimkulu constituency. When the new assembly convened, there was every possibility that Transkei's first chief minister would be Victor Poto, Sabata's ally, if a sufficient number of appointed chiefs could hold firm. Briefly, they did. The assembly's first election was for the post of

28. Brown, "Liberal Party," p. 44; Lodge, *Black Politics*, pp. 285–90.
29. Lodge, *Black Politics*, pp. 240–48.

chairman, and Poto's man won. Before the election for the chief ministership, the session was adjourned abruptly, and when it reconvened, the South African government had persuaded a sufficient number of chiefs to secure Matanzima's election.[30] The Liberal party's subsequent attempts to keep opposition alive in the Transkei were unsuccessful, partly because of inertia in the local opposition party, but above all because of Matanzima's skillful use of patronage and other forms of power. For itself, the Liberal party's reward was an increase in the government's unremitting hostility.

Bannings, "warnings," and other forms of intimidation and harassment continued at an increasing pace. Peter Brown was banned in 1964, and was to live for ten years under orders that made his attendance at public meetings and publication of his statements illegal, as well as severely restricting his rights of movement and ordinary social intercourse. In these difficult circumstances, Edgar Brookes, who had joined the party in 1962, became its national chairman, lending the weight of his distinction and formidable competence to a party under pressure.

A significant number of Liberals were among the many South Africans who left the country. Trials of members of the African Resistance Movement exacerbated matters. The police raided homes and offices; in rural northern Natal they raided the home of a party member thirteen times in one month. Cars were damaged; petrol bombs were thrown. In the second half of 1966 the party's entire rural working staff in Natal was banned. At the national party congress in 1966 Cape members were represented by a single delegate. The toll of personnel lost, and a lack of funds, meant that the party's most urgent task was simply to keep going, to keep alive the ideas for which it stood.[31]

Shortly after Vorster became prime minister in 1966, the Prohibition of Improper Interference Bill was introduced into Parliament, its aim to outlaw nonracial politics. By that time virtually all that remained to the Liberal party was an idea and a principle. When the bill passed into law in 1968, the party dissolved itself, but only after staging a final series of nonracial meetings "in that strange assortment of meeting places, many of them old wattle-and-daub houses, with which it had become so familiar over the fifteen years of its existence."[32]

On 4 May 1968, at the last meeting of the party at Hambrook, a village in northern Natal, little more than a cluster of poor houses, Alan Paton posed some critical questions:

Why have we been dealt with in this way? Why has a law been passed to make

30. Brown, "Liberal Party," p. 51.
31. Ibid., pp. 58–63.
32. Ibid., p. 64.

it impossible for us to continue? Why, long before that law was passed, were so many of our leaders restricted, and so many of our members intimidated? Why did one of our members have to be arrested at a funeral? Why did a train have to be stopped in the middle of the veld, and one of our members have to be arrested in this way, when he had been seen openly moving about on the platform of the previous station? Why did an old mother have to be visited and warned to stop her son being a member of the Liberal Party?

I'll tell you why. The Party was small and not powerful. But it was formed to give expression to ideas that were not small, and were full of power. One of these ideas is that man is not born to go down on his belly before the State. Another is that a man should live where he wishes to live, and work where he wishes to work. Another is that he should be free to move about his country, and free to take any employment for which he is fitted. Another is that if men and women of different races wish to associate together and to pursue a common purpose, it is their right as human beings to do so.

The Party was small and not powerful, but these ideas were great and powerful, and the Government was afraid of them. Therefore it took merciless steps against those who held them.[33]

33. Speech by Paton to the last meeting of the Liberal Party at Hambrook, 4 May, 1968. PP, AD 1169, D 13.

II

Liberal Interpretations of South African History

Christopher Saunders

7. Liberal Historiography Before 1945

When a school of revisionist, largely Marxist, historians arose in the early 1970s, its practitioners tended to be critical of a stereotypical liberal history. They usually did not distinguish between the early liberal historians of the 1920s, '30s, and early '40s, who form the subject of this paper, and those liberal historians who wrote in the quite different context of the 1950s and '60s, let alone between individual liberal historians.[1] Though generalizations can be advanced about the early liberal historians, each deserves individual treatment, for each had particular strengths and limitations. Here I treat only the four most important—W. M. Macmillan, C. W. de Kiewiet, J. S. Marais, and Eric Walker—in any detail.

Any discussion of early liberal historians must begin with William Miller Macmillan (1885–1974), both the pioneer and the dominant figure in early liberal historiography. Others before him had begun to criticize the pro-colonist, antiblack view in George McCall Theal's (1837–1919) accounts of the triumph of white power over African peoples.[2] But the two books Macmillan wrote when he was head of

I acknowledge the assistance of the Human Sciences Research Council, which is not responsible for anything I say.

1. Nor does Harrison Wright draw a clear distinction between early and later liberal historians in *The Burden of the Present* (Cape Town: David Philip, 1977).

2. Earlier critics include J. Cappon in *Britain's Title in South Africa* (London: Macmillan, 1902), the archivist H. C. V. Leibbrandt, and John Edgar, first Professor of History at the University of Cape Town.

the history department at the University of the Witwatersrand (Wits) in the 1920s constituted the first significant challenge by a professional historian to the views of Theal, and to those of the like-minded Sir George Cory (1862–1935). Based on the papers of the nineteenth-century missionary John Philip, *The Cape Colour Question* (1927) and *Bantu, Boer, and Briton* (1929) sought to take "full account of the weaker peoples as an essential part of the whole" and to show "the predicament of the natives . . . [which] has never been taken into account."[3] Macmillan rejected Theal's easy assumption that the blacks had brought on wars, and that the colonists always had been right. He also sought to analyze the origins of South Africa's problems in a way that would point lessons for the present: his books on Philip were weapons in the fight he was waging against the segregationist policies of J. B. M. Hertzog, prime minister from 1924 to 1939.

Macmillan's antisegregationist message was that the common citizenship given to "coloreds" in the early nineteenth century, which had meant first the removal of racially discriminatory measures affecting them and then the equal opportunity to qualify for a nonracial franchise, should now be given to Africans as well. His books told of the origins of a society at the Cape that did not discriminate by law on grounds of race, and into which "other peoples" were increasingly drawn as its economy developed. He urged upon South Africa's whites the importance of "binding the handful of rising natives to us, as we still easily can."[4] He argued that the country was essentially one, that the denial of political rights to a section of the population on racial grounds would inevitably produce a clash of race against race. His answer was equal rights for all civilized men, in the old Cape liberal tradition, and he deplored the attacks that were being made on that tradition as he wrote. Segregationism, because it would run counter to the incorporation that economic growth was promoting, would inevitably mean repression, and "sheer domination" could only "serve for a season."[5] If South Africa was indeed the "complex whole"[6] he believed it to be, its history should be the story of the creation of that single society.

Macmillan's books on Philip challenged the Eurocentric and justificatory approach of Theal and Cory in various ways. He suggested, for example, that Africans had not arrived in the country relatively late, but had long been a settled population when whites began to colonize it. He suggested that blacks had not been fighting continually among

3. W. M. Macmillan, *My South African Years* (Cape Town: David Philip, 1975), p. 167; *Bantu, Boer, and Briton* (London: Faber and Gwyer, 1929), p. vii.

4. W. M. Macmillan, *Complex South Africa* (London: Faber and Faber, 1930), p. 273.

5. Ibid., p. 279.

6. Ibid., p. 121.

themselves before white "pacification." It was not a lust for colonial cattle that had led Africans to fight so often on the Cape eastern frontier, but rather a concern to maintain their land and way of life in the face of efforts to dispossess them. The Afrikaner *Voortrekkers* (pioneers) had not advanced into an empty interior in the 1830s. The African population had been larger in the early nineteenth century than Theal had imagined, so there had been no dramatic increase in its size later in that century. On these and other matters Macmillan was to be vindicated by later scholarship.

The "Agrarian Problem" lectures Macmillan delivered in 1919 were a pioneer attempt to investigate changing patterns of production and social relations on white farms, and to chart the growth of social stratification between the wealthy farmers on the one hand and the landless white tenant farmers (*bywoners*) on the other. He was the first historian of South Africa to plead for the study of "the everyday life of the people, how they lived, what they thought, and what they worked at, when they did think and work, what they produced and what and where they marketed, and the whole of their social organisation."[7] Not until the 1970s did professional historians begin to study patterns of accumulation and dispossession in the rural areas in greater detail, and start to write the history of "the everyday life of the people" for which Macmillan had called over half a century earlier.

Nevertheless, though he was in his thinking far ahead of Theal and Cory in most respects, Macmillan like them accepted the Victorian idea of a great dichotomy between the "civilized" and the "barbarous." He pointed out that "Civilization, being of the East as well as of the West, knows no Colour Bar,"[8] but he also saw the majority of blacks as less than "civilized." Accepting the existence of discrete "races," hierarchically ordered, he spoke, in the idiom of his day, of "child races" and "weaker peoples," terms in frequent use by the white South African reading public he hoped to influence against segregationism.

Macmillan did not believe, however, that racial differences were inherent and permanent, and he always rejected discrimination on purely racial grounds. He condemned the "race obsession" of South Africans[9] and stressed how black and white had faced common difficulties in the interior in the nineteenth century, and how poverty in the twentieth century ran across the racial divide. Before he left Wits in 1932 he opposed the growth of the Bantu Studies Department there because it seemed to emphasize the different experience and "mind" of

7. Macmillan, *The South African Agrarian Problem* (Johannesburg: Central News Agency, 1919), p. 23.

8. Macmillan, *Bantu, Boer, and Briton,* Preface.

9. Macmillan, *South African Years,* p. 212, quoting what he wrote in 1931.

Africans. He expressed his dislike of the concept of "race relations" as introduced from America in the 1920s because it suggested that color was the crucial cleavage setting people apart and had to be bridged by some kind of diplomacy. Later liberal historians could no more escape racial categories in their writing than he, but did not use the "civilization/barbarism" dichotomy.

In his writings of the 1920s Macmillan argued for the extension of the nonracial qualified franchise, the development of the reserves, and a redistribution of wealth, so that Africans might be consumers as well as producers. After he left the country, his sense that time was running out became even more acute, and he rejected any form of "constructive engagement" with the Union government. On that issue he broke with the imperial theorists of the Round Table in the 1930s, who would have conceded the British High Commission Territories (Basutoland, Bechuanaland, and Swaziland) to the Union. Yet, now settled in Britain, he continued to hope against hope that reason would prevail in South Africa. "One should not assume," he wrote of race prejudice in 1939, "that the disease will be proof indefinitely against the slow seeping of truth."[10]

Unlike almost all other liberal historians before the 1970s, Macmillan stressed the importance of economics in understanding South Africa's past and present. Much influenced by the German economic historian Gustav Schmoller, under whom he had studied in Berlin, and by R. H. Tawney, whom he met in England, he began his career in 1911 at Rhodes University College as lecturer in a joint Department of History and Economics. He always believed that the economic was a more important determinant than the political or the racial. But this conviction did not mean that he wrote chiefly economic history. Based on the Philip papers, his two major historical books were necessarily focused on missionary and government policy. Nor did he understand, say, economic pressures for Cape Ordinance 50, which freed colored labor in 1828, or the economic drive behind British imperialism.[11]

In addition to economic historians, only Cornelis Willem de Kiewiet (1902–1986) of the early liberals followed Macmillan in appreciating the importance of economics: influenced by Tawney and economic historians he had met in Europe as well as by his mentor at Wits, de Kiewiet subtitled his discussion of imperial policy in the 1870s, which included a chapter on "The Economics of War," "A Study in Politics

10. *The New Statesman,* 4 November 1939.

11. See S. Newton-King in Shula Marks and Anthony Atmore, eds., *Economy and Society in Pre-Industrial South Africa* (London: Longman, 1980); Anthony Atmore and Shula Marks, "The Imperial Factor in Nineteenth Century South Africa," *Journal of Imperial and Commonwealth History,* 3 (1974).

and Economics."[12] His noted overall synthesis was a social and economic history.[13] The liberal historians of the 1950s, '60s, and early '70s still tended to separate the political and the economic, and to leave the latter to economists and economic historians, in part because economic history was not taught in the history departments of South African universities, but in departments of economics.

De Kiewiet, Macmillan's most famous student, and J. S. (Etienne) Marais (1898–1969) both followed Macmillan in challenging the intellectual hegemony of the Theal/Cory approach. It became apparent to de Kiewiet from Macmillan's teaching in the early 1920s at Wits that "the whole architecture of Theal was flawed, so that it was necessary to start rebuilding afresh."[14] When Marais, who grew up in the tradition of a southwestern Cape farm and on Theal's interpretation of the past, read Macmillan's books he thought they overstated the case against colonists and officials, but they nevertheless inspired him to tackle similar problems and further the process of refuting Theal.[15] Macmillan, de Kiewiet, and Marais all attempted to get away from Eurocentricity and to chart aspects of the development of what Marais described as "a single, if heterogeneous society"[16] based on one economy. All tried to look at the history of blacks with sympathy.

Macmillan began the task of creating an alternative vision of the South African past, and it was from de Kiewiet, a master of the broad, challenging generalization, that there came a major synthesis of all South African history, based on Macmillan's approach. The meticulous Marais, an anglicized Afrikaner, whose Oxford doctorate had dealt with the colonization of New Zealand, emerged as a historian of South Africa later than de Kiewiet. Like Macmillan's work on Philip and his times, and de Kiewiet's on British imperial policy up to the 1880s, Marais's richly detailed empirical work written from the new perspective retains its importance today.

Macmillan was aware that "intercourse" on the frontier had taken many forms, having involved trade and labor and missionary work as well as war,[17] but he did not develop the concept. It was H. M. Robertson, an economic historian who lectured in the economics department at the

12. C. W. de Kiewiet, *The Imperial Factor in South Africa* (Cambridge: Cambridge University Press, 1937).

13. C. W. de Kiewiet, *A History of South Africa, Social and Economic* (Oxford: Clarendon, 1941).

14. De Kiewiet to J. Naidoo, 1980: letter in possession of J. Naidoo of Niort, France.

15. J. S. Marais, *The Cape Coloured People* (London: Longmans Green, 1939), Preface; idem., *Maynier and the first Boer Republic* (Cape Town: Maskew Miller, 1944).

16. Marais, *Cape Coloured People,* p. vii.

17. See Macmillan, *Bantu, Boer, and Briton,* especially pp. 59, 65–67.

University of Cape Town, who in 1930 and 1935 first elaborated the theme of nonconflictive relations on the frontier, in what he called a preliminary survey of "150 Years of Economic Contact Between Black and White."[18] This way of looking at the frontier, as a "sieve" rather than a barrier, was taken up by de Kiewiet, first in *The Imperial Factor in South Africa* (1937), which was similar to Macmillan's books on Philip in that it was about British policy on the Cape frontier, and then in his *History.* That de Kiewiet, in striking prose, dwelt on the theme of "interaction" was in part because his field of vision, in a general history of the country, was necessarily much wider than Macmillan's in narrower studies.

It was the early revisionist Martin Legassick who first suggested in 1970 that the liberal historiography of the 1930s differed in emphasis from that of the 1920s. He pointed out that Macmillan, whom he regarded as "ambivalently" a founder of the "liberal school," wrote of "the remorseless advance of white agricultural colonization" and of conflict on the frontier, whereas the historians of the 1930s—especially de Kiewiet—saw the frontier as a place of cooperation where "new economic and social bonds" were forged.[19] There are other differences between Macmillan and his successors in addition to the stress he laid on economics. De Kiewiet was less morally outraged by poverty than Macmillan, and was to attribute it in part to ignorance,[20] as Macmillan never did. More radical than his successors, Macmillan did not view capitalist development as an unmitigated blessing; he wanted state intervention to bring about a more just order. De Kiewiet, writing as the world was recovering from the great depression, was readier than Macmillan to interpret economic growth as progress. The emphasis on "co-operation" in his *History* may indeed have reflected not only a general liberal belief "that the road to African 'civilisation' lay in participation in urban industrial society,"[21] but also a new appreciation of the integrative nature of the secondary industry then beginning to become significant in South Africa.

A rejection of racism and segregationism was central to the writings of these early liberal historians. But the revisionist critics of the 1970s were wrong to imply that the liberals' writings turned on the belief that capitalist economic growth inevitably worked to undermine segregationist policies. When the liberals did, relatively briefly, discuss the

18. *South African Journal of Economics,* 1934–35.

19. M. Legassick in Richard Elphick and Hermann Giliomee, eds., *The Shaping of South African Society, 1652–1820* (Cape Town: Longman, 1979), p. 244; M. Legassick, "The Frontier Tradition in South African Historiography," in Marks and Atmore, eds., *Economy and Society,* p. 63, quoting de Kiewiet's *History.*

20. E.g., de Kiewiet, *History,* p. 201.

21. Legassick in Marks and Atmore, *Economy and Society,* p. 63.

association of capitalist development with segregationism, it was to suggest that the two would be incompatible in the future, not that they had been incompatible in the past. Macmillan's writings on the past asserted no such incompatibility. De Kiewiet's *History,* in which the prediction for the future was asserted most fully, showed how racism had played an important role in the development of the mining industry, with its racially divided working class and its entrenched system of migrant labor. That racism was functional to certain capitalist interests also emerged clearly from the work of the liberal economic historians S. Herbert Frankel and Sheila van der Horst. But it also seemed self-evident to the liberal historians that the reservation of jobs for whites in the new secondary industry made no economic sense. Racism would have economic costs. When de Kiewiet wrote in the late 1930s, it was too early to know that secondary industry could prosper in a segregationist age. The new industrialization seemed, on the contrary, to offer a means of escape from the long history of racism the country had endured. In asserting a contradiction between future capitalist development and segregationist policies, de Kiewiet was expressing that hope, and trying by argument to prevent the enactment of further segregationist measures.

A decade earlier, Macmillan had allowed that a form of protective "segregation"—geographical separation of the races—might have been possible in Philip's day. But he believed that the country had since then been united by the growth of a single economy. Segregation could only now mean, in practice, continued white domination. In his later writing, Macmillan developed the more conventional liberal view that the development of the economy must, at least in the long run, work to break down segregation because of its essential economic irrationality. Writing to Margaret Ballinger in the early 1960s, he spoke of "the Nats trying, not the art of the possible, but the impossible," and said, "the answer to the Nats is not 'bust' but more and more 'boom,' to go on making the [economic] nonsense it is of apartheid." In his autobiography, compiled in the early 1970s, he had to admit that "economic strength has . . . greatly favoured the Nationalists," but he added that "economics is still their weak point and may yet defeat their ideology."[22]

How South African racism had developed was not explained in Theal's many pages. Important elements of what would become known as the frontier thesis were first presented by a professional historian in Macmillan's "Agrarian Problem" lectures. In the tradition, culture, and

22. Macmillan to M. Ballinger, 29 October 1963 and 5 May 1964: Ballinger Papers, University of Cape Town, A3.69 and .70; Macmillan, *South African Years,* p. 250.

character of the trekboer, he suggested, was to be found the essential explanation for South Africa's ills. Macmillan did not develop this thesis at length; only a few paragraphs in *The Cape Colour Question* and *Complex South Africa* touch on it. It was the highly prolific Eric Walker (1886–1976), professor of history at the University of Cape Town from 1911 to 1936, who, in a typically polished lecture delivered at Oxford in 1930, expanded the idea into a general thesis explaining the course of South African development. Like de Kiewiet, Eric Walker had fallen under the influence of Frederick Jackson Turner, whose own famous lecture had explained the course of American development in terms of the expansion of the frontier.[23]

As a historian, Walker is a more ambiguous figure than the other early liberal historians. He has recently been called "a disciple of Theal" for his interpretation of the Mfecane, the upheaval surrounding the rise of the Zulu kingdom.[24] Walker's view of the Great Trek was essentially the same as Macmillan's: as the cause of the schism, and because it carried "the frontier tradition" inland, the trek was, though the central event in South African history, nevertheless a tragedy, a "great disaster."[25] But in his detailed general history, which in part drew heavily on Theal, Walker seemed to express regret that the western Cape had not developed into "a genuine white man's country," when "the feckless Hottentots were dying or retiring" and "the sturdy Bantu were still far off." The decision to base the Cape economy on slavery, he said, had meant "stagnation in the West, dispersion in the East, and intellectual and material poverty throughout."[26]

In private, Walker qualified in another way the emphasis his Oxford lecture had laid on the importance of the frontier. William Ballinger suggested to him that the importation of big capital as a result of the mineral revolutions had done more than the frontier to shape the course of South African history, Walker replied that while he did not discount the importance of capital, he had had too little time to discuss other factors and had dealt with the principal one, which had been "longest in the field" and had "provided the atmosphere in which other and later factors have been able to flourish."[27]

The frontier thesis as Walker had outlined it in 1930 was given

23. E. A. Walker, *The Frontier Tradition in South Africa* (Oxford: Clarendon Press, 1930). See de Kiewiet's favorable mention of Turner's work in *British Colonial Policy and the South African Republics* (London: Longmans, Green, 1929).

24. J. Cobbing, "The Case Against the Mfecane," unpublished paper, 1984.

25. E. A. Walker, *The Great Trek* (London: A & C Black, 1934), especially p. 376; cf. C. F. Muller, "Die Groot Trek," in B. J. Liebenberg, ed., *Opstelle oor die Suid-Afrikaanse Historiografie* (Pretoria: University of South Africa, 1975).

26. E. A. Walker, *A History of South Africa*, 2nd ed., (London: Longmans, 1940), p. 79.

27. E. A. Walker to W. Ballinger, 28 September 1930, Ballinger Papers, F3 II.1.12.

detailed support by the historical work of the psychologist I. D. MacCrone in the first section of his *Race Attitudes in South Africa.*[28] The idea that racial attitudes emerged on the frontier, remained unchanged in the Afrikaner republics, and later developed into segregationism, was a useful one for English-speaking liberals to embrace. It seemed to place the main blame for "what had gone wrong" on the Afrikaners; the racism of the English colony of Natal tended to be forgotten, though the second half of MacCrone's book, a psychological study of the racial attitudes of students at the University of the Witwatersrand, did make clear that in the 1930s English-speakers could be as racist as Afrikaners. Segregation came to be seen as something that sprang from, and pandered to, white racism, especially the racism of the more "backward" and insecure whites, who were mostly Afrikaners.

Though the early liberals recognized that the history of South Africa was the history of all its peoples, they did not discuss all those peoples equally in their work. Macmillan called for a popular social history but did not write one. Similarly, the stress the early liberals placed on the importance of blacks in South African history was mostly mere assertion. Macmillan was a believer in the historian having a strong pair of boots and did do some interviews on historical matters, but none of the early liberal historians realized how evidence from other disciplines, and oral tradition, could be used to illuminate the internal dynamics and external relations of precolonial African societies.

Macmillan had no interest in studying the history of such societies: he aimed to influence policy, not to Africanize South African history. The early history of African societies was to him of little but antiquarian interest.[29] In his work such societies were usually treated in highly generalized terms, and were often dismissed as barbarous and inferior. His sympathies lay with the "progressive" Africans who had broken with the old traditionalism and "backwardness." For all de Kiewiet's repeated assertion of the importance of blacks in South African history, he did not give them much detailed attention in his writing. They only became his central focus in the short chapter entitled "Social and Economic Developments in Native Tribal Life" which he contributed to the eighth volume of the *Cambridge History of the British Empire* (1936), and even there he was more concerned with policy toward Africans than with internal developments in African societies.

28. Cape Town: Oxford University Press, 1937.

29. See, e.g., Macmillan, *South African Years,* p. 234. A. T. Bryant gave his lectures on Zululand—written up as *Olden Times in Zululand and Natal* (London: Longman's Green, 1929)—while Macmillan was at Wits. De Kiewiet attended Malinowski's seminar in London.

In the 1930s, inspired by Macmillan, first H. M. Robertson and then Sheila van der Horst, Robertson's protégée, began to write the economic history of relations between Africans and whites, and J. S. Marais started to trace the complexities of the history of "Coloureds" and of the Cape eastern frontier. But their work tended to describe what had been done to blacks by whites and did not investigate black experience itself sympathetically. Walker had perhaps a greater sense than any of his colleagues that Africans had a separate history, which led him to argue for a history of Africans in a 1935 article.[30] But he never thought of writing such a history, and the next year exchanged his Cape Town chair for one at Cambridge. It was not until the 1960s that professional historians first did what Walker had suggested and wrote in detail on African societies. In the late 1930s Eddie Roux, a botanist, began what became *Time Longer Than Rope: A History of the Black Man's Struggle for Freedom in South Africa,* in response to requests for historical information from African students at a night school.[31] It is likely that he read, and was inspired by, Walker's article.

The early liberal historians were products of their times. Their too-sympathetic view of British policy was a response to an orthodox historiography, by English-speakers as well as by Afrikaners, which was harshly critical of imperial meddling in South African affairs. De Kiewiet went straight from studying abroad to a teaching post in America, and was never to return to live in South Africa, and so cut himself off from South African sources other than those in the Public Record Office in London. Marais's liberalism was strengthened by his years at the University of Cape Town and in Britain, but his *Cape Coloured People,* which speaks of failings in character among "coloreds," reveals the limits of the sympathies inculcated by his rural Cape background. That both Macmillan and de Kiewiet looked to Britain for the source of the values they cherished helps explain why Macmillan, a son of the manse, saw the early nineteenth century through the eyes of missionaries and exaggerated their influence, why de Kiewiet was overready to excuse the mistakes of British policy, and why neither historian saw how missionaries, officials, and economic forces had worked to undermine African societies.

Had the leading liberal historians not left South Africa they would surely have contributed far more than they did to the reconstruction of South African history. Marais, the only central figure to remain, and to continue writing, beyond the 1930s, was the least innovative. De Kiewiet wrote his masterpiece not at the end of a long career as a

30. E. A. Walker, "A Zulu Account of the Retief Massacre," *The Critic,* January 1935.
31. London: Gollancz, 1948.

historian, but before he was forty. He then became a university administrator and wrote no more history.[32] He trained no younger historians, and such intellectual successors as there were in South Africa—some of whose careers were interrupted by the Second World War—mostly took up political-constitutional topics rather than social-economic ones. Arthur Keppel-Jones, who lectured in the history department at Wits before, during, and after the war, was distracted by the appeal of Britain and by pressure to complete a doctorate on a topic in British history begun at Oxford. He was looking over his shoulder to a future in another country even before he began to write *When Smuts Goes* in 1946.[33] The ambivalent commitment to South Africa of liberal historians—Marais excepted—because of their abhorrence of its politics helped prevent some of them from embarking on large-scale and intensive projects on the South African past. When Keppel-Jones did embark on such a project in 1949, he chose a Rhodesian topic because South Africa was too painful to write about, and he wanted to do the research in a more congenial environment.

For all their limitations, the early liberal historians broke the mold of the Theal/Cory orthodoxy, and inspired all later liberal historians, many of whom long regarded "interaction" as the central theme of South African history. Monica Wilson and Leonard Thompson acknowledged their debt to de Kiewiet's *History* in the preface to the first volume of *The Oxford History of South Africa.*[34] We have noted how in some ways the early liberals were ahead of their successors in opening up topics not to be explored in detail until the 1970s. They can hardly be blamed for what their successors failed to do, and must be judged in the context of their times. Macmillan's inspired emphasis on the importance of economics was lost in the writing of later liberal historians, as was the attention—empirical though not conceptual—that he and de Kiewiet gave to class.[35] De Kiewiet produced a one-volume synthesis that was superior to any other written before or since. The achievement of the early liberal historians was indeed impressive, and it deserves greater recognition than it has been accorded.

32. C. Saunders, *C. W. de Kiewiet: Historian of South Africa* (Cape Town: Centre for African Studies, University of Cape Town, 1986), chapter 3.

33. Interview with A. Keppel-Jones, 1985.

34. Oxford: Clarendon Press, 1969.

35. On this see John Lonsdale, "From Colony to Industrial State: South African Historiography as Seen from England," *Social Dynamics* 9 (1983): 72.

Jeffrey Butler and Deryck Schreuder

8. Liberal Historiography Since 1945

South African history, a record of conquest and continuing conflict, is subject to peculiar emphases and exaggerations. In 1937, C. W. de Kiewiet wrote of how the past in South Africa "thrust[s] itself . . . relentlessly upon the future."[1] All South African historians carry a heavy burden of the past as well as of the present.[2] Liberal scholars, preoccupied with the manifest injustices of their particular presents, have frequently written as though they wished the past could be undone so that a genuinely reforming process could begin. This interaction between history and historiography has had an important result: because many whites and blacks are understandably skeptical about the effectiveness of a reformist liberalism, they have conflated a distaste for liberalism as a program of action for the present with a negative view of its capacity for creative analysis of the past.

To come to a critically informed view of liberal historiography since World War II, we need a better appreciation of the changing content of historical liberalism. Such an appreciation should arrest the rampant teleology of contemporary interpretation which implicitly or explicitly tells what liberal scholars of the past could or should have written,

We thank Colin Bundy for comments on an earlier draft of this paper.

1. C. W. De Kiewiet, *The Imperial Factor in South Africa* (Cambridge: Cambridge University Press, 1937), p. 1.

2. For a review of the historiographical debate, see Harrison M. Wright, *The Burden of the Present: The Liberal-Radical Controversy Over South African History* (Cape Town: David Philip, 1977); R. Elphick, "Methodology in South African Historiography: A Defense of Idealism and Empiricism," *Social Dynamics* 9 (1983): 1–17.

without recognizing that they were frequently expressing the views of their day with respect to race and segregation. Contemporary virtue on these issues is both recent and insecure. Not only should historians see their predecessors in context, but historical understanding would provide a surer basis for addressing a critical issue for South Africa and the subject of this book: the reasons why liberals resist the attractions of revolution, national and/or socialist, as a means to resolve acute social crisis, and rely instead on informed and rational action. This paper is, then, about liberal historiography and liberalism.

Using D. J. Manning's excellent analysis of liberalism as a vital modern ideology, three essential organizing principles can be seen as defining liberal scholarship in modern South Africa.[3] First, a primary concern has been the conditions that allow freedom to exist and to be protected, in a harmonious social order and under an independent system of law. Second, liberals have been fascinated with the freedom and power of the individual will and personality, constantly present to "redeem" society. Nineteenth-century liberalism was liberating and reforming, not a force of mere melioration. In liberal political economy, equality of opportunity represented the search for real change, for generative collective growth and individual accumulation of capital. Gradualism was accepted–the very antithesis of a revolutionary and rapid move to an egalitarian order in state and property. Third, this tradition of liberal thought as brought to South Africa had a historicist dimension: the democratic order was attached to a developmental concept of civilization. J. S. Mill, for instance, had indicated a "hierarchical" step-by-step progress toward the highest levels of freedom.[4] Liberals in Britain accepted the individually incomplete steps of the reform acts; the long delay of female enfranchisement was not something to feel acutely guilty about.

Yet there existed at the heart of this historic liberalism a crucial tension.[5] What if a society does not progress along a line of development and reasoned understanding, with a growth of shared perceptions? In some societies, liberal social theory finds the joints of interconnectedness being pulled apart. The empires of the nineteenth and early twentieth centuries created precisely such divided "plural" societies of settlers, natives, and former slaves in Africa, America, and the Caribbean. South Africa, as a plural society founded at the same time as the thirteen

3. D. J. Manning, *Liberalism* (London: Dent, 1976), especially pp. 9–30, 139–57.

4. J. S. Mill, *Representative Government* (London: Oxford University Press, 1942); Manning, *Liberalism*, pp. 20–21.

5. Michael Oakeshott, "Political Education," in M. Sandel, ed., *Liberalism and Its Critics* (New York: New York University Press, 1984), pp. 219–38.

colonies in America, compounded the difficulties in being dominated by a racially defined minority that was itself deeply divided along historical and cultural lines.[6] A liberalism reared in Britain faced, like its heretical offshoot Marxism, a challenge in South Africa which both have still to meet adequately, theoretically or practically.

The liberal view of the world gave high priority to evolution as the preferred mode of change, but that view could be confidently held only if the recent past gave some ground for believing it to be possible. When the social reality was as intractable as it was in South Africa, liberal scholars looked for retrospective explanations of *when things began to go wrong*. History became "the making of the South African native problem," an identification of "turning points" when South African history kept on turning *the wrong way:* "When Smuts Goes," in the title of a famous liberal "history of the future," signaled a historical divide.[7] Liberals' understanding of the human prospect had this informing power of historicism, and not alone because of their sense of human compassion, or of their belief in the "role of the individual" in history.

The liberal view confronted South African realities in another way. It was an ideology with universalist implications. Although it provided for cultural differences—the rights of small nations had long been a preoccupation of liberal statesmen—it was also a call to *all* humanity, regardless of class, ethnicity, nationality, or culture, a call rather jolting to most white South Africans with their long history of division and privileged minority status. The call was to join a historical process of incorporation. Before World War II and its aftermath, many saw in the evolving British Commonwealth a benign dissolution of an empire into a family of nations: the empire, wrote de Kiewiet, had been "a spiritual achievement."[8] Reconciliation *was* being achieved between the "white dominions" and the mother country, and there were grounds for hope before the war that India, and other new "non-white" states, would one day join the Commonwealth, as most of them did.

The liberal historians in South Africa had begun their work in World War I, particularly William Miller Macmillan, who returned to South Africa from Oxford in 1911.[9] By the beginning of World War II

6. R. F. A. Hoernlé, *South African Native Policy and the Liberal Spirit* (Johannesburg: Witwatersrand University Press, 1945), p. vii.

7. W. M. Macmillan, *Bantu, Boer and Briton: The Making of the South African Native Problem* (Oxford: Clarendon, 1929); Arthur Keppel-Jones, *When Smuts Goes: A History of South Africa from 1952 to 2010, First Published in 2015* (Cape Town: African Bookman, 1947).

8. C. W. de Kiewiet, *A History of South Africa: Social and Economic* (London: Oxford University Press, 1941), p. vi.

9. Jeffrey Butler, "William Miller Macmillan: Poverty, Small Towns and the Karoo" (forthcoming in a collection edited by Shula Marks and Hugh Macmillan).

a general liberal orthodoxy existed, rejecting the frontier tradition established by G. M. Theal and Sir George Cory.[10] Liberal scholars, as Christopher Saunders shows above, had attacked the attempt to rewrite South African history to create a segregated past that never was—as a means to justify the present and to bolster the drive for an even more segregated future.[11] In 1937, de Kiewiet was explicitly historicist: historical and cultural realities were being "persistently obscured and ignored."[12] South African history, these scholars said, could be reconstructed to show that there had been, and were, better paths to take.

World War II, with its stimulation of speculation about the future, also dramatically sharpened the attention given to the themes of liberal writings on the past. The war provided an almost Pauline sense of "hope." New, if tentative, policies came from government with liberal implications in the area of labor, the pass laws, influx control, trade unionism, and further enfranchisement (related to the Indian people). J. H. Hofmeyr, after his stand against the Representation of Natives Bill in 1936, and as an innovative minister of finance during the war, emerged as the liberal hope in the Smuts camp. Just before the end of the war, the exposure of the Nazi death camps demonstrated the obscene cruelty of which extreme racists were capable. Soon after VE Day, the Labour party won an overwhelming victory in the United Kingdom. This demonstrated, in the case of the United Kingdom at least, that postwar politics were not going to be dominated by wartime leaders however inspiring they had been, but by popular demands for a new postwar order.

South African white society had been deeply divided by the war, producing two national tendencies which persisted after the war—one based on an Anglo-Afrikaner combination, the other on an Afrikaner ethnic nationalism. In the Anglo-Afrikaner camp, there was a new sense of a South African national identity, by no means uncritically following the call of empire, and having within it the possibility of its own interpretation of South Africa's past. That potentially liberal combination failed to find an effective leader and voice in the United party. Exploiting the dislocations of the postwar era, the National party swept the Afrikaner countryside in the general election of 1948 and gained a slim parliamentary majority. The loss of power by the United

10. D. M. Schreuder, "The Imperial Historian as Colonial Nationalist: George McCall Theal and the Making of South African History," in G. Martel, ed., *Studies in British Imperial History* (London: Macmillan, 1986), pp. 95–158.

11. For Saunders, see pp. 137–38; E. A. Walker, *The Frontier Tradition in South Africa* (Oxford: Oxford University Press, 1930); I. D. MacCrone, *Race Attitudes in South Africa* (London: Oxford University Press, 1937), p. 136.

12. De Kiewiet, *Imperial Factor,* p. ix.

party changed the whole style and tone of politics, bringing to an end the era of Anglo-Afrikaner conciliation begun by Sir Henry Campbell-Bannerman, Liberal prime minister of the United Kingdom, in 1905. "Campbell-Bannerman," claimed G. H. L. LeMay, "gave to white politics in South Africa nearly half a century of moderation."[13] The unexpected victory of an exclusive Afrikanerdom led liberal scholars to a new search for the origins of the "present discontents."

World War II had also reintroduced the imperial theme into the forefront of the South African public debate. The controversies over South Africa's support for the Allied war effort simply spilled over into the old arguments among scholars about the determining forces in South African history itself. Liberal scholars had before them the virulent anti-British feeling of most Afrikaners, and they had already been uneasy on the issue of imperial responsibility, especially as demonstrated in Sir Alfred Milner's role in bringing on the Anglo-Boer War 1899–1902.[14] When the papers of Sir Graham Bower, secretary to the high commissioner at the Cape in 1895, were opened in Cape Town in 1946, there was great anxiety among supporters of the Smuts government; they apparently feared that nationalists would be able to prove that the Jameson raid, a provocative attack on the Transvaal in 1895 that led eventually to the Anglo-Boer War, had been a deliberate act of the imperial government.[15] Would they be able to make political use of the fact in the election then only two years away?

These new sources highlighted a dilemma in liberal scholarship: the British imperial factor had been creative in protecting African land, but destructive in the Anglo-Boer war. "Why don't you write a thesis on Campbell-Bannerman's failure to reconcile Afrikaners in South Africa?" said an Oxford scholar to a beginning graduate student from South Africa in 1952.[16] Jean van der Poel and Ethel Drus both pursued Joseph Chamberlain, colonial secretary after 1895, to establish his complicity in the Jameson Raid, adding him to a rogues' gallery already occupied by Milner and Rhodes.[17] Jeffrey Butler, in his study of the raid, asked why the liberals had failed to use it for political purposes in the United

13. G. H. L. LeMay, *British Supremacy in South Africa 1899–1907* (Oxford: Clarendon Press, 1965), p. 215.

14. See, e.g., E. A. Walker, ed., *The Cambridge History of the British Empire* 8, *South Africa* (Cambridge: Cambridge University Press, 1936), pp. 602, 631.

15. Sir Graham Bower Papers, South African Library, Cape Town.

16. F. W. Deakin, Warden of St. Antony's College, to Jeffrey Butler.

17. Jean van der Poel, *The Jameson Raid* (Cape Town: Oxford University Press, 1951); Ethel Drus, "A Report on the Papers of Joseph Chamberlain Relating to the Jameson Raid and the Inquiry," *Bulletin of the Institute of Historical Research* 25 (May 1952), pp. 33–63.

Kingdom, especially to moderate British policy before the war.[18] J. S. Marais examined *The Fall of Kruger's Republic,* looking sympathetically, though critically, at a small, struggling state brought down in the interests of an ambitious imperial policy in the hands of Milner and Chamberlain.[19] And LeMay characterized the Anglo-Boer War as "Sir Alfred Milner's" War.[20] Here at least was one issue on which liberal and Afrikaner nationalist historians could have some limited agreement: the old imperial agents were agreed fair game.

At the core of this revived imperial history was the mixture of past and present burdens. Leonard Thompson completed his "Indian Immigration into Natal, 1860–1872" while white Natalians were debating both the restriction of land owning by Indians and a limited extension of the franchise to them.[21] Later he wrote on the Cape franchise, when the National party government had launched its final, and ultimately successful, attack on the qualified nonracial franchise in Cape Province.[22] The "disaster" of 1948 had also provoked a reappraisal of the imperial-Afrikaner relationship in the period of *the* great historical "turning point" for South Africa—the years of the raid, war, and unification, 1895–1910. The point of much of this postwar scholarship was to show how the "New Imperialism" of the Chamberlain-Milner variety had utterly alienated Afrikanerdom at a crucial moment, driving it back into a volk ethnicity, and away from a convergence with the liberal forces of modernity in South Africa. For van der Poel, the "worst outcome" of the raid was that it accelerated political processes and drove South Africa into an "artificially constructed union"—instead of relying on the "natural growth of unity."[23] Thompson, in his study of the formation of the Union, demonstrated how state-making had both excluded Africans from the polity and built a unitary constitutional structure which moved away from the Cape-liberal preference for a federal model, ignoring the experience of other federations.[24]

Most of this postwar history was political and institutional in focus, and was particularly drawn to the personal responsibilities of individuals. Largely gone was the social and economic focus of Macmillan and de

18. Jeffrey Butler, *The Liberal Party and the Jameson Raid* (Oxford: Clarendon, 1968).

19. J. S. Marais, *The Fall of Kruger's Republic* (Oxford: Clarendon, 1961), pp. 323–32.

20. LeMay, *British Supremacy,* p. 1.

21. L. M. Thompson, "Indian Immigration into Natal 1860–1872," *Archives Year Book* 15 (1952). Thompson began this work before the war.

22. L. M. Thompson, *The Cape Coloured Franchise* (Johannesburg: Institute of Race Relations, 1949).

23. Van der Poel, *Raid,* pp. 261–62.

24. L. M. Thompson, *The Unification of South Africa* (Oxford: Clarendon, 1960), pp. 480–83.

Kiewiet, of van der Poel's work on railway and customs policies, Robertson's essays on Cape society, and van der Horst's work on African labor.[25] This shift was largely due to the hammer blows of government policy after 1948, the riveting fast of an Afrikaner ascendancy by gerrymandering the constitution, and the elaboration of the blueprint for the preservation of white power, which came to be "apartheid." But the present intruded even more with the emergence of an alternate power base for change in an African nationalist and trade-union movement. This in turn had been stimulated by rapidly changing policies on the part of Great Britain in relation to tropical Africa, and by the forceful intervention of India in South Africa's affairs, via the new United Nations Organization, even before 1948.

Here, liberals were much less sure of their posture. In the early 1940s Leo Marquard, as a founder and former president of the National Union of South African Students, and later an acute analyst of rural distress in the Orange Free State, had pressed the potential of militant African collectivist action in *The Black Man's Burden,* published in 1943 under the pseudonym "John Burger."[26] But the mainstream of liberal thought and action, shaped in many ways by the liberal-dominated South African Institute of Race Relations, then in the heyday of J. D. Rheinallt Jones, preferred to focus on forms of social and political amelioration, through the modification of government policy itself.[27] That view, a depoliticization of liberalism, had a long history, coming in part from the liberals' despair in the 1920s and 1930s when they had to face the fact that they remained a tiny minority and there was little to be hoped for from the principal white political parties.[28]

This choice of the institutional path and medium was crucial for liberalism. An opponent of that choice, Solly Sachs, sharply pointed out that, both tactically and strategically, "liberalism in South Africa is doomed unless and until it learns to understand the workers' problems and finds a concrete basis of cooperation with the masses of workers, European and non-Europeans."[29] That was not to be. In the context of growing militancy of the African National Congress in the 1940s, and then the Pan Africanist Congress in the 1950s, liberals held back from proposing a universal franchise. As always, liberals were politically less

25. Jean van der Poel, *Railway and Customs Policies in South Africa* (London: Longmans, Green, 1933); H. M. Robertson, "150 Years of Contact between Black and White," *South African Journal of Economics* 2 (December 1934) and 3 (March 1935); Sheila van der Horst, *Native Labour in South Africa* (London: Oxford University Press, 1942).

26. John Burger, *The Black Man's Burden* (London: Gollancz, 1943).

27. See Paul Rich, *White Power and the Liberal Conscience* (Manchester: Manchester University Press, 1984), pp. 73–76.

28. Jeffrey Butler, "Interwar Liberalism," pp. 95–97, above.

29. Quoted in Rich, *White Power,* p. 90.

bold than radicals. The founding of the Liberal party in 1953 actually divided liberals deeply, and the party failed to make headway among whites, as it had to do if change were to come in a peaceful evolutionary way.[30]

Marquard's position appeared to have moderated from that in *The Black Man's Burden.* His widely read *Peoples and Policies of South Africa,* first published in 1952, and infused with a liberal historical interpretation, addressed the revealing self-chosen question "Can the inhabitants of South Africa arrange matters so that they may live together in harmony, that white and non-white may enjoy a common citizenship, that no one group need fear that it will have to forfeit its cultural identity?" His answer was to suggest the probability of the collapse of apartheid as segregationist economic policy and to propose a new national convention to redraft the South African constitution.[31] The mistakes which Thompson said had been made at the time of unification were to be rectified. History was to be "re-run." In 1971 Marquard was still spelling out a new version of the old Cape "lost cause" at the 1908–1909 conventions—a call for a federation of southern Africa, a call made earlier by another liberal historian, Arthur Keppel-Jones.[32] But what of the more militant or "direct action" approach, involving a united white-black pressure from *outside* the constitutional arena to force urgent change? Marquard now spoke for mainstream liberalism in answering that "constitutions and laws cannot abolish prejudice in the human mind, but they can help to create the climate in which the fears that feed on prejudice are more easily dissolved. This is what a federation of Southern Africa, built on strong realistic foundations and constructed on practical lines, could do."[33]

The institutional emphasis of this liberal reformism was so marked and looks so oligarchic in thrust that it needs an explanation. In the late 1940s and 1950s, the pace of change in Africa and in Asia became extremely rapid, and South African liberals were no less children of their time than anyone else. For liberals the orderly dismantling of the British empire showed again the capacity of the state to undertake a controlled demission of its power. It also brought to the fore articulate Asian and African leaders and their popular support. The leaders of the new states themselves raised few problems; most of them used a

30. T. R. H. Davenport, *South Africa: A Modern History* (Toronto: Toronto University Press, 1977), pp. 279–80.

31. Leo Marquard, *The Peoples and Policies of South Africa* (London: Oxford University Press, 1962), pp. 273–77.

32. Leo Marquard, *A Federation for South Africa* (London: Oxford University Press, 1971), p. 139; Arthur Keppel-Jones, *Friends or Foes?* (Pietermaritzburg: Shuter and Shooter, 1950).

33. Marquard, *Federation,* p. 139.

language of lofty statesmanship and wished to stay in the Commonwealth. The appearance of mobilized masses, however, brought visions of uncontrolled social and political change, always a bugbear for liberals, perhaps now more intense in the context of a polarized international order, with Western governments resisting the "communist menace." The Liberal party, for complex reasons, did not participate in the historic Congress of the People that drew up the Freedom Charter in 1955; liberals became divided, and the franchise became a major issue between liberals in the Liberal party and future Progressives.[34]

Liberals appeared in the 1950s to be conservative, looking back to yet another lost path of controlled political change—the Cape liberal tradition, then being dismantled by the Afrikaner nationalist government. Many South African liberals accepted the notion that the vote required a trained populace, that Africans were to be "progressively" embraced politically.[35] This fear of a too-rapid move to democracy was related to the demands of political realism: if whites were to be persuaded, then change would be dictated by the pace of persuasion. Just how slow was that pace was demonstrated by the reaction of the South African government to the new Commonwealth: H. F. Verwoerd, then prime minister, returned to South Africa from the momentous London Commonwealth conference in 1961 and declared the "triumph of commonwealth expulsion."[36] Not only had conciliation of Afrikaners failed, but South African white English-speakers soon acquiesced in the renewed move to isolation. Poor Sir Henry Campbell-Bannerman turned in his grave once more.

Liberal scholars were not only influenced by events—World War II, the election of 1948, and growing African assertion—but by developments in the historical discipline itself. While representing, as always, a minority view in South African white society, they dominated the history departments of the English-speaking universities even if none of the chairmen of these departments were social historians in the Macmillan/de Kiewiet mold. English-speaking universities in South Africa continued to maintain contact with British universities, where much historical writing was in an empirical tradition which was also institutional. The editor of the distinguished series *The Oxford History of England*, G. N. Clark, had been unapologetic about the institutional emphasis: "It is in public institutions that men express their will to control events. . . . The

34. Davenport, *South Africa*, p. 280.

35. Margaret Ballinger, *From Union to Apartheid* (Cape Town: Juta, 1969), p. 23.

36. James Barber, *South Africa's Foreign Policy, 1945–70* (London: Oxford University Press, 1973), pp. 185–89.

history of institutions must in some sense be central."[37] The faults and virtues of South African liberal scholars tended rather to be those of the genre of the time, because it was from overseas that they took their models.

British economic history was still dominated by J. H. Clapham (1873–1946), whose three-volume *History* appeared between 1926 and 1938.[38] His approach continued to dominate after the war: even the leftist orientation of E. J. Hobsbawm resulted in economic history of a fairly orthodox kind.[39] In the United States, W. W. Rostow elaborated a liberal stage theory of history, a "non-Communist manifesto," and addressed the problem of "take off," then a central preoccupation of all interested in the future of newly independent states.[40] At least one South African liberal economist, Desmond Hobart Houghton, used it as the model for an economic history of South Africa, critical of policies of segregation.[41]

The liberal-empirical approach found its shortcomings exposed in relation to what has been dubbed the "new history," a "history from below," a method to get beyond the history of minority ruling classes in any society. The History Workshop Movement in Britain built on an older tradition of British social history exemplified in the work of the Hammonds, R. H. Tawney, and others, and on the work of the Annales school in France. British historians of the left had to explain why a militant proletariat had not emerged in Britain. E. P. Thompson's work is in a long English tradition, but with a difference: whereas the Hammonds had sought to show the sufferings of the masses, Thompson showed how workers had developed their own culture—one of moderation, not necessarily of militancy.[42]

A related source of the new history, and one that was even more obviously applicable to African studies, was the impact of social-science theory. This had immense attraction in apparently offering conceptual tools that allowed the historian to probe the great questions that

37. Quoted in A. Marwick, *The Nature of History* (New York: Alfred A. Knopf, 1971), p. 200.

38. J. H. Clapham, *The Economic History of England* (Cambridge: Cambridge University Press, three volumes, 1926–1938).

39. E. J. Hobsbawm, *Industry and Empire: An Economic History of Britain Since 1750* (London: Weidenfeld and Nicolson, 1968), pp. 88–127.

40. W. W. Rostow, *The Stages of Economic Growth (A Non-Communist Manifesto)* (Cambridge: Cambridge University Press, 1960).

41. Desmond Hobart Houghton, *The South African Economy* (Cape Town: Oxford University Press, 1964), pp. 6–9.

42. J. L. and Barbara Hammond, *The Town Labourer* (London: Longmans, Green, 1917); E. P. Thompson, *The Making of the English Working Class* (New York: Knopf, 1963), pp. 830–32. See also A. Marwick, *The Nature of History,* 2nd ed. (London: Macmillan, 1981) and John Tosh, *The Pursuit of History* (London: Longman, 1984).

dominated everyday lives—prejudice, poverty, and power—in a manner broader and yet more definitive than through the old "common-sense approach" to human behavior, reliant on sources made by the literate strata of society. It also pointed to historical explanations which did not rely on individual actors. Historiography without such "theory"—a self-conscious, systematic organizing principle of inquiry and exposition—became unthinkable to many scholars of a new generation. If the history of South Africa was to become more than the history of the white, literate, and dominant classes, then a considerable challenge in method had to be faced.

There was also the growing scholarly fascination with "process" in the history of social change, those structural features and forces which could be identified by "theory," a matter of naming the essential determinants of history. Marxist theory, with its concern for capital accumulation, here offered one highly attractive way to that structural explanation of "process." It proposed definable phases or stages of historical change—largely of economic performance and class formation—which could be deployed to write about the total experience of nonliterate mass societies. These approaches to historical study were flourishing in the United Kingdom just at the time, from 1955 on, when liberals in South Africa experienced their most depressing public developments: the 1953 election had been lost to the Nationalists, D. F. Malan had been succeeded as prime minister by J. D. Strijdom and then by H. F. Verwoerd, who in turn won the election of 1958, the third Nationalist victory in a row.

A notable group of graduates from English-language universities in South Africa, most of them historians, traveled the traditional path of going to the United Kingdom for further training: Shula Marks, Stanley Trapido, Martin Legassick, Dan O'Meara, Charles van Onselen, Colin Bundy, to name a few. Some of them had been radicalized by confrontation with the South African state: to them reformism seemed to have little to offer and liberal history had become merely a dreary catalog of defeat and political misjudgment. Joining revisionist scholars from the United Kingdom and the United States, they looked for new historical models both to explain the present situation and provide a model for the future.

They could hardly have gone overseas at a better time. Within a decade there appeared major works of historical scholarship, most of them written by social scientists who had turned to history, works of large geographical and temporal scale. Barrington Moore's synoptic study of lord and peasant in the origins of modern political ideologies in 1966 and Eric Wolf's work on peasant wars in 1969 elucidated both the origins of modern political orders and the persistent challenges to

share power, another wrong road taken in the past, and still being taken today. But the British intellectual world and the South African were about to go further "out of sync" once more: with the ending of empire in colonial Africa, scholars in the United Kingdom were rapidly turning to the problems of explaining yet another failure, namely the rapid dashing of hopes for a new social order in Africa in the aftermath of imperialism. For South African liberals that aftermath was yet to come, and they failed to anticipate it in tropical Africa. Marxists, however, had an explanation for it.

A major achievement of the *Oxford History* was its determined Africanist emphasis—something like half of Volume I was devoted to African societies. For liberals the emphasis was morally and politically crucial. There was, moreover, in both *Oxford History* volumes an emphasis on "interaction," an attack on the assertion of a segregated past that liberals believed never was. But the theme of interaction did not address itself to the problem of the relation of social structure to power, a central question for the "new" historians listed above. Consequently, there was a tension between narrative—essentially the stories of white conquest of Africans and other exercises of power—and description of social structure and culture, set out in ethnic and racial divisions.

Volume II of the *Oxford History* made a major attempt to resolve this difficulty. It began with four chapters on the social and economic processes that, since 1865, had brought all South African groups closer together, in spite of Canute-like attempts by all South African governments to stop them. In doing so, the *Oxford History* anticipated the work on social and economic themes that has been such a feature of revisionist scholarship. A narrative sequence followed, made up of six chapters that gave a chronological account of the subjection of African kingdoms, the clash between Britain and the Afrikaner republics, the making of Union, and South Africa's relations with "the Modern World"—the latter a dig at what liberals regarded as the essentially anachronistic character of apartheid and separate development. Inserted between the "Compromise of Union" and "South Africa and the Modern World" were chapters on Afrikaner and African nationalism, a fairly explicit statement that these were the contending forces of the struggle for power in the future. It was clearly implied, too, that liberals should take the side of Africans: as in history, so now in politics too.

One major problem of this design can be especially noted: the lack of a description of the central role played by white English-speakers. From the beginning of South Africa's mining revolution, they had after all provided, and still provide, the bulk of the capital, technology, and overseas connections essential to the South African political economy. South African liberalism itself received brief attention as an "antinationalist" force.[49] Just as the failure of conciliation among Afrikaners had been given no adequate explanation, so the failure of liberalism remained something of a mystery. Lastly, the analytical scheme of the *Oxford History* failed to explain the absence of a black militant proletariat, an issue for certain British socialists when analyzing their own society.

Liberal historians *could* have included more social and economic material, returning to the path blazed by Macmillan in the twenties. They would, however, probably have used such material, as Macmillan did, and as the *Oxford History* did, to place actors, political institutions, and policies "in context." Having no fresh analytical scheme, and especially no new theory of society, they did not try to establish some process which they regarded as the central one that *determined* all others in society. They continued with characteristic liberal interests: with individuals, as in a major biography of John X. Merriman, the last prime minister of Cape Colony, the seat of South Africa's only liberal tradition, however limited;[50] or of Mosheshwe, a great conciliator and nation builder;[51] and with studies of political organizations, as in a study of the Afrikaner Bond, the story of the clash between an ethnic movement and an arrogant imperialism.[52]

General histories, because they attempt to paint the "big picture," frequently show the assumptions of the historian more clearly than do monographic works. T. R. H. Davenport's *South Africa: A Modern History* (1977) now replaced E. A. Walker's *A History of Southern Africa* (1957). It showed a characteristic liberal interest in chronological political and institutional history, in the institutions and movements that sustained white domination, as well as in the history of dominated peoples. Here also Davenport showed a liberal refusal to deny the palpable facts of racism—a willingness to take much of racism at face value, and thereby to resist interpretive schemes that try to explain it, or explain it away, in terms of other social variables, like class. Davenport's history was also liberal in its eclecticism, incorporating the Africanist perspective of the *Oxford History*—"the philosophical basis of this 'Africanist' school," wrote Davenport, "was indistinguishable from the liberal."[53] It was, moreover, eclectic in a deeper sense: it used the massive amounts of basic research on economic and social processes produced by revisionist historians, but always as a means of elucidating the main political story.

49. Ibid., 2, pp. 416–23.

50. Phyllis Lewsen, *John X. Merriman: Paradoxical South African Statesman* (New Haven: Yale University Press, 1982).

51. Leonard Thompson, *Survival in Two Worlds: Moshoeshoe of Lesotho 1786–1870* (Oxford: Clarendon, 1975).

52. T. R. H. Davenport, *The Afrikaner Bond: The History of a South African Political Party, 1880–1911* (Cape Town: Oxford University Press, 1966).

53. Davenport, *South Africa,* p. xiii.

It did not produce a startling new interpretation of South African history, but it has avoided a central weakness in revisionist scholarship, with the notable exception of the Poulantzian "fractionalists," namely, the virtual consignment of white politics to the historical dustbin.[54]

There is no normative way to the past "as it really was," in Ranke's famed phrase. Material forces and factors are no more certain to reveal the wellsprings of human action and social process than a range of other criteria. The *Oxford History,* with its emphasis on writing a history of *all* South Africa's peoples, was true to liberal universalism, an important milestone in South African historiography. With it, liberal historians maintained their commitment to "open-ended" and "pluralistic" history, which draws on a range of theory and disciplines.

Any assessment of the role of liberal historians since World War II has to take account of the assault on them by revisionist historians. To some extent, the two schools have been talking past each other, the revisionists castigating their predecessors for having left out so much of the "real" story, the liberals continuing with what they had done before but with changes of emphasis. Yet they were also engaged in a barely hidden battle for the hearts and minds of the black majority of South Africa, with revisionists arguing, largely by implication, that some kind of socialism, rather than modern capitalism or a "mixed" economy, should provide the basis of a future South African order. Not only had liberals as actors failed politically in the past—the failure was too palpably manifest to argue about—but they had allegedly given a misleading interpretation of that past, particularly in asserting that capitalist processes were essentially benign *if* allowed full rein in society and not obstructed by the irrational forces of racism.[55]

This so-called liberal view of capitalism has come to be known in revisionist scholarship as the "conventional wisdom," a kind of clay pigeon for students and others to shoot at. It is difficult, however, to find in postwar liberal scholarship such a naive optimism as to the consequences of growth in capitalist societies.[56] Rather, from Macmillan on, liberal historians have emphasized the questionable intellectual bases of South African segregationist policies, arguing that economic growth would increase the mutual dependencies in South African society, without suggesting that rational policies including redistribution of

54. See David Yudelman, "State and Capital in Contemporary South Africa," pp. 251–52 below. It is not insignificant that revisionist scholars have so far failed to provide a synoptic single author interpretation of the span of South African history.

55. Frederick Johnstone, "Most Painful to Our Hearts: South Africa Through the Eyes of the New School," *Canadian Journal of African Studies* 16 (1982): 5–26.

56. Richard Elphick, "Methodology in South African Historiography," pp. 1–5.

wealth and power would follow *as a matter of course.* Alone of liberal writers, Ralph Horwitz, Michael O'Dowd, and W. H. Hutt (none of them historians) have perhaps come close to the kind of liberal determinism of which liberal historians are often accused.[57] Revisionists were, quite understandably, accusing liberals of political quiescence, of relying on social process rather than demanding fundamental change, of advocating policies of social control and cooptation, of a lack of interest in *real* change—hence the failure of liberalism itself as a program of action.[58]

Modern liberal historical scholarship has had, and still does have, a basic optimism that human beings *can* respond rationally and morally to the problems they create by their own deeds. Liberals' concern for the conditions that might be conducive to freedom, their belief in the power of ongoing historical process, and particularly their belief in the power of regeneration, of the capacity of individuals and societies to make choices, necessarily implies an optimism that is more fundamental than a belief in the necessary consequences of economic growth. Even within the latter debate, it could be argued that South African society today *is* facing the consequences of sustained capitalist development, that South Africa's rulers are at last being forced to grapple, for example, with the relentless urbanization that no earlier government has been able to arrest. A significant weakness of liberal scholarship has lain in its unwillingness to be precise about when "regeneration" would take place. It has also been infused with a sometimes naive form of historicism which believed that history (and human regeneration) would ultimately happen along certain patterns. Both these notions had about them a vague optimism, and a flaccid analytic grasp, which made them easy targets for an acute generation of radical scholars.

Yet it should be pointed out that a major strength of modern liberalism has been its capacity to meet circumstances with creative change: Gladstone's laissez-faire state of morally right-minded independent citizens could become the emerging social democracy of welfare politics in the age of Lloyd George.[59] Liberalism could indeed become the New Liberalism, and remain true to itself in new circumstances. As a historic

57. Ralph Horwitz, *The Political Economy of South Africa* (New York: Praeger, 1967); Michael O'Dowd, "South Africa in the Light of the Stages of Economic Growth," in Adrian Leftwich, ed., *South Africa: Economic Growth and Political Change* (London: Allison and Busby, 1974), pp. 29–43; W. H. Hutt, *The Economics of the Colour Bar* (London: Deutsch, 1964).

58. Rich, *White Power,* pp. 128–36.

59. See accounts of such a liberal transformation in K. O. Morgan, *The Age of Lloyd George* (New York: Barnes and Noble, 1971); Peter Clarke, *Liberals and Social Democrats* (Cambridge: Cambridge University Press, 1978); and M. Freeden, *The New Liberalism* (Oxford: Oxford University Press, 1978).

ideology, vulnerable to individual pressure, it could also be turned back on its origins, to form the core of a new conservatism in economics: the unacceptable consequences of capitalism have to be kept in check by a socially responsible political order. Marxism, however, has to confront the consequences, economic and human, of *its* failures, which run from the Stalinist state to Pol Pot. The potential in liberal ideals and values for the human prospect is more valuable than the South African historiographical debate has so far allowed. As South Africa's peoples enter a new age of crisis and change, so a new liberalism, informing a social democratic state, offers a deeply valuable human vision. The very lack of a rigid social theory, which implies an ideologically defined outcome sooner or later, is, potentially, liberal history's greatest strength—given the manifest failure of any social theory so far to be accurate in its predictions. Liberal historians, if they are true to their empirical tradition, are unlikely to try and force fact to conform to theory. They are more likely to tell the human story with all its triumphs and tragedies, and in the telling create a powerful agency for social change and hope.

Richard Elphick

9. Historiography and the Future of Liberal Values in South Africa

What effect might historiography have on the prospect for liberal values in postapartheid South Africa? One's first instinct, of course, is to say "not much." After all, in South Africa most intellectuals have little influence on practical affairs, and historians, particularly liberal historians, have less influence than most. Moreover, the audience for liberals may soon shrink even further if the country lurches to the left, to the right, or into chaos.

There are, however, more hopeful possibilities for liberal historians. The role of intellectuals is greatest in times of ideological confusion, and for South Africa this is surely such a time. A new South African government, whatever its ideology, will certainly put a high premium on education and might thus grant considerable autonomy to the universities. Historians presently at South African universities, many of whom are liberals, may soon encounter a massive thirst for history, particularly among young blacks and Afrikaners; the vision they present of the South African past may well be of more than academic importance.

In discussing the relationships between historiography and social values in South Africa, the important question is whether historians can nurture in South Africans a vision of the historical process which would allow them to imagine a just society based on liberal principles.

I wrote this chapter while a fellow at the Center for the Humanities, Wesleyan University. Colin Bundy, Kenneth Hughes, and Richard Vann helped me with comments on an earlier draft.

There are three features without which a liberal South Africa will not long endure: (1) a high degree of mutual understanding among ethnic groups, and hence a high tolerance for cultural pluralism; (2) a determination to protect the rights of individuals and institutions such as the universities and the press against encroachments from the state; and (3) an openness to constant change and experimentation, combined with an optimism about the possibilities of attaining a just order in South Africa. I assume that the struggle for tolerance, freedom, and justice will continue long after the demise of the Nationalist regime.

In 1982 Shula Marks and Richard Rathbone published a collection of fourteen papers first delivered at the University of London, under the title *Industrialisation and Social Change in South Africa.*[1] The fifteen authors—most influenced to some degree by Marxism—have rendered obsolete a number of older complaints about Marxist historiography. Their papers are not excessively theoretical, nor do they build their cases on inadequate evidence; most chapters are remarkable for their empirical depth and their attention to complexity and detail. Not content merely to locate exploited classes in the "social formation," these writers have described the lives of African workers, sharecroppers, and the "petty bourgeoisie" as these lives were experienced. Moreover, they have expanded the previous Marxist preoccupation with "land, labor, and capital" to include religion, the arts, the family, music, and sports. In short, this book indicates the degree to which the Marxist historiography of South Africa has broadened, deepened, and matured.

If their book is representative of the best of recent Marxist work, it might be worthwhile to analyze it in terms of our question: What are *Marxist* historiography's implications for liberal values in postapartheid South Africa? In answering this question we must state firmly that these historians are not, on the whole, "determinists" in the sense in which anti-Marxists often use that term. Marks and Rathbone emphasize that "there was nothing predetermined about the shape of South Africa's industrial revolution."[2] By this they mean that their contributors do not simply read the details of South Africa's industrial revolution from an abstract model of capitalist development. They do not let their model overrule their evidence.

Nor, on the whole, are these authors guilty of a more modern Marxist fallacy of confounding function with cause. The essence of that fallacy is to say that because A has proven useful (or functional) to B, it was

1. Shula Marks and Richard Rathbone, eds., *Industrialisation and Social Change in South Africa: African Class Formation, Culture and Consciousness 1870–1930* (London: Longman, 1982). Hereafter cited as *ISC.*

2. Marks and Rathbone, *ISC,* Introduction, p. 11.

caused by B. This view, which is defended by Marxist philosophers like G. A. Cohen,[3] violates long-standing assumptions of the mainstream of Anglo-American historiography. In the Marks and Rathbone collection it is most notably rejected by Patrick Harries (with firm support from the editors) when he argues that the migrant-labor system in South Africa did not originate in the intent of "capital."[4] Rather, he says, it was the product of "the weakness of colonial authorities, the continued access Africans had to the land, and the cohesion of pre-colonial social formations." Thus Harries severs the origins of migrancy from the forces that benefit from it and sustain it (largely the mines). This emphasis on unintended consequences in history forms a point of contact between the latest Marxist empirical scholarship and liberal historiography.

However, this is not to deny that Marxist theory influences the authors' view of history. Behind most of the chapters looms the story of capitalist "accumulation" and the class struggles attendant upon it. This story has its own internal logic, and the authors link it directly and indirectly to their varying subject matters. To take some representative examples: Judy Kimble's analysis of labor migration from Basutoland is told against the background of "several decades of the penetration of merchant capital into the whole region." Similarly, Jeff Guy asserts that the "history of Zululand in the 1880s and 1890s can be seen as the history of the diversion of surplus labour from the service of the Zulu state to the service of developing capitalist production in southern Africa." And Tim Keegan seeks to understand the peasant-tenant economy by its "subsumption within colonial capitalism," along with its role in the "process of landlord capital accumulation."[5] Even those chapters that do not have an explicitly economic focus begin by situating their subjects in the "social formation" and describe the way they coped with circumstances caused by the development of capitalism in South Africa.[6]

I have already called this process of capital accumulation a "story." In doing so I call attention to the historian's freedom to choose themes or plots, to rank them according to their importance, and to interweave

3. G. A. Cohen, *Karl Marx's Theory of History: A Defence* (Princeton: Princeton University Press, 1978), pp. 249–96.

4. Marks and Rathbone, *ISC,* Introduction, p. 18. See also Patrick Harries, *ISC,* "Kinship, ideology and the nature of pre-colonial labour migration: labour migration from the Delagoa Bay hinterland to South Africa, up to 1895," pp. 142–43.

5. Judy Kimble, *ISC,* "Labour migration in Basutoland c. 1870–1885," p. 119; Jeff Guy, *ISC,* "The destruction and reconstruction of Zulu society," p. 167; Tim Keegan, *ISC,* "The sharecropping economy, African class formation and the 1913 Natives' Land Act in the highveld maize belt," p. 196.

6. For example, see Brian Willan, *ISC,* "An African in Kimberley: Sol T. Plaatje, 1894–1898," p. 238; and Philip Bonner, *ISC,* "The Transvaal Native Congress, 1917–1920: the radicalisation of the black petty bourgeoisie on the Rand," p. 271.

them in a finished account. These stories proceed by an internal logic which should be persuasive to the reader. Where does the logic reside—in the artistry of the storyteller or in the facts he or she is relating? For Marxists the answer to this question must be clear: it resides in the reality. That is, the Marxist historian does not imagine that he or she is imposing a story or an order upon a fragmented reality in order to reduce it to comprehensibility; rather the logic is seen as external to the historian, inhering either in a "system" (such as capitalism) or a "process" (such as capital accumulation).

I am using the terms "system" and "process" to refer to such objective entities that embody their own logic, and the words "story" and "plot" to focus on the historian's role in imposing logic and order on history. I assume that not only the objective but also the subjective contribute to the coherence and comprehensibility of a final work of history. I make no attempt here to relate the two, a forbidding philosophical task. I merely assert that liberal historiography must be conscious of the importance of the historian's role in choosing, shaping, and interweaving "stories"—much more conscious than South African Marxists conventionally are.

Marks and Rathbone give a few clues on how they envisage the internal logic of capitalist development. For example, they say it proceeded by "compulsion"; seldom did Africans freely consent to proletarianization. On the other hand, "pre-industrial societies, both black and white, could determine, sometimes in significant ways, what was and what was not possible for mine magnates, aspirant capitalist farmers and, later on, manufacturers." And not only was capital accumulation channeled by the conditions of South Africa, but even magnates like Rhodes and Beit had their options limited by "the imperatives of the capital markets and the nature of the class struggle."[7]

It would be unfair to reduce this historical vision to a simple formula. However, certain aspects of it can be identified and put in propositional form: (1) capital accumulation is the principal story; (2) capital accumulation works itself out by forcing itself on other realities, though to a lesser extent it also yields to them; (3) it operates, to some degree, out of control of all actors. For me, the key point in this vision is the consistent subordination of the minor stories to the main story. This subordination is accomplished, as I shall try to show, sometimes by explicit affirmation, sometimes by the way the stories are "emplotted."[8] This can be illustrated by looking at four other "stories" (each corresponding to putatively objective "systems" or "processes") and the way

7. Marks and Rathbone, *ISC*, Introduction, pp. 13–14.

8. See Hayden White, *Metahistory: The Historical Imagination in Nineteenth-Century Europe* (Baltimore and London: Johns Hopkins University Press, 1973), pp. 7ff.

in which the authors of *Industrialisation and Social Change* deal with them: (1) the state, (2) moral communities such as ethnicities and religions, (3) nature, and (4) the individual.

The authors do not treat the state as a mere agent of fractions of capital[9] and they regularly grant that it has an element of autonomy. Nonetheless, they rarely tell the "story" of the state in a coherent way and they thus fail to portray that autonomy. Yet one might ask whether the state does not in fact comprise a more coherent "system" than does capital. After all, the twentieth-century state, unlike capital, has clear boundaries. Its actions are prescribed and limited by laws and regulations, and the behavior of its citizens is enforced, ultimately, by the police and the armed forces. This is the issue David Yudelman has tackled in his recent history of the relations between the South African state and capital between 1902 and 1939.[10] Yudelman chastises both Marxists and liberals for underestimating the extent to which the state (under which he subsumes administration as well as politics) has interests of its own. For him, the state and capital both have a measure of autonomy; the imperatives and the logic of the state bear equal explanatory value with those of capital. The two, he feels, entered into a symbiotic relationship early in the century—a symbiosis which remained throughout the period he studied.

Thus Yudelman offers a theoretical framework in which a non-Marxist history of twentieth-century South Africa could be written. For the nineteenth century the most useful perspective is probably still the theory of British imperialism developed by Ronald Robinson and John Gallagher.[11] Robinson and Gallagher did not deny that British imperial policy was, at the highest levels of abstraction, functional to the interests of British capitalism. But at the concrete levels of most interest to practicing historians, they found definite divergences: the actions of imperial statesmen were frequently shaped by an antibusiness bias and were shaped by strategic considerations and the need to respond to local crises on the periphery of empire. Their view, like Yudelman's,

9. A failing, for example, of Marian Lacey, *Working for Boroko: The Origins of a Coercive Labour System in South Africa* (Johannesburg: Ravan Press, 1981); and Dan O'Meara, *Volkskapitalisme: Class, Capital and Ideology in the Development of Afrikaner Nationalism, 1934–1948* (Johannesburg: Ravan Press, 1983). Two examples in *ISC* of the independence of state action from the relations of production or capitalist direction are Keegan, "Sharecropping," p. 207, and Sean Moroney, "Mine married quarters: The differential stabilisation of the Witwatersrand workforce, 1900–1920," p. 268.

10. David Yudelman, *The Emergence of Modern South Africa: State, Capital and the Incorporation of Organized Labor on the South African Gold Fields, 1902–1939* (Cape Town and Johannesburg: David Philip, 1984).

11. Ronald Robinson and John Gallagher with Alice Denny, *Africa and the Victorians: The Climax of Imperialism* (Garden City, N.Y.: Anchor, [1961] 1968).

frees the historian from the compulsion to subordinate the actions of the state to the imperatives of capital.

A second realm whose autonomy needs to be asserted is that of moral communities such as ethnic groups and religions. Obviously, human affairs, even under capitalism, consist of far more than the accumulation of capital and extraction of surplus value. Most people apparently need to situate themselves in the cosmos and in history, and to identify with entities larger than themselves and their immediate families. In many societies these needs have been satisfied by religion. In modern, industrial societies nationalism (or its variant, racism) has sometimes shared this role with religion or usurped it entirely. It is obvious that in South Africa all three—religion, nationalism, and racism—have been extraordinarily prominent.

As usual, *Industrialisation and Social Change* avoids crude formulations on these matters. For example, the editors approvingly quote G. Clarence-Smith's view that "racism is a social practice with its own changing history and its own symbolic regularities," in other words, in the language of this essay, that it is a "system." But they immediately subordinate it to the class struggle: "both capital and the state—and indeed workers—can use this social practice for their own instrumental purposes." The same strategy is followed in a reference to the Christian religion of the black "petty bourgeoisie": "it was deeply felt *and highly instrumental*" (my emphasis).[12]

One cannot quarrel with the editors' conviction that both racism and religion can be used by a class to gain advantage over another. But I distrust a historiography that briefly salutes the autonomy of these areas of human experience and then hastens to focus on their instrumentality to something else. Such a sequence of thought is found in many, but not all, chapters of their book.[13] For example, Harries shows how the "cosmology of southern Moçambican society . . . changed to *accommodate* migrant labour . . ."; and Phil Bonner, commenting on the way "petty bourgeois" Africans were preoccupied with their education and "civilised" identity, goes on to say "there was more to their community of interest than [these] *mere ideological forms*" (my emphases).[14] These

12. Marks and Rathbone, *ISC,* Introduction, pp. 5, 29.

13. Deborah Gaitskell's study of African women's *manyanos* is a major exception: *ISC,* "Wailing for purity: prayer unions, African mothers and adolescent daughters, 1912–1940," pp. 338–57.

14. Harries, *ISC,* "Kinship," p. 157; Bonner, *ISC,* "Transvaal Native Congress," p. 277 (emphases added in each case). See also Guy, *ISC,* "Zulu Society," p. 171, where he assures us that the accumulation of cattle in Zulu society was "*not an end in itself* but practised in order to transform these cattle into human beings, thereby increasing . . . the amount of labour power at the command of an individual" (emphasis added).

quotations form part of interesting, and possibly valid, arguments; I quote them merely to show the direction in which the authors' and editors' reasoning tends to run. The importance and autonomy of religion and culture are rhetorically granted, only to be drowned by the undertow of materialist thinking.

Interestingly, however, four chapters of the book are not subject to this generalization: Willan on the culture of the Kimberley petty bourgeoisie, Couzens on missionary influences and black literature, Gaitskell on women's *manyanos,* and Coplan on the development of a black working-class culture. Each of these authors grants a high degree of autonomy to his or her subject. None subordinates it to the dictates of the story of capital accumulation. In fact, none shows much influence from Marxist theory at all except in the use of terminology such as "petty bourgeoisie." The editors seem apologetic about the degree to which these chapters manifest exclusive loyalty to their subject matters. In reference to them they write:

> . . . it is the essential interrelationships which we wish to emphasise: interrelationships between the political economy, imperial and local, and class formation, culture and consciousness. . . . For ease of explication we have separated out what rightly belongs together and can only be fully understood as a "total" picture. Historians should be able to write in chords, for our very medium distorts our intentions by its linear imperatives.[15]

This is a key statement, but one from which liberals can dissent at two levels. First, is it true that a "total" picture is inherently superior to a study of a single subject? Surely it is a matter of different levels of comprehension, one more sketchy but embracing, one more detailed but particular. Second, even if one chooses to strive for the total picture, or in Marks and Rathbone's words, "to write in chords," must every chord be dominated by the same note, "political economy, class formation, capital accumulation," etc.? The relentless repetition of one historical vision—a vision no less arbitrary than any other—has so numbed the sensibilities of a generation of South African scholars that many take it as a self-evident truth, a product of "common sense." Liberals, to be liberals, must liberate themselves from the tyranny of this, as from any, total and single vision.

The state and moral communities thus comprise two stories or systems slighted in much Marxist scholarship which are natural quarries for a renewed liberal historiography. A third less obvious one is "nature." There are aspects and provinces of nature that probably have a stronger case to be treated as systems with their own internal logic than have

15. Marks and Rathbone, *ISC,* Introduction, p. 9.

either the state or capitalism. In fact it was probably models of nature that suggested the idea of "social systems" in the first place.[16]

At least one author in *Industrialisation and Social Change* manifests concern lest nature intrude into his conceptual framework. Jeff Guy, in recounting the destruction of Zulu society, must confront the droughts, malaria, sleeping sickness, lungsickness, smallpox, and locusts which did such damage to African societies in the 1890s. He calls these "natural disasters" in quotation marks; but they cannot, he says, "be categorised as just 'natural disasters'; they were natural enough, but the degree to which they were disastrous depended on the social context in which they occurred."[17] That is, the relations of production, and the big story of capitalist penetration, mattered most in the end. An investigation of these natural phenomena, however, is long overdue in South African studies. Such an investigation should be sensitive to the ecological and biological aspects of the phenomena (that is, the natural systems should be treated somewhat autonomously from human history), but it should also study the complex interactions between these systems and human social, political, and cultural systems. We might decide that at certain points these disasters exercised as much influence as capitalism in subordinating African peoples to white domination.

A final sphere, emphasized by traditional liberal historiography but deemphasized in *Industrialisation and Social Change*, is that of individual character and behavior. It is perhaps significant that, except in the four "cultural" chapters, there are few prominent personalities in this book and little causal significance is given to the actions of individuals. One author, Kevin Shillington, addresses the personality of an African ruler (Jantjie Mothibi of the Tlhaping) and his Christian beliefs, but he assures us that such adventitious influences are not crucial to an explanation of the collapse of Jantjie's chieftainship:

> It may be that Christianity, economic shifts and Jantjie's personal failures combined to weaken the Dikgatlhong chieftaincy in the 1860s. What brought about its collapse in the 1870s, however, was the political and territorial encroachment of colonial officials and settlers combined with the increasing decentralisation prompted by individualist responses to the market opportunities of the diamond fields.[18]

Shillington is determined to show that Jantjie's personality was not

16. Such is the argument of Robert A. Nisbet, *Social Change and History: Aspects of the Western Theory of Development* (London: Oxford University Press, 1969).

17. Guy, *ISC*, "Zulu Society," p. 184.

18. Kevin Shillington, *ISC*, "The impact of the diamond discoveries on the Kimberley hinterland: class formation, colonialism and resistance among the Tlhaping of Griqualand West in the 1870s," p. 103.

a key factor in the decline of his chiefdom. So he argues that Jantjie had a son whose strong personality canceled out the effects of his father's weakness. But can such an argument (contrary effects) not be used equally against the assignment of causal primacy to capitalism? When capitalism is shown to have contradictory effects (e.g., when it both strengthens and weakens an African polity), Marxist scholars sometimes cheerfully acknowledge its "ambiguous" effects without for a moment dismissing it as an explanation, often *the* explanation. In other words, capital accumulation is seen as the primary explanation of contrary effects.[19] The same could be done with Jantjie and his forceful son: the interplay of contrasting personalities could be presented as the main plot, albeit a plot with an inconclusive outcome. The decision as to which plot to treat as primary is reached beforehand, in the "prefigurement of the field"[20]; it precedes, not follows, an argument such as Shillington's.

All historical explanation involves considerable selection. Every event is linked to an infinity of other events, and it is inevitable that the historian will select various sequences she or he thinks most important. It is also probably inevitable, given the metaphorical nature of much human thought, that these sequences will be arranged into "stories" which are deemed to correspond to "systems" or "processes," allegedly objective phenomena that seem to possess some intrinsic logic. Capitalism is such a system, but so is Afrikaner nationalism, the South African state, the life of Chief Jantjie, and the natural history of the rinderpest. But just as historians simplify reality by selecting systems that interest them, so they complicate it again by presenting several systems as interlocking. This interlocking is rather like the linking of subplots in a drama, which is why I have called the accumulation of capital the main plot in South African Marxist historiography. By constantly subordinating other stories to that plot, Marxist historians have drained these stories of their storylike qualities; that is, their inner coherence. Racism, nationalism, religion, the individual, nature all appear to take their meaning in reference to something else. All are rendered insubstantial, transparent, and of only marginal interest.

In justifying the primacy of one plot, historians can appeal to social theory. One of the advantages Marxists have had over liberals is that their theory is coherent, well articulated and explicit; the liberals by contrast may not have a single body of theory; if they do, it is implicit and no doubt tinged with contradiction and naïveté. It is worth

19. An example in *ISC* is Kimble, "Labour Migration," p. 119.
20. A phrase used by White, *Metahistory,* p. 30.

emphasizing, however, that the Marxist theory is by no means self-evident; it rests on as many untestable assumptions as any other. The ontological primacy of capital accumulation over other systematic processes cannot be demonstrated empirically. It can only be asserted on a priori grounds. Even on those grounds, as I have suggested, some systems (like the state, the individual, and certain natural systems) are more likely to be systems in fact as well as metaphor. The flood of literature devoted to expounding capital accumulation as the main plot by no means proves that it *is* the main plot.

As Marxism bids fair to become the new orthodoxy in South African historiography, can one speak meaningfully of a "liberal" school which is opposed to it? Surely there are a large number of historians who hold themselves aloof from the Marxists' enthusiasms, timidly pursuing their research without the comforts of an explicit "problematic." My own view is that, by temperament and conviction, these people do not constitute a school, nor will they easily become one. Their commitments are too varied, their visions of history too idiosyncratic, for a homogeneous non-Marxist vision to emerge from their efforts.

On the whole, I consider this pluralism a good thing. It suggests to me that the essence of liberal historiography is not the affirmation of a single central plot and a view of how it articulates with other, subordinate, plots. Rather it consists in cultivating many plots and experimenting with different ways of interweaving them. A liberal historiography will thus be more individualistic than a Marxist one, but it need not, therefore, be less socially responsible.

In introducing some suggestions for a renewed liberal historiography I will rely on Maurice Mandelbaum's threefold categorization of the structures of historical accounts.[21] Mandelbaum did not regard these structures as mutually exclusive in an individual work, but he did argue that one form would likely predominate in most lengthy studies. I will start from that assumption, and will simplify and adapt his typology slightly for my own purposes.

For Mandelbaum the traditional and most common sort of historical structure is the *sequential,* which is akin to what most people call "narrative" history. In a sequential history a scholar chooses an entity, like a nation-state, an industry, or a society, which he or she deems to have a continuity of its own. The task is to trace the development of that entity by describing how one event in the entity's history flowed

21. Maurice Mandelbaum, *The Anatomy of Historical Knowledge* (Baltimore and London: Johns Hopkins University Press, 1977), pp. 24–45.

into another, and how that event in turn flowed into yet another. Sequential historical reason proceeds forward in time, starting from a point in the past and moving toward the present.

By contrast, in *explanatory* history the historian begins with a problem—an event or process which needs to be explained (the explanandum). He or she then goes backward in time to trace the many antecedents of the explanandum. (The final history will be written forward in time, but the investigation must inevitably go backwards.) This method involves tracing antecedents of many sorts—say, economic, political, religious, personal, climatic—which may be quite unrelated to each other except where they converge in the explanandum. Such a history will obtain coherence from the question asked, not from the belief that all the chains of explanation pertain to an ongoing entity, as in sequential history.

Finally, Mandelbaum speaks of *interpretive* history. He finds this best typified in those introductory book chapters in which the author presents a snapshot of a society in a given year or period, ranging freely over many aspects of the society and setting out some interconnections among them. Such an author has considerable freedom in modeling the society; he or she is not constrained to maintain tight temporal connections between events as in sequential history, or by the unity of the question as in explanatory history. His or her own vision of the way society and history "work" may in fact be more formative here than in other types of historical writing.

I will suggest that liberal values would be best fostered (1) by writing *sequential* histories on important subjects neglected by Marxist historians; (2) by greatly increasing the number of *explanatory* histories; and (3) by plunging into the much-neglected area of *interpretive* history to exploit, and transcend, the best findings of the Marxist school.

My primary suggestion regarding *sequential* history is implicit in my critique of the volume edited by Marks and Rathbone. That is, while the authors show a commendable willingness to concede autonomy to "systems" other than capitalism, they have been less enthusiastic about spelling out the continuities, inner logic, and "compulsions" inherent in these systems. It is important for us to have sympathetic studies on aspects of the Western tradition in South Africa beyond those of capitalism and racial domination. Among the most obvious are histories of the universities, the private schools, the press, religious groups, the law and the legal profession, the medical profession, women, and the family. I am of course aware that work on most of these subjects has been appearing for a long time, and that (not coincidentally) a large part of it is written by liberals. The problem is this: simply because these subjects can be constituted as stories with their own internal logic (relatively separate from the history of capitalism or the state) they tend to be regarded as specialist histories and have trouble entering into the main stream of historical debate. How do we overcome that problem?

Here we encounter a built-in strength of Marxist historiography and an equivalent weakness in its liberal counterpart. The very capacity of liberals to imagine a variety of histories, written at different levels of abstraction and according to different logics, encourages rapid specialization, hence intellectual fragmentation in their work. By contrast, the considerable commonality of vision among Marxists engenders unity of discourse and makes their historiography a more truly collective if repetitive enterprise. I hope liberals will not adopt a framework as tight as the Marxists', hence I am forced to say that variety, even idiosyncrasy, must remain a liberal hallmark. There are two things we can do: we can make sure that we write specialist history in full awareness of the worlds of discourse surrounding our chosen field (something which historians of, say, business or religious bodies, often fail to do), and we can work more at interpretive history—of which more shortly.

Liberal historians also have an obligation to write histories of those bigger systems that are arguably as embracing as capitalism itself. I have already alluded to some of these. Among the most important is the state. It must be remembered that the drift away from political history in South African historiography is now of long standing. Nor has it been significantly reversed by the Poulantzian Marxist attempts to link party political events to shifting relations among fragments of capital. It may well be time to reinsert politics into a historiography which has recently become much richer in social and economic topics. I would add, following Yudelman, that the history of the state includes administration as well as legislation. Accounts of local government and of Union departments (most obviously the Native Affairs Department) are drastically needed before we can understand how white domination has worked in South Africa and how it has been experienced by its victims and its beneficiaries.

Rather different is the case of intellectual history: the history of symbols and languages of discourse. This subject has been neglected by South African historians of all schools, a neglect which has led some young historians to believe that ideas are *mere* ideological smoke screens. It is striking that for a country which the world routinely labels "racist South Africa" we have little historical work on racial stereotypes, racist language, or racial anxieties such as the fear of miscegenation. Fortunately, we do have the beginning of work on Afrikaner political ideas, liberalism, black consciousness, neo-Calvinism, and segregationism. But there is still much to be done, for example, on liberalism among blacks, socialism, temperance ideology, Gandhianism, imperial federation, republicanism. Even the massive and central edifice of Afrikaner nationalism has only just been breached. Intellectual history is a natural terrain for liberals for two reasons: first, they are more likely than Marxists to take seriously the independent force of ideas; second, they have a stake in showing forgotten aspects of past South African thought from which new inspiration can be drawn in a postapartheid era.[22]

However, it is preeminently in the field of *explanatory* history that liberals can make their most distinctive mark. In a sense, explanatory history is quintessentially liberal because it assumes a multicausal world view, in which it is not so important to rank the causes as to show their intricate interactions. A model of this approach, and one that is highly relevant to our theme, is P. L. Wickens's essay on the Natives' Land Act of 1913.[23] The Land Act had usually been treated as part of a larger story, such as the development of segregationist ideology or the imposition of a labor-repressive system. Wickens, by contrast, set out only to explain the act itself; in doing so he uncovered a variety of interest groups and motivations behind it, some of them in obvious contradiction to one another; also, he found considerable confusion among its sponsors and no shortage of unexpected consequences. His allegiance to the method of explanatory history is summed up in his conclusion "It would be naive to grasp at one particular strand in this tangled skein."[24] Newell Stultz has taken a similar approach to the apartheid election of 1948,[25] and it is probably necessary to do something of the sort for most of the high points of South African political history in the twentieth century. This is especially so for those events that have become embedded in the Marxist account of the era, like the South African Native Affairs Commission, the Native (Urban Areas) Act, the elections of 1924 and 1929, and Fusion. We should have similarly multicausal studies about some of the great conflicts between labor and management (like 1922) and between white and black (like Sharpeville).

Also, little good *interpretive* history of South Africa has been written in recent years. Of all contemporary societies, surely South Africa more than any other requires a bold historical vision that will allow its people to understand the tragedies of the past, to work through their feelings of guilt or anger, and to discern a way to a juster future. Many have

22. In the context of Afrikanerdom such is the motivation of André du Toit and Herman Giliomee in their *Afrikaner Political Thought: Analysis and Documents*, Vol. 1: *1780–1850* (Cape Town and Johannesburg: David Philip, 1983). This strikes me as a constructive move for South Africans of all backgrounds.

23. P. L. Wickens, "The Natives' Land Act of 1913: A Cautionary Essay on Simple Explanations of Complex Change," *South African Journal of Economics* 49(1981): 105–29.

24. Ibid., p. 128.

25. Newell M. Stultz, "South Africa's 'Apartheid Election' of 1948 Reconsidered," *Plural Societies*, (1972), 25–37.

called for a new de Kiewiet, but none has so far appeared. The Marxists, interestingly enough, despite the built-in interpretive structure of their theory, have yet to produce a synthetic history. No doubt they will do so soon, but they will find it hard to escape the dilemma I have pointed out in this essay: either the big story of capital accumulation will dominate, thus reducing many aspects of human experience to fragmentary accounts, or the other stories will be treated generously and the book will cease to be Marxist apart from its sympathies for workers. It may be possible to escape this dilemma, but it will not be easy.

A truly liberating interpretive history of South Africa is more likely to be written by a liberal than by a Marxist. Such a history would require that idiosyncrasy of vision which the taut conceptual world of South African Marxism is unlikely to foster. It would require a broad range of empathetic understanding—for English-speaking whites and government bureaucrats as well as for peasants and proletarians. Above all, it would require the ability to hold several plots in tension, slighting neither their autonomy nor their interrelations. Eclecticism and rigor rarely cohabit in the same mind. But interpretive history requires both—along with a large fund of imagination. The worst writer of interpretive history will be someone who has submitted so long to the discipline of a single model that its operation has become second nature. The best writer of interpretive history is likely to be someone with a varied intellectual background and a capacity for reasoning at different levels and in different modes. Since I believe such intellectual pluralism to be characteristic of many liberal historians, I am convinced that liberal commitments and a flair for interpretive history are likely to be mutually supportive.

Assuming a continuation of university autonomy, many university historians of the next decades will be liberals. They will be subject to all the temptations of liberals in other countries just emerged from colonialism. There will be pressures to serve the interests of the state or party or revolution: to glorify their country's leaders and to find antecedents for them in South African history. The liberal, always prone to self-criticism and guilt feelings, will be tempted to create a historiography which is not only antinationalist and anti-imperialist (which should come easily enough) but also anti-West, anticapitalist, even, in the end, antiliberal.

Liberal values are really too important, and too vulnerable in South Africa, to be sacrificed to the timidity or guilt feelings of liberals. It is to be hoped that liberal historians will find the courage, under any new regime, to set forth a sophisticated view of history that will make an open society first imaginable, then real.

I have suggested three social values to which a liberal historiography could lend support. The first is understanding among South Africa's ethnic groups. Such understanding will be much enhanced by a historiography which helps each group to realize the historical forces that shaped the others. I have argued elsewhere, following R. G. Collingwood, that *all* proper historical explanation must deal with the consciousness of actors.[26] It follows that the understanding of complex events, particularly conflicts, involves a re-creation of the consciousness of various parties. Such a multisubjective approach to historical understanding has been rare in South African historiography, which has almost always been designed to serve the interests of a group or party and to make not-so-subtle moral judgments on the past. This is true not only of nationalist and Marxist historiography but of much liberal historiography as well. We all know, of course, that moral commitments inevitably intrude in historical writing. But a historian can hold partisan moral judgment sufficiently at bay, without abandoning a commitment to truth and to fairness, in order to reenact sympathetically the position of each actor in a historical drama.[27] It is not necessary to excuse crimes or stupidity, much less to expunge them from the historical record. But it is desirable to show that villains and bunglers have a past; that their villainy and stupidity are neither self-explanatory nor beyond explanation.

I also said that we need to nurture respect for the freedom of the individual, the universities, the press, the courts, and the churches. Unless South Africa descends into a Lebanese-style anarchy, we can assume that the state will continue to threaten these liberties, just as it does now. That will be so whether the state is a corrupt and inefficient patrimonial regime, a tough totalitarian one, or perhaps even a relatively benign social democracy. The imperative demand for economic growth and redistribution of wealth, combined with the desire of the impoverished to make use of the state, will engender hostility toward any institutions or individuals who thwart the state or are less than zealous about its programs.

The liberal answer to this threat is not only to extol nongovernmental institutions by writing their histories sympathetically, but, a much more fundamental task, to form minds which grasp the historical process as multileveled and complex, with causal chains stretching in an infinity of directions. Such a relativism in historical vision is distinct from a

26. Richard Elphick, "Methodology in South African History: A Defence of Idealism and Empiricism," *Social Dynamics* 9 (1983): 1–17.

27. A classic statement of this view is Herbert Butterfield, "Moral Judgements in History," in Hans Meyerhoff, ed., *The Philosophy of History in Our Time* (New York: Doubleday Anchor, 1959), pp. 228–49.

relativism in values. Just as a historical understanding of different groups can foster a tolerant attitude toward them, so an understanding of, say, the force of ideas in history can foster a concern to preserve those institutions, such as the university, where ideas are born. A view of plural causation in history is a natural support for a plural society.

But it might be objected: surely a multicausal view of history leaves one baffled, dispirited, and paralyzed before the need for massive change? Possibly here we find one root of the excessive caution that has so often characterized South African liberalism. On the other hand, we should note that the Marxist model in South African studies has been far less revolutionary in its implications than one might expect. The much-repeated story of the triumphs of capitalism—its constant adaptations to new challenges; its pervasive, irresistible effects on all aspects of life—does not make plausible the basic Marxist prediction of the imminent breakdown of capitalism. Consequently, academic Marxism has proven more powerful in explaining why things never change in South Africa than in inspiring one to change them.

The view of history I have been expounding is more profoundly subversive than the Marxist. It teaches that the various spheres of human endeavor intersect so as to produce effects unpredictable by an observer who studies only one alone. Plural history is open history. And an openness to history is indispensable not only to the overturning of a regime but for the more strenuous task of creating a better social order. It is of course easy to exaggerate the importance of historical vision. But perhaps it is even easier to underestimate it. Here the Marxists have done us a real favor: they have shown us an alternative vision of history, and when all due praise has been given to their efforts, one is left with the suspicion that historiography can render yet better service to the cause of liberation in South Africa.

III

Toward a Liberal Analysis of Contemporary South Africa

David Welsh

10. Democratic Liberalism and Theories of Racial Stratification

The debates around the issues of race and class in South Africa remain intense. Liberal scholars, responding to the neo-Marxist critique, have slowly begun to refurbish their traditional conceptual tools, making, in the process, significant acknowledgments of the usefulness of class perspectives. Corresponding to this has been an equally significant acknowledgment of the force of race and ethnicity by some revisionist scholars, who seem thus to be substantially modifying their virtually exclusive focus on class. However, nothing like a consensus has been reached in the scholarly debates, and, indeed, within the broad boundaries of the two schools diversity is actually increasing. Precisely how class and race or ethnicity interrelate is still debated and will be for a long time.

The classical liberal historians of South Africa paid little attention to the concept of class as such. Classes occupy their pages only in analytically minor roles. Their major themes were rather the conflicts of race and ethnicity, and few dwelt at any length on the origins of these groupings or the processes that elevated them to basic principles of social organization. Yet, especially for C. W. de Kiewiet or W. M. Macmillan, the dominant motifs were conquest, power, exploitation, and development—all capable of being harnessed to a class analysis.

None of the liberal historians approached South Africa's history with a framework nearly as comprehensive as, for example, Marxism. None saw his or her task as fitting South Africa's evolution into a theory of capitalist development, and in turn locating class actors within such a conceptual scheme. In short, they sought to answer different questions from those posed by Marxists.

Marxist scholars have seized on some of the liberals' emphases as evidence of a perverse unwillingness to strip away the veils that hide and mystify the class relations of a developing capitalist system fundamentally oriented to the goal of capital accumulation. Liberals are also accused of seeing racial discrimination as rooted in irrational sentiment alone; as Shula Marks and Richard Rathbone say, "the radical literature of the seventies contested the [liberal] view that racist practices in contemporary South Africa resulted from 'the actions of a state bizarrely following the "logic" of irrational racial prejudice.' "[1] Harold Wolpe criticizes some liberal scholars for believing that "racial discrimination" was due to "racial beliefs emanating and operating 'outside' the economic system, but impinging upon the latter."[2]

Wolpe and others take to task the writings of the liberal psychologist I. D. MacCrone in particular. Wolpe criticizes MacCrone for holding the view that racial prejudice is the cause of racial discrimination. This is less than fair to MacCrone's position, which centered on group psychology on the South African frontier. MacCrone recognized that racial prejudice was a means whereby groups, in this case white Afrikaners, identified themselves, maintained their cohesion, and thereby became an effective political force.

> Since colour prejudice, as a social attitude, can have no reality apart from the existence of the group, much of its operation will depend upon the circumstances in which the group has developed and the conditions under which social contacts take place.[3]

While liberal scholars would generally reject many details of MacCrone's theory (for example, the emphasis he placed on the openness of South African society before the eighteenth century), they see no reason to disagree that racism can be functional to group domination.

Few if any influential thinkers on race have denied its genesis in group conflict. As a personal aside, this writer as an undergraduate in a liberal South African university in the 1950s was assigned as a standard

1. See their "Introduction," in Shula Marks and Richard Rathbone, eds., *Industrialisation and Social Change in South Africa: African Class Formation, Culture and Consciousness 1870–1930* (London: Longman, 1982), p. 4.

2. Harold Wolpe, "Industrialism and Race in South Africa," Sami Zubaida, ed., *Race and Racialism* (London: Tavistock, 1970), p. 156.

3. I. D. MacCrone, *Race Attitudes in South Africa: Historical, Experimental and Psychological Studies* (Johannesburg: Witwatersrand University Press, 1937), p. 131.

text in several courses on race relations Ruth Benedict's *Race and Racism* (1942), which represented the prevailing orthodoxies on the question of race, and this quotation was invoked to represent her point of view:

> The fact that to understand race conflict we need fundamentally to understand *conflict* and not *race*, means something much more drastic. It means that all the deep-seated causes of conflict in any group or between groups are involved in any outbreak of race prejudice.[4]

Most liberals of the time would have enthusiastically agreed with Benedict's proposition, accepting a wide range of factors in the origins of prejudice. Racism may indeed be described as "irrational" since it rests on assumptions that are palpably false. But it may also be "rational" in the sense of serving to justify goals of domination. Much of the revisionist critique of liberals' accounts of racism and racial prejudice is directed against a straw man.

Marxist revisionists might possibly agree with this reasoning while pointing out that it misses the objective of their critique, which is to demonstrate that racist ideology and racial prejudice in South Africa are not products of group conflict *in general*, but (1) are specific to capitalist development and (2) are "phenomena arising in the class struggle."[5] Even these statements are not wholly unacceptable to liberals, who would rightly claim that much of the evidence substantiating them was first collected and analyzed by liberals themselves. It is obvious that intruding white farmers benefited enormously from the alienation of black-occupied land and from the availability of black labor. As de Kiewiet pointed out, the "land wars were also labour wars."[6] Nor could the involvement of the mining industry in the structuring and refinement of highly repressive labor practices be denied. Sheila van der Horst, another liberal, recounted this involvement in detail in her *Native Labour in South Africa* (1942).[7]

Where the liberals and revisionists indeed part company is in the extent to which they endorse a view that accords analytical primacy to the needs of capitalist accumulation and development. To oversimplify, the revisionists treat South Africa's evolution as a variant of capitalist development. Their views are informed to greater or lesser extent by

4. Ruth Benedict, *Race and Racism* (London: Routledge & Kegan Paul, 1942), pp. 151–52.

5. Robert H. Davies, *Capital, State and White Labour in South Africa 1900–1960: An Historical Materialist Analysis of Class Formation and Class Relations* (Brighton: Harvester, 1979), p. 3.

6. C. W. de Kiewiet, *A History of South Africa: Social and Economic* (London: Oxford University Press, 1957), p. 180.

7. Sheila T. van der Horst, *Native Labour in South Africa* (London: Oxford University Press, 1942).

Marx's universal history, derived from dialectical materialism. As Duncan Innes puts it:

> To understand the nature of South African society we need to be able to identify its motivating forces: how it develops, what form it takes and, most important of all, why it develops. *Thus* we need to lay bare *the fundamental laws of motion of capitalist society in general* so as to expose the real nature of South African society.[8] (Emphasis added).

Similarly, for Dan O'Meara:

> The task is . . . to analyse the historical contradictions and processes of struggle around the development of capitalism through which these relations of production came to take the form primarily (though not exclusively) of racial categories.[9]

Liberal scholars, on the other hand, adhere to no philosophy of history as explicit as that of Marxists; most would jib at the determinist implications of Innes's statement (and of those of many other Marxists). But few would adopt a determinist countermodel that sees capitalism and racism as fundamentally antagonistic. Classical liberal historiography has taken the existence of capitalism more or less for granted, and accordingly has not dwelt at all on its alleged intrinsic properties or immanent tendencies (though strongly free-market scholars like Hutt[10] or Horwitz[11] were obvious exceptions). In more recent years, while admitting capitalism's enormous influence and its profound transformative effects on society, liberal scholars have declined to impute to capitalism the power that most Marxist theoreticians assume it to have. Moreover, most liberals would deny that capitalism has created, in contrast with affecting, the groups whose interrelationships form the stuff of South African political conflict. South African capitalism arose in a particular context with institutional, cultural, racial, economic, and demographic components. In significant respects it adapted itself to that context; it did not create it.

Mainstream stratification theory originated in European societies that were assumed to be relatively homogeneous. The phenomenon of the ethnic group was generally viewed as something of an exception, an

8. Duncan Innes, *Anglo: Anglo American and the Rise of Modern South Africa* (London: Heinemann, 1984), p. 16.

9. Dan O'Meara, *Volkskapitalisme: Class, Capital and Ideology in the Development of Afrikaner Nationalism 1934–1948* (Cambridge: Cambridge University Press, 1983), p. 11.

10. W. H. Hutt, *The Economics of the Colour Bar: A Study of the Economic Origins and Consequences of Racial Segregation in South Africa* (London: André Deutsch, 1964).

11. Ralph Horwitz, *The Political Economy of South Africa* (London: Weidenfeld & Nicolson, 1967).

excrescence that complicated otherwise tidy models of class conflict.[12] Both Marx and Engels notoriously underestimated the durability and dynamism of ethnicity. Equally striking was Marx's underestimation of the tenacity of religious division, in Ireland for example:

> Once the Irish church is dead, the Protestant Irish tenants in the province of Ulster will unite with the Catholic tenants in the three other provinces of Ireland and join their movement; whereas up to the present landlordism has been able to exploit this religious hostility.[13]

Marxists, like Marx himself, have had considerable difficulty in accommodating ethnicity or other communal solidarities to the mainstream of their thought. Their work on South Africa, at least in this critical area, has been unconvincing, constantly betraying a determination to force refractory data into an ideologized schema. Somehow, ethnic factors must be shown to be "basically" class-derived, even if intellectual contortions are necessary to achieve this.

Increasing numbers of Marxists, however, following earlier efforts by Austrian Marxists such as Bauer and Renner, do recognize the serious problems posed to the Marxist schema by ethnicity and the nationalism to which it frequently gives rise. Even the rigid theoreticians of the U.S.S.R. are having to come to terms with a force that is not going to be dissolved, neutralized, or transcended in the way that Lenin or Stalin supposed. For Regis Debray, Marxism's inability to explain "the national question" is a crucial gap:

> In this small gap, everything not said in Marxism is concentrated and crystallized. And when the unsaid is said, it explodes all the rest. In this sense . . . the nation is like the atomic nucleus in a general conflagration of Marxism as theory and socialism as practice.[14]

The problem for Marxism is this: if ethnicity or other communal identities cannot be causally reduced to, or derived from, the mode of production or class or the division of labor, or, indeed, "cannot be regarded as an inherent feature of a capitalist or industrial system,"[15] then Marxism's claims as an explanatory theory of society have to be scaled down.

The ethnically divided society is far more typical of today's world

12. Frank Parkin, *Marxism and Class Theory: A Bourgeois Critique* (London: Tavistock, 1979), p. 32.

13. Cited in Ian Cummins, *Marx, Engels and National Movements* (London: Croom Helm, 1980), p. 116.

14. Cited in A. W. Wright, "Socialism & Nationalism," Leonard Tivey, ed., *The Nation-State: The Formation of Modern Politics* (Oxford: Martin Robertson, 1981), p. 166.

15. Frank Parkin, "Social Stratification," in Tom Bottomore and Robert Nisbet, eds., *A History of Sociological Analysis* (London: Heinemann, 1979), p. 621.

than the relatively homogenous but class-stratified society of the classical sociological tradition. Ethnicity occurs in all types of society: traditional and modern, developed and underdeveloped, capitalist and socialist, democratic and nondemocratic. Immensely more devastating civil conflicts are caused by ethnic tensions than by class conflicts.[16] Consequently, it is no longer legitimate for the concept of class to dominate "stratification" theory as it did in the past. It has been widely noted that those societies which are "purest," i.e., uncomplicated by ethnic issues in their conformity to a class-stratified system, are also the most stable and consensual, even though class conflict is present.[17] Also, where ethnicity and class compete as foci for mobilization and popular allegiance, ethnicity usually dominates.[18] Nor can this fact be explained away by attributing it to "false consciousness."

Ethnicity often overlaps with or cuts across class divisions. Hence it seems unlikely that it is somehow generated by the process of capitalist development or that it is a division imposed by the bourgeoisie upon the working class. Ruling groups can and do exploit divisions, but it seems improbable that they can create them in the first place.

Recent analyses of ethnicity have challenged those scholars, principally within the Marxian tradition, who have sought the roots of ethnicity in economic or class relations. Thus A. D. Smith writes:

> Economic deprivation, economic exploitation, economic growth, are all grist to the nationalist mill; but in themselves they do not generate ethnic sentiments or nationalist movements. The uneven development of industrialisation, which roughly coincided with the development of nationalism, has undoubtedly sharpened ethnic tensions and contributed a new store of national grievances; but the cleavages and antagonisms, so accentuated, together with the aspirations and ideals based upon them, have their roots and inspiration elsewhere.[19]

Walker Connor argues that what he calls "ethno-nationalism" appears to operate in a way remarkably independent of economic variables, even though, he writes, economic issues invariably loom large in the programs of ethnic movements, serving as "catalytic agent, exacerbator, or choice of battleground."[20]

16. Christopher Hewitt, "Majorities and Minorities: A Comparative Survey of Ethnic Violence," *The Annals of the American Academy of Political and Social Science* 433 (1977): 151–52.

17. Parkin, *Marxism and Class Theory,* p. 32.

18. A. L. Epstein, *Ethos and Identity: Three Studies in Ethnicity* (London: Tavistock, 1978), p. 94.

19. Anthony D. Smith, *The Ethnic Revival* (Cambridge: Cambridge University Press, 1981), p. 44.

20. Walker Connor, "Eco- or ethno-nationalism?" *Ethnic and Racial Studies,* 7 (1984), p. 356.

Smith and Connor both find the roots of ethnicity in essentially psychological factors. For Smith these are "the belief in common and distinctive group origins and liberation, . . . a sense of unique history";[21] for Connor the essence of the nation is "a vivid sense of sameness or oneness of kind" derived from a myth of common descent.[22] But ethnicity is also seen by both as inherently a relational concept; it becomes of historic significance only when ethnic group A is confronted by ethnic groups B, C, and D. A sense of identity may be nonexistent until evoked by catalysts of varying kinds, including conquest and oppression. There is, moreover, nothing inevitable about this process.

There is abundant evidence that European colonists who encountered native peoples or slaves, even before the development of exploitative relationships with them, possessed a rudimentary ethnocentrism and at least embryonic racist views. As for South Africa, R. Raven-Hart's extracts from the earliest travelers' accounts are full of negative judgments of the Khoikhoi and other indigenous groups.[23] Europeans expressed revulsion at Khoikhoi customs, language, dress, and physical appearance. Repeatedly they declared the Khoikhoi to be midway between humans and beasts.[24] The sinister and negative connotations of "blackness" in the European tradition lent an added dimension to the relationship between Europeans and Africans. As Cairns has written of early contacts in Central Africa:

> Africans were darker than other tribal peoples, a factor which probably seemed to indicate greater biological difference. The symbolism of colour itself was undoubtedly detrimental to favourable European attitudes. The white-black dichotomy in western thought has equated whiteness with cleanliness, the light of day, moral purity, and absolution from sin. Black has implied sin, dirt, night, and evil. The colour contrast was also apparent in the frequent use of metaphors of light and darkness in missionary literature. The coincidence of racial divisions with the moral distinctions implicit in these metaphors helped to make skin colour an identification mark for differing levels of moral and religious attainments.[25]

These findings are congruent with those of David Brion Davis, Roger Bastide, and Winthrop Jordan, the latter's study of American slavery showing how "blackness" was one element in the cluster of negative

21. Smith, *Ethnic Revival,* p. 66.

22. Connor, "Eco- or ethno-nationalism?" p. 342.

23. See, e.g., R. Raven-Hart, ed., *Before Van Riebeeck: Callers at South Africa from 1488 to 1652* (Cape Town: C. Struik, 1967).

24. Richard Elphick, *Kraal and Castle: Khoikhoi and the Founding of White South Africa* (New Haven and London: Yale University Press, 1977), pp. 193–95.

25. H. A. C. Cairns, *Prelude to Imperialism: British Reactions to Central African Society 1840–1890* (London: Routledge & Kegan Paul, 1965), p. 75.

qualities (including culture and religion) that, in the view of labor-seeking colonists, preeminently fitted blacks for slavery.[26] By contrast, the absence of these alleged qualities in Europeans rendered them immune to enslavement, even though the class (as distinct from status) of some as indentured servants was not far removed from that of blacks, who were also subjected to indentures before their formal enslavement. Equally suggestive are Harmannus Hoetink's conclusions on the significance of the "somatic norm image," or, more simply, aesthetic factors such as the ideal of beauty in shaping the pattern of race relations.[27]

Donald Noel argues that three factors within a multiethnic society are likely to give rise to a hierarchical system of ethnic stratification: ethnocentrism, incorporating an embryonic or proto-racism; competition between groups for scarce resources; and initial inequality in power between the groups. For the hierarchical system to emerge, all three must be present, as they clearly are in South Africa.[28] Moreover, for Noel's theory to be validated, some degree of group endogamy would have to be maintained: identifiable ethnic groups imply, by definition, identifiable boundaries. Boundaries between groups may vary over time in their permeability, but massive miscegenation, as in Brazil, may obscure them to a point where they can no longer be enforced.[29] In the early days of the Cape, group boundaries were certainly quite fluid, but miscegenation, although extensive, did not occur on the same scale as in Brazil. Richard Elphick and Robert Shell say "the mixing of races was limited—far below what one would expect if there were no preference among Europeans for racial endogamy."[30] Since most instances of miscegenation involved white men and slave women whose racially mixed offspring acquired the legal status of their mothers, and since the rate of manumission of slaves was low, mixed-race people had few avenues of upward mobility.[31] The correlation of black and brown skin with low social status was simply reaffirmed.

Noel's theory underlines the inadequacy of theories of racial stratifi-

26. D. Brion Davis, *The Problem of Slavery in Western Culture* (Ithaca: Cornell University Press, 1966), p. 447; Roger Bastide, "Color, Racism, and Christianity," in John Hope Franklin, ed., *Color and Race* (Boston: Beacon Press, 1968); Winthrop D. Jordan, *White over Black: American Attitudes Toward the Negro 1550–1812* (Baltimore: Penguin, 1969), p. 20.

27. Harmannus Hoetink, *Caribbean Race Relations: A Study of Two Variants* (London: Oxford University Press for the Institute of Race Relations, London, 1967).

28. D. L. Noel, "A Theory of the Origins of Ethnic Stratification," in Noel, ed., *The Origins of American Slavery and Racism* (Columbus: Charles E. Merrill, 1972).

29. Carl N. Degler, *Neither Black nor White: Slavery and Race Relations in Brazil and the United States* (New York: Macmillan, 1971), p. 202.

30. Richard Elphick and Robert Shell, "Intergroup Relations: Khoikhoi, settlers, slaves and free blacks, 1652–1795," in Richard Elphick and Hermann Giliomee, eds., *The Shaping of South African Society, 1652–1820* (Cape Town: Longman, 1979), p. 135.

31. Ibid., pp. 139–40.

cation that rely solely on class as the critical variable. Of the early Cape, Hermann Giliomee and Elphick write:

> Emerging racial attitudes and stratification on racial lines were shaped both by the European heritage and the economic, demographic and institutional forces operating in the colony. No single "factor" can be isolated as most important. For instance, without the European's chauvinism towards different physical types and cultures there would not have been the relatively low rates of mixed marriages; but without favourable sex ratios the European community would not have been able to maintain its fairly rigid endogamy while replacing itself and growing in each generation.[32]

This analysis stresses the variety of contingent forces that shaped the context in which the South African racial hierarchy arose. It also emphasizes that *both* "material" and "ideal" factors are crucial: they may complement and reinforce each other, or they may be in tension. The possible permutations are many, just as they are in the relationship between class and ethnicity.

A difficult but intriguing task is to determine at what point core values are established in a multiethnic society and thereby give the society a relatively stable structure. In South Africa, by roughly the year 1720 the contours of racial stratification had been laid down, and the presumption of racial inequality had taken firm root among whites. All subsequent incorporations of groups that were not white occurred against this background. These groups, in effect, were slotted into a preexisting racial hierarchy.[33] To suppose that "racial categorisation" was imposed by late-nineteenth-century colonization under conditions of industrial capitalism grossly underestimates continuity from the social structure of the early Cape Colony.

Equally difficult to determine is which metropolitan European ideas about class, in particular the proper station of the lower orders, were transposed onto the indigenous peoples or slaves. J. H. Plumb has argued that racial slavery bears striking similarities to the treatment of the poor in Europe: "Slave, servant, worker were the objects of exploitation, the sources of labour, therefore wealth; hence we should not be surprised to find similar attitudes, similar social oppressions operating against the poor as against the slave."[34] Similarly, Cairns has indicated that British settlers made comparisons between Africans and the lower classes at home, though only rarely.[35] Clearly, hierarchically

32. Richard Elphick and Hermann Giliomee, "The Structure of European Domination at the Cape, 1652–1820," in Elphick and Giliomee, eds., *Shaping of South African Society,* p. 385.

33. Ibid., p. 386.

34. J. H. Plumb, *In the Light of History* (London: Allen Lane, 1972), p. 109.

35. Cairns, *Prelude to Imperialism,* pp. 92–93.

structured race societies show some marked parallels with class-stratified societies of predemocratic Europe. Aristocratic and middle-class fears of the great mass of the poor and their alleged violent proclivities and the fear that if enfranchised they would "overthrow the established order and confiscate private property"[36] have foreshadowed white concerns about blacks in South Africa.

However suggestive the parallels, there are important differences. Despite class differences, there had been in England a common sense of "Englishness," strengthened by the Reformation and by the unifying endeavors of Elizabeth I. Common religion, values, and language undergirded a sense of moral community, with the monarchy providing a transcendental focus of loyalty. Moreover, however rigid class boundaries may have been, they were seldom completely closed, and, in principle, upward social mobility was always a possibility for talented, lucky, or sponsored individuals from the lower classes. Indeed, the existence of this safety valve and other possibilities of class co-optation were major sources of stability in nineteenth-century England. A Weberian historian has contended that class, status, and party provided three competing systems of social organization which were unlikely to converge, thereby promoting stability through crosscutting cleavages.[37]

In contrast to this internal or "organic" development, stratification appears in the multiethnic society exogenously (to use David Lockwood's expression[38]) from migration and the incorporation of previously unconnected groups. Moreover, the visibility of physical differences (notably color) drastically limits the possibilities of upward mobility for individuals of color—nearly totally in castelike societies such as South Africa or the American South, while constituting a considerable handicap in more flexible systems such as Brazil.

Every attempt to export the English class systems to the colonies failed. As Walter Bagehot noted:

> There have been a whole series of attempts to transplant to the colonies a graduated English society. But they have always failed at the first step. The rude classes at the bottom felt that they were equal to or better than the delicate classes at the top; they shifted for themselves, and left the "gentlefolks" to shift for themselves; the base of the elaborate pyramid spread abroad, and the apex tumbled in and perished.[39]

36. W. E. Houghton, *The Victorian Frame of Mind, 1830–1870* (New Haven: Yale University Press, 1957), p. 55.

37. R. J. Morris, *Class and Class Consciousness in the Industrial Revolution 1780–1850* (London: Macmillan, 1979), p. 63.

38. David Lockwood, "Race, Conflict, & Plural Society," in Zubaida, ed., *Race and Racism*, p. 64.

39. Walter Bagehot, *The English Constitution* (London: Oxford University Press, World Classics edition, 1961), pp. 233–34.

Moreover, where small white minorities dominated black majorities, lower-class white immigrants could obtain status and material advantages in the colony that they could not have in the old. John X. Merriman noted this in 1908 when he observed that white workmen who, "however unjustly," had been regarded as the "lower classes" were delighted on arrival in South Africa to find themselves in a position of an "aristocracy of colour."[40] Metropolitan class distinctions were further blurred by pressures on the dominant minority to maintain a high degree of internal cohesion and hence solidarity in the face of the assumed "black threat." Invidious class distinctions jeopardized that cohesion and hence were discouraged. "Herrenvolk democracies," accordingly, were surprisingly egalitarian within the dominant group.[41]

The converse of the impulse to solidarity within the dominant group was a trend toward unity among the dominated. As early as 1851 Theophilus Shepstone could speak of "the evident sympathy of colour that exists among the Black nations," implying thereby that the process of white intrusion and conquest was beginning to evoke glimmerings of solidarity among Africans.[42] That "sympathy of colour" and the galling impact of racial discrimination were the bedrock of African nationalism. The first national manifestation occurred in 1912 when the South African Native National Congress (later African National Congress) was formed to

> encourage mutual understanding and to bring together into common action as one political people all tribes and clans of various tribes or races and by means of combined effort and united political organisation to defend their freedoms, rights and privileges.[43]

Of course, the existence of impulses to unity on either side of the white/black divide in no way implied that unity would be achieved easily, if at all. Indeed, contemporary South Africa shows that polarization *within* the broad racial categories has increased. Still, the effect of the impulse to unify, however patchy and uneven, was to mute class conflict within groups and to render difficult the formation of interracial classes. None of the foregoing should be construed as denying the existence of classes in South Africa or the salience of class issues there. The argument,

40. Quoted in Elaine N. Katz, *A Trade Union Aristocracy* (Johannesburg: African Studies Institute, University of the Witwatersrand, 1976), p. 77.

41. Kenneth P. Vickery, " 'Herrenvolk' Democracy and Egalitarianism in South Africa and the U.S. South," *Comparative Studies in Society and History* 16 (1974).

42. Quoted in David Welsh, *The Roots of Segregation: Native Policy in Colonial Natal (1845–1910)* (Cape Town: Oxford University Press, 1971), p. 204.

43. Thomas Karis and Gwendolen M. Carter, eds., *From Protest to Challenge: A Documentary History of African Politics in South Africa 1882–1964,* Vol. 1, Sheridan Johns ed., *Protest and Hope 1882–1934* (Palo Alto: Hoover Institution Press, 1972), p. 77.

rather, is that class has to be interpreted in conjunction with race or ethnicity in a context profoundly shaped by inherited social forms and other contingent forces such as the discovery of minerals.

Capitalism's development must be viewed in the same context. It exists, sometimes even thrives, in an extraordinarily wide variety of societies, democratic and authoritarian, developed and underdeveloped. A list that includes Britain, South Korea, Japan, Argentina, Ivory Coast, Sweden, and Nazi Germany serves to indicate its chameleonlike ability to adapt. The existence of flourishing "hidden economies" in Marxist-Leninist systems (often producing and allocating far more efficiently than the formal or "official" economy) is further testimony to the same proposition.[44]

Classical Marxism conveyed a picture of capitalism rising like a surging tidal wave and eroding all obstacles to its progress. In the vigorous words of the Communist Manifesto:

> All fixed, fast-frozen relations, with their train of ancient and venerable prejudices and opinions are swept away, all new-formed ones become antiquated before they can ossify. All that is solid melts into air, all that is holy is profaned . . .[45]

Of India Marx wrote:

> Modern industry, resulting from the railway system, will dissolve the hereditary divisions of labour, upon which rest the Indian castes, those decisive impediments to Indian progress and Indian power.[46]

These projected processes have not occurred in South Africa—or, for that matter, in India or Northern Ireland. Two alternative reasons may be advanced: first, that capitalism and the bourgeoisie in such societies lacked the power imputed to them in the Marxist tradition. Accordingly they could not (even had they wished to) confront the established preindustrial order, but instead had to conform to it and adapt their enterprises to existing relations of production. "Ancient and venerable prejudices" had to be respected, not swept away. The second alternative reason is that capitalism not only could adapt to the existing social order but found that order highly useful as a basis for exploitation. As the scale and requirements of capitalism expanded, so the raw material of the established system of racial inequality could be refined and labor-repressive practices elaborated. There is, of course, no reason why both

44. Janos Kenedi, *Do It Yourself: Hungary's Hidden Economy* (London: Pluto, 1981).
45. From the *Communist Manifesto.*
46. Quoted in Bill Warren, *Imperialism: Pioneer of Capitalism* (London: New Left Books, 1980), p. 43.

of these apparently contradictory arguments could not present important facets of truth. Capitalists in South Africa were, after all, whites before they were capitalists, and hence themselves embodiments of "ancient and venerable prejudices."

The presumption of inequality was shared by all classes in the entire European world, an inequality frequently expressed in social and economic terms. In South Africa that presumption was transformed by the force of racism and it was in that context that the industrial revolution took place. It was a racism that was not simply instrumental or functional for purposes of economic exploitation, but was also deemed intrinsically just. Once entrenched and established as a core value in the dominant group's social charter (or body of supporting myths), racism took on a life of its own that far transcended mere functionality. Notoriously, it even served purposes actually inimical to the economic interests of the dominant group but perceived as functional to its independent "racial" interests. H. F. Verwoerd's dictum "Rather poor and white than rich and mixed" is an encapsulation of the point.

The cross-pressuring to which capitalists were subject is well illustrated in comments by Lionel Phillips, one of the most prominent Randlords whose business career spanned a critical period of South Africa's industrial revolution, and whose thought reflected the class and racial prejudices of this era. Time and again, his correspondence shows, he wrestled with the tension between economic rationality and the entrenched forces of racism. Thus, in 1917 he wrote:

> The question of the Colour Bar is, of course, an extremely difficult and delicate one and I need hardly go into it at length because it is one of those problems we have all lived with for so many years. While there is a great deal to be said for not pushing out White men in the higher skilled positions, there is no justification for excluding the Coloured people in the lower types of superior manual work; in fact, not in those spheres where their labour is quite as valuable as that of the better trained and more reliable White man. . . . On the other hand the mining and other employers of White men in the Transvaal can do a great deal to meet the natural apprehensions of the skilled White working population in this connection by not taking every opportunity of squeezing out the White man to replace him by a cheaper Coloured man. The only solution lies in a give-and-take policy. Taking a long view of the whole question, I believe that the protection of the White man's position in South Africa would perhaps be better served by having no restrictions at all (other than competency for the jobs concerned) than by trying to hedge around the preserves of the White man by laws and regulations.[47]

Views such as these cast doubt upon revisionist contentions that

47. Maryna Fraser and Alan Jeeves, eds., *All That Glittered: Selected Correspondence of Lionel Phillips 1890–1924* (Cape Town: Oxford University Press, 1977), p. 302.

mining capital itself "imposed on the industry" the forms of racial organization,[48] hence solidifying the class structure of society. As Merle Lipton has pointed out, the Chamber of Mines opposed the first statutory color bar established in the Transvaal in 1893; it opposed the bar incorporated in the Mines and Works Act in 1911; and it opposed the entrenchment of the job color bar in the amendment to the Mines and Works Act (the so-called "Colour Bar" Act) in 1926.[49]

What conclusions can be derived from these considerations? In one crucial component of segregation, it is clear that capitalism was neither an originator nor an enthusiastic accomplice: it acquiesced, and adapted itself to a social structure not of its own making and whose integument it was powerless to burst asunder. It is futile "to analyse history in terms of utopian alternatives,"[50] but it is nonetheless intriguing to speculate what *might* have happened had no job color bar been institutionalized. Would the possibilities of upward occupational mobility have allowed increasing numbers of people of color to fill intermediate categories of work, something like the Brazilian process?[51] Or would what Frederick Johnstone has called "exploitation colour bars" (e.g., unequal wages, unequal access to education, unequal rights to unionize) have limited the process to a trickle, thereby minimizing the overall effect on the class structure?[52] George Fredrickson has suggested that a genuinely free labor market might have enabled workers to organize across racial lines.[53] Probably, too, substantially more individuals of color would have risen up the occupational and professional ladder. Had this been the case, then the substantial overlap between race and class would have diminished, as blacks became more widely distributed among classes.

As it happens, the overlap between race and class has never been complete. It is precisely those blacks whose *class* position or class expectations was higher than those of workers or peasants but whose aspirations were thwarted by *race* barriers who took the initiative in forming organizations like the South African Native National Congress. As an editorial in an African newspaper put it in 1895:

> It is not wise . . . to educate a man out of barbarism, and then to show plainly that he must remain an inferior almost chattel all his life, no matter his personal

48. Innes, *Anglo-American*, p. 81.

49. Merle Lipton, *Capitalism and Apartheid: South Africa, 1910–84* (Aldershot: Gower/ Maurice Temple Smith, 1985), pp. 112–13.

50. Warren, *Imperialism*, p. 126.

51. Degler, *Neither Black nor White*, pp. 267–87.

52. Frederick A. Johnstone, *Class, Race and Gold: A Study of Class Relations and Racial Discrimination in South Africa* (London: Routledge & Kegan Paul, 1976), pp. 23–24.

53. George M. Fredrickson, *White Supremacy: A Comparative Study in American and South African History* (New York: Oxford University Press, 1981), p. 234.

moral character, or his intellectual ability. It is neither wise nor christian like [sic] to preach the doctrine that all men are equal before the God of the white man, and then, when the Native has accepted his faith, at the sacrifice of feelings handed down to him from generations to treat him as a moral and a social pariah.[54]

To sum up, the growing lack of fit between race and class and the resulting aggravated frustrations as to status provided the impetus for modern political organization in South Africa.

The category of people represented in this intermediate and ambiguous stratum are what Marxists often term the "petty bourgeoisie." They include teachers, interpreters, clerks, ministers of religion, tradesmen, and other functionaries who are both Christian and educated.[55] Because of their intermediate position and because they have proven highly susceptible to the appeal of both Afrikaner and African nationalism, the petty bourgeoisie has been a battleground for conflicting theories of South African history.

Dan O'Meara's *Volkskapitalisme* is probably the most sophisticated structuralist class analysis on a South African theme yet to appear. Its weaknesses, however, illustrate the problems of trying to apply a purely class analysis to a society such as South Africa. O'Meara's basic argument is that the intense mobilization of Afrikaners in the 1930s and 1940s has to be understood as the economic striving of a frustrated Afrikaner petty bourgeoisie. Like all South African classes, the petty bourgeoisie has historically been divided along white-black and English-Afrikaner lines, and the impulses for interracial class unity have either been very weak or nonexistent. According to O'Meara, the reason for this division, at least within the white group, is:

The historical trajectory of capitalist development in South Africa placed the Afrikaans-speaking petty bourgeoisie in a structurally different set of roles, alliances, pressures and struggles, from those of the English-speaking members of this class. These structural differences expressed the widely divergent historical processes which formed the English- and Afrikaans-speaking sections of the petty bourgeoisie, and the differing class forces with which each was identified and allied.[56]

Undoubtedly, O'Meara (and perhaps other revisionists) would extend this analysis to explain the divisions between the white and black sections of the petty bourgeoisie as well. He accuses others of reading "a timeless ethnic concept" back into Afrikaner history so that "the

54. *Inkanyiso,* 21 June 1895, quoted in Welsh, *Roots of Segregation,* p. 244.
55. Brian Willan, "An African in Kimberley: Sol T. Plaatje, 1894–1898," in Marks and Rathbone, eds., *Industrialisation and Social Change,* p. 238.
56. O'Meara, *Volkskapitalisme,* p. 52.

past becomes the inevitable movement to the present."[57] For him the starting point is class:

> In the historical processes of class formation, the various agents of the same class are incorporated in varying sets of social relations and are subject to differing conditions and pressures. They undergo differential experiences, engage in differing struggles and form widely differing mental conceptions of these experiences.[58]

The argument seems to be that the "same class" is divided into racial or other segments because of these various different forces. Afrikaner nationalism is then explicable as

> an historically specific, often surprisingly flexible, always highly fracturated and differentiated response of various identifiable and changing class forces—in alliance—to the contradictions and struggles generated by the development of capitalism in South Africa.[59]

The problem with this argument is: why were Afrikaners subjected to these different and differentiating forces *as a category,* unless some line of ethnocentrism, however mild, was an intrinsic accompaniment of the process of differentiation? (The difficulty is reminiscent of that associated with the "split labor market" variant of class analysis: how did the split get there in the first place?) Also, how does one explain how this alliance across class lines has hung together unless it was undergirded by some common ethnic sentiment? One need not regard this sentiment as "primordial" or deny the degree of contingency in its formation to assert that ethnicity played an autonomous and growing role in Afrikaner politics in the 1930s.

In rejecting the power of sheer ethnic sentiment as an explanation, O'Meara has been forced to seek unconvincing class explanations for particular episodes.[60] Thus he emphasizes economic reasons for Afrikaner nationalists opposing South Africa's entry into World War II on the side of Great Britain. Given Afrikaner nationalists' long antipathy to British imperialism and their sympathy for Nazism, this emphasis is particularly nonpersuasive. Equally unconvincing is O'Meara's attempt to explain in class terms the stance adopted by different factions of Afrikaners in relation to Fusion (the amalgamation of the National and South African parties) in 1934. To be sure, there were economic aspects to the issue, but the overwhelming reason why the "Purified" Nationalists such as D. F. Malan refused to join Fusion was the strong sense

57. Ibid., pp. 6–7.

58. Ibid., p. 14.

59. Ibid., p. 16.

60. For examples, see Welsh, "All Brothers Together," *Times Literary Supplement*, 16 September 1983, p. 981.

that this would be a treacherous betrayal of Afrikaner nationalist principles.[61]

There can be no question that economic aspects of the Afrikaners' condition came to the fore in the 1930s and 1940s. It was, after all, a time of world economic crisis. But it does not follow that therefore there was an economic *basis* to the brand of nationalism propagated by the secret Afrikaner Broederbond. Nationalists themselves consistently stressed the theme that Afrikanerdom was an organic whole whose political, economic, cultural, and spiritual dimensions were inextricably interrelated. As the chairman of the Broederbond, Nico Diederichs, said in October 1940:

> Spiritual freedom and economic freedom are indeed two completely different things, but nevertheless they are closely connected because a people who are economically in bondage can to a considerable extent still be spiritually self-reliant, but they can never reach the highest steps of spiritual self-determination. The removal of a people's right to economic self-determination is the first step in the direction of its spiritual destruction. For us as Afrikaners it is doubly necessary to know this. It is often said to us that *business* and *economics* have got nothing to do with sentiment, culture, politics and so on. But today we know a lot better.[62] (My translation).

The conclusion to be drawn from this and much other evidence is that O'Meara's argument has to be inverted: economic motivations did not underlie nationalism; nationalism underlay, or at least provided the context for, economic motivations.

It is equally difficult to agree with the contention that Broederbond nationalism provided an organizational resource for strivings of a self-interested class, namely the Afrikaner petty bourgeoisie. Other Marxist studies of ethnic and nationalist movements make the similar point that they reap benefits for a particular class, *ergo* they are "basically" class movements. Such reasoning, however, infers causes from consequences. We may agree that most of the leadership positions in Afrikaner nationalism were filled by petty-bourgeois individuals; better-educated, better-connected people often, if not invariably, gravitate to such positions in organizations of all kinds, including ethnic, socialist, or liberation movements like the African National Congress. Expectations or hopes of material gain are by no means the only explanations of individual ambitions.[63] Status, prestige, power, and idealism are all possible sources of ambition or spurs to action.

* * *

61. At van Wyk, *Die Keeromstraat-Kliek* (Cape Town: Tafelberg, 1983), pp. 135–37.
62. Chairman's address to *Bondsraad*, 4–5 October 1940, p. 3 (mimeo).
63. Ernest Gellner, *Nations and Nationalism* (Oxford: Blackwell, 1983), pp. 60–61.

This paper has stressed that the issue of ethnicity and class should not be viewed in "either/or" terms. The interaction between class, race, and ethnicity during the Witwatersrand strike of 1922 forms an instructive case study. The Afrikaner mineworkers, who comprised approximately 75 percent of the white mine labor force, clearly had a class-based grievance, namely job insecurity stemming from the Chamber of Mines' abrogation of the Status Quo Agreement of 1918. Yet their behavior was also an expression of republican Afrikaner nationalism directed against the British victors in the Anglo-Boer War (1899–1902). The strike was perhaps even the fourth in a series of ethnic rebellions that had begun in 1914.[64] Class was woven into a racial and ethnic fabric.

A realistic reader of South Africa's history, while accepting that class has been a powerful force, must also accept that classes have usually, though not invariably, been located in, and encapsulated by, ethnic or racial categories. There have been occasional manifestations of interracial or interethnic class solidarity, but their rarity stamps them as exceptions that prove the rule. Belinda Bozzoli has said that "the economic identification of classes is not the *last* word, but merely the first."[65] If my argument is correct, then class is neither the first nor the last word, but only one among several. Individuals may have several identities, among which are race, ethnicity, and class. Their behavior in everyday life may be a complex amalgam of these identities. The exigencies of particular situations may in theory determine which identity is invoked. As Richard Sandbrook says, "it is common for people to compartmentalize their identities, in the sense that they perceive that different identities are relevant in different social situations."[66] What is needed is a dynamic approach that reifies neither ethnicity, race, nor class, but recognizes the situational salience of each.

64. A. G. Oberholster, *Die Mynwerkerstaking, Witwatersrand 1922* (Pretoria: HSRC, 1982), pp. 36–49.

65. Quoted in Marks and Rathbone, "Introduction," p. 7.

66. Richard Sandbrook, *The Politics of Basic Needs: Urban Aspects of Assaulting Poverty in Africa* (London: Heinemann, 1982), p. 194.

Norman Bromberger and Kenneth Hughes

11. Capitalism and Underdevelopment in South Africa

Much academic debate about the South African past is covert argument about the future shape of South African society.[1] This is especially true of arguments that link capitalism and apartheid, and probably also true of arguments from the more general "underdevelopment" perspective that links capitalism with poverty and inequality. We will attack these perspectives on the grounds that they are empirically false, but also because we think that the preservation of some form of capitalism in South Africa can contribute both to material welfare and to the achievement of liberal goals. At the very least, we want to combat the *reflex* rejection of capitalism rooted in simplified accounts of our economic history.

When the general secretary of the National Union of Mineworkers says that "the workers . . . have reaped nothing from the free enterprise system but poverty, low wages, massive unemployment, lack of housing, inferior education, malnutrition and inadequate medical care,"[2] he draws attention to the need for an interpretation of South Africa's economic history that vividly recounts its achievements, while acknowledging the limits of those achievements and the price paid for them.

1. See Merle Lipton, *Capitalism and Apartheid: South Africa, 1910–1984* (Aldershot: Gower/Maurice Temple Smith, 1985), especially pp. 11–12.
2. *Weekly Mail*, 13–19 June 1986, p. 8.

There are two routes by which capitalism is supposed to have "underdeveloped" South Africa, producing the backwardness of the "reserves," poverty, and relatively low incomes among Africans generally. First, the market is alleged to have *directly* provided scope for the competitive advantages of successful (white) market participants, who enjoy superior location, skills, experience, wealth, and access to new technologies—advantages that have become cumulative and irreversible. Second, it is argued that there is an *indirect* route to underdevelopment via apartheid: many of the racially defined statutory discriminations against black economic agents, and much of the racially biased pattern of public investment have flowed from the economic interests of key capitalist (white) groups. We reject both these contentions.

We dispute the direct route because changes in the geographical pattern of production and in the market-determined allocation of jobs and incomes *may* be phases in the creation of a larger integrated market-based economy and society. In such an economy and society, labor mobility, growth of education, acquisition of skills, and small-scale accumulation reduce impoverishment and many gross inequalities over time, and there is evidence that this has been the case in South Africa. As to the indirect route, it is not at all clear that capitalist interests were predominant in the creation of South Africa's modern racial order. Some were *not* significantly involved; and over time capitalist support for racial discrimination and controls has diminished and turned, in most sectors, into opposition. Finally, economic growth has empowered some of the subordinate black groups and classes in the society, enabling them to resist oppression more effectively and increasing the cost of maintaining the system.

Capitalist economic growth in South Africa has been "development," not "underdevelopment." It has laid the material basis for a large-scale modern state. Within that political framework, despite a widespread assumption to the contrary, the modern South African capitalist economy has created rising average per capita incomes for black citizens. Not only has an elite of urban dwellers benefited, but so has the reserve population, if one includes incomes brought home by migrant workers. Furthermore, in the 1970s income inequality between the races has been reduced quite markedly, though of course it remains substantial.

To assert the real achievements of capitalist development is not to deny that these achievements have been limited. Slow growth rates of per capita income since World War II and inequality of income distribution are evidence of this. These limitations are clearly not the result of the operation of capitalism per se since other capitalist economies have done better. It is important that modern South Africa was created as a "settler conquest state," and in such a state there is a pervasive problem of security which cannot be explained by capitalist interests alone and which has led to attempts to limit economic integration. Moreover, African resistance to conquest and domination inhibited complete capitalist "penetration" and enabled older institutions and practices to survive. Finally, immigrant labor at both ends of the labor market created wage differentials. Also, while increasing the capacity of the economy to grow, it lengthened the time over which growth had to be sustained before the indigenous population could be fully absorbed into the modern productive sector.

We discuss first those arguments that indict market forces for creating disparities and unequal outcomes without state intervention. Parsons and Palmer, for example, write that "Western capitalism promoted underdevelopment by permeating third world economies, reducing them to dependency, and then *creaming off their surpluses.*"[3] Similarly, Denoon and Nyeko say that "as prosperous cultivators, African families enjoyed only a very brief golden age, before they became *the chief victims of the process of agricultural capitalist development.*"[4]

It is often not clear whether the "surplus extraction" said to be taking place is caused by trade, investment, or straightforward looting. We concentrate on what is said to be capitalist "underdevelopment" after the basic colonial framework had been established and the fundamental allocation of land (and, in some areas, cattle) had been determined. Jack Lewis, writing on Colin Bundy's *The Rise and Fall of the South African Peasantry,* argues that the majority of small households in the Ciskei were "caught in a downward spiral only explicable in terms of the impoverishment that comes with conquest and the vast appropriations of land and cattle from the Xhosa and the subsequent effects of incorporations into the economic system of the Colony."[5] He distinguishes, therefore, between "appropriation" and "the effects of incorporation," and it is the second of these which concerns us here.

Since there has been no systematic theory of the market-mediated processes by which capitalism is said to have "underdeveloped" regions and groups in South Africa, we attempt to synthesize one ourselves. A substantial contribution to such a theory emerges from an analysis of "backwash" effects.[6] Growth in one region may benefit other regions,

3. Robin Palmer and Neil Parsons, *The Roots of Rural Poverty in Central and Southern Africa* (London: Heinemann, 1977), p. 3.

4. Donald Denoon and Balam Nyeko, *Southern Africa since 1800,* new ed. (London: Longman, 1984), p. 148.

5. Jack Lewis, "The Rise and Fall of the South African Peasantry: A Critique and Reassessment," *Journal of Southern African Studies* 11 (1984): 20 and 24.

6. Gunnar Myrdal, *Economic Theory and Under-Developed Regions* (London: Duckworth, 1957).

for example by providing them with a market for their products. But growth in one area may also harm others. The growing region may produce manufactures that undersell local handicrafts; it may attract investments from lower-yielding environments and attract mobile labor from areas paying lower wages. The growth of transport linkages may cause shifts in trade among neighboring regions and countries, shifts that result in losers as well as gainers. Moreover, these processes may be cumulative and self-reinforcing, particularly as agglomerations create concentrated and expanding markets, so that economies of scale in production are realized. Also, more general economies and advantages can arise as growing enterprises and populations cluster near cities or in growth centers or growth regions. Competitive advantages gained will not easily be lost, and the "drain" of resources from, and contraction of production in, disadvantaged areas will continue. It is widely suggested that some such analysis explains such crucial developments as the continuous growth of the Witwatersrand area relative to the rest of the country, especially the African reserves.[7]

However, the "drain" of labor from poor to rich areas might under certain circumstances benefit both areas—depending on the volume of incomes sent back and the uses to which they were put. The "under-development" perspective either denies such possibilities or takes them to be irrelevant in the South African case. It takes a pessimistic view of migratory labor between black rural areas and mines and towns. By the 1970s, and possibly earlier, migrant remittances are admitted to have become a crucial component of subsistence in these rural areas and a necessary source of funding for farming, but only because the decline of local production had become so marked.[8] Behind the decline lies the intersectoral and interregional transfer of labor in response to differentials in wages. Also, the average productive and entrepreneurial quality of "reserve" labor has declined, since the young, the males, and the better educated tend to migrate. So, too, the increasing competitiveness of food grown on commercial farms has weakened local production.

Economic growth involves shifts in production in response to shifts in consumer demand as incomes rise, tastes change, or new products are developed. It is intrinsic to growth that markets will turn against some producers and toward others. Growth in capitalist economies often is driven forward by wavelike bursts of innovation, opening up new techniques of production and disrupting existing markets. In the

7. See, e.g., T. J. D. Fair, *South Africa: Spatial Frameworks for Development* (Cape Town and Johannesburg: Juta, 1982), pp. 71–79.

8. James Leatt, Theo Kneifel and Klaus Nürnberger, *Contending Ideologies in South Africa* (Cape Town and Johannesburg: David Philip, 1986), p. 41.

late nineteenth and early twentieth centuries South Africa experienced such expansions and disruptions: the "mineral revolution" created large new market opportunities for *small* grain producers, transport riders and wage laborers. Then prices tumbled in some of those markets as the railways brought in foreign wheat and undercut bulk transport in wagons over certain routes. Trade networks introduced new consumer and producer goods into African societies, increasing the desirability of money incomes. Presumably Beinart has such processes in mind when he explains the decline of the South African black peasantry: "It was the very dependence on the wider colonial economies in which the terms of trade turned against the peasant . . . which first constrained the development of peasant agriculture. And the operation of capitalist markets, coupled with the action of colonial states favouring capitalist and settler interests, ultimately crushed the peasantry on a wide scale."[9]

We shall return to the question of agency later, to the indirect route to "underdevelopment" that resulted from the effective political pursuit of their interests by white capitalists and settlers. Here we begin to assess the arguments for the direct route by pursuing the question of the creation of new communities, which is related to the question of the crushing of older ones. How mobile has labor been? Has it moved permanently to new locations or continued to migrate from original locations? Why has it moved? What has been the capacity of the new economic structures and associated communities to absorb the displaced or disrupted elements of earlier structures? Our view is that the more labor has been willing and able to migrate to areas of greater opportunities, the more the new economic environments have been able to provide those opportunities, and the less the value that migrants have attached to preserving their historic communities in their original locations, so the less appropriate it is to see "backwash" and related effects as a problem: specific social communities may be destroyed, but despite the human cost there may be considerable human gain. The longer the period over which the adjustments and reabsorptions are observed, the easier it will be to detect such gains.

It is significant that migration occurred on a substantial scale *before* the subjugation of African kingdoms. Members of some polities, such as the Pedi, traveled a thousand miles on foot to the diamond fields, and there were estimated to be 60,000 Moçambicans on the Rand alone by 1897.[10] Pressures for migration emanated from rulers in these

9. W. Beinart, *The Political Economy of Pondoland 1860–1930* (Johannesburg: Ravan, 1982), p. 3.

10. For the Pedi, see Peter Delius, "Migrant Labour and the Pedi, 1840–1880," in Shula Marks and Anthony Atmore, eds., *Economy and Society in Pre-industrial South Africa* (London: Longman, 1980). For the Moçambicans see Patrick Harries, "Kinship, Ideology

precolonial societies and later from colonial governments: still, there is also evidence that workers were pursuing their own strategies and that in some cases these included permanent settlement away from the "home base." By the 1950 census about 30 percent of South African black males and 21 percent of females were in metropolitan areas or towns. Roughly a third of both sexes were on farms (some of course had never been anywhere else), with only some 33 percent of males and 47 percent of females in the reserves. This absence was most marked in the case of prime-age males: of those in the 20–29 age group, for instance, some 48 percent were in metropolitan areas and towns and 38 percent on farms.[11]

There have always been strong material inducements to work for wages, at least part time or at one stage in life. Agricultural production has always been remarkably uncertain in South Africa because of disease and drought.[12] Moreover, in the early twentieth century, agriculture confronted a long-term crisis as population increased and soils were depleted.[13] Under such conditions, wage-work might be highly rewarded by comparison with other activities or in terms of the utility or productivity of new commodities bought with cash wages. In the nineteenth century, wages for unskilled, largely black, labor were at times high even by European standards.[14] While in the first three decades of the twentieth century there was a decline in the cash value of gold-mining wages, that decline was halted after the 1930s and a new range of higher-paying jobs became available as the economy began to diversify. Simkins estimates that the industrial wage in the 1920s was *three* times the average annual agricultural output of a family of five persons in the reserves; in the 1930s it rose to *five* times and stayed at that level to the 1950s as agricultural output rose in response to abundant rainfall.[15] During this period a steady *permanent* migration was under way. There is strong evidence that over time a majority of South Africa's citizens came to wish to move themselves to new locations—urban and peri-

---

and the Nature of Precolonial Labour Migration" in Shula Marks and Richard Rathbone, eds., *Industrialisation and Social Change in South Africa* (London: Longman, 1982).

11. Charles Simkins, *Four Essays on the Past, Present and Possible Future of the Distribution of the Black Population of South Africa* (Cape Town: South African Labor and Development Research Unit, University of Cape Town), p. 53 (Table 1).

12. "Indeed, South Africa is not an agricultural country": C. W. de Kiewiet, *A History of South Africa: Social and Economic* (London: Oxford University Press, 1941), p. 259.

13. See Tim Keegan, "Trade, Accumulation and Impoverishment: Mercantile Capital and the Economic Transformation of Lesotho and the Conquered Territory, 1870–1920" *Journal of Southern African Studies,* 12 (1986):196–216, especially p. 213.

14. Patrick Harries, "Kinship," p. 143.

15. C. E. W. Simkins, "Agricultural Production in the African Reserves: South Africa, 1918–1969, *Journal of Southern African Studies* 7 (1980–81):256–83.

urban—and to constitute new communities there as part of an innovative and evolving larger society.[16]

What of the absorptive capacity of the capitalist economy, its ability to continue to provide growing numbers of jobs for those drawn to the new industrial centers? Unfortunately, our information on this is less precise than we would like. However, for the period at least until the early 1950s, before the substantial increases in the rates of growth of population and labor force, a relatively optimistic account is possible. The growth rate of the economy down to the early 1950s appears to have been comparatively high: among nineteen countries on which Simon Kuznets reported in 1959, the Union of South Africa had the fastest rate of growth of total product and the third fastest rate of growth of product per capita (after Sweden and Japan.)[17] While techniques employed were perhaps more capital-intensive and on a larger scale than turned out in the long run to be appropriate,[18] the fierce competition for labor in the 1930s and 1940s between commercial agriculture and the urban economy, and the increased importation of foreign African labor, both suggest that absorption of labor was not only keeping pace with population increase but also reducing the percentage of persons outside the capitalist economy.

Moreover, in the reserves, despite an absolute reduction in local agricultural production per household and a relative decline of living standards of resident households, absolute income levels were maintained and at times increased. Thus Knight and Lenta write of the period 1936 to 1972–73: "The total real income per capita of homeland people rose somewhat over the four decades for which data are available, but . . . this increase was due to the increase in earnings from external employment, which more than offset the actual decline in black income from homeland sources.[19] In part the reserves were sustained by the desire of Africans to maintain a particular type of community; if one ignores the injustices of influx control, the reserves would have been a defensible device by which a slower pace of transition to a different political economy might be chosen by individuals, families, and com-

16. Hermann Giliomee and Lawrence Schlemmer, eds., *Up Against the Fences: Poverty, Passes and Privilege in South Africa* (Cape Town and Johannesburg: David Philip, 1985).

17. Simon Kuznets, *Six Lectures on Economic Growth* (New York: Free Press, 1959), pp. 20–21.

18. Brian Levy, *Industrialisation and Inequality in South Africa* (Cape Town: Southern African Labor and Development Research Unit, University of Cape Town, Working Paper No. 36, 1981).

19. J. B. Knight and G. Lenta, "Has Capitalism Underdeveloped the Labour Reserves of South Africa?" *Oxford Bulletin of Economics and Statistics* 42 (1980):169. This paper is a valuable discussion of many issues we raise.

munities. Moreover, long-run countervailing developmental tendencies have now begun to emerge in manufacturing and agriculture, which are lessening the regional polarization of productivity and hence the relative deprivation of the reserves. According to R. T. Bell, since the late sixties, market forces have been inducing a shift of certain labor-intensive industries toward the "homelands."[20] We see, therefore, that the record of the reserves has not been one of universal and relentless decline, depressing though many of the statistics relating to them have been.

The direct route to "underdevelopment" we defined as one undertaken under the influence of market forces without state intervention. When dealing with "reserves," however, one cannot ignore the legal machinery of influx control, certainly since 1950 and probably earlier. In the 1950s, the full weight of state power was thrown into the effort to shift population to "the homelands" (one of the new designations for the reserves). Simkins has consistently emphasized the importance of this strategy and its success in slowing urbanization (certainly outside the homelands), though not in reducing the absolute numbers of Africans in urban areas, its stated objective. This success destroyed the "precarious" equilibrium between people and food production in the reserves, which had formerly been maintained by permanent emigration.[21] This latter-day counterrevolution certainly did not emerge from the "needs of capital," although this is less clear for the earlier phases of influx control, where there is *some* plausibility about the claim that the urban influx control system served the interests of capitalist employers by producing "cheap labor."

According the this view, both mining capitalists and commercial farmers had an interest in obtaining a wage-labor force, and in keeping it immobile: they wanted to keep wages low, or even actually to reduce them, as after the Anglo-Boer War. Some commercial farmers, as distinct from land companies, also wanted to reduce the rights of Africans to farm the land as "squatters," labor tenants, and sharecroppers. These employer interests, so the argument goes, were responsible for the legislation that imposed differential taxation on Africans, entrenched but restricted their landholdings, and curtailed their rights of urban residence and their mobility out of (white) farming areas.[22] These are

20. R. T. Bell, *The Growth and Structure of Manufacturing Employment in Natal,* Institute of Social and Economic Research, University of Durban-Westville, Occasional Paper No. 7, 1983.

21. Simkins, "Agricultural Production," pp. 270–72.

22. Martin Legassick, "South African Capital Accumulation and Violence," *Economy and Society* 3 (1974):264–65.

some of the alleged *indirect* ways by which capitalism led to "underdevelopment."

The assignment of certain lands as African reserves with associated restrictions on urban influx is here interpreted as an attempt to secure a low level of wages by preserving (or creating) a low-productivity agricultural base. There are two main explanations of the benefits that capitalists derive from the system. Harold Wolpe argued that the maintenance of the reserves saved capitalists from paying the reproduction costs of labor.[23] Giovanni Arrighi, writing primarily about colonial Rhodesia, took the view that limiting available land in a time of population growth depressed African agriculture and brought out workers at low wages.[24]

In considering this hypothesis that the reserve system and the decline in per capita agricultural production were contrived in the "interest of capital," one can lay alternative stress on the general interest of whites, or the specific interests of white workers. Radicals have emphasized the interests of capitalists but Knight and Lenta, for example, argue that "the radical interpretation of the government policy of restricting the further settlement of black families in white cities, and the imposition of the oscillatory migrant labor system which that implied, is questionable. Our interpretation is that government was concerned to reduce black competition with white workers and that it regarded migrants as being less of a political threat to the system than proletarians."[25] In the specific case of the Land Act of 1913, a cornerstone of the twentieth-century reserve system, a careful investigation by Peter Wickins into its origins revealed a complex story of conflicting expectations and conflicting interests.[26] There were also the interests of Africans themselves in the "reserves." Beinart wrote of the Pondo: "Migrancy, as a specific form of proletarianization, arose initially out of the dynamic relationship of power and authority within rural society as much as from the specific demands of capital."[27]

We also need to ask sharp questions about "the demands of capital," even when statements exemplifying these demands are produced from impeccable capitalist sources. Juan Martinez-Alier has put the argument this way:

23. H. Wolpe, "Capitalism and Cheap Labour-Power in South Africa: From Segregation to Apartheid," *Economy and Society,* 1 (1972):425–56.

24. G. Arrighi, *The Political Economy of Rhodesia* (The Hague: Mouton, 1967).

25. Knight and Lenta, "Has Capitalism Underdeveloped," p. 195.

26. P. L. Wickins, "The Natives' Land Act of 1913: A Cautionary Essay on Simple Explanations of Complex Change," *South African Journal of Economics* 49 (1981):105–29.

27. Beinart, *Political Economy of Pondoland,* p. 6.

> The existence of a rural subsistence sector in the South African economy allegedly has the function of cheapening the "cost of reproduction" of the wage labor force employed in the mines or in the plantations. The subsistence sector assumes "functions that capitalism prefers not to assume . . . the functions of social security." In this particular instance . . . one would like to know whether alternative arrangements would not really come out cheaper for the capitalists (such as, for instance, confiscation of the land in the subsistence sector, and compulsory or wage labor), and whether, therefore, the statements from spokesmen for the capitalists who assert this positive economic function of the subsistence sector are not merely a rationalization of their own misgivings when confronted with the herculean and dangerous task of depriving the whole indigenous population of access to land. Unless the costs and benefits of alternative arrangements are spelled out, it is difficult to know to what extent the capitalists' complaints (or praises) about the existing arrangements are to be taken as accurate descriptions of reality or as ideological statements.[28]

Our argument thus far has been primarily concerned with capitalists' complicity in creating and maintaining "the reserve system," but there were other controls and discriminations that, in Bill Freund's words, "kept black workers poor and unable to defend their own interests."[29] We agree with Lipton and Greenberg that mine-owners and farmers, in particular, relied on, indeed demanded, state assistance in imposing coercive labor arrangements, and in putting pressure on various forms of land tenure under which Africans still cultivated on their own account outside the reserves.[30] But both writers also note that manufacturing and commerce were never as involved as mining and farming in the creation of the modern racial order, and that all major groups of capitalists now have a much-reduced stake in that racial order and have supported attempts to reform it. Lipton writes of manufacturing and commerce:

> The growing need of manufacturing and commerce for skilled black labour, and for a larger domestic market, meant that apartheid was incompatible with continued economic growth in these increasingly capital- and skill-intensive sectors. . . . Erosion of the job bar led to erosion of the education and training bars and to pressures for stabilization, and hence to the demand for a secure and permanent African status in the "white" area; this, in turn, raised the question of African citizenship and political rights.[31]

A key aspect of the racial system in South Africa has commonly been

28. Juan Martinez-Alier, *Haciendas, Plantations and Collective Farms* (London: Cass, 1977), p. 13. The internal citation is of Claude Meillasoux, "From reproduction to production," *Economy and Society,* 1 (1972):102.

29. Bill Freund, *The Making of Contemporary Africa: The Development of African Society Since 1800* (London and Basingstoke: Macmillan, 1984), p. 186.

30. Lipton, *Capitalism and Apartheid,* chapters 4–6; S. B. Greenberg, *Race and State in Capitalist Development: South Africa in Comparative Perspective* (New Haven: Yale University Press, 1980).

31. Lipton, *Capitalism and Apartheid,* pp. 180–81.

seen as discrimination in the labor market, such as job reservation, preferential hiring of whites in the public sector, and restrictions on access to urban jobs. It is difficult not to see white workers as crucial agents in pressing for discriminatory measures. However, some radical writers wishing to resist this suggestion have argued that actual responsibility for some of these phenomena lies at the door of employers.[32] Such an argument is not easy to sustain. It faces the difficulty of explaining the early emergence of a racially structured workplace on the mines, due to initiatives from immigrant skilled labor. Moreover it is confronted by the reality of conflict between capitalists and white workers over job reservation practices and the failure of capitalists to have their way when white workers were able to exploit the power that possession of the franchise gave them.

Even if they accept that the job color bar is a protective device for white workers' interests, such writers are still able to blame the capitalists. "Non-white workers", wrote Frederick Johnstone, "have suffered far more from the exploitation color bars of the employers than from the job colour bars of the workers."[33] He was referring to restrictions on mobility and free contracting, and on access to land, and he based his comparison on the relative scale of popular protest and agitation against the two sets of measures. However, the argument falls away because we have rejected the view which sees these restrictions as primarily created in the "interest of capital."

Most of the arguments we have been considering have been concerned with the alleged culpability of capitalists for racial oppression and the poverty and inequality that results from it, but there are also more sophisticated arguments which lay the blame not on capitalists but on capitalism as a system. White workers, it will be conceded, did band together to exclude blacks from high-paying jobs, but it would only be under capitalism that worker would be pitted against worker and black workers subject to having their wages depressed by a tacit conspiracy of capitalists with a white labor aristocracy.

This argument, while superior to some of those considered earlier, does rest on some doubtful assumptions. To start with, it presumes a situation where we have limited competition on both sides of the market, and here it would appear to be true that a split in the ranks of the workers will confer more power on employers who collude with each other. But this situation is not to met with universally. Even when it is present, however, it is important to remember that the discipline of the market puts bounds on the power of both employers and trade unions.

32. See Lipton, *Capitalism and Apartheid*, pp. 112ff, for a discussion of this issue.

33. Frederick A. Johnstone, *Class, Race and Gold* (London: Routledge & Kegan Paul, 1976), p. 214.

Market agents who are concerned with profitability and the risk of bankruptcy or with employment levels and the ability of their union to survive and grow cannot just do as they please. They are constrained by the market demand for their products or their labor and by their ability to raise credit.

These constraints are peculiar to capitalism since under socialism budget constraints are "soft,"[34] that is, costs and revenues are subject to manipulation and the whole economy tends to be run as one large enterprise in which the scope for such political manipulation is greatly increased. Thus, if in 1922 the organized workers in the Rand revolt had managed to install socialism in South Africa, the society would have become more racist, not less, according to their slogan "Workers of the world unite and fight for a white South Africa!"

In rebutting the charge that capitalism (or an alliance of particular capitalist interests) has to be held centrally responsible for backwardness, poverty, and inequality in South Africa, one can sketch an alternative, more positive view of the capitalist record.

One hundred and fifty years ago "South Africa" was certainly not a state, and economic growth was a necessary condition for its political unification and demographic expansion. It is worth recalling a series of outstanding achievements that have since occurred: the construction of a railway and road transport system from the coasts across the massively elevated plateau of the interior; the feeding and material support of a heavily urbanized population in a largely semiarid land; the technical miracle of mining gold two miles down and deeper; and the creation of those myriad work environments in which populations from a nonliterate culture and without industrial skills began a linguistic, technical, and social transformation. Perhaps most impressive of all has been the rise in African life expectancy. First estimates are that average African male life expectancy at birth in Cape Colony in 1891–1904 was about 30 years;[35] for 1970–1975, it was reported as 52 years in the Republic as a whole.[36]

As regards the growth of black incomes within the relatively large-scale state and economy created by capitalist economic growth, two views are current: one that black incomes in South Africa are high by African standards, the other that the black population is absolutely and relatively impoverished, or, as, Shula Marks has recently written, that

34. For enterprise under socialism, see Janos Kornai, *Anti-Equilibrium* (Amsterdam: North Holland, 1971).

35. Charles Simkins: personal communication.

36. M. D. McGrath, *Racial Income Distribution in South Africa,* Department of Economics, University of Natal, Durban, 1977, p. 28.

in 1910 "the vast majority of black South Africans . . . were systematically excluded . . . from any share in the possible rewards of capitalist growth."[37] The first assertion is of little interest for our present purposes, since no African countries have been developed under capitalism to the same degree as South Africa. The second assertion is wrong. There is evidence of a rising trend in average real black per capita incomes for most of the twentieth century. From Union in 1910, at which date our national income estimates begin, to 1979 the gross domestic product has grown in real terms at about 4 percent per annum.[38] An average growth rate of this size sustained for seven decades implies a substantial increase in real income per head—given that the population growth rate, at least until 1950, was only half that of income.

A common response to statistics of this sort is to assert that somehow all the income growth was appropriated by whites.[39] It is clear that this cannot have been so. From 1917/18 to 1970 the data suggest a constant black share of the growing income total, while the overall black share of population was effectively constant until the 1950s (though it began to rise thereafter). Down to 1950, therefore, black per capita incomes would have grown at the same rate as overall per capita incomes, i.e., at about 2 percent per annum.[40] From 1950 to 1970 they appear to have continued to grow but at a slower rate than before;[41] while from 1970 to 1980 black per capita incomes have grown faster than the average and considerably faster than those of whites. These growth rates mean that average real black incomes more than doubled over the fifty years from 1920 to 1970 and quadrupled by 1980.

It is still possible to be skeptical: average gains are always compatible with no gains or even losses among the majority. However, we think there is sufficient evidence to suggest that gains among blacks have been reasonably widespread; the gains were not confined to an urban (or industrial) elite but were shared by people in reserves and on farms.

37. Shula Marks, *The Ambiguities of Dependence in South Africa* (Johannesburg: Ravan, 1986), p. 38.

38. Jill Nattrass, *The South African Economy: Its Growth and Change* (Cape Town: Oxford University Press, 1981), Table 2.1, p. 25. She calculates 3.8 percent per annum for the period.

39. Stanley Greenberg, "Economic Growth and Political Change: The South African Case," *Journal of Modern African Studies*, 19 (1981):678–79.

40. For constant racial income shares, see Stephen Devereaux, *South African Income Distribution, 1900–1980* (Cape Town: Southern African Labor and Development Research Unit, University of Cape Town, Working Paper No. 51, 1983), Table 1, p. 4. For population shares, see *South African Statistics 1974*, page 1.8. White share: 21.6 percent (1904), 20.9 percent (1950) but declining to 19.3 percent (1960) and 17.4 percent (1970).

41. McGrath, in *Racial Income Distribution*, pp. 24–25, suggests that for the slightly longer distribution period 1946/7 to 1970 per capita incomes of whites, Indians, and coloreds grew at over 2 percent per annum, while those of Africans grew at just on 1 percent per annum.

As for the reserves, Simkins claims that from 1918 to the mid-1950s agricultural production per head in these areas was roughly constant, though with considerable fluctuations.[42] Knight and Lenta studying the period 1936 to 1973/4, calculated a growth rate in incomes per head of 1.3 percent per annum. For an overlapping period (1960–1980), Simkins simulated the growth of household and per capita incomes in the reserves. While there is serious poverty at the bottom of the income distribution, 85 percent of households showed substantial real income gains and 70 percent experienced "just over a doubling of their 1960 per capita incomes in the twenty years between 1960 and 1980."[43]

We know less about the incomes of black farm workers on commercial white-owned farms, but in one of the few existing studies Simkins has reported that real income per head on farms (aggregating production and wages in cash and kind) was roughly constant during the 1930s, rose during the war years and early 1950s, was interrupted by a substantial drop from 1955 to 1965, then resumed its growth in the late 1960s.[44] Lipton reported an increase for real farm wages for most of the 1960s, and Nattrass confirmed this for a longer period, showing that real incomes of black wage earners on farms rose by 9.1 percent per annum during 1960–1975, though she qualified the achievement by pointing to the low initial base and the decline in the number of farm workers.[45]

The view that black incomes have been stagnant or have fallen may have some foundation in the widely noticed statistic that the cash component of the black gold-mining wage was at the same real level in 1969 as it had been in 1911.[46] We have already noted that most miners were reserve residents and we have reported rising incomes in the reserves—if wage remittances are taken into account. Mining labor force statistics indirectly confirm that average real incomes were *rising* among rural blacks—at least from the 1930s. Participation by South African–born Africans in the gold-mining industry declined markedly over the period, from 50 percent of the labor force in 1931 to just over 20 percent in 1973 (or, in absolute numbers, from 113,000 to 81,000). Participation by foreign migrants increased correspondingly. Since the

42. Simkins, "Agricultural Production," p. 262.

43. Charles Simkins, "What Has Been Happening to Income Distribution and Poverty in the Homelands?" Carnegie Conference Paper No. 7, Cape Town, 1984, pp. 13–14.

44. Charles Simkins, "African Population, Employment and Incomes on Farms Outside the Reserves, 1923–1969," Conference of the South African Historical Society, University of Durban-Westville, 1981, p. 14.

45. See Merle Lipton, "White farming: A Case-Study of Change in South Africa," *Journal of Commonwealth and Comparative Politics* (March 1974):43–61 especially 47–48; Jill Nattrass, *South African Economy,* Table 6.9 on p. 125 and discussion pp. 125–26.

46. Francis Wilson, *Labour in the South African Gold Mines 1911–1969* (Cambridge: Cambridge University Press, 1972), Table 5 on p. 46.

real value of the cash wage in gold mining was essentially constant from 1931 to 1961, this behavior is what one would predict given the emergence of increased employment opportunities at higher, and increasing, real wages in the manufacturing, construction, and service sectors in the diversifying South African economy. The 1970s saw something of a revolution in gold mining, when the real wage quadrupled between 1971 and 1982 and the ratio of white to black wages fell from 20.9:1 to 5.5:1. Concurrently the South African labor complement rose again, from 20 to 58 percent. It is clearly a serious mistake to see black mine wages for the forty years before 1970 as a reliable proxy for either black wages in general or black per capita income in *South Africa*.[47]

We believe that evidence of this kind justifies our claim that from 1910 to 1980 black per capita income gains were widespread and not confined to urban dwellers or some other elite. And where doubts about the record are clearest, from 1950 to 1970, a plausible case can be mounted that it was not so much the capitalist economy which faltered as that a substantial attack was launched by the apartheid state against full integration of blacks into the core capitalist economy. This campaign coincided with a major demographic transition: blacks had started to experience longer life expectancy and, in due course, faster growth rates of population.

Figures such as those we have been employing have a limited value. They do not go back far enough—the 1860s would be a useful starting point. They do address the issue of income distribution among the black population but somewhat sketchily, and they do not throw much light on the qualitative aspects of life. But we trust that we have made our main point. Many discussions of South Africa do not even consider the possibility that there may have been long-term gains in measured incomes for blacks. We assert that there *have* been, and this achievement will be clearly recognized when a dispassionate assessment of South African history, and of the role of the capitalist economy in it, is attempted.

The limitations of development in South Africa include, but go beyond, the features of "underdevelopment" already mentioned. The principal limitations as we see them are the persistent sharp inequalities between whites and blacks, and the relatively poor rates of growth South Africa has experienced at some stages of its twentieth-century development, notably the decades after World War II, together with related phenomena such as the exceptionally low rate of growth of

47. Lipton, *Capitalism and Apartheid,* Tables 8 and 11 on pp. 385 and 388; Greenberg in "Economic Growth and Political Change," pp. 678–79, makes the mistake referred to above.

labor productivity. Also, during at least the last decade it would appear that black unemployment, at unacceptable levels and increasing, has become a normal feature of the economic scene.

It is useful to document these limitations in a little detail before attempting to explain them. Briefly, racial shares of personal income were roughly constant for some decades to 1970, with whites, who constituted 17 percent of the population in that last year, receiving slightly over 70 percent of total personal income.[48] On criteria such as these, South Africa was, at least until very recently, at or near the top of the world inequality table. As regards economic growth rates, however, the picture is less clear. South Africa certainly had a reputation, at least at home, for relatively fast growth. As noted above, in a long-term study down to the early 1950s South Africa's track record appeared outstanding. In the subsequent periods it has been much worse. According to one computation based on World Bank statistics, South Africa's gross national product per capita for 1950–1975 grew at an average of 2.2 percent per annum. This rate was surpassed by several groups of countries: advanced industrial countries averaged 3.2 percent, Latin American countries 2.6 percent, African countries 2.4 percent, East Asian countries 3.9 percent, and southern European countries 4.5 percent.[49]

It is not possible to define or measure unemployment in South Africa uncontroversially. It is clear enough that its incidence is markedly more severe among blacks, Asians, and coloreds than among whites. It is also fairly clear that it is increasing, at least since the mid-1970s but possibly from an earlier date. Simkins put its level at 21.1 percent of the all-races labor force in 1981; since then the average annual index of employment outside agriculture has hardly increased (1981 = 103.2; 1985 = 103.8) whereas the labor force is increasing at about 2 percent per annum.[50]

Before attempting to explain these limitations we must insist that there is no fatal defect in the South African economy which makes it impossible for redistribution to take place at the same time as economic growth. For example, there is no doubt that income inequality decreased during the 1970s, the white share of total personal income falling from 71.7 percent in 1970 to 61.5 percent in 1980. Africans gained most

48. McGrath, *Racial Income Distribution,* pp. 22–23.

49. David Morawetz, *Twenty-five Years of Economic Development 1950 to 1975* (Baltimore and London: The Johns Hopkins University Press for the World Bank, 1977), Appendix A.1.

50. "Labour: Employment in the Non-Agricultural Sector," *South African Reserve Bank Quarterly Bulletin,* September 1986: S-105. The Simkins estimate of unemployment for 1981 is cited in R. T. Bell, "Issues in South African Unemployment," *South African Journal of Economics,* 53 (1985):24–25.

during this decade, their share jumping from 19.8 percent in 1970 to 29.0 percent in 1980. Comparable trends can be observed in the size distribution of South African income in these years. The top 20 percent of income *earners* received 77 percent of national *remuneration* in 1970 but only 61 percent in 1980.[51]

We do not wish to be dogmatic about most of these trends, and therefore we are hesitant about explaining them. Not only are the data difficult to establish, but the phenomena are complex. It is clear, however, that the limitations of South Africa's development cannot be attributed to capitalism *as such,* since the performance of most capitalist countries has been better than South Africa's both on the score of distribution and of the efficient pursuit of growth. (In relation to growth we confined ourselves to the long postwar boom.) Our tentative explanation turns on politics and on the peculiar way the South African economy has been inserted in the world economy.

South Africa is not merely a capitalist state but, more important, it is a *settler state* created and established by conquest and settlement. It consequently has pervasive problems of mistrust and insecurity and has constantly established and reestablished its authority through force or the show of force. The old fear of slave revolts was reinforced by the fear of frontier wars and the possibility of a general insurrection of the "natives" to drive the settlers into the sea. Twentieth-century decolonization in the rest of Africa, some of it the result of armed conflicts as in Algeria, Kenya, Angola, Moçambique, and Rhodesia, revived this specter. So long as the security of the settlement remains an issue, the distribution of power between the colonizer and the colonized must be problematic. Power, so the colonizers reason, must be retained in their hands, and so long as it is, it can be used to economic as well as political advantage. Public resources can be increasingly allocated to benefit whites primarily or exclusively. These privileged allocations must in turn be protected, thus creating a further need to keep power in the hands of the settlers.

Still, a settler population is not a given constant. It may change its size by natural increase, by intermarriage or other forms of sexual recruitment from the indigenous population, and by in- or out-migration. In the seventeenth and eighteenth centuries the rate of natural increase was initially high: although the settlers retained the Western European age-of-marriage pattern by which age of marriage and completed family size were determined by individual access to resources, their fertility

51. Devereux, *South African Income Distribution,* pp. 34–37. The 1970 figures he reports are due to Simkins; the 1980 figures are his own; Jill Nattrass first noted these trends in "The Narrowing of Wage Differentials in South Africa," *South African Journal of Economics,* 45 (1977).

was set free by the ready availability of land.[52] With the closure of the frontier and the onset of urbanization the rate of increase fell sharply. The second possibility, miscegenation, though contributing to the population even in the twentieth century, has been much restricted by racism, which both discourages miscegenation and assigns the offspring of mixed "white" unions to the subordinate category "colored," kept at arm's length.[53]

Consequently it was to immigration of whites that settlers looked to increase their security. To attract immigrants and discourage emigrants, inducements need to be offered, one rationale for maintaining white incomes at a high level. Such a consideration clearly operated in neighboring colonial states such as Kenya and Southern Rhodesia.[54] Of course, in South Africa the matter was complicated by the existence of two "vintages" of settlers—distinguished by language, by other cultural traits, and by differing relations to the process of capitalist economic growth. Nonetheless, the concern to encourage immigration and reduce emigration was not eliminated by this competition between English- and Afrikaans-speakers.

The question of real-income levels and of flows of international migration relates to the way the South African economy was inserted into the world economy. In the nineteenth century both labor and capital flowed more freely than they did subsequently. Consequently, from the time of the first mineral discoveries, money and people poured into South Africa. After the initial rush, miners and engineers with special skills were needed, and, because they were mobile on an international market in which they were in short supply, they could command a high wage.

The wages of black laborers were determined quite separately on the local market, and were much lower than those of white settlers. This was due partly to their relative lack of experience or skills, to their "plentiful" numbers especially as black labor was also available across international boundaries, and to the development of techniques to restrict competition between employers. Whatever their precise genesis, the high wage differentials between white and black workers had profound consequences. In particular, such differentials created the ever-present possibility of "undercutting" privileged white labor, in which

52. For the Western European marriage pattern, see J. Hajnal, "European Marriage Patterns in Perspective" in D. V. Glass and D. C. Eversley, *Population in History* (London: Arnold, 1965). The persistence of the European pattern has been established by Robert Shell (personal communication).

53. See Richard Elphick and Hermann Giliomee, eds., *The Shaping of South African Society 1652–1820* (London and Cape Town: Longman, 1979), pp. 126–62, 371–78.

54. Paul Mosley, *The Settler Economies: Studies in the Economic History of Kenya and Southern Rhodesia, 1900–1963* (Cambridge: Cambridge University Press, 1983), p. 234.

employers would be free to hire whom they wanted, giving further opportunities for black advancement in the modern economy. However, such a process would immediately have reduced the living standards of the white labor elite and the income prospects of that part of the Afrikaner population which, driven by the commercialization of agriculture, began to arrive in the new urban centers from before the turn of the century. White labor, always enfranchised, demanded protection and obtained it, in the form either of the standard supply-restricting devices of the labor unions or of preferential state employment policies and the quotas and statutory prohibitions of the color bar. Either way, the competitive reduction of inequality was restrained.

The role of international labor flows had ambiguous consequences in other areas also, since there were black immigrant workers as well as white. Labor practices had been harsh in colonial South Africa, in part the legacy of slavery and in part the consequence of the existence of relatively free resources, such as land, on which laborers could support themselves rather than work for another. Employers, who constantly felt their authority threatened, had recourse to harsh punishments, and demanded pass laws, and Masters and Servants legislation. Their long-established labor problems were replicated and compounded in the mines and in industry, where, as in England from the eighteenth century on, the work force had to be broken in to new rhythms and disciplines enforced by the clock and the machine and not by the sun or the task in hand.[55] African miners often deserted as the harvest approached, and new recruits sometimes fled in terror before the prospect of the descent into the earth. Nor was the quality of the labor skilful and sustained. Unpleasant conditions and danger made workers reluctant to come out at all, as did attachment to a traditional way of life. Coercion, therefore, was resorted to in the form of the poll tax payable in cash, and the sanctions of Masters and Servants laws which made desertion a criminal, not a civil, offense. Faced with these problems of supply, employers found that international labor flows might supply the lower end of the market as well as the upper. Thus, from before the mining revolution, Africans from beyond the boundaries of the states of the future Union of South Africa came to work there, and Indian indentured labor was supplied to the sugar-cane growers of Natal, from 1860 on. With the coming of mining the use of foreign labor increased at once, and for a brief period labor was recruited in China.

The effects of international flows on local populations are difficult to assess. Some were bypassed, ignored or thrust aside by the development

55. E. P. Thompson, "Time, Work Discipline and Industrial Capitalism," *Past and Present*, 38, (1967):56–97.

process; but presumably constraints on growth were thereby removed and there was the possibility that the early victims would later be integrated into the modern economy. Moreover, since the 1930s, the increased flow of foreign workers to the mines did not necessarily bypass local populations since alternative employment opportunities were being developed. But, as we have noted, their presence kept wages low for those South African–born workers who continued to work in the mines. However, within the peculiar economic circumstances of the gold-mining industry their availability also meant that ore was mined which would not otherwise have been mined—implying a longer lifetime for the industry and expanded flows of exports, incomes, and taxes. Foreign workers helped to keep mines open in the 1960s when the industry was contracting and mines were closing earlier than planned. It was in this industry and in those years that wage inequality between whites and blacks rose to an all-time peak of 20.9:1 in 1971.[56]

Since 1948 South Africa has been ruled by mobilized Afrikaners who have successfully pursued sectional and nationalist objectives. That success involved the use of state patronage and power to advance Afrikaner capital and to protect numerous whites (predominantly Afrikaners) from black competition in the social and economic domains. There has been a consequent attempt to preserve a monopoly of political control by suppressing black opposition and by attempting to impose a political version of segregation, the so-called Grand Apartheid, which hinged on a tightened system of "influx control" and on the prevention or reduction of black urbanization in the metropolitan areas.

The restrictions on black economic competition and the restraints on the family-based (as distinct from migrant-worker-based) urbanization of black people have jointly constituted a serious curb on the growth of the South African economy. By the early 1980s South Africa was underurbanized by world standards, for its average level of income;[57] it has thus foregone some of the economic advantages of extended agglomeration. Moreover, it has inhibited the entrepreneurial and accumulative activities of Indian, African, and colored businessmen by "group areas" restrictions and a range of other limitations, and has imposed something like two decades of deliberate underinvestment in black eduction. Faced with serious long-term problems of rapid population growth and the need to create from diverse elements a cultural and linguistic milieu which will sustain the common economy, South Africa chose to emphasize separateness in education; it stressed eco-

56. Lipton, *Capitalism and Apartheid,* p. 388.

57. Charles Simkins, *Four Essays,* the third essay on "Structural Change in the South African Economy and Urbanisation 1950–2000" at pp. 111 and 114–15 (Table 1).

nomically irrelevant English/Afrikaans language parity and tied increases in expenditures on black education to the black capacity to pay increased taxes. There was, surely, a significant economic cost to all this.

Of course there is another side to the story: the reduction of overt political unrest by the early 1960s, the tapping of Afrikaner economic potential, and the briefly increased flow of immigrants from Europe created an environment in which South African capitalism was able successfully to ride the world boom of the 1960s. Hence, perhaps, the allegations of the mutually supportive roles of white domination and capitalism, which were first enunciated around 1970.

It is important not to underestimate the extent to which the growth of the South African economy is dependent on the growth of the world economy. Thus Trevor Bell has pointed out that increases in unemployment in South Africa are paralleled by a similar trend (though at lower levels) in other parts of the world economy and that in both cases the proximate cause is a lower rate of growth of output and income.[58] We naturally accept complex influences of this kind, but wish to maintain our hypothesis that the *net* effect of the major political policies of the postwar period has been to slow economic growth below its maximum achievable level, within the restraints of the world economy.

During the most recent decade, the economic costs of government policy have risen dramatically. The level of political conflict in the country has had a negative effect on the rate of economic growth and on employment, and the settler state and society are in crisis. How does such a social and political system transform itself into an order acceptable to the colonized majority without precipitating chaos and economic retrogression? In the absence of a clear way forward, investors do not commit funds to the expansion of the capital stock and employment stagnates or contracts, and disinvestment and sanctions simply reinforce the negative spiral. Over a long haul, capitalist growth has subverted the government's attempts to balkanize the country and society, and has slowly swung the balance of social and economic power in favor of the masses of the population no matter what employers intended. The crisis itself has an inescapable political core. The economic gains we have sought to document may be preserved and extended or may crumble and diminish, for growth cannot be sustained in conditions of chronic disorder. The outcome will be determined, not by economic forces, but by the presence or absence of political courage and imagination, and a reasonable amount of luck.

58. Bell, "Issues in Unemployment, pp. 26–27.

Charles Simkins

12. Democratic Liberalism and the Dilemmas of Equality

"We want everything whites have." So said a school pupil in Soweto in 1985. Perhaps the best way to begin a review of liberal ideas about equality in the South African context is to distinguish the various meanings within this pupil's claim. In doing so, one exposes not only a number of the many faces of equality but also some of the different faces of liberalism; there are disagreements within liberalism itself over the conceptualization of equality and the justification of claims to it. The argument here will be in the tradition of what is sometimes called "egalitarian liberalism," outstandingly expounded by John Rawls in his *Theory of Justice;* other views, both liberal and nonliberal, will be considered in order to indicate what is at stake at certain important points.

A key problem for everyone is the assessment of realized conditions ("outcomes") in a context where people desire different ends. It is a particular problem for liberals because they regard such a diversity as desirable, ends being chosen by the confident, innovative individuals who should flourish in a liberal society. That A owns an expensive car while B does not is not necessarily a cause for complaint. B may have a bigger house than A. A and B may have identical command over resources but different tastes; in maximizing their utilities, i.e., their self-chosen ends, they make different choices (which may involve inequality in their money incomes). Any effort to equalize outcomes will make them both worse off in terms of their utilities. Many liberals have concluded that any attempt to equalize outcomes would be tantamount to fitting individuals to a Procrustean bed. Equality is relevant not at this level but at the level of opportunity, equality of opportunity being defined as "open competition for scarce opportunities," the career open to talents.[1] At first sight this approach might seem adequate for dealing with the claim of the Soweto pupil. The first move would be to say that if the claim were a claim for equality of outcomes, it would involve the adjustment of black culture and tastes until they corresponded to white culture and tastes. Since the speaker in particular or black people in general would be unlikely to want that, the claim cannot refer to equality of outcomes; it must refer to equality of opportunity.

Now it is certainly true that any liberal account of equality must include equality of opportunity as defined above. It is equally certain that the requirements of this equality are far from being satisfied in South African society at present. In regard to open competition for scarce jobs, a number of public-sector jobs are closed to black people at present; and, while black people are legally excluded from only a few private-sector jobs, customary barriers and recruitment practices mean that access to many more is far from equal. Change here must be part of any liberal program.

Yet, leaving political arrangements aside, it is unlikely that these changes alone would exhaust the meaning of the claim for equality of opportunity. The terms on which people compete for scarce opportunities also have to be part of the discussion. Radical critics of the concept of equality of opportunity have often charged that its implementation would end up in a hopelessly rigged game. At no stage are competitors for scarce resources equally placed, so that winners cannot attribute their victory to their deserts, or, more exactly, to their deserts alone. For instance, it may be argued that even if South African education were to be reformed in such a way that every pupil had access to educational resources of the same quality, differences of class and culture would still work against the claim that equality of opportunity had been established. The appropriate liberal response is not to deny the criticism a priori, nor to abandon the concept of equal opportunity. Rather, equal opportunity should be regarded as an abstract term whose concrete content may change with the advance of knowledge; relevant to the debate on equality of opportunity in education, for example, is research into its effects.

1. Anthony Flew, *The Politics of Procrustes: Contradictions of Enforced Equality* (New York: Prometheus, 1981), p. 45.

Radical egalitarianism, on the other hand, is grounded in nonindividualist assumptions. As Amy Guttman puts it, "the radical egalitarian argument is that an understanding of what constitutes an individual's interest cannot precede an understanding of what constitutes a desirable political community. Equality is considered a primary value insofar as it is constitutive of a fraternal social order, regardless of whether fraternity is in the interest of all individual citizens."[2] Here liberals must be on their guard against a theoretical and practical propensity of radical egalitarianism to discount individual judgment, dissent, and criticism.

But is there a liberal way forward? If a narrow equality of opportunity, usually accompanied by a possessive individualist[3] account of property rights, is inadequate to liberals, and if radical egalitarianism is equally so, can another view of the matter be advanced? The first challenge is to deal with the diversity-of-ends problem. Rawls's introduction of the notion of primary goods is designed for the purpose: Primary goods "are things which it is supposed a rational man wants whatever else he wants. . . . With more of these goods men can generally be assured of greater success in carrying out their intentions and in advancing their ends, whatever these ends may be. The primary social goods, to give them in broad categories, are rights and liberties, opportunities and powers, income and wealth. A very important primary good is a sense of one's own worth. . . ."[4] This move makes it possible to focus the discussion of equality on a limited number of issues, particularly on enabling conditions for the realization of ends (conceived by Rawls to be embedded in rational plans of life) rather than on the realization itself, maintaining a distinction necessary to a liberal account.

Rawls's first category of primary social goods comprises rights and liberties; according to his first (and prior) principle, these should be distributed equally within a system of liberty which is as extensive as possible consistent with equal liberty for all persons. The second category of goods comprises such things as opportunities and powers, income and wealth. Under the second principle these may be distributed unequally provided that the distribution is to the long-term benefit of the least advantaged persons in society, and that there is fair equality of opportunity. These principles are derived from the Rawlsian version of the social contract. Suppose individuals knowing general social laws were to agree on a particular social form ignorant of the particular

2. Amy Guttman, *Liberal Equality* (London: Cambridge University Press, 1980), p. 219.

3. The phrase "possessive individualism" is taken from C. B. McPherson's *The Political Theory of Possessive Individualism* and refers to the "conception of the individual as essentially the proprietor of his own person or capacities, owing nothing to society for them," p. 3.

4. John Rawls, *A Theory of Justice* (London: Oxford University Press, 1971), p. 92.

position they would occupy in it. Then that form would be just, argues Rawls, and further it would satisfy his two principles. This hypothetical agreement accords with ordinary notions that fairness is a product of disinterested analysis and judgment according to general rules.

Rawls's work has been much discussed and there are criticisms at every stage in the argument. Radical critics have charged that the notion of the abstract individual party to the hypothetical agreement is incoherent, a view consonant with their refusal to impute interests to individuals prior to their incorporation into a political community. Libertarian critics on the right complain that Rawls does not give adequate consideration either to the rights of property or to moral deserts. Indeed, one of the differences between Rawls and his right-libertarian critics is that Rawls's system implies that property rights are to be deduced from the principles of justice whereas they suppose them to be supplied, independently of distributive considerations, by Lockean arguments.

The radical critique deserves some attention at this point. Attempts have been made to conceptualize a "social subject" whose existence is in some sense prior to the individual subject. A sophisticated Marxist analysis (in this case, of the "class subject") was provided by Georg Lukacs;[5] a more accessible discussion of many of the issues is provided by Michael Sandel.[6] Sandel argues that it is equally justifiable to aggregate desires into "systems of desire . . . an order or structure of shared values partly constitutive of a common identity or form of life" as it is to conflate desires within individuals, as Rawls does. He further argues that the Rawlsian self is too thin to be morally robust and that it is without capacity for serious relationships with others, and he backs his arguments by criticism of the Rawlsian analysis of benevolence, friendship, and love. Now, a liberal could concede that individuals are partly constituted by their enduring attachments and affections and that plans of life are affected by these. Because we are social beings, the view of the good society as one in which our entire duty is to act in accordance with social norms has much to commend it. Liberals can learn much from Charles Taylor's analysis of Hegelian thought.[7] Visions of this sort offer a more richly expressive account of the good society than the drier accounts common within liberalism. They also offer accounts of the relationship between individual and society which are worth taking seriously. Nonetheless, in all actual situations, and in South Africa in particular, the normative promptings of our collective

5. Georg Lukacs, *History and Class Consciousness* (London: Merlin, 1971).
6. Michael Sandel, *Liberalism and the Limits of Justice* (New York: New York University Press, 1984), p. 161.
7. Charles Taylor, *Hegel* (London: Cambridge University Press, 1975).

attachments often point away from the requirements of justice, whose demands can only be discerned by an effort of abstraction of the type described by Rawls (What if everybody . . . ? Would I think it fair . . . ? and especially, Would I agree to . . . if I could turn out to be a party in the agreement?) If liberalism in South Africa is to make progress it must be constituted by individuals from the greatest variety of contexts proposing answers to these questions. South African liberals may be called precisely not to be spokesmen of particular group or class interests. The attraction is the search for a just constitution within which these interests may first find expression and compete.

A use of the Rawlsian framework, therefore, is the most fruitful way to proceed; what is now needed is a consideration of what justice requires in respect of the distribution of each of the primary goods. The priority of the first principle of justice implies that the constitutional question is the most important aspect of equality for liberals. Our Sowetan pupil was probably in no doubt about the political aspect of his claim; in this he would be in agreement with much of black opinion. The principle of equal liberty, says Rawls, "requires that all citizens are to have an equal right to take part in, and to determine the outcome of, the constitutional process that establishes the laws with which they are to comply. Also the constitution is to be framed so that of all the feasible just arrangements, it is the one most likely to result in a just and effective system of legislation."[8] This implies: a constitutional regime, with a representative and accountable legislature; free and fair and regularly held elections; freedom of speech, assembly, and political association; the same weight for each vote, each adult having one; equal eligibility for public office; and limits on the ability of the wealthy to influence the political process.

All these (except perhaps the last) are standard liberal positions and by now have become part of South African liberalism. But an important question remains: Can there be a liberal justification for a system of racial estates—a legal imposition of racial identity—within the South African constitution? Alfred Hoernlé argued in 1939 that segregationist, parallel, and assimilationist policies could all be provided with liberal justifications in principle, because they all could provide an end to domination by one group if they were pursued with the necessary resolve.[9] He doubted, however, that the necessary resolution for any of the paths would be found. Certainly, the current South African constitution is a hybrid of segregationist (the homelands) and parallel (the tricameral Parliament) forms which denies large sections of the African

8. Rawls, *Theory of Justice,* p. 221.

9. R. F. A. Hoernlé, *South African Native Policy and the Liberal Spirit* (Lovedale: Lovedale Press, 1939), Chapter IV.

population any representation at all. It is far from satisfying the principle of equal liberty.

Here it might be argued that segregationist and parallel forms are capable of taking on a more liberal aspect. After a generation of separate but plainly unequal policies, some now propose a policy of separate but equal. Against this, South African liberals have long been fond of quoting the 1954 U.S. Supreme Court finding in *Brown v. Board of Education* that separate education is inherently unequal. The reason for this finding is less well known: that segregation inevitably induces feelings of inferiority in less advantaged groups and so prevents them from making the best use of opportunities. Segregation, often defended as a means to "group self-determination," functions to preserve relations of inequality; if it had not the latter effect, it would be harder to account for its imposition. Many of the illiberal aspects of the present constitution are there precisely to deny equal liberty: that is the reason for segregationist and parallel forms.

More interestingly, Rawls holds that "the most extensive political liberty is established by a constitution that uses the procedure of so-called bare majority rule (the procedure in which a minority can neither override nor check a majority) for all significant political decisions unimpeded by any constitutional constraints. Whenever the constitution limits the scope and authority of majorities, either by requiring a greater plurality for certain types of measures, or by a bill of rights restricting the powers of the legislature, and the like, equal political liberty is less extensive."[10] Rawls is not saying that bills of rights, entrenched clauses, or minority vetoes are out of the question for the egalitarian liberal, but that they have to be argued for in particular circumstances.

There would appear to be a case for these constraints in an attempt to construct a liberal constitutional order in South Africa. It would have to be constructed in a society of originally separate groups interacting with varying degrees of dominance and subordination and hostility as well as cooperation. It would have to contend with the lack of an overarching political tradition and with attitudes left over from decades of apartheid. For an initial period, at least, there might be substantial shifts in political identity. Moreover, the destructive tradition might be continued whereby a parliamentary majority holds even the most basic rights and liberties of others in contempt. This could be guarded against by both a justiciable bill of rights and by allowing for a veto by a substantial minority on a range of issues covered by Rawls's first principle of justice and the equality-of-opportunity portion of the second. Two other provisions would be important: proportional representation, which

10. Rawls, *Theory of Justice*, p. 224.

would not penalize smaller groups and would facilitate regroupings as identities changed; and entrenchment of the constitution, which would stabilize a new system while actors become accustomed to it, while permitting later amendments having firm popular and widespread support.

It should be noted that these constraints do not one-sidedly protect a particular group of people. They do not deal with social and economic inequalities. They do not protect whites only, or even whites, coloreds, and Asians only. Unless the support required for a minority veto were to be set at an unjustifiably low level, none of these groups alone would be able to exercise it. And there is no reason to suppose that any of these groups would return a politically homogeneous set of political representatives, any more than to suppose that black opinion would be homogeneous. It is not so now, and there would be less reason for it to be so once the disabilities on black people as a class are removed. One can see no reason why any group might not need the protection of the constraints: that they bear equally on all citizens is a powerful argument for their adoption.

Historically, South African liberals have differed in their conceptions of a desirable economic system, some advocating an unencumbered free market and others something close to democratic socialism; and even those who accept the Rawlsian formulation of liberalism may disagree over the precise nature of economic institutions best fitted to improve the position of the poorest as quickly as possible. However, the list of particulars involved in political equality would not, on the whole, be contested by liberals who favor a pure "free enterprise" system except perhaps for the last of Rawls's constitutional provisions, namely the constraint on the use of wealth for political purposes and the corresponding public duty to supply resources to encourage free public discussion. The purpose of this provision is to admit all citizens to the public forum in which proposals can be made and debated; without it, the wealthy are enabled to purchase what money ought not to be able to buy—a disproportionate influence on the course of legislation.

And what of the liberal response to radical egalitarianism? We have now and shall have in the future a range of groups offering their vision of freedom and fulfillment. Some will ask for the power to force dissenters to be free for their own good. Liberals have two duties here: first, to work for conditions under which these visions can be articulated and tested by being brought into the civilized conversation (Michael Oakeshott's fine phrase) that politics in a liberal society ought to be. Second, they ought to resist firmly those visions that threaten to restrict liberty to a level below what it might be. The liberal response to the

Freedom Charter is a case in point.[11] It may be seriously doubted whether all the items in the Charter are capable of simultaneous realization; it is even more questionable whether the demands of the Charter are compatible with any robust concept of freedom at all. But the argument cannot properly be had at all until institutions are designed to allow free speech and an open political debate. Our history means that many of the utopias proposed will have the narrowness associated with limited education and isolation, and a harshness born of frustration and resentment; there will, almost certainly, be much to criticize in proposed new arrangements. Mere criticism, however, will not suffice; a liberal political style will seek to take people from where they are, to make them aware of the range of possible alternatives, to overcome the extreme fragmentation of opinion and organization and to create a unified national forum for debate.

At the constitutional level, then, the liberal response to the claim "We want everything whites have" is that it at once may claim too much and too little. On the one hand, if it is a claim for the kind of power that, while certainly exercised before 1948, has monstrously grown since that date into a naked coercion, disguised by a corrupt political discourse in which opponents of the government are denied access to places of public discussion—if it is that sort of claim, then it claims too much, because that kind of power should not exist. On the other hand, it should be noted that even among white people the political liberties enjoyed fall short of the maximum that is possible, even subject to equal liberty for all. A liberal system would extend, not contract, the range of liberties envisaged by the first principle of justice.

A further discussion of equality of opportunity and equality of respect is now needed. Anthony Flew's[12] notion of equality of opportunity as open competition for scarce resources contrasts with Rawls's view in that it assures that the social system (the "system of cooperation" as he terms it, arising from the hypothetical agreement) is one of pure procedural justice. Under suitable background conditions, social processes may in themselves guarantee just results: if there is equality of opportunity, there is no need and no justification for amending the outcomes of these processes. In general, Rawls's principle will permit inquiry into the background conditions that produce competitors for scarce resources, whereas Flew's principle is designed to shut such inquiry off. Rawls's principle, therefore, makes space for the justification

11. The Freedom Charter was adopted by a Congress of the People at Kliptown, near Johannesburg, in 1955. The Charter is given in full and discussed in detail by Sean Archer in chapter 20 of this volume.

12. Flew, *Politics in Procrustes.*

of, say, affirmative action programs, though whether a particular program would be justified depends on arguments about the particular case. The general test is: would a society with or without the program be judged superior by parties in the original (hypothetical) position—i.e., from the point of view of fairness?

For Rawls one of the primary goods is self-respect, which he sees as including the formulation of a rational plan of life, confidence in its value and in one's ability to carry it out. It is not fanciful to suppose that the worst damage done by apartheid is not to the material conditions of life, but to the self-respect of most South Africans. The issue surfaces from time to time but is not discussed in proportion to its importance. Lack of self-respect leads to apathy and cynicism; it creates a moral and intellectual wasteland. It robs social institutions of the moral significance they might have and it saps the self-confidence to strive for just social arrangements. On the recovery of self-respect and the ability to see social institutions as, and to shape them into, systems of cooperation, the whole South African liberal project depends. In this respect, current circumstances are not auspicious. A case in point is the loss that South Africa has inflicted upon itself in the last couple of years because of the loss of foreign confidence in the economy and the growing set of political restrictions on trade.

At this point a note on the relationship between liberalism and nationalism is appropriate. If nationalism at the cultural level is constituted by the attempt to define an "imagined community," as Benedict Anderson suggests, one can easily see its relevance in terms of the adoption of a rational plan of life, which, after all, is not decided upon in solitude. The imagined community has places and tasks for people, the content of which needs to be subjected to evaluation. South African liberalism came into conflict with Afrikaner nationalism because the nationalist sense of community was exclusive and entailed the imposition of economic and political injustice as well as an unwarranted cultural hegemony. Liberalism will also have to deal with a *black* nationalism which logically cannot adopt the same unjust policies as Afrikaner nationalism; however, it may adopt others and will have to be evaluated on its own performance. Liberals may find much cause for approbation if self-respect is increased. Nonetheless, a certain critical distance is essential. It would be as well to be vigilant on behalf of fair equality of opportunity, the right of dissent, and the compliance of economic policies with the Rawlsian criterion discussed below.

Rawls's stress on a self-chosen plan of life can be contrasted with alternative views. One alternative is utilitarianism which sets up the satisfactions of individuals as a social welfare function to be maximized. It is well known that utilitarianism has difficulty in supporting a theory of rights and justice; what is important here, however, is that, although it is capable of giving an account of a plan of life in terms of an intertemporal structure of preferences, it attaches no more importance to this than to any other set of desires. Utilitarianism does not, in other words, support such a clear account of self-respect and individual autonomy as the Rawlsian notion that justice is produced by reflection on what would be agreed to by persons devising social arrangements without knowledge of their particular circumstances. On the other hand, radical egalitarianism often proposes a plan of life but without provision for individuals to choose to adopt it for themselves or not, this omission being justified by a theory of where people's real interests lie.

There remains the discussion of equality of income and wealth. This has been left for last precisely because the Soweto pupil's claim is most likely to be interpreted in an economic sense. The preceding discussion has been designed to illustrate how much more there is to a liberal account of equality than this. But while liberals are not vulgar materialists, they have no grounds for refusing to attend to economic inequality.

If the pupil's claim is regarded as a claim to income and if "everything whites have" is interpreted as "everything whites have now," then the claim is impossible to satisfy and will be so for the next two generations. (Proof: In 1980 whites constituted 16 percent of the population and absorbed 62 percent of personal income. White per capita incomes were therefore 3.87 times as high as average per capita income. The claim could be satisfied when average income has grown 3.87 times. At a respectable real per capita growth rate of 2 percent per annum, this would take 68 years.) There is a subtler point that will need to be borne in mind in the coming years. Part of what whites have now is a discrimination premium, originating from an ability to restrict supply in one way or another. The labor market has been growing more competitive in recent years; nonetheless, premiums of this sort certainly still exist. They cannot be generalized to the whole population; we cannot all be discriminators, and the result of equal access will be a downward pressure on many job-specific earnings. All over Africa the complaint has been heard: "Just when we get the jobs, they become less well paid." Ah yes; it is precisely greater access which has rendered supply more plentiful and depressed the wage.

If there are senses in which it is impossible, for reasons of logic or scarcity, to satisfy our claim, there is also a sense in which all liberals would agree that it is justified. The claim can be interpreted as a claim to equality of entitlement in respect of publicly supplied goods. Liberals will disagree as to the proper scope of entitlements; where these exist, however, they must be awarded in accordance with the equal opportunity part of Rawls's second principle. There can be no liberal justification, for instance, of the present racial pattern of educational spending. One of the most important tasks of the coming years in South Africa is the reform of entitlement expenditures to make them conform with the requirements of justice.

But the economic component of our claim cannot be given only this interpretation. There is a more general claim about the distribution of income and wealth which, when considered, shows up the tension within liberal thought very sharply. The division is between those who, like Rawls, consider property rights variable, to be defined and redefined as social circumstances change so as to maximize the position of the least well off, and those, like Robert Nozick,[13] who wish to justify a set of property rights on fixed grounds regardless of social circumstances. Nozick derives the fixed bundle of property rights using Lockean arguments. For him, an asset is justly held if it has been created justly or transferred justly; if holdings do not arise from a sequence of just creations and just transfers, they are not held justly and those wronged are entitled to compensation. Critics assert that these arguments are simply unsupportable in a great number of societies, including industrial societies. The Rawlsian position assumes that property is a relation rather than a thing, a relation whose elements are constantly changing. Changes in legislation controlling pollution or regulating industrial relations constitute amendments to property rights. The Rawlsian approach is essentially prospective; a measure is just if it leads to a long-term improvement in the prospects of the least advantaged. In the end, entitlement to assets and the form of the collection of rights implied by that entitlement is conditional upon holders putting those assets to the best possible use in terms of the interest of the poorest.

In general, the Nozickian position has been interpreted as the more conservative of the two, involving as it does a defense of a fuller and more unconditional range of property rights. Ironically, this may not be the case in the special circumstances of South Africa. Arguments are certainly possible about the details, but it can hardly be denied that historically a great deal of property has been transferred unjustly, largely from blacks to whites. Application of the compensation principle would therefore involve a great deal of asset transfer, not necessarily from the richest whites or to the poorest blacks. On the other hand, while a Rawlsian would certainly advocate some asset transfer, especially of land, and while he would also want the institution of compensation to rectify clear and present wrongs, it might be that the process of adjustment in property rights and holdings implied by Rawlsian principles would

13. Robert Nozick, *Anarchy, State and Utopia* (Oxford: Blackwell, 1974).

be a good deal less abrupt than a rigorous application of the Nozickian principle of rectification. This implication may not be entirely understood by some South African Nozickians.

More important are the implications of the Rawlsian interpretation of our claims. Existing economic arrangements ought to be subjected to a Rawlsian critique. The indications are that such a critique would yield the result that much has to be done, without necessarily having to overturn the entire present order. In a number of respects the structure of the South African economy has reached a point where rapid reduction of poverty would be possible if Rawlsian policies were followed. The division of labor is changing to produce a larger proportion of better jobs and is already inducing substantial social mobility in some communities. There are considerable opportunities in agriculture for higher production, more employment and better wages. However unsatisfactory the quality of education, capacity for handling increased numbers of pupils has been created—opportunities for improving quality can be exploited in a liberal dispensation, some of them quite rapidly. Labor absorption is a major problem, but even this can be alleviated by means (such as public works programs and small business promotion) which would have a direct impact on the poor.[14] South African income distribution has been very unequal for most of this century; yet in the last fifteen years more progress has been made toward equalization than is often supposed. The continuation and strengthening of this trend is the task that lies ahead. It is not fanciful to imagine that the removal of remaining illiberal policies would lift a number of constraints on growth. More growth accompanied by greater equality: what better formula for the improvement of the material position of the poor could there be?

It is sometimes supposed that there is something spoiling about an emphasis on equality, that it involves a commitment to "leveling down" and a destruction of excellence. An egalitarian must reply that what really spoils human lives is lack of respect, lack of the power to participate in the political life of the society, and economic disparities not justified by the difference principle. We have seen where inequality in all these dimensions has landed us. Realization of South Africa's potential to support a rich and diverse social fabric depends on the implementation of an egalitarian program. As it proceeds, the use of "what whites have," especially at present, will come to seem more and more inadequate as a standard.

14. For a more detailed account, see Charles Simkins, *Reconstructing South African Liberalism* (Johannesburg: South African Institute of Race Relations, 1986).

Johan Degenaar

13. Nationalism, Liberalism, and Pluralism

The possibility of large-scale conflict in South Africa has been a subject of anxious discussion for years, but especially since the Second World War. Some authors such as Alan Paton have seen liberals, black and white, playing a crucial role in mitigating that violence: "If Black power meets White power in headlong confrontation and there are no Black liberals and White liberals around," he wrote, "then God help South Africa."[1] In the hope of contributing to effective change, I here explore the rhetoric of nationalism, liberalism, and pluralism in search of an appropriate political model for South Africa that will avoid headlong confrontation. I look at the nature of white and black nationalisms in South Africa, discuss the nature of liberalism in relationship to nationalism, and then introduce the notion of pluralism as a means of clarifying two crucial political terms, ethnicity and group rights.

Nationalism is an ideology, an action-oriented system of ideas, according to which the highest political loyalty is owed to the nation. If I had to reduce nationalism to one basic principle, my choice would be that of self-determination. Of course, manifestations of nationalism are historical phenomena and each manifestation requires analysis on its own terms, within its context of historical, social, and economic influences. I write here, however, not as a social historian, but as a

1. Alan Paton, *Knocking on the Door* (Cape Town: Philip, 1975), p. 258.

philosopher. I introduce ideal-typical descriptions of ideologies that enable me to identify ideas that are in clearcut opposition.

Among the various kinds of nationalism, for example, I concentrate here only on the distinction between constitutional nationalism and nationalism-of-the-people, also called *volk* nationalism. Constitutional nationalism combines the liberal principle of the freedom of the individual with the national principle of the autonomy, the self-determination, of the nation-state. In order to protect the freedom of the individual while adhering to the sovereignty of the nation, constitutions frequently include a bill of rights as a guarantor of individual freedom. *Volk* nationalism, on the other hand, gives priority to the *volk,* viewed as a historic, culturally homogeneous group, with the result that the individual is invariably depreciated in favor of the collective personality.

Liberalism in South Africa has to cope with both Afrikaner and African nationalism if it is to achieve constitutional nationalism. Neither Afrikaner nor African nationalism has a monolithic structure. Nationalism has manifested itself in the history of the Afrikaner in at least five areas: self-determination, *volk,* race, structure, and power;[2] all of these forces are mobilized by the Afrikaner in the process of identifying himself with nationality as the primary source of political obligation. Here, however, I concentrate only on the first two of these areas, self-determination and *volk.*

The historian F. A. van Jaarsveld has documented numerous examples of liberation rhetoric and self-determination terminology used by Afrikaner nationalists in the nineteenth century: expressions such as "*ontwakening van den Afrikaansche geest*" ("awakening of the Afrikaans spirit"), "*de tegenwoordige nationale herleving*" ("the present national revival"), and "*barensweën van die nationale wedergeboorte*" ("labor pains of national rebirth").[3] In his summary of the characteristics of the awakening national consciousness, van Jaarsveld referred to: a sense of injustice and an offended dignity; an attachment to the *volk* and the fatherland, which leads to pride in achievements; an urge toward self-preservation and national identity; a sense of destiny and predestination; and a love for the past of the *volk,* which projects a national consciousness backward in time, true to the precept that a nation, of necessity, creates its own past. All of these sentiments were mobilized by Afrikaner intellectuals and political leaders in the twentieth century, especially during the 1930s, and in 1948 the National party (NP), using the

2. J. J. Degenaar, *The Roots of Nationalism* (Pretoria: Academica, 1982), discusses these five categories.

3. F. A. van Jaarsveld, *The Awakening of Afrikaner Nationalism 1868–1881* (Cape Town: Human and Rousseau, 1961).

apartheid policy as its platform, exploited its victory in the election to consolidate the position of Afrikaner nationalism. In 1961 Afrikaner nationalism, which was the most appropriate vehicle for self-determination, reached its zenith by achieving its historic constitutional objective, the creation of the Republic.

There is a close connection between the realization of having one's own language, the recognition of being involved in a unique history, and the claim to being a people with a divine calling, for, as in many other nationalisms, the myth of the chosen people functions in the Afrikaner's self-definition. Many examples can be given of the nationalist view that the individual Afrikaner finds his true identity through the act of identification with the *volk.* It is this ideological commitment that has made it so difficult for the Afrikaner to define himself in liberal terms.

Since 1961 certain changes have taken place within the ideological framework of the NP, for example, the broadening of Afrikaner nationalism toward an inclusive white nationalism, and even toward a co-optative multiracial nationalism, through the admission of colored and Asian leaders into a tricameral Parliament. This latter creation is not a genuine sharing of power, and the government remains unwilling to really share the governing process with anyone, and still excludes blacks from the new co-optative scheme. While Afrikaners may be willing to share a measure of power with other groups, they do not want to lose control. Afrikaner nationalists have clearly not yet made the crucial choice for constitutional nationalism, by which the constitution would become an agent in the creation of an all-embracing South African nation rather than simply the embodiment of a nation already in existence.

Nationalism among Africans, like Afrikaner nationalism, is also a complex phenomenon: there are several movements in which national consciousness can be clearly discerned. According to Leo Kuper, the basis of African nationalism is "a perception of a common racial identity, a shared historical experience of subordination, and a common civic status in South African society."[4] Of these perceptions there are many examples, but how they will be integrated into a single story of African nationalism is not yet clear.[5]

4. L. Kuper, "African Nationalism in South Africa, 1919–1964," in Monica Wilson and Leonard Thompson, eds., *The Oxford History of South Africa* 2 (Oxford: Clarendon, 1971), p. 424.

5. Some of the ideas and formulations used in this section on African nationalism are taken from my article on "Nationalism" in D. J. van Vuuren and D. J. Kriek, eds., *Political Alternatives for Southern Africa. Principles and Perspectives* (Pretoria: Butterworths, 1983), pp. 69–83. For a discussion of some of the problems related to the use of the concept of

Africans were not accepted as full and equal participants at the founding of Union in 1910. In 1912 in protest they formed the South African Native National Congress (later the African National Congress or ANC), with the purpose of representing all Africans in a central organization. They rejected ethnic parochialism by blacks in favor of a potentially broad South African nationhood, inclusive of all racial groups, that was still to evolve. This ideal, they hoped, would come about through a process of reform and would therefore have to be realized within a white-dominated state. Important divisions among Africans in their commitments to nationalism began to develop: the "integrationist" nonracist nationalism of the ANC was opposed by black-power nationalism, which emerged during the Second World War. Its slogan "Africa for the Africans" regarded South Africa as the home of the blacks; whites were the intruders. Within the ANC itself, the Youth League also rejected the concept of a (black) nation within a (white) nation. "Africans comprised not *a* nation within the boundaries of South Africa, but in fact were, by right of indigenous origins and preponderant numbers, *the* nation, and the only nation, entitled to claim and to rule South Africa."[6] In 1949 the Youth League adopted a radical program of action, which gave birth to terms like "nation-building," "national freedom," "political independence," and "self-determination," all examples of typical nationalist rhetoric.

However, the ANC remained a moderate organization. The Freedom Charter of 1955, whose drafting was heavily influenced by the ANC, states that "South Africa belongs to all who live in it, black and white, and . . . no government can justly claim authority unless it is based on the will of all the people." The Africanists within the ANC, rejecting this so-called "realistic" approach, adopted a more radical line; they opted for an exclusive African nationalism as the only ideology that could mobilize blacks. Nationalism, "the political philosophy of the man in the kraal," was seen as the cornerstone of the African's struggle for liberation.[7] In April 1958 the Africanists founded the Pan-Africanist Congress (PAC). Its slogan was also "Africa for the Africans," its program an explicitly *African* nationalism which referred to Africans' "deep, undefined yearning for self-realization, self-expression, and nationhood," to the "divine destiny of nationhood," and to the inner logic of "national nationalism."[8] Both the moderate ANC and the more doctrinaire PAC were banned in 1960. In the late 1960s the black-consciousness

nation, see N. Alexander, "Approaches to the National Question in South Africa," *Transformation* 1 (1986):63–95.

6. Gail M. Gerhart, *Black Power in South Africa: The Evolution of an Ideology* (Berkeley: University of California Press, 1979), p. 67.

7. Ibid., p. 148.

8. Ibid., pp. 217, 232.

movement revived the liberation rhetoric of African nationalism, including a broader conception of a nationalism of all oppressed groups, which found particular success on black campuses. Consequently, the continued banning of these and other organizations during the 1970s did not succeed in extinguishing the struggle for national emancipation. For example, in April 1978, when the Azanian Peoples' Organisation was founded, it placed itself unequivocably in the black-consciousness camp under the banner "One people, one Azania."[9]

The period since the Soweto uprisings in 1976 was one of rising political consciousness, especially among black youth. The ANC has been a major beneficiary of this process, and since 1985 has gained ascendancy as one of the chief contenders for power in South Africa. By way of summary one can say that since that time the South African scene has been dominated by the dialectic of the struggle for liberation by African nationalism and the suppression of this struggle by Afrikaner nationalism, each manifestation of nationalism claiming supreme loyalty. Liberals need to understand what African nationalism means to the ANC, but unfortunately the banning of ANC publications has made it impossible for other South Africans to come to the necessary critical assessment of its thinking on this issue.

It would be an oversimplification to define the conflict in South Africa primarily in terms of a clash between Afrikaner nationalism and black nationalism, but the conflict between white and black cannot be historically divorced from claims made by two opposing nationalisms in the same country.

One of the many tasks of liberals in South Africa is to define their own position in relation to both of these opposing nationalisms. Afrikaner nationalists, for their part, see liberalism as a threat because it entails equal rights for blacks. Black nationalists striving toward power, on the other hand, see liberalism as a drawback because it tends to insist on peaceful change and on guarantees for all individuals and all minorities.

The liberal regards as his ultimate objective the protection and enhancement of individual freedom from constraints, a freedom usually viewed as based on natural rights. He therefore opposes the choice of the nation as the primary value, as that choice is expressed, for example, in one extreme statement by an Afrikaner nationalist that "the individual in itself is nothing, but only becomes itself in the nation as the highest

9. R. Davies, D. O'Meara, and S. Dlamini, *The Struggle for South Africa* 2 (London: Zed, 1984), pp. 308–10.

(human) community."[10] The idea of individual freedom is as old and respectable as Western civilization itself. The world of liberalism is rich and complex principally because the value of freedom is linked to so many other values that came to the fore in Western culture, for example, the values of human dignity and development of the personality, all to be secured by freedom of association, freedom of speech, the rule of law, representative government, an independent judiciary, and an institutional pluralism that divides church, state, and university from each other.

Tension between liberalism and nationalism can become acute when nationalism takes an extreme form, as in *volk* nationalism. However, South African history includes examples of a nationalism among Afrikaners that showed signs of being influenced by liberal principles. The notion of liberal nationalism as explored by N. P. van Wyk Louw, for example, represented in a limited way a realization among Afrikaner intellectuals that the concept of *volk* had become for other groups a symbol of domination because the Afrikaner had defined his nationalism in exclusive terms, inevitably entailing domination of those excluded. Louw, in speaking of coloreds as Afrikaners, showed a willingness to introduce a concept of nationalism that was based on mother tongue rather than on race. He nonetheless fell short of true liberalism because for him blacks remained outside the *volk*.[11] The government itself in including coloreds and Asians in the tricameral Parliament, has made a similar, partial move, but also in a halfhearted way. It continues to exclude blacks and therefore must take responsibility for any violent eruptions that occur among those excluded from full citizenship. This exclusion was a fatal mistake on the side of Afrikaner nationalists: it has triggered for the majority of the population total rejection of the government's claim to legitimacy. It has further evoked the demand by many black nationalists for transfer of power without negotiation.[12]

The choice of the liberal, on the other hand, must be constitutional nationalism, based on a constitution that fosters a process of political negotiation toward the establishment and maintenance of an inclusive nationality. Constitutional nationality, therefore, cannot be the organic extension of a dominant ethnic group; it must be the product of a constitution and of processes of creative cooperation which it in turn

10. Quoted by W. A. de Klerk, *The Puritans in Africa: A History of Afrikanerdom* (Harmondsworth: Penguin, 1976), p. 204.

11. N. P. van Wyk Louw, "Voorwoord" in D. P. Botha, *Die Opkoms van ons Derde Stand* (Cape Town: Human en Rousseau, 1960), pp. v–x.

12. E.g., the statement in *The Leader* as quoted in the *Cape Times*, 21 April 1986: "Azapo, and indeed of late, Nelson Mandela himself, are of the opinion that there is nothing to discuss but the method of transferring power to the majority."

protects and encourages. The drafting of such a constitution by joint effort would itself be an important first step both in creating an inclusive nationalism and in arriving at constitutional arrangements that could be called just.

To achieve a more just political order, Afrikaner nationalists must transcend racist nationalism, and black nationalists will need to resist the lure of a racist exclusivism of their own. Both need to channel their national fervor into a broader South African nationalism.

If liberals are to play a role in a process of constitutional nationalism, they must come to grips with the reality of ethnicity in politics, and with the controversial notions of group and minority rights. Historically, liberals have underestimated the force of ethnicity in politics, because of their political focus on individual freedom. They have assumed that the individual possesses inalienable natural rights to be respected by the state, to which the individual stood in a direct relationship. The intermediate relationship of ethnicity, that is, of individual to ethnic group, was viewed as a retrogression in the individual's self-development. Even today, many liberals still view the conflicts that result from opposing group interests as prejudices which impartial use of reason should readily resolve. Yet liberals should not, I believe, ignore ethnicity in favor of a concept of abstract rationality; the sense of belonging that ethnicity fosters should be respected as a legitimate way in which individuals can define themselves.

The liberal, especially in South Africa, is inclined to apply to politics the Westminster model of democracy, one effective in culturally homogeneous societies, to culturally heterogeneous societies where its limitations are exposed. In the 1930s Alfred Hoernlé pointed this out with regard to South Africa. South Africa's founding fathers might have been advised to use a federal constitutional model such as that in the United States, which might better have accommodated South Africa's social conflicts.[13] An institutionalized pluralism, a process of accommodation of intermediate ethnic groups into politics and of incorporating them effectively in the political process, is perhaps capable of solving this problem.

Two types of pluralism must be distinguished. In structural pluralism, the emphasis is placed on a plurality of institutions, e.g., state, church, and university, and of organizations, e.g., in business, the arts, and sports. In cultural pluralism, the emphasis is on the plurality of ethnic groups that constitute a society. Within the context of cultural pluralism

13. L. M. Thompson, *The Unification of South Africa* (Oxford: Clarendon, 1960), pp. 482–83.

Arend Lijphart distinguishes majoritarian democracy, institutionalized in the Westminster system, from consociational democracy, based on four principles of coalition government: a grand coalition of the political leaders of all significant segments, mutual veto, proportional representation, and autonomy of the segments; all four of these principles deviate from the principle of majority rule.[14] To this one might add the principle of equal economic distribution.

A principle of liberalism that is consistent with cultural pluralism is the notion of voluntary political association. Free association would lend flexibility to ethnicity, but it would also raise a crucial issue of free choice if, in fact, ethnic groups regard their ethnicity as anything but voluntary. The pluralist resists the notion of imposed ethnic identities and claims equal opportunities for members of all ethnic groups. He supports negotiation among ethnic groups in defense of their own interests. Since ethnicity inevitably plays a role in politics, it should, for the time being, be accommodated to play a positive role. However, the crosscutting of ethnic affiliation with institutional affiliation and the transcending of ethnic boundaries, say, through intermarriage, can eventually lead to ethnicity's progressive depoliticization.

In the present political climate in South Africa it is risky to raise the problem of ethnicity because it has been abused through servitude to the policy of apartheid as an integral part of nationalism, and has consequently been rejected by blacks as a symbol of oppression. Yet, referring to Lijphart's consociational model, Heribert Adam states: "In theory there seems nothing objectionable to the principle of *communal* representation, as compared with *individual* participation in the political process. . . . " Adam, however, points out that the consociational model is based on a depoliticized public, hardly a realistic assumption in South Africa. He notes that since both urbanized and rural blacks have become increasingly politicized, Lijphart's principle of the coalition of elites could have only a limited application there.[15]

Consociationalism would have more application in South Africa if politicized blacks were permitted to channel their political interests into the bargaining process without advance prescription on how the various pressure groups should be constituted. If Inkatha, the predominantly Zulu organization, led by M. G. Buthelezi, chooses to come into the bargaining process on the principle of communal representation and the ANC on pure ideological grounds, then both should be free to do

14. A. Lijphart, "Majority Rule versus Democracy in Deeply Divided Societies" in *Politikon*, 4:2 (1977), pp. 113–26.

15. Heribert Adam, "The Failure of Political Liberalism in South Africa" in H. Adam and H. Giliomee *The Rise and Crisis of Afrikaner Power* (Cape Town: David Philip, 1979), p. 52.

so. If, however, the majority are unwilling to enter into negotiation on any form of communal representation, the bargaining process can be organized instead on the basis of competing political parties, deliberating then the best way to protect the cultural interests of voluntarily organized ethnic communities. Adam argues in favor of this institutionalized multiculturalism as follows:

> One could ask why should there not be an exclusively Zulu, Afrikaner, Islamic or Hindu TV station and broadcasting facility in place of a state regulated uniform institution, espousing a correct line of official propaganda, as exists from Pretoria to Cairo at present? As long as such multiculturalism is supported by a large enough constituency and does not infringe on the common, overriding individual citizenship rights of its adherents, the diversity of "meaning-conferring activities" can only enrich the whole society. There are various legal forms and precedents which such cultural self-determination can emulate in a new non-racial South Africa. The PFP [Progressive Federal party] proposal of corporate "cultural councils," represented in an Upper House, is the most widely known suggestion. . . . The examples of legitimate cultural self-expression in South Africa are inextricably tied to two prerequisites: (a) that group boundaries and membership are no longer imposed but self-chosen; and (b) that no unequal political power and economic privilege is publicly bound up with private ethnicity and heritage maintenance.[16]

In this discussion of the political function of ethnicity I have deliberately refrained from introducing the controversial concept of group rights. I wanted rather to illustrate that the notion of ethnicity can be analyzed and evaluated positively without presupposing group rights. Yet because these two concepts have often been linked politically, our task is to assess the validity of this linkage.

"Right" in the sense of "human right" is a moral concept. A right (within an individualistic context) can be defined as a quality or value ascribed to human beings on the basis of which they can claim respect and equal treatment as persons. These values should not be seen as derived from a metaphysical reality but rather from the moral consciousness of human communities in their historical development. It is wiser to say that rights are *ascribed* to persons than to say that they *have* rights. Rights are values ascribed to persons by a community as it becomes conscious of its moral responsibility. But rights need not be ascribed only to individuals; rights become values ascribed also to human groups, and not only to human beings but also to animals and to nature as a whole.

Nathan Glazer and Daniel Patrick Moynihan refer to "the pronounced and sudden increase in tendencies by people in many countries and in many circumstances to insist on the significance of their group distinc-

16. Heribert Adam, "South Africa after Apartheid," *Cape Times*, 31 March 1986.

tiveness and identity and on new rights that derive from this group character."[17] Pluralism can overcome the individualistic bias of liberalism by granting that groups have a life of their own and can function as intermediates between individuals and the state. To these groups rights can be assigned; e.g., groups can not only claim (negatively) a space in which they can foster self-realization for their members, but they can also claim (positively) that the state should provide benefits to them, such as education in the mother tongue. Advocates of pluralism cite various examples of corporate groups that claim moral rights. Van Dyke distinguishes four kinds of groups to whom rights are ascribed in one way or another: racial (in Fiji, New Zealand, and the United States); linguistic (in Belgium and Switzerland); religious (in Northern Ireland and Cyprus); and national, as in the declaration of the Rights of Man, which states: "All sovereignty resides in the nation," that is, "the nation has a collective right to act as a unit, and the word 'essentially' suggests that the right is intrinsic, not delegated by individuals and not reducible."[18]

Many historic precedents and contemporary examples of racial, linguistic, religious, and national groups can be cited as corporate units to which moral rights are ascribed. The question can therefore be asked whether ethnic communities cannot equally be judged to be such groups. Van Dyke defines ethnic community as "a group of persons, predominantly of common descent, who think of themselves as collectively possessing a separate identity based on race or on shared cultural characteristics, usually language or religion."[19] Ethnic communities, by such a rationale, can be seen as corporate units with moral rights and thus deserving of legal status and legal rights.

The arguments for and against the practice of affirmative action illustrate the tension between liberal and pluralist ideologies. "Affirmative action" refers to a range of desegregation programs designed to help minorities gain access to institutions that would otherwise remain closed to them because of discriminating traditions and strong competition. The liberal individualist may be involved in a contradiction if he or she accepts the group orientation of affirmative-action programs; from an individualist point of view, such programs may seem to be reverse discrimination. A pluralist, however, may accept discrimination in favor of an underprivileged group as advancing compensatory justice: the community then would take responsibility for those groups which

17. N. Glazer and D. P. Moynihan, eds., *Ethnicity: Theory and Practice* (Cambridge, Mass.: Harvard University Press, 1976), p. 3.

18. V. van Dyke, "The Individual, the State and Ethnic Communities in Political Theory," *World Politics* (April 1977):351.

19. Ibid., p. 344.

have been discriminated against and left behind in a highly competitive society, accepting that certain individuals will be discriminated against as a result. Some individuals then gain special attention as members of an ethnic group which can claim a moral right to be treated differently because of past discrimination.[20]

The South African government has interpreted the concept of group rights over a long period to the advantage of whites. Yet such distortions of the concept of group rights in favor of group privilege should not invalidate the concept. One should rather introduce the principle of justice, to help evaluate the applications of the concept of group rights. Charles Simkins, who argues in favor of group rights, formulates three requirements of justice to be applied to the educational system: the basis of financing should be the same throughout the system; there should be a unitary system of public examination; and different cultures and groups should be accorded equal respect, a respect institutionalized within the educational system.[21]

Adam, in a positive assessment of constitutional group rights, similarly states that "a good case may be made for state recognition of collective cultural rights."[22] Various other writers have used this concept, with terminological shifts from "collective cultural rights" to "minority rights" to "the right to cultural self-determination," and with qualifications such as "voluntary membership," "availability to all groups," and "non-contravention of individual rights."[23] Although writers differ in the way these rights should be institutionalized, they agree that the concept is coherent and politically appropriate for plural societies. Still, most such writers admit that the theory of constitutional group rights remains a controversial concept, principally because it has been used by the South African government to justify group privileges and to fragment black

20. J. J. Degenaar, "Normative Dimensions of Discrimination, Differentiation and Affirmative Action," in H. W. van der Merwe and R. Schrire, eds., *Race and Ethnicity: South African and International Perspectives* (Cape Town: David Philip, 1980).

21. C. Simkins, "Reconstructing South African Liberalism" (unpublished lectures, University of Cape Town, August 1985), lecture 2, p. 21.

22. Adam, "South Africa after Apartheid."

23. N. Glazer, "Individual Rights against Group Rights," in E. Kamenka and A. E. Tay, eds., *Human Rights* (London: Edward Arnold, 1978), pp. 37–103; A. Lijphart, *Power-Sharing in South Africa* (Berkeley: University of California Press, 1985); L. Schlemmer, "South Africa at a Crossroads" (presidential address, South African Institute of Race Relations, Johannesburg, 30 November, 1985); F. van Zyl Slabbert and D. Welsh, *South Africa's Options: Strategies for Sharing Power* (Cape Town: David Philip, 1979); V. van Dyke, "Justice as Fairness; For Groups?" *American Political Science Review* 69 (1975):607–14; and M. Walzer, "Pluralism in Political Perspective," in M. Walzer, ed., *The Politics of Ethnicity* (Cambridge, Mass.: Belknap, 1982). It is worth noting that the second point of the Freedom Charter carries the heading "All national groups shall have equal rights" and that the second sentence of this section reads, "All people shall have equal right to use their own languages, and to develop their own folk culture and customs."

unity, and because most black liberationists have rejected the theory outright.[24]

Most pertinently for our present purpose, the pluralist concept has also been criticized from a liberal point of view.[25] Ian Macdonald argues in favor of the sovereignty of individual rights and asserts that all privileges which can legitimately be claimed by groups can be covered by a concept of individual rights. He cites the example of the rights of the university. However, since a university is an autonomous institution consisting of a group of people and organized according to a fixed set of rules, this amounts, it seems to me, to making a pluralist point. I do not see how the group rights of the university that originate and operate in the relationship between university and state can be translated merely into the rights of individuals to associate freely with this institution.

The nonpluralist liberal view allows Zulus to claim freedom of association to found a school based on mother-tongue education but denies them the right to claim that the state should provide public funding for such an education. The pluralist, by contrast, allows the Zulu community the group right to claim such provision from the state. A language community is an illustration of a communal dimension that structures an individual. Children are born into a language, and before they can freely choose what language they want to speak and which school they want to attend, they should be educated in their own language as a matter of right. The precontractual communal dimension of language can be expressed as follows: the individual does not choose his language, his language chooses him. Because of this, being born into a language community cannot be described merely in terms of a contractual model.

The nonpluralist liberal is also limited in his or her definition of religious rights, if he or she defines them primarily as freedom of conscience ascribed to the individual rather than as the rights of the collective body of the faithful, a preexisting community into which a believer is born. The importance of this difference can be illustrated by the practice of Catholicism and Protestantism in Northern Ireland. Of this group conflict Glazer says: "It would be play-acting . . . to try to solve the serious problems of group conflict by legislating the freedom of the practice of religion, for that is not the issue. The issue . . . is the relative economic and social positions of the two religious communities, not the free practice of religion."[26]

24. Schlemmer, "South Africa at a Crossroads," p. 12.

25. I. Macdonald, "Group Rights." This unpublished paper consists of comments on the first draft of my paper and is a good example of a philosophical exploration of some of the problems related to the concept of group rights.

26. Glazer, "Individual Rights against Group Rights," p. 90.

Macdonald seems to me correct in pointing out that not all claims by groups can be accepted as rights since the principles of justice must also apply. He summarizes five "tests" for group rights: "(a) group membership must not be imposed but must be self chosen; (b) no unequal political power and economic privilege is publicly bound up with the recognition of rights of a group; (c) if a right is made available to one group it must, in principle, be made available to all groups; (d) a right for one group must not contravene a right for another; and (e) group rights must not contravene individual rights."[27] It is not difficult to apply these criteria, for example, to a claim to a right to mother-tongue education. My application follows Macdonald's criteria systematically: (a) although a child is born into a language community, the adult members of the community are members voluntarily; (b) no unequal political power and economic privilege should be bound up with mother-tongue education, as is the case with white education in South Africa where group rights have been distorted by group privilege; (c) if mother-tongue education is made available to the Zulus, for example, similar education should also be made available to other ethnic groups; (d) this right should not contravene a right for another group to choose either for or against mother-tongue education; (e) this right should not contravene the individual right of a member of the group to join an integrated school that provides education in English, for example.

On the basis of these considerations I propose the following:

(1) The concept of group rights is a coherent concept that enables us to confront the state with its duties in more than only individual cases.

(2) If necessary, we can distinguish between rights in a strong and a weak sense: the concept of rights in a strong sense refers to individual rights, the accepted liberal tradition, while the concept in a weak sense refers to the broader application of rights to include human groups, animals, and nature as a whole.

(3) It is not sufficient to downgrade communal rights into mere social utilities or cultural interests that could be catered to on the basis of freedom of association, for the group has then no claims vis-à-vis the state and is left on its own to protect its own cultural values. Under majority rule a minority can be excluded from all levels of power and can remain perpetually excluded. Even if it is represented indirectly, on an individual basis, there is no guarantee that its cultural values will be protected. But if cultural values are translated into rights they can be protected in a democratic way.

(4) A distinction should be made between group rights and minority rights. Liberal thinking rejects the concept of group rights based on a

27. Macdonald, "Group Rights," p. 4.

preexisting ethnicity and on statutory demarcation of groups, which carries a threat of rigidity and resistance to individual choice of membership. The concept of minority political rights is evaluated positively by liberals since the minority group is constituted as a party on the basis of free elections, not on a preexisting or imposed definition. This liberal strategy can help to draw the boundary of group membership clearly if the party is capable of effectively laying claims in favor of cultural values.

(5) Because of its linkage with apartheid, the concept of group rights, unfortunately, has been rejected by black liberation movements. But so too has the concept of minority rights. And of late the rhetoric of black liberation also rejects the priority given to a bill of rights in liberal thinking. It emphasizes instead the emotionally loaded nationalist slogan of "the power of the people." "The people," entrusted with sovereignty, becomes the source of justice.

Must we allow white or black nationalists to prescribe our use of liberal-democratic concepts? We should remain true to our belief that minority and group rights can and ought to be protected. In the politics of the near future, the interplay of pressures from groups and classes will result in fruitful negotiation only if there is some pragmatism and willingness to compromise. In this situation, liberals, though not in command of the big battalions, could provide a crucial service to others in advancing reasonableness and the use of conceptually coherent terms.

David Yudelman

14. State and Capital in Contemporary South Africa

In South Africa serious discussion of the state-capital or business-government relationship has until very recently been subsumed under the rubric of "economic growth and political change" or, even more crudely, "capitalism and apartheid." This has resulted in a debate about the degree to which business, or capital, or economic growth is, has been, or will be responsible for the perpetuation, intensification, or erosion of racial discrimination and apartheid in South Africa.

The debate is important in ideological terms, since both antagonists—until recently, largely liberals and Marxists who evolved into neo-liberals and neo-Marxists as they refined their argument over the decades—sought to establish the particular relevance of their vision to the eradication of apartheid. But the events of 1984–1986 have at last made clear just how secondary a part of the unfolding reality was encompassed by that debate. Ahead lies a far more fundamental struggle over power. The death of apartheid will merely be a milestone on the road to determining the future shape of South African society, and will not mark the end of the struggle.

A new approach to an analysis of South African conflict is now focusing on the South African state's legitimation crisis, its lack of accepted authority whether deemed moral or not, and increasing inability to perform its everyday functions without the exercise of naked force. An examination of the legitimation crisis, however, must be augmented by analysis of South Africa's little-understood but increasingly critical accumulation crisis: the growing inability of the economy to generate the revenue or jobs necessary to underpin social and political programs. The accumulation crisis is more than the economic problems that arise from contemporary political issues such as sanctions, divestment, insurrectionary violence, and war. More important, there is a structural crisis in the economy itself.

This structural crisis, and its convergence with the state's crisis of political acceptance and control, has opened up a new role for business in formulating political policy. Business has always had a large voice in determining policy, but the current mutually reinforcing economic and political crises, and the government's weakness, have enabled business increasingly to influence fundamental policy changes instead of confining itself, in public at least, simply to reacting to government's initiatives. Business has also begun publicly to influence "horizontal" policy, i.e., policy issues that cut across sectors of society and affect the interests of all groups, not merely those of business.

The convergence of distinct but mutually reinforcing political and economic crises has also been central in generating the critical mass of support in state and capital for such radical changes, in South African terms, as the proposed phasing out of influx controls. The convergence of crises is pivotal to the proposed new strategy of "inward industrialization," which, if implemented, could fundamentally transform South Africa demographically and politically, as well as economically. Inward industrialization would necessitate turning the policy of separate development on its head by abandoning the attempt to reverse the flow of blacks to towns, and even encouraging permanent urbanization. This change in policy would be a transformation akin to a revolution. One of the keys to understanding it and contemporary South Africa is the analysis of the relationship of business and government, of state and capital.

The serious analysis of state and capital in South Africa started comparatively recently. In the mid-seventies a group of neo-Marxists emerged who attempted a comprehensive analysis of South African state and capital, basing their work heavily on theoretical underpinnings provided by a European neo-Marxist, Nicos Poulantzas. Strikingly, a great deal of Poulantzian theory is wholly consistent with (1) liberal interest group theory, which concentrates on the contention of groups for control of the state and (2) the "policeman state" in which the state has the minimal function of ensuring a stable environment for contending groups. Poulantzian theory seems to do little more than translate liberal interest group theory into Marxist terms. The South African Poulantzians became known as fractionalists, because of the emphasis they placed on the Poulantzian theory that the state is to be understood in terms of the fractions of capital and of the bourgeoisie that dominate it. These dominant fractions of the bourgeoisie form a power bloc and contend for hegemony within it, sometimes seeking the support of nonbourgeois classes when deadlocks arise. Such alliances can result in state policies that appear to contradict the interests of capital; but Poulantzas, and the fractionalists, would argue that ostensibly antibusiness policies are, ultimately, in the real interest of capital.

The problem with applying the fractionalist theory to South Africa was its equation (in true liberal fashion) of state and government. Wherever the fractionalists observed a change of government they looked for and usually found a change in the nature of the state. Their periodization of the South African state was therefore littered with "turning points," most notably those of the election of new governments in 1924 and 1948, which were in all important respects identical with the turning points noted by liberals and interest group analysts generally. This analytic focusing on 1924 and 1948 radically overemphasized the importance of party politics, the divisions in capital and state, and the lack of continuity in state-capital relations. Moreover, it continues to distort the literature on South African state and capital.

The convergence between the fractionalists and liberal-pluralist analyses has been noted by various commentators, including more orthodox Marxists who derided fractionalism as liberal mystification. Conversely, Merle Lipton's recent neo-liberal analysis of the so-called victory of national interests over foreign capital, of agriculture and manufacturing over mining, differs from that of the fractionalists only in terminology, and in the degree of blame she attributes to capitalists for racially discriminatory policies. Both the fractionalists and Lipton reduce the state to an instrument of various fractions, and compound the error by exaggerating the power of the weaker fractions, i.e., manufacturing and agriculture, rather than mining.[1]

As the debate on the state and state-capital relations was developing, I undertook a detailed critique of theories of the state and these "turning points," and I proposed an alternative theory, emphasizing the concepts of state legitimation and capital accumulation and the resulting symbiotic relationship of state and capital.[2] These concepts drew on and synthesized the work of such theorists as James O'Connor and Jurgen Habermas,

1. Merle Lipton, *Capitalism and Apartheid: South Africa 1910–84* (Totowa, N.J.: Rowan and Allenheld, 1985).

2. David Yudelman, *The Emergence of Modern South Africa: State, Capital and the Incorporation of Organized Labor on the South African Gold Fields, 1902–39* (Westport, Conn.: Greenwood, 1983), passim.

making a Weberian distinction between: (1) the state including not only the executive but also the legislature, civil service, judiciary, police, and army—the institutions that make and enforce public policy, both symbolically and actually; and (2) the government, i.e., the government of the day. The starting point, then, was a description of the state, by presenting a detailed empirical picture of the nature of the South African state, focusing in particular on its relations to capital and organized labor.

The results suggested that the South African state was exposed earlier than most modern states to the necessity of resolving the tension between legitimation and accumulation. It needed to legitimate itself vis-à-vis the white population—to win at least minimal acceptability—by mobilizing political constituencies; this was done not only by the development of an ideology, but also by broadening representative institutions, trade unions, and access to the vote. At the same time, both for itself and others, the state needed to protect the accumulation process in order to ensure continued enonomic growth. Because the state needed private enterprise to optimize the accumulation function, and because capital needed the state to perform the legitimation function, a relationship of mutual dependence was the natural outcome. This symbiotic relationship was therefore not essentially that of a dominant to a dominated party; nor was it a "zero-sum" relationship. But this mutual dependence does not necessarily imply equality. Rather it emphasizes that the relationship of the state to capital is neither solely instrumental, in which the state merely represents the interests of capital or other classes or groups, nor arbitrational, in which the state acts as a neutral arbiter among conflicting interests of which capital is merely one. Liberal, Marxist, and nationalist theories of the state, in contrast to the symbiotic theory, all see the state as representational, regardless of whether they see it as representing the general interest, a particular class, or a particular ethnic group.

Symbiosis suggests that the state can be seen in some senses as an actor in its own right. This is not to argue that it is, or could ever be, autonomous: even the so-called totalitarian states did not come close. Nor is it to foreclose options, as does the fractionalists' concept of "relative" autonomy, which extends only as far as the ultimate interests of capital as a whole are served. Rather it is to suggest that the state can represent both itself and its major constituencies, and make limited choices where there are clashes. Symbiosis does not predict outcomes between contenders, but does suggest that mutual dependence will survive most disputes no matter how acrimonious they emerge in public debate. Thus symbiosis survives most electoral contests, and most historical "turning points." Turning points in any case have the same relationship to history that UFOs have to science: they are sighted far more often than they appear. Certainly the symbiosis of state and capital has a long history stretching back before the unification of South Africa in 1910 and—though state and capital today are radically different from their counterparts of seventy-five years ago—continuing unbroken until the present. If, however, the state were consistently to fail to legitimate, or capital to accumulate, symbiosis would face a genuine challenge.

It has been suggested that symbiosis is a highly elastic concept, as if that were a criticism. In fact, symbiosis does appear to offer a far more convincing account of state-capital relations in a wide variety of cases than those provided by its logical alternative, the representational theories. But surely, in a world where social scientists expend so much sweat to design clothes that cover all bodies, elasticity is a positive characteristic, particularly as it will not conceal differences by overemphasizing similarities. Symbiosis between state and capital, for example, is quite consistent with radical changes within each and in the balance of their relationship. Though mutual dependence might, and usually does, persist, continual changes in the balance of the relationship are likely to result both from changes in state and capital and from changes in their environment. For example, the South African government is currently confronted by a dramatic erosion in its traditional support from the white working and lower middle classes, particularly from Afrikaners in those groups. At the same time, it faces a militant black population—both in urban and rural areas—which for the first time is rejecting, by force and in a sustained fashion, the very legitimacy of the state. This is what I have designated here as a legitimation crisis: not only the lack of acceptance of the moral authority of the South African state, but the active, ongoing attack on its very viability.

In this legitimation crisis the South African government and state has had to look to other constituencies for support, most notably to business. Big business has recently taken on its most explicitly political role in South Africa since the 1920s. Whereas it previously could confine itself largely to the actions of government and state as they affected the economy, business has now become vitally concerned with the legitimation crisis of the state and the way that crisis is threatening the very future of the free-enterprise system and of capitalism. This new situation could ultimately pose a threat to the mutual dependence of state and capital; but the threat is not imminent. While the relationship of business and government has changed in important and identifiable ways, it is still preeminently symbiotic. The expansion of international economic sanctions and the onset of a "siege economy," moreover, will strengthen rather than weaken this symbiosis.

* * *

The South African state in the early 1980s faced a legitimation rather than an accumulation crisis.[3] This did not merely mean that a new ideology had to be formulated: to legitimate a state requires an ideology, but it also requires extensive policy measures, particularly in the area of co-optation. The South African state was successful during the twenties and thirties in co-opting and depoliticizing white labor. In the eighties, if it wished to resolve its legitimation crisis, it had to attempt the same thing in the case of blacks. How could it do this? Any action along these lines would face major difficulties because although the practice of apartheid constituted a highly effective and ruthless use of power, the ideology of apartheid appealed only to the converted and had delegitimated the state from the blacks' point of view. The state could co-opt blacks but, given the exclusionary nature of virtually the entire constitutional and legal fabric, this would require unprecedented state intervention (both coercive and co-optative) at precisely the time that state withdrawal was being preached.

The ideology of the free market, developed to take the place of the apartheid ideology, called for the progressive removal of the state role in the economy and its replacement by the sovereignty of the market. Behind the move toward free-market ideology was the hardheaded recognition that massive state intervention, so successful when used on behalf of whites, and of Afrikaners in particular, would shortly be demanded by blacks as well. There are three possible responses to such a demand. First, one might choose to follow the old methods of coercion, though this has become increasingly difficult with the growing politicizaton of blacks, which, in turn, requires more intensive and expensive repression and also accelerates the delegitimation of the state in black eyes. Second, one could follow the method used in the relatively rich societies of post–World War II Europe, of radical increases in state microeconomic intervention and the creation of a welfare state, in effect buying legitimation. Third, one might minimize the role of the state in the economy, relying on so-called free markets in which supply and demand and collective bargaining determine the levels of wages, employment, and even welfare. Theoretically such a policy might depoliticize such issues and create nonpolitical zones in which they could be fought out "economically" or even administratively.

Options one and two are simply too expensive to be feasible. Neither could option three be implemented without enormous effort. States are not fond of emasculating themselves, and free-market ideology would

3. Ibid., pp. 281–88.

not have the desired effect without free-market policies to complete the legitimation process. The ultimate objectives of state withdrawal would be to prevent the state from having to take political responsibility for "economic" issues such as low wages or unemployment, thus preempting serious threats to the legitimation process; and to remove from the state's sphere of jurisdiction a number of areas which could, under a black government, constitute a threat to capital and to whites generally. Neither the state formulators of the new ideology nor capital wish to see blacks seizing control of the state and using it to redistribute wealth and economic leverage as the Afrikaner nationalists once did so effectively.

Stanley Greenberg, in his more recent work,[4] has compared South Africa as a developing and ethnically divided society with other developing capitalist societies which have contrived to separate economics and politics by removing the state from a direct role in markets. The market is sometimes regarded, especially in divided societies, as an alternative to the naked exercise of force by the state. He points out that as modern market and capitalist societies develop there is an almost universal tendency to differentiate or disentangle state and economy. This involves four ideological processes: the separation of the political and the economic; the establishing of a distinct private sphere; the diminution of the political; and the universalizing of the state. Paralleling the expansion of the market is the contraction of the state responsibility for producing material welfare, a contraction which allows the state to extricate itself from particularist issues and to claim to stand for society as a whole.

In divided societies, however, the previous ideology had frequently explicitly called for, and achieved, state intervention on behalf of particularist interests (this is the essence of apartheid in practice: a policy of massive and sectionalist social engineering). This earlier interventionism greatly intensifies the problems both of actual withdrawal and of legitimation through free-market ideology.[5] One possible approach to this dilemma, suggested by Jan Lombard,[6] is to decentralize and fragment power, disperse functions regionally, and entrench these decisions in constitutions that can be altered only by all regions or all groups, or both, unanimously agreeing to the changes. But if anyone

4. This work includes the following unpublished draft chapters: "Legitimation and control: ideological struggles within the South African state," 1982; "The political economy of illegitimacy," 1983; and "State against the market: prelude to crisis," 1984. For the final version, see *Legitimating the Illegitimate: State, Markets and Resistance in South Africa* (Berkeley: University of California Press, forthcoming).

5. See Greenberg, "Political economy of illegitimacy," especially pp. 5, 11, 16–20.

6. J. A. Lombard, "The evolution of the theory of economic policy," *South African Journal of Economics* 53 (1985).

should understand the frailty of constitutions and entrenched clauses it is the National party in South Africa with its checkered career in finding ingenious or simply coercive ways to override them. It would therefore be difficult to persuade the aggrieved segments of society, especially blacks, that these arrangements were not merely devices to preserve existing privilege, which would in turn result in a decidedly fragile, changeable constitution.

The difficulties in the way of a successful implementation of a free-market strategy in South Africa seem virtually insurmountable, particularly in a climate of economic decline which, it will be argued below, may be structural rather than cyclical, and of political violence and repression which may be on its way to becoming endemic. On the other hand, there may be few viable alternatives.[7]

Significant differences exist between the structure of business generally in the industrialized market economies and the special features to be found in South Africa. The state plays a fairly extensive role, directly producing between 20 and 30 percent of the gross domestic product. In line with free-market ideology, however, it proclaims the intention to privatize significant sectors and has already begun, for example, to sell off shares in the oil-from-coal parastatal corporation, Sasol, without jettisoning control. But there is nothing particularly unusual about the balance between public and private sectors in South Africa.

Another major division is the conventional one between sectors of business, i.e., between primary industries (such as agriculture and mining), secondary industries (such as manufacturing and construction), and tertiary or service industries (such as commerce, trade, and services). South Africa's resource sector is proportionately larger than in most industrialized market economies, with mining accounting for over 21 percent of the gross domestic product in 1985, agriculture about 6 percent, and manufacturing just under 20 percent. Exports are dominated by the resource sector, the degree of dominance fluctuating with the gold price, but usually around 60 percent of total exports. The mix itself is not unique, however, and there are significant comparisons to be made with other small, open, export-reliant economies such as those of Australia and Canada. Nor should any direct equation be made between the size of the contribution of any particular sector and its influence in the state, or its ability to make the state act in its behalf. In South Africa in the sixties the manufacturing sector expanded rapidly while mining stagnated in the wake of a fixed gold price and rising

7. Greenberg, "Political economy of illegitimacy," p. 25; Yudelman, *Emergence of Modern South Africa*, p. 287. For an outline of the corporatist alternative, see the concluding section of this paper.

costs. Analysts such as Rob Davies took this to indicate the dominance of the manufacturing sector or "national fraction" of capital. In fact the issue of power and influence is far more complex than that, with factors such as degree of international competitiveness (frequently inversely proportional to degree of dependence on state support and subsidies) of central significance.

Mining capital worldwide tends to be unusually concentrated. South African mining capital, largely for historic and geological reasons that were first outlined in J.A. Hobson's famous studies of the industry and taken up as a model by Lenin, is an unusually concentrated variant of an internationally concentrated industry. Few, if any, industrialized market economies are so dominated by one industry, both quantitatively and, more important, qualitatively (mining is internationally competitive, needs no state subsidies, and earns the bulk of the country's foreign exchange). The rapidly rising gold price and the successful expansion into international coal and ferro-alloy markets in the seventies heightened the importance of mining in South Africa, but that importance is not new: mining has enjoyed a unique and symbiotic relationship with the South African state ever since unification in 1910.

The final division within capital which is unique to South Africa is the ethnic division between Afrikaans- and English-speaking white capitalists, characterized by the greater support among Afrikaners for the National party government since 1948. This is an important distinction, particularly because of the role of the state in helping create Afrikaner capital and capitalists since World War II. The move of Afrikaner capital into the mining industry came late, with the takeover (encouraged by Harry Oppenheimer, the chairman of the Anglo-American De Beers stable) of General Mining by Federale Mynbou in the early sixties. Oppenheimer hoped for and achieved a more cordial relationship at an institutional or public level between the mining industry and the government. He also hoped for, but did not achieve, closer intercorporate ties between the Federale and Anglo-American groups.[8] While the importance of the English-Afrikaner ethnic division should not be ignored, the bigger danger is for it to be exaggerated. Even during the days when the relationship between mining capital and the Afrikaner government was characterized by fairly regular public threats of nationalization, particularly in the fifties, a solid structural relationship of symbiosis between state and capital persisted.

The same point may be made in more general terms about the importance of all the white ethnic divisions elaborated above. Afrikaner capital has been more politically significant, in being influential among

8. Interview with Harry Oppenheimer, Johannesburg, 10 February 1986.

the government's major political constituency, the Afrikaners. And Anglophone capital has been more economically significant, being larger and better connected internationally. The greater contribution of Afrikaner capital to the state's legitimation imperatives and of Anglophone capital to the state's accumulation imperatives has led to significant policy differences at times, and to far greater toleration within Afrikaner capital until recently for direct state participation in the economy.

Nevertheless, while the differences between Afrikaner and Anglophone capital cannot and should not be ignored, it would be equally mistaken to lose sight of the remarkable degree of centralization and concentration of capital in South Africa, dominated by two massive aggregations: the Anglo-American/De Beers stable, and the Sanlam/Federale Mynbou/Gencor stable. While there will obviously always be divisions within business and capital, business in South Africa is more able to talk with a united voice—and act in concert—than virtually anywhere else.

One way to distinguish between business and government, on the one hand, and state and capital on the other is to distinguish the levels on which they tend to operate. Broadly speaking, business-government relations are most appropriately analyzed at the public, institutional level with examination of party political debates and published statements of business associations, corporation executives, government leaders, and bureaucrats. At this level there is public debate and interchange between recognized, defined institutions. Equally broadly speaking, state-capital relationships are best analyzed at the structural level. Structural relationships are, by their nature, not conducted in the public arena, and are more difficult to define. They are best analyzed at the macro-level dealing with issues such as the relationship of an economy to its polity.

The degree of importance of the "political" and the "economic" at each level is a matter for empirical investigation rather than a priori assertion. For example, the contemporary debate about the color bar in the mines has a long history of intense and public institutional interchange. Many observers, if not most, tend to analyze it primarily or only at this level. The liberals and nationalists in particular (but to a surprising extent the neo-Marxists as well) have been consistently guilty of doing this in analyzing South Africa's past and present. This is an error of considerable importance in that it accepts political posturing at face value, ignoring the fact that "politics is the means by which the will of the few becomes the will of the many."

In the area of state-capital relations this is a particularly crippling error, in two respects. First, it leads to a wholly misleading impression of the relative strengths of the two: government and state will lose support from citizens if they publicly bow to a particular interest group, and capital shares the state's interest in not being indentified as advancing its selfish interests against the "general will." Second, overemphasis of the political frequently leads to a fundamental misconception of the relationship of state and capital in that the political process is usually set up as adversarial ("government and opposition"), leading to the perception that state-capital relations are adversarial whereas in fact they are basically symbiotic.

The second misconception, because it is both pervasive and largely unconscious, is the more insidious. Not only does it distort our perceptions of the past and present, but it also limits our creative imagination in planning for the future. The tendency to exaggerate the importance of the political process is almost endemic in South African studies.[9] An extended example is supplied below because of the centrality of the issue to understanding the relationship of state and capital and the potential role liberalism may have in South Africa's future. The example draws on Merle Lipton's recent detailed treatment of state-capital relations, *Capitalism and Apartheid,* which is singled out not because it is worse than others (it is probably better than most), but because it had the opportunity to build on the numerous recent publications on the topic, and because it is ambitious in scope and comprehensiveness.

Lipton says that the mining industry's failure to erode the color bar in the twenties demonstrated its lack of political power: "Hence [the mineowners'] repeated attempts to erode the job bar. Their failure was due to their lack of political power" (p. 115). The clear implication is that the mining industry has to do what it is told by the government, even on issues it sees as fundamental to its well-being. Capital proposes, but state disposes. In fact, it is only by defining political power merely at the level of public debate that one can make such a statement even vaguely convincing. At the structural level, Lipton fails to take into account the fundamentals of the state-capital relationship. For example, many if not most of the costs and burdens of the color bar were quietly transferred back from the mineowners to other sectors, first to white labor in general: mining was excluded from the burden of the civilized labor policy, it retained exclusive rights to recruit migrant labor abroad, and it was not compelled to form an industrial council. More specifically, the costs of employer privilege were borne by white miners: although they remained among the best-paid sections of white labor, they were left with a toothless co-opted union, stagnant membership, perpetual

9. Yudelman, *Emergence of Modern South Africa,* pp. 1–49.

job fragmentation, and an industrial-relations system that virtually precluded effective strikes. While the industry grew, the Pact government did not succeed in improving the conditions of service or wages of white miners compared to the "capitalist," South Africa Party government labor policies. In fact they lost considerable ground to the employers during the Pact's regime. Real wages of white mine labor actually fell: using an index, 1910 = 1,000, white real wages in mining fell to 794 in 1922, recovered to 833 in 1925, and to 1,010 only in 1933, remaining close to 1,000 to 1939.[10] The white miners also lost ground to their black counterparts with proportionately more blacks continuing to be employed under the Pact government than before the 1922 upheaval. Finally, the government, forced to allow mineowners to continue to recruit substantial numbers of black workers from foreign countries, had to create the largest part of sheltered employment for the poor whites in the state sector rather than in mining, though the latter was highly labor-intensive.

Thus, in dealing with the institutional relationships of business and government one needs to keep in mind the need to place these relationships within the context of the structural relationships of state and capital. It is true that the mining sector was forced to keep a low profile at the political level because the government needed to avoid alienating the white working voters (i.e., given the government's legitimation imperative), and it is also true that the government would at all costs avoid superficial favoritism on mining's behalf. But this caution was exercised by government precisely because mining enjoyed and enjoys unmatched access to the state at the structural level, a fact that would not have been at all popular with voters if publicized.

Nor is this an isolated instance in Lipton's work. Because of her failure to understand the nature of the importance of mining (and capital as a whole) she makes a number of other sweeping and unsubstantiated assertions, some of which are patently wrong. For example, she argues (p. 188) that the decline of the white workers' militancy after 1924 "was not because they had been politically castrated, but because they could get what they wanted by easier, institutionalized means." This could hardly be further from the truth, and there is an abundance of evidence, both statistically and in official and unofficial private correspondence, that indicates the diametrically different reality of a splintered, supine labor movement after 1924.[11] The assertion that the white workers "could get what they wanted" is pivotal to Lipton's analysis of state-capital relations: yet it is based entirely on citations of

10. Ibid., pp. 26, 194, 255.

11. Ibid., pp. 190–248.

secondary material which does not in fact support her case. As with so many who have written in the field before, the "facts" appear to emerge from the preconception.

Why is it that it is so generally thought that the state is the instrument of capital, or vice versa? In general, one could argue that business, most liberal academics (at least until the neo-Marxist assault of the sixties and seventies), and the fractionalists tend to pose the question of political power too narrowly at the institutional level of public debate. If, for example, the minister of mines stands up and says the color bar will remain no matter what the mining bosses say, and if it is not formally abolished, this is widely and erroneously interpreted as evidence of the impotence of the mining industry.

In 1986, though most of the statutory color bar on the mines have gone, many of the issues remain the same. The government still has to balance the threat to its electoral support entailed in abolishing the white monopoly over blasting certificates (its legitimation imperative) against the threat to the employment and state revenue generated by the industry if the provision is allowed to stand (its accumulation imperative). What has changed is that the state is now far more concerned than ever before about legitimating itself and the industry to the newly unionized black workers. The industry and capital generally are equally concerned to legitimate themselves to organized black labor, particularly in view of the potential militance of the National Union of Mineworkers and the possible impact of serious trade sanctions against South Africa's resource exports in a world where the secular terms of trade have turned against resources generally.

The structural factors, then, have moved even more strongly against the retention of the last vestiges of the statutory color bar: both state and capital, as a whole, need this change. Though this means the blasting-certificate monopoly is likely to be phased out, the timing and the trade-offs will also be heavily influenced by the *government's* need, at least in the short to medium term, to keep the militant white working and lower middle classes under some semblance of control. When government and state imperatives clash, the resolution of the issue is always liable to be fudged or mystified by contrasting or contradictory solutions at the institutional and structural levels, as happened when the 1926 amendment to the Mines and Works Act took the color bar from the regulations into the statute itself. What makes a comparatively clear-cut resolution more likely in the eighties is the fact that, even at the public political level, the state can no longer address itself and its legitimation endeavors merely to white voters and miners. It needs the acquiescence, and increasingly the tacit support, of the black miners as well.

Why, then, have the mining industry and business generally downgraded their power and influence when they are manifestly aware of the myriad of ways of exerting both at the structural level? Two answers suggest themselves, though more are probably needed to be fully convincing. First, until recently (and with some notable exceptions, such as the Urban Foundation) business has defined political power as the ability to win public debates and achieve its goals publicly. Neither state nor government is in a position to allow this, particularly in a system of government that gives a vote to far more employees than employers. Second, it is also true that it is to the advantage of both business and government to portray business as a supplicant. Government cannot generally afford to be seen to be dominated by *geldmag*, or money power (a lesson the state president P. W. Botha doesn't seem to have fully learned from all his predecessors, to his cost at the polls), and industry wants government to be able to mobilize its followers and thus to legitimate mining policy. The industry also finds it convenient at times to be able to blame its problems on government policy.

So, to some extent, there is a pervasive conspiracy of silence between business and government on their symbiotic relationship. Once one moves toward an ideology of the free market as happened in the late seventies, however, it becomes increasingly difficult to deny the symbiosis. In fact, it becomes increasingly necessary for the government to proclaim the special relationship of business and government as a positive good. It is ironic that the structural changes and political crisis occurring at the same time in South Africa impelled business to distance itself, at least symbolically, from the government. It would be wrong, however, to mistake this distancing process for a termination of the symbiotic relationship.

In conclusion, let us identify some of the salient changes in the actual relationship of state and capital in South Africa in recent years and ask what role, if any, liberalism might play in the changing relationship.

Recent changes in the relationship of state and capital can be considered at the institutional level of public debate, and at the structural level. In the case of the former, government and state have actively and very publicly courted business, the most notable instances of which were the summit conferences at the Carlton Hotel in Johannesburg in November 1979, the Good Hope Conference in Cape Town in November 1981, and in Pretoria on November 7, 1986. These were only the top of a very large iceberg, however, being accompanied by extensive swapping of ideas on public platforms.

As the political crisis has grown, however, business has become increasingly concerned to put some distance between itself and the government, particularly because of foreign sanctions and divestment pressures, and because of its fear that capitalism itself might become identified, particularly in the minds of the black majority, with the regime and with racial discrimination. In earlier years, when the state appeared to be fully in control and performing its order and legitimation functions, capital tended to confine itself to business, at least publicly. The exceptions all prove the rule: they occur precisely when the legitimation process—and the state itself—is seen to be threatened, for example during the 1920 black miners' strike, during the Sharpeville riots, during the Soweto insurrection, and during the 1984–1986 period. The prolonged nature of the latest crisis and the failure of the state to perform its legitimation function efficiently has led to more and more outspoken business interventions in political issues. Most of these interventions have been of a declamatory nature, intended more to establish business bona fides and express its frustration than to achieve any really concrete objectives.

Increasingly, however, business has been prepared to publicly threaten action. For example, the "chairman of the leading industrial group" was recently reported to have threatened an investment and tax strike in an international financial journal.[12] And there was the famous visit of leading businessmen to the headquarters of the African National Congress in Lusaka. There have been dozens of manifestos from business organizations over the last two years, and they have adopted an increasingly adversarial tone toward government. The *Financial Mail* of 25 April 1986, having just praised the government for announcing the scrapping of influx controls, goes on brutally on the same page to say, "we don't need another Carlton or Good Hope conference. The State President has talked too much as it is. . . . We need to get down and reform the law, not listen to more of P.W.'s jaw."

A publicly adversarial business-government relationship has long been the norm rather than the exception. What is new is the doubt creeping into business whether capital can, in its most literal sense, live with the present state, whether the latter can reform itself sufficiently to resume performing its legitimating function. Whatever its doubts, however, capital would be very hard put to come up with a viable alternative government it would find acceptable. State-capital symbiosis is likely to continue for the medium-term future at least.

Does this mean that the Chilean option is the only credible one, an alliance of a strong repressive state and untrammeled business? The problem in South Africa is, first, that the state needs to legitimate itself in the face of increasingly radical rejection by blacks and can no longer

12. "Big Business prepares for change," *Euromoney*, December 1985, p. 79.

indefinitely maintain itself through force; and second, that state-capital symbiosis is beginning to look inadequate, in itself, to hold the polity together. In the past, a combination of this symbiotic partnership and a co-opted organized (white) labor force proved enduringly viable. Today's black trade unions do not, however, fit comfortably into this model. In less than a decade they have emerged as the third force in South Africa, with both a strong political and economic base; thus, as has been obvious for some time, they are unlikely to be co-opted. They have demonstrated the leverage they can exert for their members even during a time of acute unemployment, though they have not demonstrated a capacity as yet to represent blacks other than their members. Given the precarious and unstable balance of forces prevailing in South Africa today, no viable strategy can exclude central participation by the black unions, and it seems possible that, if they cannot be co-opted, they could enter in the next decade into a corporatist or tripartite regime, in which state, capital and organized labor work out, at least temporarily, a new modus vivendi.[13]

What is the role of liberals and liberalism in such a situation? It should be emphasized that we are talking of two distinct groups of liberals. To simplify somewhat, there are the liberals who are primarily concerned with individual human rights and the morality of race discrimination: let us call them political liberals. And there are the liberals who are primarily concerned with economic freedoms, the primacy of markets, and the necessary restriction of the economic role of the state: let us call them economic liberals. In some cases, individuals are both economic and political liberals, but there is no reason that one has to be both.[14]

Political liberals have always been few in number and without any power base. Thus those who really aspired to present a politically feasible alternative had to seek some outside support, and they did so by appealing to business. The two major figures in the sixties, who played a central role in keeping liberalism politically alive, were Helen Suzman—for many years the lone Progressive party member of Parliament—and Laurence Gandar, the then editor of the *Rand Daily Mail.* Both argued that apartheid and racial discrimination were not only morally repugnant

13. The new book by Heribert Adam and Kogila Moodley, *South Africa Without Apartheid: Dismantling Racial Domination* (Berkeley, University of California Press, 1986), is far more at home with ethnic than economic issues, but it contains (almost in passing, and contradicting to some extent the analysis of the bulk of the book) an excellent short summary of the potential significance of the black unions, even under a white or mixed government (p. 260), which sounds very much like a corporatist scenario. See also Yudelman, *Emergence of Modern South Africa,* p. xvi.

14. David Yudelman, "Industrialization, race relations and change: an ideological and academic debate," *African Affairs,* 74 (1975):88–89.

but economically a pipe dream. The issue that enabled them to appeal to both economic and political liberals was that of black labor: with a great deal of courage and persistence they argued for at least a decade that if blacks were allowed to work where they wished, to acquire skills, and to earn higher wages the result would be accelerated economic growth and higher incomes for the entire population, without any need for the whites to pay for black advances. An expanding cake, they argued, would result in larger pieces for all.

Much of the liberal analysis of the 1950s and 1960s has proved remarkably prescient, and its plea for a radical expansion of South Africa's internal market by upgrading black skills and wages should be seen as a harbinger of today's proposed "inward industrialization" policy. The South African government, though not necessarily the South African state or Afrikaner nationalists generally, has now adopted, in many essentials, the liberal position of twenty-five years ago. This major change is reflected in government policy, which has been fundamentally transformed to allow freedom of association of black workers through legally entrenched trade unions, and is about to allow at least formal freedom of movement to blacks in general, through the abolition of influx control. Government policy in the mid-1980s, moreover, is going further than "allowing" what it can no longer physically prevent and is beginning seriously to envisage what is in important respects an actively *anti*-apartheid program. The proposed new policy of inward industrialization, for example, would actually encourage permanent urbanization (starting with a massive campaign to build urban housing for blacks) in the hope of creating a growing internal market as the new generator of economic growth.

The about-face of the government on basic issues of principle has also embarrassed another group that had been highly influential from the late 1960s to the early 1980s: the neo-Marxists. The central argument of the neo-Marxists, which became something of an orthodoxy, was that apartheid and the restriction of market freedoms were not only consistent with capitalist economic growth in South Africa, but were also germane to it. The new rush to discard the central economic tenets of apartheid, led by the dominant sectors of big business and their peak associations, has therefore led to considerable disarray among the neo-Marxists. They now have to develop a convincing explanation why black resistance to the current regime should be focusing on socialist transformation rather than black nationalism. For if it is not true that capitalism and apartheid are one, then the rationale for socialism has to be based on something other than mere antiracism.

Even if the lip service paid to the free market by the current government is followed through systematically, however, the new situation is still fundamentally problematic for political liberals. In the same way that the government will not be able to guarantee the "rights" of Afrikaner nationalists under the new dispensation, the liberals will not be able to offer guarantees to individuals or groups. Perhaps the freeing of markets thirty years ago could have been accompanied by the significant expansion of individual human rights which remains so important to liberals; but in today's situation it is more likely that the conditions necessary for the changes will have to be imposed from above by force, the so-called "Brazilian option."

A generation ago, liberals could argue that rapid expansion of the economy would result in more for all via a mechanism known as "trickle down" (the prosperity of the whites was automatically to trickle down to the blacks). Today, income redistribution is already taking place, encouraged by state policy and with the open acquiescence of senior business leaders such as the chairman of Barlow Rand, Mike Rosholt.[15] Where Rosholt has drawn the line (and other businessmen will certainly agree) is on the need to prevent income redistribution from becoming capital redistribution. Economic liberals will have no trouble agreeing on this, but political liberals are likely to face an agonizing dilemma. They will be forced to make a choice between liberal democracy and democratic socialism, a choice they have always been able to avoid in the past. Whatever the similarities and affinities, Fabian socialism is not economic liberalism.

Finally, and most likely, liberals will be forced to compromise on their central values in a number of areas, not only in the areas of wealth redistribution and free markets, but also of constitutional democracy, and of individual and minority rights. It is almost certainly going to be necessary to aim at a "second-best" solution. Theodor Lowi, the noted U.S. liberal, has argued that the best that post-Vietnam liberalism in the United States can aim for at present is a neo-laissez-faire alternative, which he calls a "liberal statist" solution. Liberal statism combines continued, even intensified, government regulation in some areas with an attempt to preserve limited liberty and market freedoms in others.

If that is even partly true in the United States, it gives an indication of how radically South Africa's embattled liberalism must be revised if it is to aspire to any relevance in the future. In fact, given the current weakness of the South African state and its inability to gain even marginal acceptance as the representative of society as a whole, it is clearly necessary to go beyond liberal statism. The unenviable task of the next generation of South Africa's liberals could well be to seek a role, however marginal, in mitigating widespread authoritarian reform—

15. *Beeld*, 11 July 1986; *Pretoria News*, 11 July 1986.

only some of which will be genuine reform—and in mediating between state, big business, and big unions, a mediation complicated by the force of African nationalism.

State and capital in contemporary South Africa are being transformed by enormously multifaceted and volatile processes, the understanding of which requires the development of new conceptual road maps. In this situation, creative destruction of past approaches is essential. The long-standing quarrel between the neo-liberals and the neo-Marxists about the relationship of capitalism and apartheid should now give way to the more central and pressing issue of the relationship of state, capital, and organized labor in contemporary South Africa.

IV

Central Institutions of Democratic Liberalism: Law, Press, and Education

John Dugard

15. Human Rights and the Rule of Law, I

The rule of law and the advancement of civil liberties (or human rights in modern parlance) have always ranked among the main priorities of liberals in South Africa. In the first thirty years of National party rule, protests against the abrogation of the rule of law and pleas for the recognition for human rights from liberal quarters were largely ignored as the government set about rewriting the statute book to give effect to its policies of white domination and racial separation. Today there are signs of a change of attitude among certain Afrikaner thinkers and, perhaps, National party politicians. Cynics may ascribe this new interest in human rights to the dawning realization that the Afrikaner will soon need the protection of the law against majority rule. But this is not the only reason. The liberal belief in the rule of law and the recognition of human rights as necessary pillars of a decent society have at last penetrated Afrikaner nationalist thought and begun to influence the legal process and the constitutional debate. International opinion is partly responsible for this new approach. But liberals must also take some of the credit. Their perseverance and commitment to liberal values in the law have to some degree triumphed over an ideology that exalted the state over the principle of equality before the law and individual liberty.

I shall describe the interaction between Afrikaner nationalist thought and liberal ideas over the rule of law and show how the liberal position has gradually gained acceptance among Afrikaners and, albeit to a lesser degree, among National party planners, and then consider the implications of this for the role of liberals in South Africa. I am conscious that not all white nationalists are Afrikaners and that not all Afrikaners are nationalists. Consequently my portrayal of Afrikaner nationalist attitudes, based upon the statements and writings of Afrikaner judges and academics, in addition to the more authoritative positions and pronouncements of National party spokesmen, is open to the criticism that I have attributed "nationalist" views to persons who are not or are no longer supporters of the National party. This is a risk inherent in any attempt to describe contemporary "Afrikaner nationalist thought," since the institutions of Afrikanerdom—particularly the Afrikaans-language universities—are today politically fractured and no longer reflect the "party line" completely.

In 1910 South Africa opted for a constitution that failed to provide safeguards for individual liberty or racial equality. Thereafter little attention was paid to the rule of law and human rights. South African public life was dominated by white political conflict; the denial of basic liberties to the black population seldom attracted attention. Moreover, the League of Nations, preoccupied as it was with European affairs, refrained from questioning the domestic policies of South Africa, one of its most loyal members. This state of affairs came to an abrupt end in 1945 when, in the postwar period of change, a new world order was established in which decolonization and the promotion of human rights were to feature prominently. Now even the moderate United party government, headed by the respected Jan Smuts, experienced difficulty in defending its racial policies before a hostile United Nations. When, in 1948, the National party government was elected on the platform of apartheid, the scene was set for a confrontation between the upholders of liberal values, both at home and abroad, and the exponents of Afrikaner nationalism.

That there was no place for the rule of law and human rights in the new ideology was soon demonstrated by the enactment of a series of racist and repressive laws[1] and by South Africa's refusal to associate itself with the Universal Declaration of Human Rights of 1948.[2] This came as no surprise—in 1942 newspapers supporting the National party had published a draft constitution[3] premised on political absolutism, racial domination, and Calvinist antihumanism. Although this consti-

1. For a description of these laws, see John Dugard, *Human Rights and the South African Legal Order* (Princeton: Princeton University Press, 1978).

2. South Africa, along with the Soviet bloc and Saudi Arabia, abstained from voting on this declaration in the General Assembly.

3. This constitution was published in *Die Burger* and *Die Transvaler* on 22 and 23 January 1942. The text appears in *South Africa and the Rule of Law* (Geneva: International Commission of Jurists, 1960), Appendix B.

tution never became official party policy it clearly enjoyed support among many party supporters.

During the 1950s the legal debate was dominated by the constitutional crisis arising from the attempts of the National party government to remove colored voters in the Cape Province from the common electoral roll.[4] The government's strategy manifested a distinct lack of respect for constitutional safeguards and for the role of the courts as a protector of individual rights. The packing of the appellate division of the Supreme Court in 1955[5] and the repudiation of any suggestion of judicial review of acts of Parliament in 1956[6] indicated clearly that the government saw itself as above the law in matters affecting human rights.

The National party did not publicly formulate a coherent policy toward human rights and the rule of law. Instead it allowed its critics to judge it by its legislative and administrative actions. Its philosophy is, however, reflected in the writings of academic apologists and sympathetic judges and in a pamphlet on *South Africa and the Rule of Law* published by the Department of Foreign Affairs in 1968. The following principles emerge from these writings:

(1) The rule of law as expounded by A. V. Dicey, and developed by British constitutional lawyers, is a political and not juridical concept; and the necessary implication is that it is not therefore to be seriously considered. In 1956 the first constitutional text in Afrikaans was published, written by J. P. Verloren van Themaat, professor of law in the University of Pretoria and close associate of the government; he was later to serve as agent to the South African government in the dispute between South Africa and Ethiopia/Liberia over Namibia before the International Court of Justice. He claimed that the rule of law as a concept embracing the absence of arbitrary executive power, the maintenance of personal freedom, equality before the law, and trial by independent and impartial courts, was not a juridical concept but simply a pious expression of the wish that Parliament would not infringe on certain rights and liberties.[7] This scholarly diminution of the value of the rule of law is echoed in the curial and extracurial statements of Judge J. H. Snyman, generally regarded as a supporter of the National party government, who declared that the rule of law "is very much the tool of the politician and the politically-minded lawyer."[8]

(2) The rule of law is unacceptable on grounds of its humanist basis.

4. See generally on this crisis, Dugard, *Human Rights,* pp. 28–34.

5. Appellate Division Quorum Act 53 of 1955.

6. South Africa Act Amendment Act 9 of 1956.

7. J. P. Verloren van Themaat, *Staatsreg* (Durban: Butterworth, 1956), pp. 116–22.

8. The South African Broadcasting Corporation: "The News at Nine," 1 November 1972. See further on Mr. Justice Snyman's views, Dugard, *Human Rights,* pp. 43–45.

According to this view, first clearly propounded in 1973 by François Venter of the University of Potchefstroom, the doctrine of the rule of law is based on "the broad fundamental humanistic assumption of "human rights." Since the South African state is based on the sovereignty of God, "which stands in radical opposition to the humanistic point of departure," it follows that the rule of law, and for that matter any doctrine of human rights, has no place in South Africa.[9] In 1982 the president's council gave support to this argument when it opposed the inclusion of a bill of rights in the 1983 constitution, inter alia, on the ground that "the humanist emphasis of individual rights *vis-à-vis* the authority of the State" was unacceptable to "the Afrikaner with his Calvinist background [who] is more inclined to place the emphasis on the State and the maintenance of the State."[10]

(3) The rule of law is synonymous with rule *by* law. This view accepts that the arbitrary exercise of power is incompatible with the rule of law but holds that the rule of law is satisfied whenever the political authority acts in terms of a law enacted in accordance with the correct constitutional procedure, however evil, repressive, and discriminatory the law may be.[11]

The rule of law is limited to fair-trial procedures and does not concern itself with arbitrary extrajudicial administrative action or the advancement of substantive individual rights. This conclusion may be drawn from the following statement made by the Department of Foreign Affairs in its publication *South Africa and the Rule of Law* issued in 1968:

> The rule of law may mean different things to different people, but there is general agreement that it requires that a person on trial be accused in open court; be given an opportunity of denying the charge and of defending himself and that he be given the choice of counsel. These rights are at all times assured by the South African courts.[12]

Ideas of this kind are indicative of a determination not to be guided by conventional notions of justice and human rights. Certainly there is no evidence to suggest that the National party government has allowed itself to be influenced by such considerations.

The early years of National party rule were dominated by the constitutional crisis that resulted from the government's actions aimed

9. "The Withering of the Rule of Law," *Speculum Juris* 68 (1973), pp. 86–87.

10. Second Report of the Constitutional Committee of the President's Council PC 4/1982, chapter 9 (para. 9.10.1).

11. This approach has been endorsed by many political figures. It also enjoyed the support of Mr. Justice J. H. Snyman: see Dugard, *Human Rights,* pp. 43–44.

12. (Pretoria: Government Printer, 1968), p. 47.

at the removal of the colored voters from the common electoral roll in the Cape Province. Before the formation of Union in 1910 the Cape Colony had a qualified but nonracial franchise, and in the compact of 1910 this nonracial franchise was maintained for the Cape Province alone. In order to secure this franchise against the northern provinces, which favored a franchise for whites only, a number of sections were included in the constitution of 1910 which might be amended or repealed only by a two-thirds majority vote of both houses of Parliament sitting together. In 1936 African voters in the Cape Province were removed from the Cape electoral roll by the correct constitutional procedure. When the National party government came to power in 1948, determined to remove the colored voters from the common roll, it lacked the necessary parliamentary support to give it a two-thirds majority vote in a joint session. Consequently it attempted to remove the colored voters by the normal parliamentary procedure of a majority vote in both houses sitting separately. This legislative action was declared to be unconstitutional by the appellate division of the Supreme Court in *Harris* v. *Minister of the Interior,*[13] as was a subsequent attempt to deny the Supreme Court's testing power by subordinating it to a "High Court of Parliament."[14] Still unable to muster the necessary two-thirds parliamentary support after the 1953 elections, the National party government resorted to the devious stratagem of packing the Senate with its own nominees and increasing the membership of the appellate division of the Supreme Court to include a number of judges sympathetic to the government. With its new parliamentary majority the government was able to remove the colored voters from the common roll. This questionable scheme was held to be constitutional by the "packed" appellate division in 1957.[15] In this way the National party government succeeded not only in eliminating coloreds from the common roll but also in establishing the principle of parliamentary supremacy over the courts. Indeed, during the constitutional crisis, as the National party saw its absolute power threatened by the courts, the principle of parliamentary supremacy assumed greater importance to the National party than the removal of the colored voters. In order to emphasize the subordinate role of the courts and the supremacy of the legislature, Parliament in 1956 passed a law expressly excluding the testing power of the courts.[16]

Although the challenge to the removal of colored voters from the

13. *Harris* v. *Minister of the Interior,* 1952 (2), South African Law Reports 428 (A.D.).
14. *Minister of the Interior* v. *Harris,* 1952, (4), South African Law Reports 769 (A.D.).
15. *Collins* v. *Minister of the Interior,* 1957, (1), South African Law Reports 552 (A.D.).
16. South Africa Act Amendment Act 9 of 1956.

common electoral roll was mounted by political bodies, it was inspired by the writings of two liberal Cape Town scholars, Ben Beinart[17] and D. V. Cowen;[18] argued by distinguished liberal counsel, Graeme Duncan and Donald Molteno; and upheld in the two *Harris* cases by an appellate division that included two of South Africa's greatest liberal judges, Albert van der Sandt Centlivres and Oliver Deneys Schreiner. Although the view that Parliament itself was bound by the law was ultimately bypassed, the arguments raised by liberal lawyers and judges in the two *Harris* cases served to highlight the lawlessness of government action and to create a new awareness of the need for vigilance in defense of the rule of law.

After the government had succeeded in removing the colored voters from the common roll in 1956, liberals turned their attention to broader issues. In 1962, the newly formed Progressive party set up a commission of experts, chaired by Donald Molteno Q.C.,[19] which recommended a bill of rights to be enforced by judicial review.[20] This recommendation, accepted as policy by the Progressive party, stimulated a new interest in the constitutional protection of individual liberties among liberal lawyers;[21] in more recent years such protection has received public support from several liberal judges, including M. M. Corbett,[22] A. J. Milne, R. Leon, and J. M. Didcott.

While some liberals focused attention upon constitutional models for a democratic South Africa, others preferred to examine the harm done to the South African legal system by the racist and repressive laws enacted by the National party–controlled Parliament. Brookes and Macaulay,[23] Beinart,[24] Molteno,[25] Mathews,[26] Schreiner,[27] and Arthur

17. Ben Beinart, "Sovereignty and the Law," *Tydskrif vir Hedendaagse Romeins–Hollandse Reg* 15 (1952), p. 101.

18. D. V. Cowen, *Parliamentary Sovereignty and the Entrenched Sections of the South Africa Act* (Cape Town: Juta, 1951).

19. This commission included a number of prominent liberal figures in addition to its chairman, such as Edgar Brookes, Leonard Thompson, and Arthur Suzman Q.C.

20. Final report of the commission set up by the Progressive party to make recommendations on a revised constitution for South Africa extending franchise rights to all civilized subjects of the republic (Johannesburg: Progressive Party, 1962).

21. See, in particular, D. V. Cowen, *The Foundations of Freedom* (Cape Town: Oxford University Press, 1961).

22. M. M. Corbett, "Human Rights: The Road Ahead," in *Human Rights: The Cape Town Conference*, C. F. Forsyth and J. E. Schiller, eds. (Cape Town: Juta, 1979), pp. 4–5.

23. Edgar Brookes and J. B. Macaulay, *Civil Liberty in South Africa* (Cape Town: Oxford University Press, 1958).

24. Ben Beinart, "The Rule of Law," *Acta Juridica* (1962), p. 99.

25. Donald Molteno, "The Rules Behind the Rules of Law," *Acta Juridica* (1965–1966), p. 135.

26. A. S. Mathews, *Law, Order and Liberty in South Africa* (Cape Town: Juta, 1971).

27. Oliver Schreiner, *The Contribution of English Law to South African Law; and the Rule of Law in South Africa* (London: Stevens, 1967).

Suzman[28] persuasively argued that the rule of law had been seriously undermined by laws that conferred wide discretionary powers on government officials, that authorized detention-without-trial, and that allocated fundamental rights unequally on grounds of race. At the same time they showed that the principles inherent in the notion of the rule of law—controlled executive power, equality before the law, the maintenance of personal freedom, and independent and impartial courts—were essential to good government. Another liberal attack was directed at the courts. As pro-executive judicial rulings in the interpretation of the race and security laws became more frequent, liberal critics questioned the judiciary's commitment to the rule of law and argued that judges were obliged, in accordance with the liberal traditions of Roman-Dutch law, to interpret ambiguous statutes benevolently in favor of individual liberty and equality.[29]

Although most of the laws that run counter to the principles inherent in the rule of law remain unchanged, Afrikaner nationalist attitudes toward notions of justice and human rights have certainly altered. However, it is difficult to assess the extent of this change. On the one hand, there is positive government rhetoric, starting with the plea of the foreign minister, R. F. Botha, in 1970 for an acceptance of the principles contained in the Universal Declaration of Human Rights[30] and culminating in the address of the state president, P. W. Botha, at the opening of Parliament in 1986, in which he declared:

> We believe in the sovereignty of the law as a basis for the protection of the fundamental rights of individuals as well as groups. We believe in the sanctity and indivisibility of law and the just application thereof. There can be no peace, freedom and democracy without law. Any future system must conform with the requirements of a civilized legal order, and must ensure access to the courts and equality before the law. We believe that human dignity, life, liberty and property of all must be protected, regardless of color, race, creed or religion.[31]

On the other hand, the government has refused to translate this rhetoric into reality. Racist and repressive laws, draconian emergency regulations, and arbitrary administrative action give the lie to the government's rhetorical flourishes. Moreover, the government has in recent times refused even to consider the introduction of a bill of rights. In 1982 the president's council rejected suggestions that the new constitution should

28. Arthur Suzman "South Africa and the rule of law," *South African Law Journal* 85 (1968), p. 261.

29. Dugard, *Human Rights*, Part 4.

30. Republic of South Africa, *House of Assembly Debates* (*H. of Ass.*), vol. 29 (21 August 1970), cols. 2164–66.

31. *H. of Ass.*, Weekly Edition 8:1 (31 January 1986), cols. 13–14.

contain "a declaration of human rights,"[32] and in 1983 the government opposed a proposal by the Progressive Federal party that a bill of rights be included in the constitution.[33] Surprisingly, however, in April 1986, the government instructed the Law Commission, a body charged with the reform of the law, to investigate the role of the courts in the protection of group rights and individual rights and to consider the desirability of introducing a bill of rights.

Significant changes have taken place in the attitudes of prominent Afrikaners outside government who in earlier days were (or were perceived to be) part of the Afrikaner nationalist legal establishment. The following examples illustrate the nature of the change. In 1975 Johan van der Vyver of Potchefstroom University published the first text on human rights in South Africa written in Afrikaans,[34] which catalogued the statutory invasions of human rights and concluded with an appeal for a bill of rights. In 1979 D. P. de Villiers, the leader of the South African legal team in the 1960–1966 and 1971 proceedings before the International Court of Justice over Namibia, declared in a major address at the Rand Afrikaans University that the doctrine of the rule of law, which has roots in both English and Roman-Dutch law, was threatened by the security laws. He called for a commission of inquiry into these laws.[35] In the same year, at a conference held at Potchefstroom University, Ignus Rautenbach of the Rand Afrikaans University, shortly before his appointment as head of constitutional planning in the department of constitutional development and planning, advocated the inclusion of a bill of rights in a new South African constitution.[36] In 1981 Marinus Wiechers of the University of South Africa produced a new edition of the standard Afrikaans work on constitutional law in which he completely revised the section on the rule of law and fundamental freedoms.[37] Unlike the author of the original work, J. P. Verloren van Themaat, he acknowledged the juridical nature of the rule of law and deplored the extent to which South

32. Second Report of the Constitutional Committee of the President's Council PC 4/1982f, chapter 9.

33. *H. of Ass.*, vol. 108 (15–17 August 1983), cols. 11181–11494.

34. Johan van der Vyver, *Die Beskerming van Menseregte in Suid Afrika* (Cape Town: Juta, 1975). This was soon followed by the same author's *Seven Lectures on Human Rights* (Cape Town: Juta, 1976).

35. D. P. de Villiers, "The Rule of Law and Public Safety in Contemporary South Africa," *Tydskrif vir die Suid-Afrikaanse Reg* 83 (1979).

36. Ignus Rautenbach, "The Juridical Operation of a Bill of Rights and the New Constitutional Dispensation," in S. C. Jacobs, ed., *'n Nuwe Grondwetlike Bedeling vir Suid-Afrika*, (Durban: Butterworth, 1981), p. 151.

37. J. P. Verloren van Themaat, *Staatsreg*, 3rd ed., Marinus Wiechers, ed. (Durban: Butterworth, 1981), pp. 135–56.

African statutes had violated basic human rights. Wiechers[38] and other Afrikaans writers[39] have, moreover, breathed new life into the rule of law—still widely perceived as a British concept among Afrikaners—by buttressing it with the German notion of the *Rechtsstaat,* which envisages a just society based on the protection of fundamental rights, the separation of powers, the principle of legality, and an independent judiciary. Finally, Afrikaners have played a major role in the establishment of Lawyers for Human Rights, an association of lawyers committed to the promotion of human rights in South Africa. Johan Kriegler, now a judge of the Supreme Court, was the first national president of this organization and was succeeded by van der Vyver.

It is difficult to measure the significance of this new approach to law and justice in South Africa. Already it has had some tangible results: de Villiers's call led to the establishment of the Rabie Commission of Enquiry into Security Legislation[40] and the amelioration of South Africa's security laws.[41] Bophuthatswana included a bill of rights in its constitution in 1979, largely on the advice of Wiechers. Probably the intangible results are more significant, however. Today there is a new mood among legal academics on the Afrikaans campuses and there are signs that it is spreading to the legal profession and judiciary. Indeed this probably explains the new interest in a bill of rights. The advocacy of human rights and the criticism of government and judiciary for failing to show sufficient concern for this priority is no longer the preserve of liberal politicians and academics. If not part of the mainstream of Afrikaner legal opinion, it is at least an important tributary.

Liberals may take credit for the fact that the concern for human rights survived the bleak years of Verwoerd and Vorster to become a principal priority on the current political agenda. The voice of Helen Suzman in Parliament, the crusade of the women's activist organization, the Black Sash, the vigilance of newspapers such as the *Rand Daily Mail* and *Cape Times,* and the firm stance of human-rights lawyers and scholars have served to highlight injustices, to encourage the judiciary to adopt a more watchful role, to initiate a debate over a bill of rights, and to transform Afrikaner attitudes toward law and justice. These achievements of liberals in the sphere of justice are a matter of public record.

Unhappily, there is today a mood of despondency among liberals,

38. Ibid., p. 139.

39. For example, D. H. van Wyk, "South Africa and the Notion of a *Rechtsstaat,*" *Tydskrif vir die Suid–Afrikaanse Reg* 152 (1980).

40. RP 90/1981.

41. Internal Security Act 74 of 1982.

who see their role as the guardians of human rights and the rule of law denigrated by the left and by the right. The radical right is a well-known force: nearly forty years of struggle have taught liberals to withstand its racism and repression and to resist the treachery of its rhetoric. The threat from the radical left is more insidious and has clearly disturbed many liberals who never wavered under attack from the right. The radical left increasingly portrays any form of working within the present "system" as collaboration. Liberal judges are called upon to resign rather than to pursue an activist course in defense of human rights;[42] human-rights lawyers are accused of legitimizing an evil system; and participation in the debate over future constitutional models is labeled as reactionary or unprogressive. Happily the first two charges have had little impact, largely because the liberation movements themselves still seem to have some confidence in the legal process and human-rights lawyers. However, there are indications that liberals have abstained from involvement in the debate over a constitutional blueprint for the future for fear of ostracism from the left, a highly unfortunate development since there is today a desperate need for new ideas and proposals for constitutional models to accommodate the rival forces within South African society. The left argues that the Freedom Charter of 1955 provides such a constitutional blueprint. This is absurd since the Freedom Charter is a statement of principles to which a democratic South Africa should aspire and does not purport to be a constitutional instrument. Equally absurd is the idea that the only constitutional model worthy of consideration is unfettered majority rule in a unitary state. Even if the federal option is discarded in favor of a union, there remains a need for checks and balances and a bill of rights if a truly democratic society is to be attained. Liberals must therefore resist the intolerance of the left and persist in their efforts to construct a constitutional model for South Africa that will restore equality before the law and individual liberty under the governance of the law. Liberals cannot falter now that the cracks are opening in the edifice of Afrikaner nationalism. They must maintain their role as the principal guardians of human rights in South Africa.

42. Raymond Wacks, "Judges and Injustice," *South African Law Journal* 101 (1980): 266.

A. S. Mathews

16. Human Rights and the Rule of Law, II

The "rule of law," or what E. P. Thompson has described as "the negative restrictions of bourgeois legalism,"[1] has always been a prominent article of faith of Western liberalism. This is true of South African liberals too, but their approach to the rule of law has always supported the traditional, more conservative theory associated with A. V. Dicey, which concentrates strictly on the legal protection of basic civil rights through the ordinary courts. Oliver Schreiner, a name associated with impeccable liberalism in South Africa and one of its great judges, was firmly committed to the conservative view of the rule of law.[2] He announced and justified his belief in the Diceyan model in the Hamlyn lectures in 1967 at Cambridge.[3] The rule of law, in its traditional form, seeks to guarantee civil rights in the restricted sense of personal, spiritual, and political freedoms—what Ralf Dahrendorf has felicitously called the civil element of citizenship.[4] This encompasses personal freedom and freedom of belief, expression, movement, assembly,

1. E. P. Thompson, *Whigs and Hunters* (London: Penguin, 1977), p. 266.

2. Schreiner's adherence to the traditional concept of the rule of law sometimes wavered in his political judgments: see Christopher Forsyth, *In Danger for Their Talents* (Cape Town: Juta, 1985), p. 151; *Tumpelmann v. Minister for Justice and Minister for Defence,* 1940, TPD 242.

3. O. D. Schreiner, *The Contribution of English Law to South African Law, and the Rule of Law in South Africa* (London: Stevens, 1967).

4. Ralf Dahrendorf, *Society and Democracy in Germany* (New York: Doubleday, 1967), p. 70.

and association. It confines the rule of law to "the position of the individual in political society."[5] It does not seek to "embrace the whole area of good government"[6] or propound the theory that "good should triumph."[7]

Liberal commitment to the traditional theory of the rule of law implied the rejection of alternative theories. It will be helpful to examine what liberals avoided when they eschewed post-Diceyan models, and whether they were wise to do so. One of the chief advocates of the transformed theory of the rule of law has been the International Commission of Jurists. Though the commission's first pronouncement on the subject at Athens in 1955[8] was cast in a Diceyan mold, it soon committed itself to an altogether grander approach, first at Delhi in 1959[9] and later at Lagos in 1961, where it declared that

> The rule of law is a dynamic concept which should be employed to safeguard and advance the will of the people and the political rights of the individual and to establish social, economic, educational and cultural conditions under which the individual may achieve his dignity and realise his legitimate aspirations in all countries, whether dependent or independent.[10]

The reason for this grandiose enlargement of the area of concern of the rule of law is clear: the traditional doctrine emphasizing basic civil rights (the so-called fundamental freedoms) has nothing to say about the concern of the third-world representatives at Delhi and Lagos with social, cultural, economic, and political justice. The preoccupations of those at Delhi and Lagos may be epitomized as bread, shelter, and a job before freedom of speech and conscience, and this was an emphasis that the "rule of law" was expected to reflect.

The priority of socioeconomic development over the more intellectual and spiritual concerns of the Diceyan approach is not the only basis for attempts to widen the focus of concern of the rule of law. The development on the European continent of the material *rechtsstaats* idea is due in part to the perceived failure of the narrower doctrine, with its emphasis on the legal control of the executive, to withstand such phenomena as Nazi totalitarianism. The material *rechtsstaats* theory would put the rule of law at the service of the search for justice in the

---

5. T. R. S. Allan, "Legislative Supremacy and the Rule of Law: Democracy and Constitutionalism," *Cambridge Law Journal* 44 (1985): 111, 134.

6. Schreiner, *Contribution*, p. 83.

7. Joseph Raz, "The Rule of Law and Its Virtue," *Cambridge Law Journal* 93 (1977).

8. The so-called "Act of Athens" adopted by a congress of the commission on 18 June 1955.

9. The "Declaration of Delhi" adopted at the Delhi congress on 10 January 1959.

10. From the "Law of Lagos" adopted on 7 January 1961.

broadest sense, including the realization of the goals of the modern welfare state.[11]

Considering that the broader theories were developed specifically to further the achievement of socioeconomic justice and to counter totalitarian trends in government, it is surprising at first sight that South Africa's liberals were not attracted to them. After all, one of their prime concerns has been about socioeconomic injustice and authoritarian and totalitarian trends under National party rule. Still, the liberals were reluctant to make the rule of law a vehicle for all those concerns. In the first place, Dicey's doctrine is wider than the formal *rechtsstaats* idea in Europe, which requires mainly the subjection of executive authority to clear rules enforced by the courts. The Diceyan theory goes beyond this by demanding that the basic rights of the citizen be recognized and protected by public authority; and this material content of the theory means that it stands in opposition to totalitarianism. The entire purpose of the rule of law, conceived as Dicey did, is to resist jackboot-style incursions into the rights of speech, assembly, association, and the like. In the second place, to expand the rule of law to embrace socioeconomic justice in the fullest sense, or, as Hayek would have it, to apply it to the government in *all its actions,* would be to cast it into a sea of troubled waters which are bound, sooner or later, to submerge it.

There are several reasons why liberals, notwithstanding their commitment to material justice for all citizens, have shown great wisdom in refusing to saddle the rule of law with these broader concerns. The reasons may be summed up as follows:

(1) While judicial enforcement of rights is an essential feature of the rule of law, the broader (or material-justice) approaches to it would place a burden on the courts which they could not sustain. The courts are asked to perform a manageable task when a constitution or legal system requires them to protect personal freedom by granting a writ of habeas corpus, say, but *not* when they are expected to guarantee fair wages or a decent education.

(2) The rule of law seeks to regulate official conduct by pre-announced, clear, and specific rules; and whereas such rules are quite workable in relation to the fundamental freedoms, they are inappropriate in other areas of government. As Lon Fuller said, there are certain areas of human endeavor which cannot endure a delimiting in terms of formal claims of right and wrong.[12] Clear examples of such areas of decision-

11. See Eikema Hommes "De Materiele Rechtsstaatsidee," *Tydskrif vir Suid-Afrikaanse Reg* (1978): 42.

12. Robert S. Summers, *Lon Fuller* (London: Edward Arnold, 1984), p. 91.

making are fiscal policy, economic decentralization, and wage and price determinations.

(3) The effect of the introduction of fixed norms into such inappropriate areas of government is to "detach legal thought from social reality,"[13] to freeze social development, and to stabilize and sharpen existing disparities between those who possess economic power and those who do not.[14]

(4) The narrow doctrine of the rule of law has a far greater chance of cross-cultural acceptance than one which seeks to commit it to specific socioeconomic policies. The broader theories tend to politicize and polemicize the rule of law and to deprive it of general if not universal respect.

We may sum up the argument by saying that liberals, while committed to socioeconomic justice, have sensibly (though with some inconsistency) refrained from seeking to pursue it through the rule of law, a task that is essentially a political one with law playing only an ancillary or handmaiden role.

Once this is understood, the misdirected nature of the Marxist critique of legality becomes clear. The essence of Marxist thinking on this point is that the law, while ostensibly a neutral arbiter between competing claims or interests in society, actually protects and entrenches ruling-class interests. One commentator on the liberal doctrine of the rule of law expressed the problem in these terms:

> Far from an autonomous, egalitarian sphere, the legal realm for classical Marxism was rooted in the social relations of production whose oppressiveness it not only did not counteract, relieve or even escape, but indeed which it ratified, mystified and enforced.[15]

Or, as Bob Fine has said, the law "puts its social weight behind one claimant or another and so 'resolves' disputes by virtue of its power rather than its impartiality."[16] The reason why Marxist critiques are misdirected is that what they seek to expose, frequently with success, is the false neutrality of law in society, not of the rule of law. They do not distinguish between the *role* of law in general and the *rule* of law in particular. Moreover, the Marxist critique is concerned mainly with the economic sphere and specifically with the role of law in the "social relations of production." The focus of the rule of law, on the other hand, is on the political relations between ruler and subject. It is in

13. Q. Nonet and F. Selznick, *Law and Society in Transition* (New York: Harper & Row, 1978), p. 64.

14. Anthony T. Kronman, *Max Weber* (London: Edward Arnold, 1983), p. 94.

15. M. Mandel, "The Rule of Law and the Legislation of Politics in Canada," *International Journal of the Sociology of Law* 13 (1985): 273, 274.

16. Bob Fine, *Democracy and the Rule of Law* (London: Pluto, 1984), p. 157.

Marxist states that this relationship is characterized by pure oppressiveness and in which the subjection of the individual to public authority is "ratified, mystified and enforced."

The irony of it all is that had liberals responded to radical pressure to extend the traditional doctrine into the economic sphere, they would have become vulnerable to the very radical criticism they avoided by their conservatism. That conservatism has invested the rule of law with a formidable claim to neutrality, since it associates the doctrine with those basic rights that grant citizens the freedom either to support or to attack the existing economic and social order. And while the neutrality of the law in the confined area of basic rights may sometimes falter, this is due to human failings, which are remediable without doing violence to the Diceyan model.[17] The reason why a Marxist like E. P. Thompson has decribed the liberal doctrine as an "unqualified human good," and why Bob Fine has advocated an interim alliance between liberalism and Marxism on the issue of civil rights, is that the rule of law is not a sham or a bourgeois "fetish" as its radical critics have frequently claimed. It is indeed, as G. Treves has said, "an achievement of mankind."[18]

Unfortunately, the good sense and moderation reflected in the liberal ideal of the rule of law has been accompanied by a lack of discernment and realism in the program for its achievement in the divided South African society. Even though liberals have conceived of the rule of law as a restraint on power, they have failed to appreciate the reality of power relations in the context in which they desired the rule of law to operate. Their failure, as the report of the political commission of the Study Project on Christianity in Apartheid Society (Spro-cas) has said, has been to distinguish between liberal-constitutionalism "as a normative requirement and as a practical proposal in a given situation."[19] Sometimes liberals spoke as if the rational appeal of the rule of law, and of constitutionalism in general, were sufficient to ensure its victory, whereas, in truth, it has little relevance or appeal either to a group intent on consolidating its power in a plural society or to a rival group committed to the unseating of the power-holders.

In a nutshell, the rule of law is a predictable casualty in the intense nationalistic power struggle that has dominated South African politics for decades. An analysis of the demise of liberal "bourgeois legalism"

17. Measures to ensure the impartiality of judges (including the avoidance of class bias) are quite consistent with the liberal doctrine.

18. G. Treves, "The Rule of Law in Italy," *Annales de la Faculté de Droit d'Istanbul* IX (1959), p. 118.

19. *South Africa's Political Alternatives: Report of the Political Commission of the Study Project on Christianity in Apartheid Society* (Johannesburg: Ravan, 1973), p. 130.

will be helpful in evaluating the past, present, and future relevance of liberal thinking in South Africa.

There can be no doubt that many liberals were guilty of advocating the doctrine of the rule of law in such a way that they alienated the supporters of both rival nationalisms in South Africa. Afrikaner nationalism, though correctly perceived as hostile to liberal constitutionalism, was presented as the sole and exclusive threat to the maintenance of legality and basic rights. Liberals failed to perceive that black nationalism, whether or not spurred on by oppression under National party rule, might in time present as serious a threat to democratic constitutionalism. In Zimbabwe today, the security apparatus created by Ian Smith's minority regime has been taken over by the Mugabe government and is being applied with even less regard for individual rights than was the case in the former Rhodesia.[20]

Liberals also failed to appreciate that any government in a divided society, including a government of liberals, would be forced into deviating from pure rule-of-law principles as the contending groups struggled for dominance, equality, or greater justice, especially during a period of transition toward a better dispensation. Black nationalism has been alienated by the liberal doctrine because, as the Spro-cas report has pointed out, the constitutional measures advocated by many prominent liberals would operate as a conservative force and "would tend to inhibit political changes in the unequal status quo."[21] In advocating these constitutional measures, liberals were in practice untrue to the narrow doctrine of the rule of law to which they gave intellectual adherence, since they sought to preserve the economic and property rights of the privileged by entrenched restraints of law. The liberal failure, in relation to their advocacy of the rule of law, was essentially a failure to test their beliefs against the realities of the social and political life of the country. It is not surprising that they were seen by both sides as the adherents of a theory of "airy-fairy" unreality and that they have failed to persuade either most Afrikaner nationalists or most African nationalists of the relevance of the rule of law.

If the rule of law is to be more relevant, liberals must in the first place acknowledge that it has only *limited* applicability in an unequal, divided society in transition toward a new order. The old liberal notion of full civil rights backed by law in normal times, with occasional deviations during emergencies of short duration, has proved unequal to the security demands of a plural society. Amnon Rubinstein has expressed this well for the state of Israel:

20. See the fair-minded, objective assessment by David Caute in the *Weekly Mail*, 18–24 October 1985.

21. *South Africa's Political Alternatives*, p. 140.

> Because Israelis believe that this war or semi-war situation is not a short-term affair, they think that the country cannot afford the excesses of other countries in time of war. In other words, because we perceive our semi-war situation as a permanent feature of our national life, we have had to regulate, modify, and moderate the measures that would otherwise have been justified by the grave emergency situation.[22]

In other words, the continuing security demands of conflict-ridden societies make the return to full freedom under the law a remote possibility, and some more permanent way of tempering and moderating those demands must be found. Thus in Israel, preventive detention is reluctantly accepted on security grounds but every detention requires confirmation by the ordinary courts within forty-eight hours or else it will be illegal. The task for liberals in South Africa is to generalize this concept of a compromise between the demands of order and of liberty in such a way that the maximum freedom consistent with stability is permitted and guaranteed.

In the second place, liberals need to examine the social conditions under which full adherence to the rule of law will become possible and to work actively toward the achievement of such conditions. The specification of such conditions is a difficult task, but it has been suggested that the rule of law has flourished only in societies in which a roughly equal balance of forces made an appeal to the law attractive to all sides.[23] This finding gives clear direction to the liberal quest for a *political* solution in South Africa. If the liberal doctrine of the rule of law is to survive, its pursuit must be allied in a realistic way to the broader search for political and social justice in our society.[24] In other words, a return to the full guarantee of basic rights through law can be envisaged only as the outcome of a settlement of the broader economic and political issues that divide South Africans.

22. Amnon Rubinstein, "State Security and Human Rights: The Israeli Experience," in *Human Rights: The Cape Town Conference* (Cape Town: Juta, 1979), p. 138.

23. Roberto Unger, *Law in Modern Society* (New York: Free Press, 1976).

24. Though the quest for a return to legality has to be allied to general reform, the two tasks must not be conflated and confused as in the material-justice approach to the rule of law.

Gerald Shaw

17. The English-Language Press

The South African English-language press is rooted in a nineteenth-century liberal tradition that accords a high value to freedom of the individual in political and economic life. The record of this press has been as flawed as that of any other human institution and its performance today falls short of universal excellence, yet the liberal newspapers have made a useful contribution toward the creation of a more humane order in South Africa. They remain indispensable in a stormy transitional phase of South African history, and their survival in strength will be an index of the health of that society. Their demise, if the tradition does not survive, will reflect its degeneracy.

The liberal tradition of free expression came to South Africa with the 1820 British settlers. The story of the battle between 1823 and 1829 of John Fairbairn, Thomas Pringle, and George Greig to establish the freedom of the press in the teeth of the hostility of despotic colonial authorities has been frequently told,[1] as has the growth of a vigorous settler press under Robert Godlonton on the eastern frontier in Grahamstown.[2] Not until the mineral revolution in the last quarter of the

1. A concise history of the early days of the press in South Africa may be found in William A. Hachten and C. Anthony Giffard, *Total Onslaught—The South African Press Under Attack* (Madison: University of Wisconsin Press, 1984), pp. 23–28.

2. B. A. LeCordeur, "Robert Godlonton As Architect of Frontier Opinion 1850–1857," *Archives Year Book for South African History*, 2 (Pretoria: Government Printer, 1959).

nineteenth century, however, could a vigorous daily press be established on a permanent footing throughout the country.

The *Cape Times*, established in 1876, the first paper to begin as a daily, has continued in unbroken publication. The discovery of diamonds in Kimberley in 1870 was beginning to transform the economic landscape and railways were racing into the interior. As gold discoveries from 1886 on added further momentum to trade and industry, daily newspapers prospered in the ports and inland in centers such as Kimberley. These newspapers were founded as commercial undertakings by individual entrepreneurs in close association with the burgeoning commercial communities of the time. Supported with advertising by local traders, they tended to favor economic freedom rather than the protectionist policies promoted by groups such as the Afrikaner Bond in the Cape which represented agrarian interests. Such newspapers in the ports were the *Cape Times* and the *Cape Argus* in Cape Town, the *Natal Mercury* in Durban, the *Eastern Province Herald* in Port Elizabeth, and the *Daily Dispatch* in East London. In smaller centers inland, independent papers such as the *Midland News* in Cradock and *Grocott's Mail* in Grahamstown were important institutions in their own communities. In the Natal interior, the *Natal Witness*, one of the oldest papers, established a vigorous daily newspaper tradition which, with the *Daily Dispatch* of East London, still flourishes under independent ownership.

The Argus Company, under the control of mining-financial interests, is a publishing giant dominating the English-language press in South Africa.[3] The Johannesburg Consolidated Investment Company, at present under the chairmanship of Gordon Waddell, and a subsidiary of the Anglo-American Corporation, is today the controlling shareholder in both Argus and South African Associated Newspapers (SAAN), the other major newspaper group. Duncan Innes accords Anglo-American a 40 percent controlling interest in Argus, which in turn has a large share in SAAN. Robin McGregor argues that Anglo-American is the ultimate controlling shareholder in both SAAN and Argus, with a share of SAAN, via Argus, of 37.91 percent. Innes notes that Harry Oppenheimer, until recently the chairman of Anglo-American, has often claimed that Anglo-American does not interfere in the editorial policy of the newspapers, but he suggests that because Oppenheimer owns

3. *Report of the Press Commission 1964* (Pretoria: Government Printer, 1964), annexure IV, portion I, pp. 54–60; Robin McGregor, *McGregor's Who Owns Whom* (Johannesburg: McGregor, 1984), pp. 54, 254, 255; *The Argus* 3 March 1981; *Cape Times*, 7 September 1984; Duncan Innes, *Anglo: Anglo American and the Rise of Modern South Africa* (Johannesburg: Ravan, 1984).

the papers anyway such interference is unnecessary.[4] Much of the radical critique of the "monopolist" English-language press is based on this link of the press to mining-financial interests, with ultimate financial control of most of the country's English-language newspapers in a few hands.

Both radical and Afrikaner nationalist hostility toward the English-language press goes back a long way, much of it deriving from the writings of J. A. Hobson before and during the South African War of 1899–1902.[5] Hobson's assertion that the war was caused by a mineowners' conspiracy, working through a "kept press," has long been accepted by radicals and Afrikaner nationalists alike and is still cited by both.[6]

Some recent research suggests, however, that Hobson's view was based on faulty assumptions and information.[7] As does Innes today, Hobson tended to assume that financial control of a newspaper necessarily brings with it effective day-to-day control of editorial policy. But apart from the proprietor's critical role in appointing and on occasion discharging the editor, there is also the role of the editor, and of the readers, whose inclinations can sometimes determine what line a paper will take.[8] It is an imprudent proprietor who interferes in the editorial prerogative in order to inject his own notions and fancies into the control and management of a newspaper, and an unwise editor who loses touch with his readers. A newspaper operating in the liberal tradition, competing in the marketplace of ideas, is much of the time reflecting the opinions of its readers as much as forming them, although it may in crisis situations move somewhat ahead of them. Editors or proprietors alike who lose sight of this are courting disaster.

In South Africa, where a newspaper such as the *Cape Times* today finds its readership rather evenly divided between white (45%), colored (45%), and black (10%), the editorial function is especially demanding. In any society, it helps a great deal if a paper's readers are on similar levels of income and share similar interests, tastes, and patterns of

4. Innes, *Anglo-American*, p. 205, and McGregor, *Who Owns Whom*, pp. 54, 254, 255.

5. J. A. Hobson, *The War in South Africa* (London: James Nisbet, 1900), pp. 206, 229; J. A. Hobson, *The Psychology of Jingoism* (London: James Nisbet, 1901), pp. 197ff.

6. See, e.g., G. Blainey, "Lost Causes of the Jameson Raid," *Economic History Review* 18 (1965), pp. 350–56; Shula Marks and Stanley Trapido, "Lord Milner and the South African State," *History Workshop* 8 (1979); *Commission of Inquiry into the Mass Media RP/1981*, pp. 773, 760.

7. A. H. Duminy, *The Capitalists and the Outbreak of the Anglo-Boer War* (Durban: University of Natal, 1977); G. Shaw, *South African Telegraph versus Cape Times, An Examination of the Attempt by the South African Telegraph, Financed by J. B. Robinson, to Challenge the Dominance of the Pro-Rhodes Press at the Cape, August 1895 to September 1896* (Cape Town: Centre for African Studies, University of Cape Town, 1980); G. Shaw, ed., *The Garrett Papers*, Van Riebeeck Society, Second Series, No. 15 (Cape Town: Van Riebeeck Society, 1984), pp. 19–39.

8. Shaw, *South African Telegraph*, pp. 61–65.

consumer behavior; a paper with a readership divided by class *and* race faces an uphill task.

In the liberal tradition of newspaper publishing, the control and direction of a newspaper's policy is a complex three-way process. The power of the proprietor is properly exercised in the initial choice and appointment of an editor. Proprietors appoint editors whose views and attitudes are known to them in general terms. They appoint editors they believe will maintain the traditional practices and attitudes of the newspaper and will do so at a profit. The proprietors can discharge the editor, but if he is established in his post and respected by his staff and the community, and if the paper is at the same time commercially successful, dismissal is an option proprietors approach with the greatest reluctance. On the *Cape Times,* where there is a strong tradition of editorial independence, contractually entrenched in the letter of the appointment given to the editor, the latter's position is very strong indeed.[9]

Independent editorship is invariably associated with editorial excellence and tends to be more viable commercially than its opposite. Interference in the editorial function leads to faltering morale, to intellectual inconsistency, and to a lowering of standards, quickly perceived by the readership. Dismissal of a respected editor and a rapid succession of changes of editorship can incur great odium, undermining a newspaper's credibility and standing. The role of the readership and the market must never be left out of account. If the readers lose interest in a paper and its circulation goes into decline, advertisers soon withdraw from its columns, robbing the newspaper of the revenue which is its lifeblood. It is the readers who have the final word, exercising a check upon editor and proprietor alike. This is a sound tradition, I believe: it renders newspapers responsive to social reality and curbs any tendency to editorial self-indulgence or proprietorial delusions of grandeur.

The liberal tradition has long been, and remains, under attack from both the left and the right. On the right, the hostility of the National party rulers of South Africa toward the English-language press has been sustained without respite since D. F. Malan's accession as prime minister in 1948. One of the first actions of the new regime was the appointment of a Press Commission, under a judge, Helm van Zijl, which labored for fifteen years before producing a voluminous report in 1964 calling for a national register of journalists and a statutory council to control the press. These recommendations were not translated into legislation.

9. G. Shaw, *Some Beginnings: The Cape Times 1876–1910* (Cape Town: Oxford University Press, 1975), pp. 164, 165.

The newspaper industry, having been told to "put its house in order," felt it expedient to introduce a form of self-discipline, preempting government action. A press council was set up by the newspaper industry to receive and adjudicate complaints against infringements of a code of conduct that laid down ethical and professional standards for newspapers. As a result, members of the Newspaper Press Union were exempted from the censorship provisions of the Publications Act that was brought into force at this time.[10]

Again, in the 1980s, amid a feeling among Nationalists that the press council had been deficient in disciplining the press, another commission of inquiry was appointed, this time under the chairmanship of another judge, M. T. Steyn, which revived the idea of a register of journalists and a statutory council to watch over the press. Again the newspaper proprietors and editors came together to preempt government action and, under intense government pressure, revamped the old press council and renamed it the media council. This remains as a voluntary body under the chairmanship of a retired judge. It has the power to reprimand newspapers, to instruct them to publish retractions or corrections, and even to impose fines up to 10,000 rands for infringements of a new and expanded code of conduct.

There have been significant amendments to the code of conduct, prescribing more comprehensive guidelines for editorial comment as well as for news coverage. A statute known as the Registration of Newspapers Amendment Act passed by Parliament in June 1982 empowered the state to de-register newspapers that declined to subject themselves to the discipline of a "voluntary" media council. The effect of this legislation, if enforced, would be to transform the voluntary media council into a statutory body. For the first time in South African history, arrangements for ethical and professional discipline of the press—discipline which to a liberal should be strictly domestic and voluntary—would be enshrined in the law. Existing law lays down that newspapers may not be published unless registered with the authorities, so refusal to be subject to the media council would mean the closure of the newspaper concerned. This statute, although enacted by Parliament, has never been brought into force by proclamation in the *Government Gazette* and remains as a sword of Damocles to concentrate the minds of editors. The proposal for a register of journalists was again not enacted. Nevertheless, if the Newspapers Amendment Act is brought into force, the principle of statutory control of the press will be

10. Elaine Potter, *The Press As Opposition: The Political Role of South African Newspapers* (London: Chatto and Windus, 1975), pp. 102–12.

established, and further encroachment on press freedom will be that much easier.[11]

In its dealings with Western visitors the South African government is quick to claim that South Africa, almost uniquely in Africa, has a vigorous free press. The reality is rather different. The press is operating in a twilight zone between freedom and unfreedom. Since 1948 a host of restrictive statutes have been passed; they are discussed below.[12] Recently, the legislative onslaught has been augmented by a second process of attempted co-option of the press in a kind of gentlemen's agreement not to rock the boat, an insidious process almost imperceptible to the untrained eye. It is to some extent institutionalized in written agreements, such as that between the Newspaper Press Union and the South African police, in terms of which the police make news available to the papers, and maintain a system of accreditation of journalists who may be given such news.[13] This agreement can become a telling weapon against the press. The police, if displeased by a particular newspaper, have been known to cut it off from all police information, a severe penalty for a publication that must rely on news of crime and catastrophe for much of its circulation. The threat of police displeasure no doubt acts as a check against vigorous investigative reporting of police activities in the townships, especially of allegations of overreaction, reckless use of tear gas or firearms, and so on. And it can, if it is allowed to do so, exercise a marked inhibiting effect on editorial comment.

Left-wing critics dismiss the English-language press contemptuously as the "commercial" press, assuming, I imagine, that the English-speaking mining-financial interests that own the English-language press have by now made common cause with the Afrikaner nationalist rulers of the country. The closure of the *Rand Daily Mail* and the *Sunday Express* by the proprietors is taken as proof positive of this contention.

The distrust of the English-language newspapers in the ranks of the radical left is not surprising, given their belief in the fundamental connection between ownership and control. But why the intense hostility felt by Afrikaner nationalists toward the English-language newspapers, and why the corrosive suspicion and distrust that have led to the appointment of two judicial commissions of inquiry into the press

11. For the Steyn Commission, see M. J. Richman, W. H. B. Dean, and D. M. Davis, *Distrust in Democracy: A Lawyers for Human Rights Comment on the Report of the Steyn Commission of Inquiry into the Mass Media* (Cape Town: Lawyers for Human Rights, 1981); for the media council, see K. W. Stuart, W. Lane, D. Hoffe, D. Dison, and C. Tatham, *Kelsey Stuart's Newspaperman's Guide to the Law*, 4th edition (Durban: Butterworth, 1986), pp. 19–34.

12. For details of restrictive statutes, see Stuart et al., *Newspaperman's Guide*.

13. Ibid., pp. 157, 158, 159.

since 1948 and a sustained barrage of antipress rhetoric, characterizing these newspapers as biased, slanderous, pro-communist, and unpatriotic?

The roots of the Afrikaner nationalist hostility to the English-language press are to be sought in a cast of mind that derives from the eastern frontier in the nineteenth century when the Dutch frontier farmers became convinced that the English secular and missionary authorities would invariably side with the blacks against them. Even today many Afrikaner nationalists are convinced that the English-speaking press is purposefully stirring up the blacks to undermine the Afrikaners. The frontiersman's suspicion and distrust of English missionaries and philanthropists became fastened upon the English-language newspapers in the early twentieth century and especially in the years before and immediately after the Anglo-Boer War. This distrust was steadily reinforced at the time of the general strike of 1922, when newly urbanized Afrikaner workers again detected the sinister hand of Hoggenheimer—the caricatured Anglo-Jewish capitalist—this time perceived as employing cheap black labor to undermine them.

After 1948 this demonology was strongly reinforced by the nationalists' perception of the English-language newspapers as the main channel through which black grievances and aspirations were being articulated. Now, more than ever, nationalists saw liberal newspapers such as the *Rand Daily Mail* as deliberately mobilizing black industrial and political power "to plough the Afrikaner under." Similarly, they saw the battle put up in the 1950s by the English-language newspapers to save the colored common-roll franchise from abolition as evidence of a determination to retain and develop the colored franchise as a means of driving Afrikaners from power.

All these considerations became intensified a thousandfold as black resistance to apartheid gathered momentum in the 1970s and 1980s. Because most blacks get their news about national events from the English-language press, many Afrikaner nationalists increasingly see the more forceful English-language newspapers as the handmaidens of black revolution. Given such hostile perceptions in the highest levels of government, is there any role left for liberal newspapers? Can a liberal press survive in South Africa, in a situation of incipient or low-intensity civil war?

Against a liberal yardstick, how do the proprietors of the English-language newspapers fare? What does the record show?

The proprietors, having lived since 1948 under an Afrikaner Nationalist government, have been acutely sensitive to the neo-Hobsonian charge that they might be abusing their power as owners of the English-language press to dictate editorial policy and manipulate public opinion. In practice they have been scrupulous most of the time in not interfering in the editorial or managerial policies of the newspapers and, on the assumption of continuing profitability, have been content to leave management to professional managers and editing to editors. In recent times the failing economic fortunes of the SAAN group have led to an unprecedented degree of managerial intervention by proprietors. But such intervention has been the exception rather than the rule.

There are a few notorious exceptions in which proprietors have stepped in to curb an editor's independent discharge of his duties. In the most celebrated case, in 1938 at the time of Munich, such attempted interference, when resisted, led to the forced resignation of Dominic McCausland as editor of the *Cape Argus* on account of his opposition to the appeasement policy favored by the financial establishment of the time. No single other incident in the history of the Argus Company has attracted such odium. The removal of McCausland was carried out on instructions sent by telegram from London by John Martin, then chairman of the Argus Company and also a governor of the Bank of England.[14]

The McCausland case was a warning to other editors that if they stepped too far outside the current assumptions of their mining-industry owners, they could get the chop. As Anthony Heard has written, it was one thing to be right, it was another thing to be right too soon.[15] Another celebrated case was that of Morris Broughton, an Argus editor who kept up a brave editorial stand during the Sharpeville state of emergency in 1960. Broughton incurred the wrath of his proprietors by editorials calling for an open-minded attitude toward the National party's proposal to declare the country a republic. Believing the Nationalists were determined to introduce a republican constitution, Broughton thought that English-speaking South Africa might achieve more for the liberal cause by accepting the inevitable gracefully in the 1961 referendum and securing concessions in the apartheid policy in return. The Argus Company brought intense pressure upon him to abandon this editorial line and join the chorus of outright opposition to the change.[16] The Nationalists won the day by a narrow margin in the referendum, and South Africa became a republic outside the Commonwealth. Not long afterwards, Broughton was appointed as an Argus correspondent in Europe and went to live on an island off the coast of Spain. The fact

14. E. Rosenthal, L. E. Neame, eds., *Today's News Today* (Johannesburg: Argus, 1956), pp. 264–69.

15. Anthony H. Heard in *Business and Society Review: A Quarterly Forum on the Role of Business in a Free Society* (Boston: Warren, Gorham and Lamont, 1985).

16. Information given by M. Broughton to G. Shaw in Cape Town in 1961.

of South Africa's republican status was quickly accepted by the English-speaking white community.

There was also the case of one of the most clear-sighted and courageous newspaper critics of apartheid, Laurence Gandar, editor of the *Rand Daily Mail* in the 1960s. Gandar was eased out of the editorship after losing a costly court case over his paper's disclosure of alleged abuses in the country's prisons. Gandar's strong opposition to apartheid would be unexceptionable today, but the *Rand Daily Mail* found itself attracting intense hostility in the English-speaking business community on the Witwatersrand. This hostility, plus the Nationalist government's clandestine funding out of the taxpayer's pocket of a competitor newspaper, the *Citizen* (established in 1976 seven years after Gandar had left the paper), meant loss of advertising revenue and led to eventual closure in 1985, following a rapid succession of changes of editorship. The *Rand Daily Mail's* circulation remained healthy throughout, but its share of the advertising cake declined steadily and the paper was massively in debt at its demise.

The state's role in the funding of the *Citizen* came to light in the so-called Information or "Muldergate" scandal in 1978–1979, which led to the downfall of the minister of information, Connie Mulder, and exposed the South African Department of Information's use of secret defense funds to influence the formation of opinion in South Africa and abroad. But the establishment of the *Citizen* was only one factor in the demise of the *Rand Daily Mail,* an unmitigated tragedy. In the years ahead, a daily paper like the *Rand Daily Mail,* trusted and respected in the black community, will be sorely needed.

It is too early to assess the impact of the current program of rationalization embarked upon by the Argus/SAAN groups to counter the effects of economic recession on the newspaper industry. After closing down the *Rand Daily Mail* and the *Sunday Express* and establishing a new business-oriented daily, *Business Day,* in their place, SAAN remained burdened by a large overdraft, causing it to sell its presses and to enter into a joint plant-sharing, distribution, and (to some degree) marketing operation with the Argus Company while retaining editorial independence for its publications. The signs are that the fortunes of SAAN will be successfully restored and the company placed on a sound footing.

Assuming that the SAAN-Argus rationalization program is benevolent in its effects and succeeds in securing the economic future of the English-language press while enhancing the development of outspoken, vigorous, and liberal-minded publications, what further hazards remain?

The main statutory restraints on the press are in the areas of reporting on defense, police, and prisons. The ban on publishing defense information without the approval of the minister of defense is almost total, but by informal agreement newspapers are exempted from prosecution when publishing official statements or news reports already published abroad, as long as the source is given and the department of defense is given prior opportunity to comment—and as long as the report does not deal with the acquisition of armaments.[17] There is a total ban on publishing without permission reports about oil supply and strategic minerals such as uranium. The reporting of any activities of the South African police is legally hazardous. It is an offense to publish any "untrue matter" about the police without having reasonable grounds for believing it to be true, on pain of a fine of 10,000 rands or imprisonment of up to ten years. In all, there are about one hundred laws on the statute books that impose restrictions on newspapers.

An important restriction in the Internal Security Act makes it a criminal offense for newspapers to quote any statement made by banned people, including leaders of the banned African National Congress, such as Oliver Tambo. The ANC, established in 1912, was declared a prohibited organization after the Sharpeville crisis in 1960 and has since then pursued a policy of "armed struggle" against the Pretoria government. This restriction on quoting banned persons became particularly irksome during 1985 when business leaders, churchmen, and other influential South Africans, seeking black-white rapprochement, took part in a series of exploratory meetings with the ANC leadership in Lusaka, Zambia. South African newspapers found themselves unable to report the ANC contributions to these discussions or to explain their significance. The editor of the *Cape Times,* Anthony Heard, interviewed Tambo in London and published an extended report of their conversation in the *Cape Times* in November 1985, believing that it was in the public interest for South Africans in all groups to be informed of the policies and attitudes of the major black nationalist organization in the country. Heard was charged under the Internal Security Act, but the hearing was continually postponed until July 1986, when the attorney general of the Cape announced that it was withdrawing the charge against him. South African Associated Newspapers in their capacity as publishers of the *Cape Times* paid a fine of 300 rands.

Harassment of reporters and photographers in the field, and restrictions imposed in terms of emergency regulations or other statutory provisions, made coverage of the "unrest" that began in September 1984—and continued through 1985 and into 1986—extraordinarily difficult. Large parts of the country were under a state of emergency for much of this time, with progressively more restrictive measures in force to curb the

17. Stuart et al., *Newspaperman's Guide,* pp. 159–62.

press. Reporters and photographers were locked out of emergency areas and forbidden to take pictures or make tape recordings. Journalists were detained, whipped, warned off, and generally harassed by hard-pressed police, and some also suffered assault, stoning, or petrol-bombing at the hands of demonstrators. The lifting of the state of emergency in March 1986 brought brief respite—until its reproclamation in June as a general state of emergency covering the entire country.

The most sweeping press curbs ever experienced in South Africa were brought into force under the emergency regulations of June 1986, taking South Africa far across the borderline from a free to an unfree press. The emergency regulations and the orders promulgated under them rendered nonofficial news coverage of police and army action in the unrest punishable by summary seizure of the publication concerned, with some or all issues of particular newspapers liable to be taken off the streets for the duration of the emergency. It became an offense to publish anything that might fall within the vaguely worded definition of a "subversive statement." The effect was to prohibit almost all independent reporting of the disorder and to limit coverage to the official handouts of the government propaganda machine, the Bureau of Information.

In mid-1985 legislation was rammed through Parliament to enable the minister of law and order—without declaring a state of emergency—to exercise the emergency powers vested in the state president. Under the Public Safety Amendment Act, the minister may declare certain disturbed areas in the country "unrest areas" and then issue such emergency decrees and regulations as he thinks fit to assist the police to deal with the disturbances. This legislation creates permanent powers for the police to override the ordinary law of the land and to enforce state control of the press by decree. So whether or not a formal state of emergency is in force, the South African police enjoy powers to curb the press as they choose. Regulations to restrict the press could become a permanent feature of the legal landscape and could take even more restrictive forms.

Against this background, liberal newspapers may expect to face sustained harassment and prosecution under emergency regulations or permanent statutes. The costs of answering such charges in court mounts up steadily and can become crippling to a newspaper industry only marginally profitable. Newspaper executives already find themselves spending hours preparing legal briefs for court or media council hearings instead of doing their job as journalists.

The English-language newspapers are, therefore, embattled on many fronts. The purely economic impact of television as a competitor for advertising revenue and the squeeze of prolonged recession, which could be faced in a free society, are as formidable as the more obvious politico-legal threats to their existence.

Reliance on market forces does not provide universal answers to the ills of mankind, but the market does offer opportunities to those who discern them. The challenge to English-language newspaper proprietors in South Africa is to keep as many publications as possible in existence in vigorous life and editorial independence. Apart from journalistic excellence, this calls for business acumen, vision, and exceptional management and marketing skills, with a good measure of entrepreneurial courage.

New ways must be found to enhance the viability of newspapers without resorting to gutter journalism. For liberal newspapers the road ahead seems to lie in the rapidly expanding market in colored/black readership, which brings with it the prospect of rising circulation figures and a chance to perform a useful service in intergroup communications. It is lamentable that no means could be found to keep the *Rand Daily Mail* in business long enough to reap the benefit of this steadily more lucrative market. Black buying power has a growing clout as black standards of living and education rise. This clout could be mobilized in consumer boycotts, which, it should be noted, have already been successful in the Eastern Cape and elsewhere. Newspapers are as vulnerable as any other commercial undertakings dependent on colored/black support for economic viability. Editors may face the threat of a black boycott if they fail to report news their black readers feel is relevant. The prospect of a boycott imposes a useful discipline, requiring newspapers to provide fair and balanced coverage that enjoys credibility in all communities. The discipline of the market, here again, is salutary.

Critics who are cynical about the value of newspapers published in the tradition of free-enterprise liberalism might care to consider the alternatives. Let the evils of trivialization, sensationalism, and "yellow press" profiteering be admitted, but what are the alternatives to newspapers run for profit which can support themselves in vigorous independence? State control or state subsidies are surely unthinkable, as are subsidies from private quarters. A newspaper must be able to stand on its own feet, otherwise its editorial "independence" may prove to be nominal. As has been argued here, liberal newspapers are dominated neither by their proprietors nor by their editors but by their readers as much as anyone else.

The English-language press in the liberal tradition in South Africa, by and large, has upheld an honorable record of operation in the public interest; there has been and remains a significant degree of editorial independence. At the time of the watershed constitutional referendum of 1983 there was a noteworthy demonstration of this within the SAAN and Argus groups, both of which, as we have seen, are ultimately controlled by the Anglo-American Corporation. Voters in the referendum were called upon to accept or reject P. W. Botha's controversial new constitution. In editorial comment, newspapers in both groups took a variety of positions—some equivocated, others called for outright rejection of the constitution on principle, while others urged its acceptance on the grounds that it was a "step in the right direction." In the SAAN camp, for example, the *Sunday Times* was strongly in favor of a "Yes" vote, while the *Cape Times* took the opposite view, rejecting the proposed constitution out of hand. This was a political issue of fundamental importance, affecting the direction of South African politics. Yet it is plain that a uniform policy was not dictated by the Anglo-American Corporation or anyone else. Policy was made by editors rather than forced upon them behind the scenes by monopolist proprietors.

It would be wrong to overstate the degree of independence, however. It is obviously not absolute and the role of the proprietors and of market forces cannot be left out of account. There have been striking instances of unwarranted proprietorial interference. Editorial independence will not survive if proprietors lack vision and editors lack resolution. A strong editor, established in his chair and respected in his community, is well placed to hold his own in determining what goes into the paper and laying down the line of editorial policy. The best of the editors in this tradition have also managed to strike a balance between the sometimes conflicting demands of commercial viability and decent standards. The *Cape Times* and *The Star,* to name two of the best of the dailies, have demonstrated this capability consistently down the years. As long as the proprietors continue to acknowledge a public responsibility to maintain the editorial excellence of their publications, skilled and dedicated editors can resist the temptation to take the easy way out, maximizing revenue and profits at the expense of standards. Commercial pressures that depress standards can be insistent. With some exceptions in the Sunday newspaper field, however, the English-language press has avoided the excess of circulation-building "yellow press" journalism, but in an economic recession it is not easy to bring out good newspapers which can yet pay their way.

In a time of political crisis the difficulties are compounded. Yet South Africa badly needs liberal-minded newspapers which are in touch with readers in all communities. The ranks of such newspapers are sadly depleted. The good ones that remain should be cherished. The building of a great liberal newspaper is not the work of a day.

Jane Hofmeyr

18. Liberals and the Education Crisis

The continuing crisis in South African education is so severe, and the challenges of ideological, political, social, and economic forces so powerful, that liberals are in danger of becoming irrelevant in the transition to a new educational order. To avoid irrelevance and to win credibility they must urgently examine and use the available strategies for effective involvement in the process of change.

Since the unrest and student riots of 1976, observers have pointed to a crisis in South African education. For most of the last decade, black education has been in a state of turmoil; it now faces "creeping disintegration."[1] The turmoil has characterized mainly the urban areas and, particularly, African and colored high schools. The spate of boycotts, riots, repression, detentions, bannings, violence, and deaths since 1976 has resulted, in K. B. Hartshorne's words, in a "probably irreversible breakdown of the black education environment" in the main metropolitan areas.[2] Among those who still attend school in these areas, little formal learning takes place. Increasing numbers of young blacks are not in school at all; they are the "street children" who have dropped

I thank my husband, Karl, and my children, Kate and André, for their support, and Robin Lee, Penny Enslin, Ros Jaff, and Jenny Marcus for comments and assistance.

1. K. B. Hartshorne, "Educating the People," *Leadership: Human Resources* (1985/6), p. 20. In this paper, "black" is used to refer to Africans, Asians, and coloreds.

2. K. B. Hartshorne, "The Boycott Classes of 1980–1984," *Indicator South Africa*, Vol. 3, No. 3, (1986).

out, failed, rejected the system, or chosen the path of "liberation before education." For them there are few "safety nets" or "second chances" and fewer jobs. Growing numbers of young blacks with or without school leaving certificates cannot find employment.

Black pupils have made it clear that they are rejecting their education as a reflection of the entire oppressive and discriminatory system of apartheid.[3] African education is separate and inferior and it lacks legitimacy at two levels: without political representation in the central government, Africans have no power or say over their education nor do they enjoy meaningful participation within their education system. Pupils have become increasingly politicized as they link their educational struggle with the national struggle for liberation. Their teachers, underqualified on the whole and often under pressure from all sides, are also becoming politicized as they are drawn into the struggle. The same remarks apply to colored and to a lesser extent to Asian education. Although funding of their schools is greater than that for Africans, and although they are represented in the central government, many colored and Asian students and parents make common cause with Africans.[4]

Recently, black rejection of the existing system of education has found expression in the articulation of an alternative—"people's education for people's power." The goal of this People's Education is a free, compulsory, unitary, nonracial, and democratic system of education, relevant to the establishment of a free, nonracial, democratic South Africa. It aims to achieve this via the collective strength of the community: the People's Education movement is intended to mobilize and empower black communities to take control of their schools.[5]

The government, on the other hand, is determined to maintain its control of the schools: Afrikaner history provides concrete evidence of the value of education as a mobilizing base, and the government is loath to relinquish this base to other groups. Furthermore, the regime insists on segregated education systems, a principle that lies at the heart of its ideology of separate development.[6] Since June 1986, the authorities

3. See Republic of South Africa, *Report on the Commission of Inquiry into Unrest in Soweto and Elsewhere 1976–77* (Cillie Commission) (Pretoria: Government Printer, 1980); and P. Christie, *The Right to Learn* (Johannesburg: Ravan, 1985).

4. If, according to a government ruling in 1983, a qualified teacher has a senior (school-leaving) certificate and a three-year professional qualification, then 80 percent of African, 60 percent of colored teachers, and 4 percent of white teachers are underqualified.

5. Z. Sisulu, "People's Education for People's Power." Keynote address, Second National Consultative Conference, Durban, 29 March 1986.

6. J. Hofmeyr, "An Examination of the Influence of Christian National Education on the Principles Underlying Black and White Education in South Africa: 1948–1982," (unpublished M. Ed. thesis, University of the Witwatersrand, 1982); J. Shingler, "Education and Political Order in South Africa 1902–1961" (unpublished Ph.D. thesis, Yale University, 1973).

have moved into an openly coercive mode, with new, strict regulations for teachers, introduction of identity documents for pupils, use of police and soldiers in the schools, and the subsequent closure of thirty-two schools. "The message is clear," writes Hermann Giliomee, "Government provides education—take it on their terms or leave it."[7]

Schools, therefore, are sites of confrontation between the authorities and communities, and education has become an arena for political conflict in the absence of an adequate constitutional structure. It is increasingly a contested area, caught up in a spiral of violence and the process of polarization which has developed momentum in South African society during the last few years. The roots of the educational crisis lie in a complex interaction of many factors—educational, political, ideological, socioeconomic, with ramifications far beyond the educational sphere itself.[8] It is not just a schooling crisis: indeed, "black education under apartheid is a focus, a symbol and a cause of the present national crisis."[9]

Given the salient features of the education crisis and the positions of the main actors, it is possible to identify certain trends that probably will obtain during the next few years. The government will almost certainly introduce no structural change in education. Since 1976, it has squandered many opportunities to introduce significant reforms. If, under better conditions, meaningful reforms were not introduced, then, in the present climate of coercion, confrontation, and retreat into the "laager" (a circle of wagons), structural change is unlikely; indeed, many observers believe that education will be the last bastion of apartheid. Even the Group Areas Act is likely to be removed before the government gives up its control over education and before it desegregates the schools.[10] Instead of changing the basic structure and power relationships in education, it will continue to introduce piecemeal, technocratic reforms and limited concessions: for example, racial quotas for private schools have been abandoned, affecting only 5 percent of white children and a smaller proportion of blacks.[11] In addition, it will

7. "The Pattern of Politics," *Business Day,* 1 August 1986, p. 4.

8. Main Committee of the HSRC Investigation into Education, *Education Provision in the RSA* (Pretoria: HSRC, 1981). (De Lange Committee). See also P. Christie, *Right to Learn;* P. Kallaway, *Apartheid and Education* (Johannesburg: Ravan, 1984); and J. Marcum, "Black Education in South Africa: Key or Chimera," *CSIS Africa Notes,* 15 April 1985; J. Hofmeyr, "The Education Crisis Re-examined: Challenges, Options and Strategies," The Urban Foundation, November 1986.

9. University of the Witwatersrand, "University Policy and the Current Crisis," 6 December 1985.

10. For example, see K. B. Hartshorne, "Post-Apartheid Education: A Concept in Process. Opportunities in the Next Five Years," McGraw-Hill Seminar, Indaba Hotel, Johannesburg, 19 September 1986.

11. E. G. Malherbe, *Education in South Africa* 2 (Cape Town: Juta, 1977), p. 282.

spend more money on African education in an effort to increase the efficiency of the system—in the last eight years, the total budget for African education has increased eightfold, but the ratio of white to African per capita expenditure is still 7 to 1.[12]

The impetus in black communities for participation in and control over their education will grow. The locus of change is shifting from the government to the black communities. It is possible that the initiative has already passed to the students, black communities, and the crisis committees, and that the government has adopted an essentially negative, reactive position in which the influence of conservative elements and the security forces is evident.[13] The crisis has mobilized and united some communities, particularly African and colored ones, as have few other issues. It is significant that almost every important predominantly black organization from trade unions to women's movements has included the education crisis on its agenda.

Because of its broadly based grass-roots support and its national network, the National Education Crisis Committee has emerged as a most significant community organization in education. It has shown itself to be influential, committed to principles of consultation, negotiation, and mediation, and willing to interact with a broad spectrum of educators. Pupil power will remain an important factor in the communities' role, but there is evidence of attempts to organize and discipline this power through crisis committees, student organizations, and trade unions.[14]

During the next few years, the clash between government and black communities is likely to produce an educational version of the "violent equilibrium" that has been predicted generally in South Africa. The opposing forces are at a confrontational stalemate because both have different sources of power and both want to control the schools.[15] Within the violent equilibrium between government and black communities, the relative balance of power will shift from time to time and will differ from region to region. The effect could be a patchy, uneven map of spheres of influence and control. In certain areas (rural, peri-urban, and some urban) the authorities will maintain strict control; in some (the Eastern Cape, parts of the Western Cape, and parts of urban

12. Research Institute for Education Planning, *Education and Manpower Production (Blacks)*, no. 5, University of the Orange Free State, Bloemfontein, 1984.

13. Z. Sisulu, "People's Education" and interview in *Leadership*, Vol. 5, No. 4, 1986.

14. S. Nyaka, "The Afternoon Classroom Flip," *Weekly Mail*, 18–24 April 1986.

15. H. Giliomee, "Pattern of Politics"; L. Taunyane, "Dealing with the betrayal of the essence of education," *The Star*, 16 September 1986; M. Bot and L. Schlemmer, "The Classroom Crisis: Black Demands and White Responses," *Indicator South Africa, Focus Issue* (July 1986).

townships), the communities could acquire effective control of the schools; in others, the homeland governments will be in charge.

The debate about alternative education, especially People's Education, is growing and producing a position on the left which is a rejection of the existing system and white models of education. Hostility to capitalist norms of competition, to individualism and elitism, is coupled with commitment to socialism, a demand for liberating curricula relevant to the community, and an emphasis on democratic processes and structures. Many blacks do not necessarily want "exactly what whites have" in education any more. In many quarters, white models are seen as oppressive, irrelevant, and inadequate for a new nonracial, free, democratic South Africa. The crisis in education thus extends to white education as well.[16] Although initially People's Education seems to have served largely a mobilizing function, the concept could acquire more substance. Since March 1986, working groups under the aegis of the National Education Crisis Committee have been developing syllabi to flesh out its philosophy.[17] With the preparation of a curriculum, People's Education will enter a new phase of evolution.

The quality of African education nevertheless will continue to deteriorate as it has for a number of years. The government's Ten Year Plan to bring about equal educational opportunity for all groups will not reverse this trend against the background of continuing disruption, huge backlogs in provision, a rising number of pupils, shortage of qualified teachers, impoverishment of the rural areas and the homelands, and the multiple effects of the economic recession. Lost generations of high school pupils will be the result, particularly in the urban areas. Increasing total education expenditure by at least 4.1 percent per annum, as the plan provides, will not, as the minister of national education has admitted, be sufficient to achieve equality after ten years.[18] Government does not have the resources to equalize educational expenditure at the level of the white norm, not even in twenty years' time, given competing claims on the budget, recession, and resistance of whites to redistribution of expenditures.[19]

Legitimacy, now a crucial issue in education, depends on the effectiveness of a program, who controls and funds it, and primarily on community sanction. The government no longer has legitimacy, nor

16. HSRC, *Education Provision in the RSA* (1981).

17. S. Pleming, "Pessimism over Education," *The Star*, 14 October 1986.

18. Republic of South Africa, *House of Assembly Debates* (*H. of Ass.*), vol. 7 (1986), cols. 3423–25.

19. C. Simkins, "Public Expenditure and the Poor: political and economic constraints on policy choices up to the year 2000," Paper No. 253, Carnegie Conference on Poverty (Cape Town: University of Cape Town, 1984).

can it confer it. Its ability to deliver material benefits is limited; it has failed to incorporate education symbolically into a single united ministry of education; and it has resorted to coercion and repression to maintain its control of the schools. Because the government has lost credibility with most people in black communities, projects and initiatives linked to "the system" become contaminated by association. Consequently, alternative education strategies and structures are urgently needed as parts of the formal learning environment disintegrate. Technology and networks in the nonformal and informal sectors of education have a crucial role to play in this regard. Those networks will have to be nurtured by agents outside government, and here the private business sector will become increasingly important. It will be called upon to intervene in areas of crisis or neglect, to facilitate and fund community initiatives, to provide alternative formal and nonformal education, and to pressure government for structural change. Yet the business sector alone, despite goodwill, resources, and expertise, cannot make its programs legitimate, because communities now have virtual veto power over the programs that affect them and the say of pupils has become an important factor in their acceptability.

In the future many additional projects will originate within black communities, and the "why," "how," and "what" of other initiatives will be scrutinized by community groups. Obtaining sanction for a project will involve negotiation and cooperation with groups enjoying high credibility within communities. Community representatives will want at least an equal partnership in initiatives. Blacks are no longer prepared to accept programs designed, implemented, and managed for them by whites.

Finally, everyone will be debating programs in a worsening context because socioeconomic factors will continue to fuel the education crisis. Economic recession and structural changes in the economy will exacerbate the high rate of unemployment of young people, and the accelerating urbanization of the African population, the high African and colored fertility rates, and the growing proportion of young blacks in the population will place enormous demands on the schooling system.[20]

Given the daunting challenges posed by projected trends above, what contribution can liberalism make to the creation of a legitimate and effective system of education?

Historically, liberal values in education have been associated with

20. E. Postal and T. Vergnani, *Future Perspectives on South African Education,* occasional paper no. 4, Institute for Future Research, University of Stellenbosch, 1984.

institutions like the mission schools, some private schools, the South African Institute of Race Relations, the "open" universities, and, more recently, the Urban Foundation. The liberal contribution to education in the past has been attacked from both the right and the left.[21] However, as I believe that the important focus is liberalism in the present and future, I shall leave that debate to historians, and ask first, what is the meaning of liberalism in education today; and second, what can it offer the future?

Two contemporary accounts of liberalism by Charles Simkins and Penny Enslin are relevant to these questions.[22] Simkins has examined the theoretical content of contemporary South African liberalism. He uses the principles derived from John Rawls's theory of social justice as the basis for his exposition of an egalitarian liberalism: all social primary goods (for example, rights and liberties, opportunities and powers, income and wealth, self-respect) are to be distributed equally unless an unequal distribution is to the long-term advantage of the least favored.[23] For Simkins, the crucial issue for liberalism is equality, and in the educational context this means equality of access and entitlement. Equal access and opportunity is denied by direct controls like segregationist legislation, and indirect controls like patronage prevent equal access by blacks to senior posts in administration. Meaningful reform, therefore, will necessarily entail the removal of these direct and indirect controls.

Equal entitlement involves equal spending of public monies on educational goods and services. Thus, the basic principle should be equality and impartiality in public spending on education. However, the available resources are insufficient to enable the present white standards in education to be extended as a general norm to all groups. Thus, rules and norms at an affordable level should be established for equal public spending on the education of all children but with provision for private additions by local communities. In the long run, however, because the capacity for private additions is greater in the wealthier communities, this practice will not work to the advantage of the deprived communities. Thus, Rawls's second principle—the difference principle—must be invoked: extra compensatory monies could be invested in the education of historically deprived groups to their long-

21. See J. Robertson, *Liberalism in South Africa* (Oxford: Clarendon Press, 1971); P. Rich, *White Power and the Liberal Conscience, Racial Segregation and South African Liberalism 1921–1960* (Johannesburg: Ravan, 1984); Kallaway, *Apartheid and Education.*

22. C. Simkins, "Reconstructing South African Liberalism" (Johannesburg: South African Institute of Race Relations, 1986); P. Enslin, "In Defence of a Liberal Theory of Education," (unpublished Ph.D. thesis, University of the Witwatersrand, 1986), p. ii.

23. Simkins, "Reconstructing South African Liberalism."

term benefit and affirmative-action programs could be allowed. In other words, the education system, like every other system, should be designed so as to maximize the position of the least well-off members of society.

Simkins reminds us of the technical constraints on the speed at which inequalities of entitlement can be removed. For instance, African education requires a stock of properly trained teachers and teacher educators and it will take time to build enough teacher training institutions and even more time to produce a flow of trained people at the desired rate.

Simkins's central concern is with liberalism in general and its application to different sectors of society. Recently, Penny Enslin has focused specifically on a liberal theory of education. She argues that the "central and most fundamental feature [of liberalism] is the defence of the principle of individual freedom."[24] This central commitment, she argues, must be distinguished from particular expressions of the liberal point of view which vary according to historical circumstances: it is a mistake, says Enslin, to treat one of these particular expressions of liberalism, such as Locke's views on property, as a timeless statement of the liberal position. Likewise, the liberal theory of education should not be identified with, for example, the assumption of capitalists (and others) that schooling contributes to economic growth: growth may be a consequence but it is not the fundamental objective.

Enslin challenges the view of contemporary radical writers that the "liberal theory of education" has been successfully discredited, a view based, she argues, on an erroneous characterization of various educational philosophies as liberal when they are conservative. Indeed, contrary to current radical opinion, the dominant tradition in studies of education in South Africa is conservative, not liberal.[25]

Enslin believes that the liberal notion of education is "fundamentally concerned with the good of the individual, which consists primarily of helping her to exercise autonomy."[26] The development of the autonomy of the individual includes three important features. First, personal autonomy revolves around the individual's ability to choose her own life plan and develop her capacities as she wishes. Second, moral autonomy implies the principle of impartiality or equality in taking into consideration the good of others and the principle of respect for persons and their human dignity. The individual who has achieved personal autonomy has "an enlarged sense of her own well-being which includes a concern for the good of others." Each person with needs and goals

24. Enslin, "Defence of a Liberal Theory," p. ii.
25. Ibid, chapters 4 and 5.
26. Ibid, p. 5.

of her own is entitled to moral consideration. And third, democratic participation (both in broad political terms and in institutions) is necessary for one to achieve personal and moral autonomy. Education for democratic participation means that authority would not be accepted unquestioningly; individuals would need to acquire skills of critical thinking to be able to participate rationally and with independence; and they would need to be well informed about social, political, and economic issues.[27]

Enslin's defense of a liberal theory of education calls for a serious reexamination, especially in radical circles, of the relevance of liberal ideas to the study and development of education in South Africa. She believes that a liberal theory of education has much to contribute to the education debate:

> What we need to ensure we don't lose during the process of transformation in South Africa during the next few years is a sense of the important principles that the liberal tradition has given us: that in the end, individuals are the final authority on what they want and need; that individual freedom is a good thing; that participating democratically with other people is a good thing.[28]

While Simkins emphasizes equality, Enslin emphasizes freedom, a difference that shows the continuing vitality of the long-standing debate within liberalism about the relative claims of liberty and equality. Both are necessary components of the liberal position. Given the present gross inequality in educational provision, equality is a crucial emphasis for liberals. But in view of the existing authoritarian educational culture and the coercive and violent confrontation over education, the call for individual freedom and autonomy must also be heard. Although Simkins and Enslin have different emphases, both argue for a liberalism which embraces liberty and equality.[29]

Simkins and Enslin explore the meaning of liberalism in education at the level of principle. But what is the meaning of liberalism at the level of action: in practice, what options and strategies are available to liberal individuals and institutions in education?

Where liberals should position themselves in the polarizing situation in South Africa is a matter of current debate. As Van Zyl Slabbert writes, liberals have a choice between only two options—to side with the forces of "repression" and "stability" or with those of "liberation" and

27. Ibid, pp. 146–248.

28. "Attacked from all sides: Liberal Education Theory," *Weekly Mail*, 25–31 July 1986, p. 9.

29. Enslin, "Defence of a Liberal Theory," pp. 146–48; Simkins, "Reconstructing South African Liberalism," pp. 17–18.

"freedom"; Heribert Adam argues that business has a similar option, with the choice of allies on the left as the key issue.[30] Or liberals can try to occupy the middle ground—the terrain typically chosen by liberals, who tend to prefer nonalignment and the opportunity to criticize both the right and the left. Unfortunately, the middle ground is steadily eroding and liberals who remain there are likely to be caught in the crossfire between two opposing nationalisms. Leo Kuper has noted that in situations of racial polarization, the middle ground becomes increasingly untenable as the conflict unfolds and remains so until it has run its course (at which time the original middle ground often becomes irrelevant to the new, changed situation).[31] Furthermore, the "middle ground" typically is defined in negative terms, i.e., that which is neither the right nor the left, so that liberals have tended to let the field be defined for them by others. This position carries the negative connotations of "trapped in the middle," of "fence-sitting," and compromise between villains. There is therefore a strong case for liberals to reject this notion of a middle-ground positioning altogether, and to delineate their terrain positively as an additional dynamic dimension, and another viable option. Moreover, they must communicate it in clear and direct terms accessible to the mass of people in South Africa.

Historically in South Africa there have been radical and conservative strands in liberalism. In the present circumstances, liberals must avoid the danger of any "pale" form of liberalism. Simkins notes that if liberalism is to become a meaningful social and political force in South Africa, it must *not* be a second-line defense of white cultural and political dominance or a first-line defense of a capitalist system marked by great inequality.[32] Rather, liberals must find the radicalism inherent in liberalism in their search for a relevant and legitimate response to the South African crisis. Moreover, they must recognize that the future of South African liberalism lies largely in black hands because blacks are the overwhelming majority of the population.

Thus in broad terms it could be argued that liberal sympathies should be with the struggle of blacks for equal liberty with whites; the rise of black political power must be welcomed from a liberal point of view.[33] The issue then becomes: to what extent can liberals identify with a particular side without ceasing to be liberals? There is the danger of compromising core liberal principles. "Central to the liberal project,"

30. For Slabbert, see "Incremental Change or Revolution?" p. 401. For Adam, see "Apartheid and the Future of Capitalism," mimeo, 1986.

31. L. Kuper, *The Pity of It All: Polarization of Racial and Ethnic Relations* (London: Duckworth, 1977).

32. Simkins, "Reconstructing South African Liberalism," p. 3.

33. Ibid., lectures 1 and 6.

Simkins says, "is the formulation of *universal* and *impartial* principles which maximise liberty, subject to the conditions required by justice" (my emphases).[34] Liberals will have to guard against compromising these principles and will therefore need to criticize illiberal policies and practices on both the right and the left.

If the debate about options for liberals is translated to the education context, I want to argue that a liberal institution must make an overt choice and broadly identify itself with the forces on the left. Since 1976, some liberal actors, influenced by the arguments of pragmatic liberalism, have pursued a reformist strategy in education which identified government as the locus of change. The Urban Foundation, for instance, aimed to effect key changes in the government's education policy in order to bring about a single national policy-making ministry and equal educational opportunities for all. The De Lange Committee (1981) represented the best hope of reformists for significant change in the education system, but the government has consistently refused to introduce the most crucial recommendations of this committee, in particular, a single ministry of education with its high symbolic significance. In fact, all the evidence suggests that structural reform from government is a vain hope and that links in the cause of reform involve severe legitimacy problems with government.

Even to do nothing is no longer a workable option. To stand aside until the dust settles is to presuppose that the dust will settle. The government and black communities are locked in a complex and shifting confrontation over education that will be protracted and violent; the educational system will face slow deterioration rather than improvement for some time. Furthermore, education has become such a focus in the struggle for a new South African society that to withdraw from it would seriously damage any organization's credibility with the majority of South African people.

Liberal institutions must respond to the crisis in education and they must seek legitimation of their response in the black communities, to which the locus of change in education is shifting. Because the future of South African liberalism is largely in black hands, black communities are the crucial arena for liberal mobilization and activism. Thus, liberals should identify with black communities in their desire to control and participate in their own education and to develop alternative models to those in the system. Liberal actors should signal their commitment to black communities' struggle and then, from that position, search for actors on the left with whom they can deal, and explore strategies that will allow for an effective involvement in change.

34. Ibid., p. 9.

The use of terms like the "left," "community," and "the struggle" conveys a monolithic sense of these entities, when in reality they are fragmented and contain a diversity of points of view and strategies. Because of the general polarizing process, many actors who were once in the middle ground have now moved to the left, and consequently there is a spectrum of moderate to radical actors on the left. If we follow Heribert Adam's and Kogila Moodley's arguments about the trade unions as the preferred players on the left, then the nearest equivalents in education are the National Education Crisis Committee and the teacher associations.[35] Liberals should forge links with church groups, and with other agencies and organizations with strong community credibility, to encourage dialogue and collaborative efforts.

In the general debate about the education crisis, there are four broad strategies potentially available to liberals: (1) engagement with the left, (2) pressuring the government, (3) exploiting the gaps in government policy, and (4) preparing for education beyond apartheid. Some of these strategies may be especially relevant to particular liberal institutions, such as businesses or universities, and many of them are already in use.

(1) What does engagement on the left mean? Although liberals should generally identify with the forces of freedom on the left, they do not have to accept the entire paradigm. J. Muller and N. Cloete discuss the stance of "committed non-alignment" on the part of academics who identify with the struggle but who do not join specific strategic movements or political parties.[36] The notion carries the idea, therefore, of some sort of "critical distance," of being free to pose questions, to engage in debate and dialogue with actors on the left.

What, then, might engagement as a strategy involve for liberals? It could include finding the radical elements in liberalism and exploring the conjunction between liberal and radical thought in education. For instance, Enslin examines this issue and suggests that there is considerable common ground between a genuinely liberal notion of education and Marxist theory of education.[37] Liberals must engage in dialogue and debate about education on the left. "People's education has offered us all both a challenge and an opportunity to consider, debate and negotiate the future of education in a post-apartheid non-racial and

35. Heribert Adam and Kogila Moodley, *South Africa Without Apartheid* (Berkeley and London: University of California Press, 1986), pp. 258–63.

36. J. Muller and N. Cloete, "Academics in a State of Confusion In Defence of Committed Non-Alignment," at ASA regional conference on Sociology in Education, The Stad, near Mafikeng, 27 April 1985.

37. Enslin, "Defence of a Liberal Theory," chapters 7 and 8.

democratic South Africa."[38] Liberals should build new contacts and alliances with community groups, develop new practices, styles, and models of interaction. They can fund, support, and strengthen alternative education initiatives and efforts "that are part of the process leading to post-apartheid education in a non-racial, democratic and just society and that are seen by the communities involved in them as relevant both to that and the intervening transitional period."[39] For educational initiatives to be truly *enabling* they must help black organizations to increase their own capacity to analyse issues, identify priorities, set agendas and assume leadership.

Liberals can inform the debate with values, skills, and critical rationality. They have an important contribution to make in terms of the resources and expertise at their disposal in areas like curriculum design, strategic planning, policy development, and management training. As the recent "Perceptions of Wits" report of the University of the Witwatersrand has shown, this fact is appreciated and recognized by community organizations who believe that the university "is a potential resource that can respond now to their needs."[40]

Certain problems, however, are inherent in this strategy. Liberal values may clash with the values of the left. Hartshorne believes that "a main concern with the position of People's Education as it is articulated at present is the clear presence of an underlying tension between the statements on critical and creative thinking, active participation, democratic practices on one hand and implied alternative ideological pressures, educational controls and 'power' issues on the other."[41] While welcoming the many positive aspects of People's Education, Ashley also indicates that there are some problematic implications with regard to standards, education of the critical intellect, and culture.[42]

There is a basic tension between the individual ethic of liberalism and the collective ethic of many movements. An extreme example of this is the evidence that for many radical black students anything that serves to separate the individual from the group is unacceptable.[43] However, it is also true that this tension is often exaggerated by a

38. K. B. Hartshorne, "Education Beyond Apartheid," *Sunday Times,* 21 September 1986.

39. Hartshorne, "Post-Apartheid Education."

40. "Perceptions of Wits: The Role of the University in a Changing Society" (Johannesburg: University of the Witwatersrand, 1986), p. 80.

41. Hartshorne, "Education Beyond Apartheid."

42. M. Ashley, "Syllabus for a New South Africa," *Sunday Times,* 27 September 1986.

43. See record of discussions between an unnamed project and black students in Alexandra, background reading material for Ford Foundation Conference on Education and the Church, Long Island, USA, 30–31 May 1986.

particular characterization of liberal individualism as self-seeking attitudes and behavior. Enslin and Simkins both reject this interpretation. Simkins suggests that individualism be seen as "self-cultivation, self-confidence and self-expression"[44]—all of which find a strong echo in Marxist theory of education and in People's Education.

Will the engagement between liberals and community organizations be an equal partnership? Many liberal and business organizations have been autocratic and paternalistic—deciding what is best for blacks. Nattrass suggests new approaches to community relationships that could be participatory, reciprocal, equal partnership models that go far beyond "consultation."[45] Unfortunately, the force of old habits and distrust on both sides will have to be overcome. There is also evidence of an unwillingness on the part of black organizations to accept involvement of liberal or business actors' with any qualifications or strings attached.[46] Liberal organizations may not be admitted to an equal partnership on the left. There is also the possibility that only a temporary partnership can prevail, that liberals and business will be used for their expertise and money and then jettisoned.[47]

(2)Pressuring the government will require a tougher stand than that taken on the reform path, inevitably less "consultative" and more "confrontational."[48] Liberals must not be seen as collaborating with government. They cannot afford to be associated with the government's technocratic reforms and must clearly and publicly distance themselves from this approach. The private business sector and liberal actors must both press home to the authorities the urgent need to address the larger issues of legitimacy, inequality, separateness, and relevance in the educational system and the wider society. Purely educational or technical answers are simply inadequate responses to a crisis that is political, social, and economic.

Confronting and pressuring government in education could involve the following elements: principled public protest; building alliances to act in concert with clout; lobbying; applying leverage with "the carrot and the stick"; civil disobedience; and legal challenges to government through the courts. There are obviously serious difficulties associated with this strategy. Liberals as lobbyists (particularly those in the private business sector), will have to balance opposing needs in maintaining a distinct and clearly perceived independence from government, and

44. Enslin "Defence of a Liberal Theory," chapters 6 and 7; Simkins, "Reconstructing South African Liberalism," p.8.

45. See J. Nattrass, "Political Change and Capitalism in South Africa," pp. 359–61.

46. See F. Mazibuko, interview in *Die Suid-Afrikaan*, Summer 1985, pp. 31–32.

47. The private business sector as a whole cannot be regarded as liberal. However, there are actors within the sector that identify with broadly liberal values.

48. A. Bloom, "Two Small Steps for Peace," *The Sunday Star*, 24 August 1986, p. 14.

keeping some channels of communication with government open. A community mandate for negotiation would seem to be essential. Acting with clout will demand alliances between liberal institutions and with community groups. Historical resentments and present circumstances, with competitive relationships between the actors, will make this task extremely difficult. Even with alliances, it would be difficult, to say the least, to persuade government to effect structural change. Indeed, governmental retaliation against a challenge is probable, as evidenced by its withdrawal of a proclamation in 1986 which allowed students of all races to stay in university residences.

(3) The third strategy involves searching for and exploiting the loopholes, the unintended consequences of the government's reforms, the innovative possibilities, and the room to maneuver in the present system. Because of the increasing costs of violent equilibrium for the ruling minority, it is forced to reform as the pressure rises.[49] "The existence of a powerful extra-parliamentary opposition means that the state will not be able to implement a reformist strategy on terrain of its own choosing. The final outcome will be crucially determined by the way in which oppositional groupings interpret and respond to state initiatives."[50] Present and future opportunities must be used to widen the gaps in apartheid-education. This strategy could involve exploiting the known loopholes such as the provision in the White Paper of 1983 for interdepartmental cooperative services which could be used to establish resource centers for all teachers in an area.[51] Liberals could operate in more fluid areas such as preschooling, private schools, homelands, farm schools, and universities. They could out-research the government in areas where it clearly lacks a "vision," "know-how," or an adequate data base: for example, national priorities in education financing, preschool provision, multicultural curricula, and in-service education and training for teachers. A major problem here, of course, is the possibility that government will close some of the existing gaps as it attempts to entrench its control in a coercive mode.

(4) Liberals must define, articulate, and disseminate a liberal vision of education beyond apartheid that provides adequate response to the historical inequalities, the developmental problems, and the multiple political, economic, and social factors. The work of Simkins and Enslin has begun this process. John Samuel has suggested that the radical left

49. Adam, "Apartheid and the Future of Capitalism," p. 12.

50. W. Cobbett, D. Glaser, D. Hendron, and M. Swilling, "Regionalisation, federalism and the reconstruction of the South African State," *SA Labour Bulletin*, 10 (March/April 1985): 96, quoted in Simkins, "Reconstructing South African Liberalism," lecture 6, p. 11.

51. Republic of South Africa, *White Paper on the Provision of Education in the RSA* (Pretoria: Government Printer, 23 November 1983).

has fallen short in this task and that "liberals are significant as a shaping forces of the imagination."[52] Liberals must plan for the needs, and particularly the socioeconomic imperatives, of postapartheid education: for example, nonformal education and training for life skills in urban environments; training in leadership and management skills; and youth opportunities programs. There is need also for implementing, sponsoring, and assisting initiatives that are truly innovative and that address postapartheid realities.

The high emotion and politicization of the education debate makes it difficult to engage in rational planning and to give attention to issues beyond the immediate political crisis; persons who focus on the long-term view may suffer a loss of credibility. However, by linking the long-term view of postapartheid education with more immediate, credible actions, liberals could counteract this problem.

Certain common themes run through all of the four strategies described above. They all imply that liberals will have to become involved in several spheres of action. Within liberal circles, they will have to define and clarify their principles, programs, and vision of the future. They also will have to consolidate the liberal base by strengthening and mobilizing liberal actors in cooperative relationships. Beyond liberal circles they will have to articulate and publicize the liberal position, without necessarily labeling it as such; they will need to seek out groups with whom they can work, and forge alliances for concerted effort and influence on government. Liberals must translate their ideals into concrete projects, programs, and initiatives that will demonstrate the viability of liberal principles in education and prepare for a postapartheid future.

Developing a strategic plan of action will not be easy. Adam and Moodley predict a future of uneven zigzag change as the forces of repression, revolution, and reform all affect the society.[53] In the constant change that this scenario implies, it is unlikely that any one strategy will be adequate for all situations. In showing their support for black communities' educational struggle, liberals probably will have to explore and use a combination of some or all the four strategies. There are dangers inherent in all of them, but, in the quest for legitimacy and relevance, can liberal organizations afford not to explore them?

Contemporary expositions of liberal thought show that liberalism is a flexible living tradition that can reorientate itself to new challenges. Liberal principles can offer relevant responses to the present crisis in

52. J. Samuel, quoted in *Race Relations News,* July 1986, p. 6.
53. As elaborated in Adam and Moodley, *South Africa without Apartheid,* pp. 248–63.

education, but to construct a liberal future will involve considerable energy, imagination, and moral courage. The process will be painful: "the hurts are deep, emotions run high, and the obstacles to understanding and shared debate are massive."[54] Liberals cannot be passive, "waiting for Godot." It is critically important that all who share a vision of a nonracial, democratic, free, and just society participate in the development of an education system for all the people of South Africa. The liberal contribution is needed in the interests of finding a balanced solution that will enrich the education of the future; "to stand back from the process, to dissociate oneself from it, because some of the 'threads' in it are not to one's liking, would be particularly barren and irresponsible."[55] Liberal principles must be translated into action: by seizing present opportunities, liberals could have a decisive influence on South African education in the future.

54. Hartshorne, "Post-Apartheid Education."
55. Ibid.

V

Democratic Liberalism in the Current Crisis

Heribert Adam

19. Black Unions and Reformist Politics

The South African economy risks becoming a comparative industrial backwater. A worldwide decline in the price of raw materials has plunged South Africa's extractive industries into recession. Its domestic demand is underdeveloped, a consequence of systematic past discrimination against its majority population which fostered low wages and unemployment. Without domestic economies of scale, South African manufactures remain uncompetitive in the world market except as a continuously declining currency gives them an edge in pricing. Such Latin-Americanization with hyperinflation undercuts investment confidence in South Africa, and the slackening of fixed investment, particularly in manufacturing, undermines the basis of the modern economy. Until the mid-1970s South Africa attracted capital and achieved a high growth rate, but since then there has been a slow outflow of capital, accelerated by more recent perceptions of investor risk and by international political pressure for disinvestment, which has made the country less able to cope with its multifaceted problems.

Demographic trends and economic crisis have combined to increase the number of the permanently unemployed. With a population accelerating at 2.3 percent annually, it would take a growth rate of 4 to 5 percent to provide employment for the newcomers to the labor market, yet the current growth rate lingers around 2 percent, with little prospect of a substantial improvement in this time of political insecurity. The social disintegration of black communities, particularly in the cities, will inevitably lead to direct consequences for the quality of life of all, including the dominant group.

From the mid-1970s on, government and business have grudgingly and incrementally recognized the necessity of empowering black labor with the rights to organize and to strike, rights that white workers have always enjoyed. This liberalization, which has yet to be extended to blacks in the political sphere, changes the nature of the political struggle in South Africa. It gives Africans an organizational base rooted in the economy which irreversibly shifts the balance of power in their favor; how much of a shift is yet to be determined. No longer is that base in the relatively small middle-class group of teachers, ministers, clerks, and their followers which characterized all African political organizations until recently. Organized black labor is now an autonomous force of growing strength and experience: government, opposition, business, organized white labor, political organizations in all groups, and the ANC in exile have only begun to accommodate themselves to it. In industrial societies elsewhere, the emergence of organized labor as an economic and political force and the strategies adopted by its leaders have been critical in determining the kind of politics which emerge, and especially in mitigating the violence frequently involved in social change.[1]

Organized labor appeared as a force in the context of the deep politicization of large segments of the subordinate population, the unprecedented international revulsion against apartheid, and the increasing cleavages within both white and black politics. Together with a new political resistance among township populations, new legends and new heroes have emerged of which white society is largely ignorant. Consumer boycotts, strikes, and agitation are fueling a heated atmosphere in which many township residents believe that an end to white power is in sight. The call to make the country ungovernable aims at creating liberated areas (in contrast with anarchy) which the opposition forces would control. With the collapse of many township administrations, in the wake of the attacks on black councillors and policemen, the state has, in turn, retreated to sporadic intervention by police and soldiers in armored vehicles but no longer governs many areas effectively. The civil war, as it is frequently described, is so far only in an incipient stage, especially with the government's opponents so far having had little access to weapons. So, too, the black educational system is in disarray. The initial slogan "liberation before education" has given way

1. This essay is a more focused treatment of a theme in Heribert Adam and Kogila Moodley, *South Africa without Apartheid: Dismantling Racial Domination* (Berkeley and London: University of California Press, 1986).

to notions of alternative "people's education." The educational system is increasingly used for overt political purposes. A new curriculum, stressing political relevancy, has emerged. Unsympathetic teachers are harassed and unable to continue in the old authoritarian style, and pupils often teach themselves. Classrooms have become the new sites for mobilization for liberation. Many schools are guarded by soldiers.

A new dimension of the protest is the involvement of previously uninvolved large segments of the urban black population. People are warned not to report crimes or grievances to the police but to submit them instead to people's courts, which mete out instant justice. A parallel sovereignty is increasingly emerging in the black society. The legitimacy of the political order, though long in doubt, is now explicitly and vociferously denied. The racial categorization of the entire population ensures the institutionalization of illegitimacy; government policy has created a permanent emergency.

In the past, the state has managed dissatisfaction with a mixture of co-optation and coercion. But the Group Areas Act has locked the black middle class into the townships without allowing for individual upward mobility; an artificially constrained black businessman or professional is unable to develop a vested interest in a status quo that grossly restricts him. Indeed, it is the black middle class, not the unions and blue-collar workers, which has been in the forefront of the United Democratic Front protest. Theirs is above all a psychological and not necessarily a material grievance, and of the two the psychological may be the more compelling. A moral dimension characterizes the complaints of white-collar, educated labor.

Co-optation of urban blacks has three prices that the government is hard-pressed to pay, partly because its resources are limited. First, the government has moved increasingly toward elimination of differential racial spending formulae. But in the process of budget cutting it has also moved to reduce a number of subsidies for blacks: rent and transportation-fee increases triggered many of the upheavals of 1984 to 1986. Second, successful co-optation depends also on symbolic incorporation, but as long as the government is unwilling to scrap the Population Registration and Group Areas Acts, the politicized have to reject even "sincere" attempts to buy them off. Economic advances, in effect, do not compensate for illegitimacy. It is precisely those who are better off who nourish the deeper grievances and who can afford to take political risks. Third, there is a price of co-optation that is not merely symbolic; if equal political incorporation would take place, it is doubtful, to say the least, that the black middle class could now be "bought off" without a substantial redistribution of power and resources in their favor.

The options open to Pretoria have become limited, and all the while in the industrial heart of the economy the processes of unionization continue relentlessly on, with labor organizations developing greater coherence and producing an experienced leadership of the privileged employed. Their unions are constrained by the economic recession but simultaneously politicized by the larger context described above. The policies of liberalization already adopted are simply compounding problems and raising the prices to be paid. For example, the massive expansion of higher education for blacks has at the same time raised expectations that are hard to fulfill anywhere. Some third-world countries with similar problems, such as Egypt, have neutralized the political potential of overeducated but unemployed youth by guaranteeing every university graduate a civil service job. An analogous substantial Africanization of the South African bureaucracy or of the parastatals would, however, touch the very power base of the National party.

Can business break through the obstacles to provide progressive leadership in a time of polarization and heightened tensions?

To date, South African business has endorsed nonracial employment efforts only rhetorically, and its accommodation of unions has been hesitant and grudging. Few affirmative-action programs are in place; adherence to the various employment codes remains uneven. Business has not really employed its clout effectively in support of a nonracial capitalism which recognizes its interest in effective and independent trade unions.

Business in South Africa has, it seems to me, several options, only one of which has the potential for contribution to constructive and less violent social change. First, it could support repression of blacks in an effort to sustain order, but that would lead to further domestic violence and increased international isolation. Even though such a course would find support among the ultraconservative elements of Afrikanerdom, the more sophisticated strategists of white power clearly recognize the limits of military might. "We must avoid destruction of the townships and the black communities in our efforts to destroy the ANC," declared a prominent former security police major.[2] Even the state has at last recognized that it cannot afford to alienate all blacks indiscriminately. Such a condition has already made the country partially ungovernable. Furthermore, the economy is utterly dependent on black labor, for which no replacement exists. Productivity cannot be coerced; it depends on voluntary identification and a basic contentment with living conditions.

2. Craig Williamson, *Leadership,* Vol. 5, No. 1, 1986, p. 66.

Second, faced with an intransigent government, business could adopt such a drastic course as relocation. This option is increasingly exercised by multinational corporations which are under consumer and shareholder pressure in their main markets abroad. The sale of their South African assets to local interests has concerned unions who fear that the social-responsibility programs and labor codes of foreign firms will disappear under South African ownership.

Retrenchment in the wake of disinvestment, too, does not strengthen the bargaining power of unions. Many union leaders have quietly entertained second thoughts about the political wisdom of the disinvestment campaign. Above all, the withdrawal of foreign firms does not seem to be able to change government policy for the time being, let alone destroy the South African economy. A siege economy merely increases Pretoria's hold over the private sector through interventionist measures and state patronage. In any case, relocation as an option does not exist for the vast sector of South African business whose assets are not portable.

Although the great majority of South African businessmen still prefer to remain apolitical, supporting neither the government nor its opposition, but simply making money, such a stance becomes increasingly untenable. Sooner or later they must decide whether to throw in their lot with the government, beating sanctions and essentially retaining a modified status quo, or press for a race-free society.

This third, essentially political option, is to develop alliances with two major power bases in South African society, the organizations of African nationalism on the one hand, and the black trade unions on the other. On a strictly economic level, business has an interest in conciliating the African National Congress, whose present leadership is ideologically divided about socialism in postapartheid society and could help to prevent anarchy, which is anathema to business. But business leaders, though some of them have made the pilgrimage to Lusaka, do not appear yet to trust emerging black leadership to endorse free enterprise. Business therefore hesitates to risk its present modus operandi in favor of a problematic future.

This last approach is to give increasing support to organized black labor, to the institutions of black unions, which are symbiotically—even if adversarially—related to the institutions of ownership and management.[3] Business is supporting the status quo not so much because of ideological conviction but because of its perceived need for stability. Unions in open societies share a similar nonrevolutionary tendency.

3. See David Yudelman, *The Emergence of Modern South Africa* (Westport: Greenwood Press, 1983).

They have focused largely on the material interests of their members, though lending crucial muscle to political, usually social democratic, parties. Unions in South Africa, like business, operate within the same whole; both, therefore, require order and capital investment, and have an interest in a stable and progressive society. Both are, at heart, pragmatic. The black unions, like business, have a strength that is rooted in practical affairs, and their strength is real, not imaginary or only symbolic.

Although many union leaders have joined the political clamor under community pressure, they have also guarded their organizational independence and most have not affiliated formally with political alliances, such as the United Democratic Front (UDF) or the National Forum. An ongoing debate within the unions about "workerism" and "populism" is far from conclusive.

The state of emergency and the recession seem to have strengthened those shop stewards who counsel caution about contests the unions are likely to lose. The very existence of unions could be at stake if military and right-wing sentiments in government circles prevail, although so far only some individual union organizers have been detained.

Business leaders have already shown that they take the ANC and the unions seriously, as evidenced in the daylong discussions between South African delegates and the ANC in Zambia on 13 September, 1985:

> Gavin Relly said that as far as the unions were concerned we were going through a learning curve, as indeed were the unions. He strongly urged the ANC to keep their fingers out of the unions. (Mac Maharaj interjected by saying they already had their fingers in) and said that the Anglo American Corporation had been rather proud of the fact in which the mine workers' strike had been averted as far as they were concerned. But he felt that the trade unions should be left to themselves to work out a spirit of negotiation with management whatever problems may arise, and that they should not be influenced by political considerations.[4]

South African employers, most of them raised in South Africa, have had little experience so far with black unions. They are accustomed to hierarchical relations with Africans and adversarial relationships with unions generally, and do not therefore find the spirit of negotiation easy to achieve. They do, however, share an interest with the black unions in a stable and productive society. Workers and management together represent class interdependency. The bargaining process is one that both sides understand, and at its best it is a disciplined and orderly contest

4. "Notes of a Meeting at Mfuwe Game Lodge, 13 September 1985," no author (allegedly Tony Bloom).

among interests which respect each other's strength. It can transcend or cut across racial and ethnic self-interests and reach, even help to define, a larger common interest.

Political processes take place in two major arenas, workplaces and living places. Unions are particularly concerned with organization of the workplace, and it may well be that it is in the mines, the factories, and ultimately on the farms that the dominant political forces in South Africa will be generated. What are the indications for the role of unions in the future, particularly in producing an alliance for stability and for a humane order in a postapartheid South Africa?

All three competing ideological tendencies in black politics are reflected in three major black union formations. At the left on a broad left-right spectrum are the black-consciousness-oriented union federations of the Council of Unions of South Africa (CUSA) and the Azanian Confederation of Trade Unions (AZACTU), both broadly committed to the National Forum (NF) and to the Azanian People's Organization's (AZAPO) philosophy; they stress Trotskyite-like black working-class leadership and are suspicious, above all, of accepting any bourgeois elements, whether black or white, as allies in their struggle.

In the middle are the much larger and better organized nonracial but mostly black Confederation of South African Unions (COSATU), a new federation formed in December 1985, mainly from former "workerist" FOSATU unions. COSATU strongly endorses ANC and UDF policies. It advocates a nonracial democracy in the postapartheid state combined with some nationalization of key industries. Their "socialist" model is less orthodox Marxist (of either the Trotskyite or Leninist version) than it is social-democratic, after the model of the British Labour party. (Ironically, the small Moscow-oriented South African Communist party supports a similar approach because it assumes that a bourgeois democracy must be created in the first stage as a precondition for a socialist transformation in a second stage.) Though formally not affiliated to the UDF, COSATU entered the political fray openly in 1986. By publicly criticizing Inkatha, the major political predominantly Zulu organization led by M. G. Buthelezi, and by endorsing disinvestment, some Confederation leaders abandoned the political caution that had characterized the more pragmatic stances in COSATU's predecessor, the Federation of South African Trade Unions (FOSATU). Some Confederation leaders responded to the heightened township politicization by shedding the previous "low profile" toward Inkatha and by openly taking the "populist" side.

This stance in turn led to the development of a force on the right, the United Workers Union of South Africa (UWUSA), initiated by Inkatha supporters. On May Day 1986 the new union was launched with a rally in Durban attended by 70,000 Buthelezi loyalists, while a smaller gathering of COSATU members held a competing rally nearby. The UWUSA unions advocate a free-enterprise system, and they regard responsible confrontation as a last resort to use with recalcitrant employers. While they are not in fact company unions, as their critics charge, the initial key figures in this movement were veterans in Kwazulu politics with management or business backgrounds. The constituency of this emerging grouping will probably not come from their poaching on the grounds of rival unions but from recruitment among now unorganized and traditional and religiously oriented workers. They lack shop stewards and experienced organizers for this stage of activity, but this lack could be compensated, at least partly, by outside support. The battle for the hearts and minds of the politically unincorporated South African proletariat will largely shape the outcome of the postapartheid state.

The extent of support for these three contrasting positions is difficult to ascertain in the absence of free political activity. We do not know whether people join a strike or consumer boycott because they identify with its goals or feel intimidated by youthful "comrades" should they fail to conform, or for some other reason. However, the impressive success in stay-away calls, even for such symbolic events as May Day, and in gaining official recognition, testify to a new effective union pressure, regardless of origin or ideological preference. Continuous, and increased, strike activities during the severe recession also indicate a surprising worker militancy.

Several patterns have emerged when for the first time black workers challenged their white managers, and not only over wage demands. Several court rulings have afforded protection to workers from dismissal for lawful striking, and this in turn has encouraged unions to follow carefully the legal route in developing disputes that is laid down in the Labor Relations Act. Workers have frequently acted precipitately, however, in wildcat strikes, with the unions left to try to mend the damage and with employers accusing the unions of losing control.

The responses of employers has been mixed. The success of management in some cases in subduing those unions that are weak or split has boomeranged, because the rivalry of competing unions has simply encouraged factions to "outradicalize" each other. South African employers still have not appreciated that a strong united union provides a better negotiating partner and better guarantee of predictable labor relations than an insecure and weak workers' organization. Many have yet to learn, as Hermann Giliomee has recently written, that "there is one thing worse than having a powerful black organization, and that is to have no organization at all."[5]

On the other hand, management for the most part has simply tended to sit out disputes rather than dismiss strikers, as it used to do. Lacking the resources for a lengthy trial of strength, the strikers have usually returned to work after a few days. Nor have employers generally resorted to the use of scabs to break a strike. When strikers for the first time used occupational sit-ins to prevent scabs from working in their place, employers showed reluctance to call in the police for fear of aggravating the dispute. It may seem remarkable that little industrial sabotage has been reported so far, but the moderate tactics used by workers probably reflect a desire to hold on to scarce jobs in spite of strong grievances. Even though township resistance spills over into the factories, many workers cannot afford to lose their only source of livelihood, and employers in turn cannot afford to alienate their work force.

Various commentators have noted that the gap between the visions of business and those of its so-called socialist opposition in the ANC has been steadily narrowing: "The powerful, capitalist, Federated Chamber of Industries," the Durban *Sunday Tribune* wrote, "has distilled its blueprint into a charter remarkably similar to that of the socialist African National Congress."[6] Organized capitalism will not, however, suddenly embrace socialist solutions, nor could radicalized insurgents be expected to shed their dreams of a nationalist takeover. Above all, conciliatory statements by business do not affect perceptions of the politicized townships, and if they are noted there at all they are dismissed as another meaningless ploy. As long as business fails to back up its interests with tangible action in the workplace that symbolizes dramatically where it stands in the struggle, employers will be considered synonymous with government. Sooner or later they will be as much a target of black frustrations as police stations and other symbols of the regime are at present unless they adopt a decisively different stance. If they do, there would be a real possibility of a joint worker-business alliance to achieve a more stable society.

What is the relation of black trade unions to the rapidly developing black political movements, and especially the ANC? Will the political organizations not inevitably dominate the unions?

Although politicization has clearly shifted from antiracist protest to

5. Hermann Giliomee, "Seven Thoughts on the Political Crisis," *Cape Times*, 13 April, 1985.

6. *Sunday Tribune*, 26 January, 1986.

socialist economics in the rhetoric of black leadership,[7] the visions of socialism expressed range from mild social welfare democracy to orthodox abolition of all private ownership in the Azanian People's Organization program. In the latter model, wealth could not be inherited, private property would be confined to a house and articles of personal consumption, and no land or rental property could be privately owned. Freedom Charter adherents, on the other hand, speak more ambiguously about the economic future of postapartheid society. In this vein, Oliver Tambo almost assured the visiting South African businessmen at their Lusaka meeting in 1985 that there would be a place for them beyond apartheid:

> He said he was often asked whether the new South Africa would be socialist or capitalist? It was not possible to say that the fight was for a capitalist state or a communist state—the fight was simply to be free. The "haves" cannot continue to exist the way they do so today at the expense of the "have nots". Freedom must reflect a difference in the conditions of life. What would happen to the wealth of the country? Monopoly capital would be nationalised, but beyond that private capital would exist. The details had neither been worked out nor spelt out. It will be a democratic country and they would nationalise say, 51% of certain organisations. One of the conditions will be that circumstances would need to be taken into account as to how the economic situation had reached that state. But it would be submitted to the people and the view of the majority would prevail. If at that point the Communist Party wanted to argue for total domination, they would have to do so.[8]

As Nelson Mandela sees it, "a prosperous non-European bourgeois class" would emerge in a position of leadership.[9] Officially, the ANC perceives itself as an all-class alliance to achieve equal citizenship and democracy but not socialism. What economic policy will be pursued beyond the vague prescriptions of the Freedom Charter will depend on the exigencies and the political forces once liberation is achieved.

The debate between "socialists" and "capitalists" in South Africa, as elsewhere, is focusing on how economic growth, which is dependent on individual initiative can be reconciled with economic justice. Social democracy as practiced in several European states so far seems to have found the most successful formula for achieving material improvement without stifling economic initiative through excessive state interference and bureaucratic regimentation. If the demand for "socialism" by most

7. Lawrence Schlemmer, "Black Workers and the Alternative: Attitudes Towards Socialism," *Indicator SA*, Vol. 3, No. 4, Autumn 1986.

8. "Notes of a Meeting."

9. Nelson Mandela, "In Our Lifetime," in Thomas Karis, and Gwendolen Carter, eds., *From Protest to Challenge: A Documentary History of African Politics in South Africa 1882–1964*, vol. 3, Thomas Karis and Gail Gerhart eds., *Challenge and Violence 1953–1964* (Palo Alto: Hoover Institution Press, 1977), pp. 245–50.

South African black spokesmen is made concrete, it probably means the Swedish or British Labour party model, in both of which unions play a critical role. For example, the new president of COSATU, Elijah Barayia, when asked whether he would describe his organization as socialist, answered: "Yes, I believe COSATU is a socialist organization and I would like to see a socialist state in South Africa. I speak of socialism as practiced by the Labour Party in England."[10]

Progressive capitalism has long learned to tolerate and coexist with labor parties in power in advanced industrial societies. A democratically organized socialist party à la Kinnock, Mitterrand, or Helmut Schmidt not only would keep a Trotskyite "militant tendency" in check but might also successfully control Moscow-oriented bureaucratized Communist parties, as the French example has shown. Even if the Marxist influence in the ANC were as strong as its detractors make it out to be, the ANC's essentially conservative constituency in South Africa would make it a reformist, nationalist movement, so long as it is democratically organized. The relevant question is not then about the degree of socialism in the ANC but the commitment of the ANC to internal democracy and rejection of authoritarian centralism. Will the unions be autonomous under an ANC government? Will the unions have the right to strike, which the Freedom Charter curiously does not mention?

In the present absence of foreseeable negotiations between Afrikaner and African interests at the national level, an important trend of gradual progress and compromise can, however, be discerned in what may be called the "localization of black politics," which has analogies to developments in mines and factories. Regional and local options have gained greater credibility despite the shriller rhetoric of no negotiations. After the collapse of imposed township administration boards, white municipalities, business associations, and other institutions have been compelled to negotiate with the only legitimate civic organizations available, particularly in some Eastern Cape towns. Successful consumer boycotts, lawlessness, or rent strikes have necessitated recognition of the force of organized opposition. For the first time, white local authorities have had to deal formally with independent associations, a development that represents as significant a shift in the local political balance of power as the formal recognition of independent unions in the economic arena half a decade earlier.

The strength of the unions compared with that of the political organizations lies not only in their tighter organization but in their principled policy of always achieving a firm mandate for actions from

10. *Leadership*, 5 January 1986.

their membership. Usually unions go for winnable contests. Most analysts are unanimous about the "strategic sophistication" of unions compared with the moral zeal of civic and student groups, which frequently act regardless of costs.[11] The revolutionary climate tends to pressure unions into more precipitate political stances at the expense of realistic or economistic calculations, a tendency likely to increase intra-union cleavages. Paralyzed by slow constituency politics on the one hand and recessionary threats on the other, many unions will try to escape the predicament by rhetorical militancy. Despite frequent moves to restore unity, rhetoric will in turn trigger further splits of memberships divided by ideology and loyalty to leaders, as the emergence of the Inkatha unions indicates.

The current union scene provides the most reliable indicator of what would happen in the political arena if there were free political activity. The most likely long-term outcome would be the emergence of a union-based social-democratic labor party and a smaller socialist as well as conservative black-middle-class party supported by the strong religious traditionalists, particularly the Zionists. There is the possibility, too, that some smaller Bantustan-based ethnic parties would emerge. Most likely, the populist ANC will eventually split up, since among its present adherents are those of diverse aspirations and orientations. In any case, an ANC in power in a postapartheid society will inevitably change, because national liberation will be replaced by the goal of concrete improvement in many aspects of the economy and society.

Analysts of radical opposition politics have noted an almost "fundamentalist" feature, an uncompromising rejection of potential reforms as dangerous co-optive domination.[12] Such a principled stance always entails unfulfilled opportunities. Uncompromising subjective fervor often coexists with objective weakness. With little organizational clout to challenge the entrenched establishment effectively on its own ground, media politics and fantasies of government collapse have taken the place of real power for many blacks. Even some usually sober union leaders seem to have been affected by the revolutionary ecstasy. Asked "how long the South African government can last," COSATU president Barayi replied: "I believe in three to four years the South African government is going to collapse."[13] Radical rhetoric can create revolutionary political expectations without the assurance of a revolutionary takeover, which will be bound to come into conflict with the realist stance of other

11. See, e.g., the excellent analysis by Steven Friedman, "Black Politics at the Crossroads," South African Institute of Race Relations, *Topical Briefings,* 1 February 1986.

12. See, e.g., L. Schlemmer, "South Africa and the Problem of Social Change," manuscript, 1986.

13. *Leadership,* 5 January 1986.

union leaders and the economic concerns of most rank and file members, as has so frequently happened elsewhere.

With its recent diplomatic success and strengthened self-confidence, the exile movement has shown a far greater flexibility in engaging itself with potential allies than has opposition within South Africa. By discussing the crisis with concerned businessmen, church delegations, liberal students, or disillusioned Nationalists abroad, the ANC shrewdly erodes the official definitions. Without embracing gradualism explicitly, the organization enlists the liberal establishment as allies. The onus is on the reformists to deliver without the revolutionaries having to concede anything in turn. The ANC now prudently distinguishes between "revolutionaries" and what is called the "forces of change" that can be mobilized and used for weakening minority cohesion. This realistic political maneuvering stands in sharp contrast to the apolitical purity of internal boycott politics which refuses to be soiled by recognizing the strength of "the enemy." Pretoria, in turn, by treating each legal concession or material improvement as a substitute for central political rights, reinforces the moral fervor of an all-or-nothing stance. With a fragile organizational base, the extraparliamentary opposition is vulnerable to volatile swings in support. In a context still strongly influenced by a powerful state, successful reform politics requires as its precondition free political activity. Only in a free contest can leaders gain the demonstrated support to deal confidently with an opponent without the fear of being constantly outradicalized by less responsible competitors. Only free political activity allows black leaders to control anarchists, provide guidance in the crippling school boycott and generally discipline rage into constructive resistance. Both from following and inspiring township sentiment, the ANC could then truly lead the opposition.

Since the conflict in South Africa concerns power and privilege even more essentially than ideology or racism, power-sharing is open to bargaining and compromise. Herein lies the basis of realistic optimism about a comparatively less violent ongoing transformation, which in the end may make liberation a less-than-spectacular affair despite the inevitable outbursts of fire. South Africa represents a configuration in which neither side can defeat the other. In this violent stalemate, revolution, repression, and reform continue in an inseparable mixture for the time being. Each policy decision and resistance strategy, however, creates its own dynamic.

While it is certain that institutionalized racial discrimination will give way to a legally integrated but still informally segregated society, it is much more difficult to predict whether the postapartheid economic order will be a free-enterprise capitalism, an orthodox Marxist socialism, or a social-democratic welfare capitalism. In these three options lies the real future of South Africa. The legitimate liberal concern with civil-rights violations has postponed the debate about these economic and social alternatives, and perhaps has masked the true significance of black labor organization. With fading racial discrimination, class stratification, particularly within each racial group, will be placed on the political agenda again. In all likelihood, a nonracial alliance of white and black forces will carry the day, an alliance in which unions could be a major partner.

Sean Archer

20. Economic Means and Political Ends in the Freedom Charter

Is the Freedom Charter of 1955 system-specific? Are its objectives realizable in only one kind of economic system, or in many? To answer such questions we need to adopt an instrumentalist perspective and to assess alternative concrete ways to meet the Charter's aspirations, in order, first, to enhance the likelihood of their realization in the near to medium future, and second, to allay the fears of those who think most reallocative and redistributive actions will be irrational and growth-inhibiting.

In the past, perhaps less so now, proponents of noncapitalist systems have offered an abstract and somewhat utopian perspective on the economic alternatives. They have presumed that devising methods and institutions for an order without private ownership and exchange of productive resources is a technical and secondary problem, certainly much less important than political organization. Often this attitude is coupled to skeptical dismissal of mainstream economic thought as a vulgar rationalization of the existing order. This is indiscriminate and wrongheaded.

This essay advances two propositions: first, that the Freedom Charter is a programmatic statement couched in open-ended terms, not an

This is a revised version of my paper "Alternative Economic Mechanisms and the Freedom Charter in South Africa," UCT Centre for African Studies, *Africa Seminar Collected Papers* (1986).

operational blueprint grounded upon or compatible with only one mechanism or form of economic organization; second, that to identify the best economic mechanism for a democratic South Africa one must take a clear-sighted look at what is already in being, at "actually existing" socialism, and at capitalism, for that matter.

Four of the ten clauses in the Charter have predominantly economic content and two others bear on the discussion. (The text of the Charter appears on pp. 350–52.)

Clause 3 states, *"The people shall share in the country's wealth."* Redistribution is to be effected in two ways: first, by nationalization, that is, by transferring to the public domain ("to the ownership of the people as a whole") assets held by foreigners, together with individually and corporately owned resources (in mining, banking, and "monopoly industry"); and second, by control of remaining economic activity in the social interest ("to assist the well-being of the people"). Ownership has many variants, especially if we include, as we should, not mere possession of things in the colloquial sense but rights as enforceable claims. Outside the socialist bloc, thirty years after the Charter's drafting a greater range in ownership forms has already emerged in the postcolonial third world and with the extension of the welfare state in developed capitalistic societies. Existing national economies span a spectrum of forms of state- and private-capital collaboration, such as joint ventures, concessions, leasing, licensed operations, and management contracts.

As to regulation, that is, control of private production and exchange by a public agency, the range of possible variations is no less wide. Overt political commitment to socialism correlates only weakly, if at all, with size of the public sector and extent of government control over the private sphere. The state's program of taxing, spending, regulating banking, and directly productive actions is no less effective in resource allocation and decision-making in "free market" Brazil and South Korea than in "socialist" India and Algeria. In all likelihood, adaptation to a postapartheid situation will require an amalgam of and balance between ownership forms and innovative regulation and deregulation for which specific precedents for the overall system may be rare but separate components are not.

Clause 4 states that *"the land shall be shared among those who work it."* The demand for redistribution of land in one form or another will be irresistible, on political grounds because of the symbolic and emotional accretions the land issue has acquired and sustained over generations, and on economic grounds because large-scale agriculture will shed rather than absorb labor if concentration of land holdings and capital intensity are left to market forces. The wide disparities between labor-intensive subsistence agriculture and capital-intensive commercial agriculture make no economic sense. In subsection 1 of clause 4, the Charter is extremely open-ended—". . . all the land [shall be] redivided amongst those who work it"—and nonspecific about form, so the possibilities here include ownership by the state, by groups, or by individuals; and with further variations in the legal basis of tenure. Where public ownership ends and private ownership begins is not easily determined. The interesting "Morogoro gloss" on the Charter,[1] adopted at an ANC Consultative Conference in 1969, envisages subdivision of some land into individual, presumably private, plots and dispersion of them alongside areas of expanded "communal ownership." Whether "communal" means just that—equal distribution of product irrespective of work input—or is used generically for all forms of nonprivate farming, including collectives and cooperatives, is unclear. Another interesting speculation is whether the drafters of the gloss envisaged large state farms with capital-intensive crop production and extensive stock grazing alongside small-holder units.

Clause 6 of the Charter reads, *"All shall enjoy equal human rights."* The economic dimension here is the asserted right of individuals to respond without restriction to economic stimuli and perceived need. In combination with clause 7, it stipulates conditions for the functioning of a "free" labor market: "The law shall guarantee to all their right to speak, to organise, to meet together . . ." (6.1); "All shall be free to travel without restriction from countryside to town . . ." (6.3); "Pass laws, permits and all other laws restricting these freedoms shall be abolished" (6.4). But under what circumstances may the state legitimately interfere in the exercise of these rights in the wider interest? There are no easy answers, yet what is peculiarly obfuscatory is the presumption that conflicts and contradictions between individual and group would not arise if ownership and production relations ceased to be predominantly capitalist. This a priori view is common despite the contemporary experience of "actually existing socialism," in Bahro's phrase.

The seventh clause is little more specific: *"There shall be work and security."* Though the Charter emphasizes social security, minimum wages, improved working conditions, and other legislation favorable to workers, surprisingly it nowhere states clearly that full employment is a macro-objective, nor, therefore, that paid work is an individual right under stipulated conditions. Such an interpretation might nevertheless

1. A. la Guma, ed., *Apartheid: A Collection of Writings on South African Racism by South Africans* (London: Lawrence & Wishart, 1972), pp. 229–44.

be placed on subsection 2: "The state shall recognise the rights and duty of all to work, and to draw full unemployment benefits."

Universal access to unemployment compensation is hardly feasible if a large segment of the economically active population is continuously without work. Together clauses 4 and 9 contain the standard elements of welfare-state capitalism, none of which are near realization for the majority of the population thirty years after the Charter. These ordinarily include a social-security system to make income transfers between contributors, taxpayers, and recipients; formalized collective bargaining and protected employment contracts; the provision of benefits in kind, such as health care, education, and personal or household social services (welfare work, home visiting, counseling); and price subsidies to decrease the consumer cost of commodities judged socially meritorious, such as food and other wage goods, transportation, housing, and cultural facilities. Additional components of the welfare state, some implicit in the Charter, are macroeconomic steering and the maintenance of employment levels; market regulation, including bank controls, credit guarantees, and antitrust provisions; infrastructural support to the private sector; general governmental activism in certain industries and foreign trade, and in stimulating investment.

Are these objectives commendably brave but unattainable in view of the country's dual economy and chronic labor surpluses? Advocates of these objectives tend to overlook the fact that prior accumulation on a considerable scale appears to be an absolute precondition for a welfare state. Workers cannot be paid more simply because they are poor; they must be more productive. The logic of the market or the law of value requires that the individual either be more skilled, or have available more capital equipment, or work harder, or all these in combination. Extensive recourse to the tax-transfer mechanism is not possible unless there is fat in the system. To be more egalitarian under capitalism, you must be rich first.

Guaranteed full employment hitherto has proved feasible only in a planned economy. In its absence, one must ponder that in situations of labor surplus a forty-hour week, wage minima, annual leaves, sick and maternity leaves, and the like on a *national* basis would be distinctly second-best goals. They would favor sectional interests, that is, workers already in occupations covered by social-security provisions, and in unionized industries where they are capable of acting collectively. In a social ranking of priorities, full employment is likely to take precedence over the package of fringe benefits listed in 7.4. Also, full-employment guarantees imply both individual security and persistent labor shortages, with serious drawbacks for discipline, morale, and productivity. Hungarian experience throws up the question pertinent to all planned economies: "Can a society achieve high efficiency exclusively by means of *positive* material and moral incentives, that is, by rewarding good work? Are *negative* economic incentives—the fear of failure, and of individual material and moral loss—dispensable?"[2]

Clause 8 urges that *"the doors of learning and of culture shall be opened."* Insofar as provision of education has a privileged status under all existing systems, with state intervention virtually unquestioned, this clause is clearly not system-specific.[3] Despite New Right rhetoric in advanced capitalist countries about enhanced choice through privatization, through voucher and other similar schemes, no national education arrangements are organized by market means. Rather, issues of priority and strategic allocation bulk large in discussions of education as an instrument of national integration and redistribution of social opportunities. One must decide what resources to devote to education, and what breakdown of that investment is most desirable on grounds of equity and efficiency by type of education, such as formal schooling and informal skill formation (apprenticeship, learning-by-doing, adult literacy), and by educational level.

Subsection 4 is a key subclause, given the explosive political significance acquired by education in the past decade: *"Education shall be free, compulsory, universal and equal for all children."* A first comment is that a compelling economic rationale for investment in education does exist: its private and social profitability is comparable to or higher than that of other avenues of investment; also, the ranking by rate of return, primary over secondary over higher levels, appears to hold in all countries irrespective of income-per-capita differences between them.[4] Second, a rapid expansion of education, including an assault on illiteracy (8.6), may illustrate the unpalatable truth that all good things do *not* go together. To widen and deepen the structure means attracting an inflow of new teachers into the profession, and moving "old" teachers into less attractive jobs and schools, with a consequent upward pressure on salary levels. To facilitate such mobilization, pay differentials must be introduced, despite the goal of decreasing inequality, particularly in the public sector. Every skill-intensive activity advocated by the Charter

2. J. Kornai, "The Dilemmas of a Socialist Economy: The Hungarian Experience," *Cambridge Journal of Economics* 4 (1980): 153.

3. The rationale for the free or subsidized supply of education as a merit good is normally couched in terms of (1) distributional considerations, in that some pupils (and parents), ignorant of schooling's benefits, ought as a matter of compulsion, not merely as of right, to attain minimum standards of literacy and numeracy; (2) externalities, meaning income and nonpecuniary gains to others than those receiving education; and (3) the melting-pot theory that schools break down class and ethnic barriers.

4. G. Psacharopoulos, "The Contribution of Education to Economic Growth: International Comparisons," in J. Kendrick, ed., *International Comparisons of Productivity and Causes of the Slowdown* (Cambridge: Ballinger, 1984), pp. 335–60.

will pose this dilemma, nor will the importation of "specialists" from abroad solve it costlessly, as decades of development experience elsewhere have borne out. Third, education does not serve the economy best if its content is predominantly vocational or narrowly technical. To raise employability in active age ranges, to make people adaptable and independent in work, and to generate self-reliance and creativity, education of a broader nature is indicated.

The final economic clause, the ninth, states, *"There shall be houses, security and comfort."* Faced with the listing of objectives in this clause—food and housing subsidies, rent control, welfare payments, free medical care, slum clearance and social overheads—the role of the economist is unenviable for the same reasons Carlyle a century ago called political economy the "dismal science." As expressed more recently, "We frequently have to point out the limits of our opportunities. We have to say, 'This or that, not both. You can't do both.' What's worse, we have to point out . . . that the economic system is complex in its nature. . . . a step which on the face of it is an obvious way of achieving certain desired values may in fact frequently lead to their opposites."[5] On reflection these may appear truisms; what is not is the realization that this is equally true of economies without capitalists. The idea of cost as an alternative foregone is fundamental, and in every system the problem is to devise mechanisms that reflect this in decision-making. Extension of state enterprise and control, a reordering of priorities, and redistributive measures would release resources for pursuing the objectives of clause 9. Yet how much immediate need would be satisfied and how transitory or enduring the long-term effects would be, are as yet unanswerable questions.

Does the Charter embody socialist goals? Yes and no. If socialism is interpreted to be socialization of ownership together with an equitable disposition of power and resources, then clauses 1, 3, and 4 constitute necessary but far from sufficient conditions for its realization. Concern with individual consciousness, autonomy, and personal values—central components of socialist ideology—would be overlooked or negated. Furthermore, ever since the foundation of the Soviet state a wide spectrum of self-identified socialists has asserted that nationalization is not socialization but at most a starting point for that process.[6] Sociali-

5. K. Arrow, *The Limits of Organization* (New York: Norton, 1974), p. 17.

6. "The notion of socialism entails a particular concept of property rights—a system of ownership whereby *society* is genuinely in control of the means of production and benefits from their use . . . if a substantive, and not formal, meaning is attached to this concept, the act of taking capital into *public* ownership (nationalization), should not *eo ipso* be identified with socialization." W. Brus, "Socialism—Feasible and Viable," *New Left Review* 153 (1985): 44–45.

zation means the establishment of social control, in contrast to sectional and elitist control by a class or bureaucracy, over the conditions and results of productive activity. In the history of political economy, "socialization" came to connote the use of productive means in the interest of society as a whole, and of democratic participation by immediate producers in their administration. As such, it remains an abstract ideal.

The German terms *gesellschaftlich* (belonging to society) and *öffentlich* (belonging to a public institution) bring out the distinction. In South Africa, Iscor, a steel corporation, Sasol (an oil-from-coal corporation), and the Industrial Development and Armaments Corporations are public, not social, bodies. As agencies of the present state they represent particular interests, and many citizens would see their activities as less than benign. The public-sector share in annual gross investment has hovered around 50 percent since the late 1960s, with fluctuations due to the volatility of private investment expenditure. But this is hardly an index of socialization or "creeping socialism," the views of market ideologues notwithstanding. Nationalization, therefore, may be propagated for a variety of populist or nationalist motives which might or might not coincide with those that underlie socialization. Such reasons include the acceleration of industrial growth, the restraint of foreign interests, the arrest of structural economic decline, and perceived "imperfections" in the domestic markets—for example, high risks and incomplete information—and yet where positive externalities may exist.[7] The nationalization drive in France under President Mitterrand illustrates the range of possible motivations, in that "As a project, nationalization could be all things to all people. Therefore it was a powerful unifying device."[8]

We have identified certain problems in interpreting and assessing the Charter's economic clauses which affirm that a democratic economy ranks equally with a democratic polity. What institutions the drafting committee envisaged to realize these wider aspirations are not clear. They worked in the international context of the Cold War and McCarthyism and, alternately, of admiration in certain progressive circles for the Soviet Union's achievements during World War II, its success in developing material and human resources, and its high economic growth rates. The manifest deficiencies of this economic performance still lay

7. R. Vernon, "Linking Managers with Ministers: Dilemmas of the State-Owned Enterprise," *Journal of Policy Analysis and Management* 4 (1984): 39–55. Externalities in production or consumption manifest themselves as costs and benefits outside the price mechanism and therefore require political intervention.

8. P. Hall, "Socialism in One Country: Mitterrand and the Struggle to Define a New Economic Policy in France," in P. Cerny and M. Schain, eds., *Socialism, the State and Public Policy in France* (London: Pinter, 1985), p. 89.

in the future, as did the 20th Party Congress of the following year, 1956, at which de-Stalinization was launched officially with Khrushchev's report "On the personality cult and its consequences." Although evidence cannot be found in the Charter itself, certain of its drafters probably had in mind planned growth along Soviet lines. Because preconceptions and misconceptions about centrally planned economies still abound on all sides of the divide in South Africa, an appraisal of their record will be useful with the Charter's goals in mind.

What are the distinguishing features of the economies of "realized socialism," by which we mean the thirteen countries that currently claim to follow Marxian precepts? In combination and in varying proportions they comprise: planning and central coordination; state and cooperative ownership; an enunciated stress upon equality; and predominantly vertical flows of information and decisions. Their deformations at the political and bureaucratic level—repression, cultural stagnation, repudiation of individual rights and civil liberties—are better known, so discussion here concentrates upon the economic dimension. Nonetheless, as we shall see, the two spheres are intimately linked.

Viewed in a long-term perspective, central planning has been highly successful. Countries that had been among the most backward economically and socially have been industrialized rapidly; education, health, science, and certain arts have approached levels comparable with those of developed capitalist countries; and full employment of labor has been maintained, with the price level held constant. This list of achievements is long, and its rapidity—thirty to sixty years, taking China and the U.S.S.R. as examples—is unique. Using U.S. congressional figures, the achievement of Soviet economic growth can be gauged roughly. Depending on the choice of price base, in 1976 the ratio of Soviet to U.S. national product varied between 50 and 74 percent, with a mean of about 60 percent compared to 40 percent in 1955 and 15 percent in 1928.[9] Two simple lessons have been drawn. First, where production targets are few, homogeneous or relatively similar, and require a uniform technology, with economies of large-scale output, central planning has proved efficient. Examples of such outputs are fuel and power, housing, medical care, transportation, schooling, and basic wage goods like clothing. Second, when sacrifices from the population are needed, a planned economy apparently can impose greater demands and deliver more rewards than the free-market mechanisms.

Nonetheless, these systems are rather less attractive today as devel-

9. S. Gomulka, "The Incompatibility of Socialism and Rapid Innovation," *Millennium: Journal of International Studies* 13 (1985): 15.

opment models than they were thirty years ago. Why? Because on a technical level, their vaunted growth performance has waned; they appear more dependent upon capitalism for technology, food imports and export outlets; consumption per capita has leveled off, both of goods and services purchased privately and of education, health care, and other items supplied collectively; agriculture remains the poor relative despite the diversion to it of huge investments. The picture is one of general deterioration even with the high rates of saving built into the system—a quarter to a third of the income flow is invested annually. A "centralized socialist" economy is like a vehicle locked into low gear: large quantities of accumulation pass through, yet only low speeds can be attained.

Some reasons for these negative trends are clear enough. No transition from extensive to intensive growth processes has occurred. Profligate use of labor, energy, natural resources, and capital cannot be sustained, and gains must come instead from increasing output per unit of input. Further growth, that is, has to emerge from the rising productivity of units of labor and capital through innovation, technical progress, and increased allocative efficiency. The essential feature of a centrally planned economy is the detailed allocation of goods and services among producing and distributing units by a centralized and hierarchical decision-maker. The planning agency, authorized by the political leadership, instructs each organization to use certain inputs and to attain certain levels of output. This arrangement can inhibit or even penalize the introduction of new techniques. Furthermore, the excessive aggregation of information leads to bottlenecks and risk-averting behavior; producers, unsure how much they are going to get, ask for more than they need, thereby producing waste, low labor productivity, and consequently, sterile investment.

To break out of their stagnation, some socialist countries have turned to importing trade and technology from market economies. Significant gains have been achieved, but at the cost of enmeshing these countries in global capitalist cycles, in balance-of-payments disequilibria, external debts (e.g., Poland), and, therefore, a series of "stop-go" policies. Another telling indicator is the composition of their foreign trade, which differs little from that of developing countries in the export of energy, materials, and simpler manufactures and in the import of machinery and electronic equipment.[10] Finally, an equally serious problem—and a cause for concern among socialists elsewhere—is the tendency of the faulty economic system to generate cynicism, disaffection, alienation,

10. W. Brus and T. Kowalik, "Socialism and Development," *Cambridge Journal of Economics* 7 (1983): 250; Movement for Socialist Renewal (MSR) (Moscow) "Manifesto," *Guardian Weekly* (London) 3 August 1986, p. 9.

self-seeking behavior, and "the privatisation of economic interests."[11] This cynicism can be seen in the bitter political humor emanating from these countries. For example: "*Six contradictions of socialism* [are:] There is no unemployment but no-one works. No-one works but the Plan is fulfilled. The Plan is fulfilled but there are no goods in the shops. There are no goods in the shops, but everyone lives well. Everyone lives well, but everyone is discontented. Everyone is discontented but everyone votes 'yes.' "[12]

In centrally planned economies many trained and gifted advisers, intellectuals, technocrats, and leaders at many levels are acutely aware of their systems' inadequacies.[13] Why, then, has reform been so halfhearted? One answer is that the technical problems of coordinating an economy are now much more formidable. Growing and unavoidable complexity in production generates exponential growth in the demand for information. Existing planning methods cannot meet this demand, even with more planners and more computers. What appears to be needed is decentralization of authority, devolution of decision-making, and some legitimation of enterprising activity, along with equilibration of social need and availability through the market mechanism.

The primary obstacles are in fact political. Great centralization of power is a fundamental precept of the orthodox interpretation of socialism in these systems. It is upon this rock that attempted reforms have come to grief, and continue to do so. The need for a feedback mechanism created through the decentralization of power can be summarized in the following terms:[14] A planned economy requires a higher degree of politicization among its participants than any other economy does, because a free flow of information is essential for efficient calculation by the central planners. For this to occur there must be a high order of democratic control of the economy, so that the population can identify with the goals of the system, and maintain *social* control over accumulation and growth.

Any serious attempt to develop an "economics of feasible socialism," to use Nove's phrase, has to address three issues: coordination in resource allocation; accumulation and participation; and distribution and incentives.

Every economic mechanism makes use of a price system to coordinate

11. W. Brus, J. Cooper, M. Ellman, and M. Nuti, "Outlook for the Socialist Economies," *Marxism Today,* February 1982, p. 24.

12. Quoted in *Critique* (University of Glasgow) 16 (1984): 122.

13. T. Zaslavskaya, "The Novosibirsk Report," *Survey* 28 (1984): 88–108; MSR, "Manifesto."

14. W. Brus, *Socialist Ownership and Political Systems* (London: Routledge, 1975); A. Nove, *The Economics of Feasible Socialism* (London: Allen and Unwin, 1983).

information and generate signals so that production, consumption, and exchange can proceed efficiently. This means that the economy comes into balance at a level and composition of output that cannot be improved upon—it is "optimal"—given the tastes and resources, including the skills, of all its individual members. Mainstream economics can demonstrate this property of prices to be the result of market processes, but only on the basis of rather strong assumptions. Among these are certain restrictions on production technology and individual preferences; the requirement of price-taking behavior on the part of every single agent (no one can profitably influence the price at which he or she transacts as buyer or seller); and the existence of all markets necessary for future transactions. Although elegant, this construct provides no justification for presuming that actual market economies will approximate idealized models in which competitive prices keep the system on a path of equilibrium and growth. It is not a useful model for constructing in Dobb's phrase "some organic fusion of planning with market-relations" superior to capitalism. Furthermore, one does not have to buy the ideological baggage of idealized markets, private property, and adherence to individualist goals: a committed socialist like Maurice Dobb accepted that a price system and *some* market institutions are necessary for efficient allocation.[15]

Economically relevant information is highly decentralized, incomplete, asymmetrical, and costly. Designers of every economic mechanism have to devise a way of pulling together information dispersed among direct producers and consumers, so that the outcome reconciles the potentially conflicting choices of all economic agents. A system of relative prices is such an instrumentality if it broadly reflects the amounts of economic resources embodied in the various commodities and their utilities to the community. As we remarked, the problem with administrative allocation in planned economies is that prices perform a passive accounting and recording function; they do not synthesize information; they generate disincentives; they reward waste; and they inhibit innovation. Opportunity cost—"what is given up" rather than "what is put in"—would also be reflected more accurately in a properly functioning price system. Political leaders and planners could still use resources in accordance with social preferences and democratic choice, but they would know better the cost in alternatives forgone by society.

These ideas about coordination can be made compatible with the economic demands of the Freedom Charter. A price system is an instrumentality, the major one in the economic sphere, used to realize

15. For an illuminating discussion, see Dobb's last paper, "Some Historical Reflections on Planning and the Market," in C. Abramsky, ed., *Essays in Honour of E. H. Carr* (London: Macmillan, 1974), pp. 324–38.

a set of social values whatever they may be at any historical juncture. Alternatives to it, whether existing or hypothetical, are either deficient or too abstract and do not respect the logic of the economic situation. Any expectation that market mechanisms in a democratic economy can be accorded wholly passive functions would be illusory and seriously misleading.

The second issue, accumulation, raises a systemic feature of economies planned hierarchically, their capital-using bias, what is termed "investment good fetishism." In the U.S.S.R. the share of accumulation devoted to investment has been high throughout the planning period from 1928, but with declining efficiency. Since the fifties in particular, the incremental capital-output ratio has been rising: where a one-ruble increase in output in 1928 required a capital stock increment of two or three rubles, in the early eighties it required six or seven. So to sustain a respectable growth rate, capital inputs must be raised further when the fraction of the income flow devoted to investment is already high. To increase that share would be unbearably burdensome and politically dangerous.[16] The long-term effect on living standards can be gauged from the Chinese experience: according to Lardy, "between the end of the First Plan [1957] and 1977 per capita output grew at 3.4 percent per annum (in real terms) while consumption—on the broadest possible measure, including personal and collective consumption—grew at only 1.3 percent annually (in real terms). In large measure the disparity in the growth rates reflects the rising share of national output allocated to investment."[17]

Overaccumulation is also simply wasteful, because "to carry out investment faster than the digestive system of the economy can absorb it is a vain sacrifice," as Joan Robinson put it.[18] This is one consequence of the centralization of power in the political sphere which admits no kind of pluralism or response mechanism like independent institutions to channel social preferences and protests. This enables the state "to pursue disastrous policies (overaccumulation being one) until they lead to catastrophe as in Poland."[19] The pertinence of this to our principal theme again should be clear, as the Freedom Charter's objectives carry high accumulation costs. When autonomous and participatory mechanisms for the expression of social choice—if need be in a countervailing direction—are absent, to set a pace in capital formation that requires

16. Brus and Kowalik, "Socialism and Development," p. 249.

17. N. Lardy, "Consumption and Living Standards in China, 1978–83," *China Quarterly* 100 (1984): 849–65.

18. J. Robinson, *Collected Economic Papers* 4 (Oxford: Blackwell, 1973), p. 43.

19. Brus et al., "Outlook," p. 23.

force to implement will be ultimately self-defeating as well as profoundly undemocratic. Democratization cannot be an afterthought, a dispensable luxury, but it is an essential prerequisite for rational economic outcomes.

With regard to the third issue, distribution and incentives, socialist thinkers in the past expected capitalism to be transcended through three key changes: the ultimate abolition of wage labor; the disappearance of unearned income from ownership of natural assets, capital, and private intellectual property; and community control of distribution. These changes would not mean immediate equality, nor that the new socialist men and women would be imbued with idealism and altruism. The effects were expected to come from social change, not from the moral transformation of individuals.

While sympathetic to such impulses, we have expressed a certain skepticism about their operational relevance. On incentives, in particular, a measure of compromise seems inescapable. What motives in addition to self-interest can realistically be expected to spur economic action? And under what conditions will individuals see their interests, not as complementary to those of society, but as divergent? Wishful thinking about altruism and the community-mindedness of ordinary people can lead to painful disillusionment for those subscribing to socialist goals. Experience elsewhere has shown the difficulty of devising incentives that reconcile productive efficiency and equity in distribution: ". . . greed can be replaced by apathy and lassitude when greed has nothing to bite on. . . . To ask individuals or groups of individuals to act in the common interest is, except in well-defined exceptional cases, not to ask anything comprehensible of them at all."[20]

Furthermore, the pricing and allocation of labor in accordance with market signals is indispensable, both to preserve individual autonomy and choice and for its rational use in production. The only workable alternative appears to be administrative direction by authority. Also, a measure of material inequality, like pay differentials, subsidies to groups, and toleration of informal sector activity, seems unavoidable for achieving efficiency. But *what* minimal degree will suffice is the hard question. The Hungarian experience is salutary: "For a long time and by many people the future of the socialist economy was thought to be such that a growing proportion of needs would be satisfied by various specialized large organizations (enterprises or public non-profit institutions). . . . This vision has proven to be extreme and one-sided. A considerable number of people want to satisfy a sizeable portion of their personal

20. F. Hahn, "Reflections on the Invisible Hand," *Lloyds Bank Review* 144 (1982): 17–18.

needs within the family, within the household, or on the basis of personal ownership and self-determination either because of their own preferences, or because they are forced to by necessity."[21]

This discussion has highlighted the cardinal issue for planning: whether the centralization of economic authority in a socialist state is compatible with decentralization of information and responsibility in a complex economic system. It seems that some amalgam and compromise between plan and market arrangements is essential to make a democratic economy workable. The visible hand of the state should manifest itself in the sphere of investment, in raising its volume and coordinating its composition; in taxation and transfer payments; and in specific price and wage interventions. On the other hand, markets are integral to a redistributive strategy, on grounds of their efficiency and consistency with ends broadly socialist. Market instruments do not imply embodiment in market-driven private-property systems.

In noting the consistency of market arrangements with socialist institutions, it is essential to distinguish between the allocative and the distributive functions of prices. The former is connected with their use to achieve economic efficiency, the latter with their determining the income to be received by individuals in return for what they contribute. It is perfectly consistent for a socialist regime to establish an interest rate, to allocate resources among investment projects and to compute rental charges for the use of capital and scarce natural assets such as land and forests. Indeed, this must be done if these means of production are to be employed in the best way. For even if these assets should fall out of the sky without human effort, they are nevertheless productive in the sense that when combined with other factors a greater output results. It does not follow, however, that there need be private persons who as owners of these assets receive the monetary equivalents of these evaluations. Rather these accounting prices are indicators for drawing up an efficient schedule of economic activities. Except in the case of work of all kinds, prices under socialism do not correspond to income paid over to private individuals. Instead, the income imputed to natural and collective assets accrues to the state, and therefore their prices have no distributive function.[22]

An even stronger proposition emerging out of the literature on "feasible socialism" is that markets are not only compatible but also necessary devices for realizing fundamental components of the socialization of production, like individual autonomy and participation.[23]

21. J. Kornai, "Comments on the Present State and the Prospects of the Hungarian Economic Reform," *Journal of Comparative Economics* 7 (1983): 237.

22. J. Rawls, *A Theory of Justice* (Cambridge: Harvard University Press, 1971), p. 273.

23. Nove, *Feasible Socialism*, pp. 233–36, Part 5; Brus, "Socialism—Feasible and Viable," pp. 47ff. One needs to recall also a more complex tradition of thought concerning markets. "The idea of a market for goods has figured in political and economic theory, since the eighteenth century, in two rather different ways. It has been celebrated, first, as a device

If we interpret the Freedom Charter as a minimal program in the economic sphere, a reading of its fine print evokes the key strategic question, namely what economic arrangements will best allow the pursuit of equity without jeopardizing long-term growth? We do not have an answer, and it would be surprising if we did. We are right, though, to distrust all unitary theories which insist on purity, because we need to adopt an instrumentalist perspective and talk less about systems and more about mechanisms. Yet we have also to beware of the "supermarket fallacy."[24] System construction does not resemble pushing a trolley down the shelves of system components—economic instruments, policies, incentive schemes, institutions—in order to put together that composite whole which we rank most highly by some set of criteria. The acid test has always to remain the question, posed in the light of historical precedent and current circumstances: But will the contraption fly?

The Freedom Charter is a point of departure, a statement of goals, not a blueprint for system construction. Insofar as its clauses entail particular means, these imply a mixed economic formation with the state's role quantitatively greater than at present, though by how much remains unclear. A reasonably determinate mix of economic objectives is both explicit and implicit in the document. Furthermore, we should not presume that, should political developments lead that way, a planned economy could be set up in South Africa free from the distortions and irrationalities that mark those already realized elsewhere. Such views are infused with wishful thinking and evoke skepticism even among those in broad sympathy with the Charter's goals. In the long run this could do a profound disservice to its ideals and aspirations.

---

for both defining and achieving certain community-wide goals variously described as prosperity, efficiency, and overall utility. It has been hailed, second, as a necessary condition of individual liberty, the condition under which free men and women may exercise individual initiative and choice so that their fates lie in their own hands. The market, that is, has been defended both through arguments of policy, appealing to the overall, community-wide gains it produces, and arguments of principle that appeal instead to some supposed right to liberty.

But the economic market, whether defended in either or both of these ways, has during this same period come to be regarded as the enemy of equality, largely because the forms of economic market systems developed and enforced in industrial countries have permitted and indeed encouraged vast inequality in property. Both political philosophers and ordinary citizens have therefore pictured equality as the antagonist or victim of the values of efficiency and liberty supposedly served by the market, so that wise and moderate politics consists in striking some balance or trade-off between equality and these other values, either by imposing constraints on the market as an economic environment, or by replacing it, in part or altogether, with a different economic system." R. Dworkin, "What is Equality? Part 2: Equality of Resources," *Philosophy and Public Affairs* 10 (1981): 284.

24. Kornai, "Dilemmas," p. 156.

Appendix

The Congress of the People was organized by members of the African National Congress, the South African Indian Congress, the South African Coloured Peoples Organization, and the Congress of Democrats. About three thousand people met at Kliptown, near Johannesburg, on 26 and 27 June 1955, and adopted the Freedom Charter.

The Freedom Charter

We, the People of South Africa, Declare for All Our Country and the World to Know:

That South Africa belongs to all who live in it, black and white, and that no government can justly claim authority unless it is based on the will of the people;

that our people have been robbed of their birthright to land, liberty and peace by a form of government founded on injustice and inequality;

that our country will never be prosperous or free until all our people live in brotherhood, enjoying equal rights and opportunities;

that only a democratic state, based on the will of all the people, can secure to all their birthright, without distinction of colour, race, sex or belief;

And therefore, we, the people of South Africa, black and white together—equals, countrymen and brothers—adopt this Freedom Charter. And, we pledge ourselves to strive together, sparing neither strength nor courage, until the democratic changes here set out have been won.

1. The People Shall Govern!

1.1 Every man and woman shall have the right to vote for and to stand as a candidate for all bodies which make laws;

1.2 All people shall be entitled to take part in the administration of the country;

1.3 The rights of the people shall be the same, regardless of race, colour or sex;

1.4 All bodies of minority rule, advisory boards, councils and authorities shall be replaced by democratic organs of self-government.

2. All National Groups Shall Have Equal Rights!

2.1 There shall be equal status in the bodies of state, in the courts and in the schools, for all national groups and races;

2.2 All the people shall have equal right to use their own languages and to develop their own folk culture and customs;

2.3 All national groups shall be protected by law against insults to their race and national pride;

2.4 The preaching and practice of national, race or colour discrimination and contempt shall be a punishable crime;

2.5 All apartheid laws and practices shall be set aside.

3. The People Shall Share in the Country's Wealth!

3.1 The national wealth of our country, the heritage of all South Africans, shall be restored to the people;

3.2 The mineral wealth beneath the soil, the Banks and monopoly industry shall be transferred to the ownership of the people as a whole;

3.3 All other industry and trade shall be controlled to assist the well-being of the people;
3.4 All people shall have equal rights to trade where they choose, to manufacture and to enter all trades, crafts and professions.

4. The Land Shall Be Shared Among Those Who Work It!
4.1 Restrictions of land ownership on a racial basis shall be ended, and all the land redivided amongst those who work it to banish famine and land hunger;
4.2 The state shall help the peasants with implements, seed, tractors and dams to save the soil and assist the tillers;
4.3 Freedom of movement shall be guaranteed to all who work on the land;
4.4 All shall have the right to occupy land wherever they choose;
4.5 People shall not be robbed of their cattle, and forced labour and farm prisons shall be abolished.

5. All Shall Be Equal Before the Law!
5.1 No one shall be imprisoned, deported or restricted without a fair trial;
5.2 No one shall be condemned by the order of any government official;
5.3 The courts shall be representative of all the people;
5.4 Imprisonment shall only be for serious crimes against the people, and shall aim at re-education not vengeance;
5.5 The police force and army shall be open to all on an equal basis, they shall be the helpers and protectors of the people;
5.6 All laws which discriminate on grounds of race, colour or belief shall be repealed.

6. All Shall Enjoy Human Rights!
6.1 The law shall guarantee to all their right to speak, to organise, to meet together, to publish, to preach, to worship and to educate their children;
6.2 The privacy of the house from police raids shall be protected by law;
6.3 All shall be free to travel without restriction from countryside to town, from province to province, and from South Africa abroad;
6.4 Pass laws, permits and all other laws restricting these freedoms shall be abolished.

7. There Shall Be Work and Security!
7.1 All who work shall be free to form trade unions, to elect their officers and to make wage agreements with their employers;
7.2 The state shall recognise the rights and duty of all to work, and to draw full unemployment benefits;
7.3 Men and women of all races shall receive equal pay for equal work;
7.4 There shall be a forty hour working week, a national minimum wage, paid annual leave, and sick leave for all workers, and maternity leave on full pay for all working mothers;
7.5 Miners, domestic workers, farm workers and civil servants shall have the same rights as all others who work;
7.6 Child labour, compound labour, the tot system and contract labour shall be abolished.

8. The Doors of Learning and of Culture Shall Be Opened!
8.1 The government shall discover, develop and encourage national talent for the enhancement of our cultural life;
8.2 All the cultural treasures of mankind shall be open to all, by free exchange of books, ideas and contact with other lands;

8.3 The aim of education shall be to teach the youth to love their people and their culture, to honour human brotherhood, liberty and peace;
8.4 Education shall be free, compulsory, universal and equal for all children;
8.5 Higher education and technical training shall be opened to all by means of state allowances and scholarships awarded on the basis of merit;
8.6 Adult illiteracy shall be ended by a mass state education plan;
8.7 Teachers shall have all the rights of other citizens;
8.8 The colour bar in cultural life, in sports and in education shall be abolished.

9. There Shall Be Houses, Security and Comfort!

9.1 All people shall have the right to live where they choose, to be decently housed, and to bring up their families in comfort and security;
9.2 Unused housing space shall be made available to the people;
9.3 Rent and prices shall be lowered, food plentiful and no one shall go hungry;
9.4 A preventive health scheme shall be run by the state;
9.5 Free medical care and hospitalisation shall be provided for all, with special care for mothers and young children;
9.6 Slums shall be demolished, and new suburbs built where all have transport, roads, lighting, playing fields, crèches and social centres;
9.7 The aged, the orphans, the disabled and the sick shall be cared for by the state;
9.8 Rest, leisure and recreation shall be the right of all;
9.9 Fenced locations and ghettos shall be abolished, and laws which break up families shall be repealed.

10. There Shall Be Peace and Friendship!

10.1 South Africa shall be a fully independent state, which respects the rights and sovereignty of all nations;
10.2 South Africa shall strive to maintain world peace and the settlement of all international disputes by negotiation not war;
10.3 Peace and friendship amongst all our people shall be secured by upholding the equal rights, opportunities and status of all;
10.4 The people of the protectorates, Basutoland, Bechuanaland and Swaziland, shall be free to decide for themselves their own future;
10.5 The rights of all the peoples of Africa to independence, and self-government shall be recognised, and shall be the basis of close co-operation.

Let all who love their people and their country now say, as we say here:
"THESE FREEDOMS WE WILL FIGHT FOR, SIDE BY SIDE, THROUGHOUT OUR LIVES, UNTIL WE HAVE WON OUR LIBERTY."

Jill Nattrass

21. Political Change and Capitalism in South Africa

South Africa is an extremely unequal society in both the economic and political spheres, an inequality related to spatial allocation of resources, and to race and sex.[1] The extreme wealth of the few rubs shoulders with the abject poverty of the many, and does so in a social order in which the wealthy minority hold the political power and in which the economic system is organized along capitalistic lines of the market system and private ownership of property and wealth. As a result, it is hardly surprising that both white political domination and capitalism are seen by the dispossessed as instruments that generate inequality and poverty.

The past decade has seen an ongoing escalation of social action by politically deprived groups aimed at redressing, through either reform or revolution, the political inequalities in South Africa. Given the obvious linkages between a group's political power and its ability to change the economic system and redirect economic resources in its direction, a highly pertinent question to ask is: Will, or can, the capitalistic economic system survive the political changes that are now inevitable in South Africa?

Although certainly not unique in this respect, capitalism is, as Karl Marx pointed out more than a century ago, an economic system that inherently generates conflict and, indeed, is driven by the outcomes of

1. Jill Nattrass, *The South African Economy: Its Growth and Change* (Cape Town: Oxford University Press, 1981).

the conflicts.[2] Conflict exists in the workplace between capital or management and labor (or perhaps between profits and wages) and in the marketplace between buyers and sellers. Because the outcomes of these conflicts directly affect the living standards of the combatants and are clearly apparent, economic class conflicts often spill over into wider social or political conflicts. This is happening to a significant extent in present-day South Africa, and as blacks gain political power the inherent economic conflict can be expected to escalate. It is virtually certain that people who find they have political power but lack economic muscle will use the former to seek to gain the latter.[3] Increasingly needed in the future in South Africa will be a framework for effective conflict management.

Changes in political power structures inevitably affect the social fabric of any society in which they take place. The nature and extent of the change will depend upon the extent to which the existing social structures deviate from those desired by the groups who are gaining political strength and of the relative bargaining strength of the new power groups and those who oppose them. This means that two factors will determine the ultimate impact that political changes will have on the economy: first, whether or not the people coming into power in the political arena want the economic system to remain as it is, and second, if they do not, whether or not they have the ability to implement changes in the system. In the present, rapidly changing, South African scene, those interested in ensuring the survival of capitalism need to ask and answer a number of questions: (1) How likely is it that the winners will be interested in the survival of the capitalist system? (2) What are their chances of materially changing the economic system should they so wish? (3) What are the trade-offs that can be successfully offered to them as a compromise by those who want to maintain the system?

One of the negative spinoffs from the present government's longstanding, but shortsighted, policies of attempting to eliminate political opposition by means such as "banning" and "listing" is that it is now extremely difficult for social analysts to gauge the relative strengths of the different black political groupings. Indeed, it is even difficult to identify clearly the overall policies of the various parties and, in particular, their economic aspirations. Apart from the Freedom Charter of the African National Congress, and a number of generalizations emanating from the writings of members of the South African Communist party,

2. Karl Marx, *Capital* (New York: International Publishers, 1967).

3. Jill Nattrass, "Economic Growth and Social and Political Change—A Suggested Theoretical Framework," in Lawrence Schlemmer and Eddie Webster, eds., *Change, Reform and Economic Growth in South Africa* (Johannesburg: Ravan, 1978).

virtually no information is available on the economic strategies of the new political groupings. Indeed, it is not even clear how the economic aims listed in the Freedom Charter are intended to be implemented.

This gap in information means that one must speculate rather than analyze specific proposed economic strategies. A new political order based on Marxian socialism or on communism would be clearly antipathetic toward the present economic order and could be expected to seek substantial change in the short term and radical change in the long term. A less left-wing black majority government might, however, seek to leave the basic economic organization in place but aim to improve black access to the economic system and to distribute wealth among all South Africans more equally. Given the extent of economic inequality and the present depth of black poverty, even a conservative black-dominated government can be expected to seek economic reform through wealth redistribution. In short, unless the new rulers turn out to be totally despotic, self-centered, and corrupt, and provided they are able to turn the present system to their advantage, it seems certain that the present economic order will be materially affected by any political reform or revolution that takes place.

If capitalism, or private enterprise, is seen to be the major cause of the present inequality in the distribution of wealth and in access to the economic system in general, then clearly those who have been adversely affected by it and who gain the power to control the economy can be expected to seek to destroy the system and replace it with one that appears to offer more equal opportunity. For private enterprise to survive under such circumstances, the system will have to be adapted so that it is seen to offer a much greater degree of participation in its activities to everyone in the wider society.

Any new group seeking to change an existing economic order has, of course, to start from that order. The economic structure of present-day South Africa will significantly influence the possibilities for its own evolution.[4] The major economic characteristics of South Africa's present order are: first, the economic system is highly concentrated in respect of both its control over economic resources and their spatial location; second, there is wide disparity between the living standards of those who have access to the economic centers and those who do not; and third, the state has widened rather than narrowed these disparities in living standards. Given the extent of the unequal access and excessive concentration in the economy, it is clear that any reform measures will have to address these three aspects to a greater or lesser degree.

4. Nattrass, *South African Economy,* pp. 306–38.

Any economy has a physical component comprised of people, and of capital in the form of buildings, plant and machinery, and social overhead capital such as roads, dams, schools, hospitals. In the implementation of changes at the grass-roots level, the physical aspects of the economy, and their relationships to one another, will significantly influence the extent to which the rhetoric for change can be actually translated into meaningful physical and economic change.

A major cause of persistent black poverty and inequality in the distribution of income and wealth in South Africa is the lack of adequate access to the growing modern economy.[5] Access is limited both by the wider workings of the apartheid system and by the geographical separation of the mass of the population from the major economic plant. Analysts studying the causes of social inequity have overlooked the fact that roughly half of the population lives in the eastern seaboard region, while nearly two-thirds of the manufacturing output originates in the Pretoria-Witwatersrand-Vereeniging triangle. They have tended to concentrate on the impact of apartheid and have underestimated the influence of the physical separation between plant and people and the difficulties to be met in bringing them together. While one can undo the apartheid legislation reasonably easily, it will not be a simple matter to relocate either the people or the physical economic plant. Certainly, with the removal of influx control and the proper provision of urban facilities, a significant proportion of the rural population can be expected to resettle in the towns. However, many in the black population use the rural areas as a "social welfare cushion," and unless they can be assured of a reasonable, lifelong income in the towns, they will be likely to retain their rural ties. As for relocating of capital, the experience of thirty years of decentralization policies shows how difficult it is to move economic plant to any significant extent. Consequently, it seems unrealistic to assume that political change in any form can exert a significant influence on this source of poverty and inequality, in the short term at least.

Economic access is also limited by the distribution of the control of capital. Control of South African business is concentrated in a few hands and is becoming more so. Concentration leads inevitably to the exercise of monopoly power, and this in turn further limits accessibility by those outside the monopoly. A solution proposed by the Freedom Charter is nationalization of "monopoly industry."[6] However, although at first sight this may look attractive, by nationalizing an already highly concentrated industry, one is simply transferring the control of the

5. Ibid., chapter 2.
6. For the Freedom Charter, see pp. 350–52.

concentration from private enterprise to the state, and in fact doing nothing about the source of the problem—the concentration itself.

Further, experience with the nationalization of large-scale industries in other countries has shown how difficult it is to maintain management efficiency in the absence of the discipline of a profit motive. While socialists may be correct that the loss of efficiency without the profit motive is simply a reflection of the degree to which personal economic gains have been socialized as desirable in a capitalist system, it will not be a simple matter to resocialize the community to a different set of values. Reeducation is a time-consuming and expensive exercise in the best of times and often provides an excuse for the abuse of power. A better approach than nationalization, and certainly one more suited to the maintenance of liberal values, would be to introduce into the private-enterprise system, through legislation, a greater degree of democratization. This could be done through the introduction of measures to ensure a higher degree of participation by both workers and community leaders, in both the ownership and management of business.

In South Africa the growing importance of financial institutions like insurance companies and pension funds in the capital market is another factor limiting an individual's access to the private-enterprise system. These institutions are taking a growing share of South Africa's limited investment funding, and, because they seek to place the funds that they manage in "secure" investments, they concentrate the funding in particular areas and economic sectors. They favor the expansion of large-scale industry in urban areas over the provision of venture capital that might allow a small entrepreneur to start up a business in a higher-risk economic sector or region of the country, thus making it increasingly difficult for such enterprises to get started. A further disadvantage of the growth and investment activities of pension funds and insurance companies is that, because of the size of their growing demands, they have caused a substantial rise in the value of stocks and shares on the Johannesburg stock exchange. These increased security prices have had the effect of diverting investment funds that could have been placed in bricks and mortar and machinery into funding the profits made on stock market transactions as a result of this upward pressure on share prices.

Clearly, reform in the area of financial investment could do a great deal to improve the level of economic access. Indeed, in this case, unlike that of concentrated capital control, for reform to be achieved one does not need a socialist input since significant improvement could be achieved by legislation requiring financial institutions to place a specified portion of their funding into social overhead capital and venture enterprises.

One of the areas in which a black government, no matter what its economic persuasion, can be expected to press for significant changes is the allocation of land. The ownership rights of black South Africans are now restricted by law to 14 percent of South Africa's land area. This restriction has generated a great deal of bitterness. Although historically, white South Africans, backed up by the state, have placed considerable importance on maintenance of "white only" land rights, there is evidence that this priority may be changing. Whites have been leaving the rural areas steadily throughout this century. The initial exodus comprised the uneconomic farmers and the tenant farmers (*bywoners*) who were pushed off the land as a consequence of the capitalization of agriculture. Their exodus led to an increasing degree of concentration in agricultural land ownership and a growth in the average size of the commercial farm, which is today larger than its equivalent in the United States.

A number of farming commissions have commented that farms are now too large to be efficient.[7] On economic grounds there seems to be no reason why black access to agricultural land should remain limited. In the interests of economic progress in South Africa, the Natives' Land Act of 1913 and the Native Land and Trust Act of 1936 should be repealed. Agricultural educational institutions should be opened to all races, extension services should be extended on a nonracial basis, and generally an efficient commercial farming sector should be developed.

There is also an urgent need to open up black access to land in the urban areas. Urbanization rates among blacks have been rising throughout this century and, with the removal of the influx-control laws, can be expected to continue to do so. A failure to provide additional access to urban land for blacks can only increase the "pressure cooker" effect of the present black urban areas, as people continue to flock into them from the rural areas, with the concomitant increased pressure for social action.

Finally, it must be remembered that one of the areas of greatest economic concentration is the public sector. The South African government controls roughly half of the capital invested annually in the economy and produces between 28 and 33 percent of local output of goods and services. Simply to continue to run the government sector will require a large, reasonably well trained management group. The challenge to any new, relatively inexperienced government will be to provide such a management cadre and to do so in a manner that will ensure that the public sector itself continues to function.

This will not be a simple matter, and any significant restructuring of

7. See, e.g., the views expressed in Republic of South Africa, *The Second Report of the Commission of Inquiry into Agriculture* RP 34/1970 (Pretoria: Government Printer, 1979).

the economic system will place an even greater management burden on the new government. If it is unable to meet this burden, output levels and living standards will inevitably fall. Indeed, the simple task of assuming the reins of government may place such a burden on the administrative capabilities of a new group that it will be virtually impossible for them to restructure the economy successfully, at least in the early stages of assuming control.

Although the public sector has been a significant force in redistributing income from the wealthy to the poorer white groups, it has not been as successful with regard to blacks. Indeed, as the situation now stands, the public sector provides an adequate safety net of social welfare functions for whites but does not do the same for blacks. What is worse, with present levels of economic resources, there is no way in which any government, black or white, could afford to extend an identical net to cover the black communities.

It seems that no matter whether the new government comes in on a socialist or a communist ticket or not, and whatever its economic aspirations, in practice its ability to restructure the economy radically will be severely limited. A sensible strategy for the people who want to see the continuation of the capitalist system would be to engage in negotiation with the intention of maintaining capitalism in the long term, but at the same time to offer reforms that will have the effect of changing the nature of the economic system from one of exclusion and exploitation to one of participation and concern. Reforms could be implemented in a number of areas, aimed at establishing a more open access to the economic system as a whole. The ultimate objective is to increase the level of participation in the system at all three levels of economic operation, individual, community, and government. One could say that the proposals are intended to establish "participating" or "concerned" capitalism.

For such capitalism to be successful, it is important that the new participatory relationships run in both directions, i.e., from the capitalist system to the community and from the community to the capitalist system. Private enterprise must participate and, even more important, be seen to participate in the community on a wide basis, and, conversely but equally important, the community must be given real participatory rights in private enterprise.[8]

Capitalism can improve its access to the community in a number of ways: (1) Business management could actively participate in community

8. See the proposals and arguments presented in Jill Nattrass, "Towards Racial Justice—What Can the Private Sector Do?" in David Thomas, ed., *Towards Economic and Political Justice in South African* (Johannesburg: South African Institute of Race Relations, 1980), pp. 40–62.

affairs and development. Corporate employees could be encouraged to take civic administrative posts and carry out their functions in a manner that highlights their dual role. Business could openly provide funds for community projects such as buildings, schools, or sporting programs. (2) Proceeds from pension fund contributions could be invested in the development of the community. For example, provision of housing for blacks, openly financed by the large pension funds and insurance companies, would indubitably help to defuse some of the present social tensions. (3) Business could take a community-oriented view of the services it provides, rather than a view based solely upon generation of short-term profits.

On the other side of the coin, the community's access to the capitalist system could be significantly improved in a number of ways. Worker ownership could be introduced on a widespread basis, whereby firms would assist their employees financially to buy their shares. At present this is not legal in South Africa, but, in view of the potential that these schemes have for reducing worker-management conflict, the legislation should be amended, as a matter of urgency, and steps should be taken to encourage their growth. If workers were also major shareholders, then the inherent conflict between management and workers over the division of the surplus into profits and wages would be greatly reduced. Another approach to the reduction of conflict could be the establishment of management/worker cooperation through the creation of worker/management factory floor committees, and employee directorships. While these schemes would not eliminate the profit/wage conflict, they would help to give the work force a much clearer idea of management's aspirations and problems, and so would provide a vehicle for the control of shop floor conflicts.

Access could be further enhanced by the provision of venture capital, by private enterprise for private enterprise, in a manner that would ensure that the capital provided was actually made available to would-be venture capitalists. This would encourage the growth of entrepreneurship and facilitate the development of a black middle class, which again would improve black access to private enterprise. Large firms could subcontract at least a portion of the services and inputs they needed to small firms. This too would encourage the growth of small firms and improve individual access to the economy.

Voluntary behavior by large firms would not, however, be enough especially in the case of monopolies. To eliminate these, the state would have to exert real control over the exercise of monopoly power, and refrain from actions that would encourage the development of monopolistic power in the first place.

Finally, communities (in addition to workers) should become involved in the management of major enterprises, through the establishment of community/worker/management committees or community participation at the directorship level. This involvement in management could be supplemented by the development of effective buyer/consumer organizations, as a means of countervailing the power of the large suppliers. Small suppliers and craftspeople could be helped in marketing by the development of selling organizations.

At present these proposals are, on the whole, opposed by management, which often argues that they would introduce practices totally contrary to the ethics of private enterprise. This may be true of private enterprise as we know it today in South Africa. However, times are changing, and if capitalism is to survive in South Africa, economic attitudes in general, and those of management in particular, will have to change with them.

It is not only in the urban, commercial and industrial sectors that changes will be needed and, indeed, demanded. One of the areas of greatest inequality is agriculture. The discriminatory legal basis of ownership could be removed, as suggested above, by the repeal of the land acts of 1913 and 1936, thereby releasing the market mechanism to begin to change the racial face of commercial farming in response to changing patterns in the demand for farm land. But in the context of rapid political change, slow redistribution by the market would not be sufficient even if it were effective: white-owned land would almost certainly also have to be purchased or expropriated for resettlement by black smallholders, as was done through the implementation of the Swynnerton plan in Kenya. A land commission, financed by the state, could also be established with the power to purchase land on the market, to subdivide it where necessary, and to resell it to small-scale black farmers.[9]

It is, however, not only a matter of private ownership. White-owned farms could also be purchased or expropriated for operation on a cooperative basis, with entry into cooperatives based on nonracial criteria; some cooperatives could be developed into communal farming settlements like the kibbutz system in Israel.

One of the side effects of more than a century of racial discrimination is a legacy of a black agricultural population without adequate formal education and training. Therefore it will be essential to train black farmers before handing over to them a significant portion of the commercial farming land. Failure to do this would be virtually certain to erode South Africa's capacity to feed itself, with consequent disastrous long-term effects on economic and social development.

9. The Buthelezi Commission, *The Requirements for Stability and Development in KwaZulu and Natal. The Report of the Economic Development Sub-Committee* 2 (Durban: H & H Publications, 1982), pp. 134–254.

Finally, since the economic role of the state seems likely to grow as a result of political change rather than to decline, it will be important to ensure genuine democratic input into the day-to-day running of the public sector. This can best be done through decentralizing the public sector as far as possible by giving to the communities themselves the authority and the responsibility for running the decentralized areas. Zimbabwe is experimenting with moves in this direction. South Africa, too, should move in this way rather than continuing to centralize control of the public sector on an increasing scale, since, if this policy continues, it will negate all other efforts to improve economic participation. However, given the inequality in wealth distribution, central government should remain responsible for the funding of regional spending, since to do otherwise would simply mean that the poor regions would remain poor.

It has been fashionable in the past to argue that any interference in the capitalist system must introduce economic inefficiencies and, by doing so, slow down the rate of economic development. The period since 1980 has, however, been one in which economic development has been significantly hindered by the lack of adequate political progress. Political reform has become an absolute prerequisite for continued economic development, even though the introduction of such reform may itself include some economic restructuring.

A restructuring of the economy could in fact be a force for economic development. Virtually all studies of the growth of the South African economy have shown that the limiting factors on growth have been the constricted size of the domestic market and the difficulties of exporting manufactured products. Political reform will help on both counts. First, with regard to the limited size of the local market, improved access to the economy will redistribute wealth to blacks, enhance the purchasing power of the low-income groups, and increase the size of the domestic market. Second, since the international movement for sanctions and boycotts appears to be advancing steadily, political reform may be a prerequisite for the creation of a healthy and stable export market.

Not only is political reform desirable from a moral and social viewpoint, but political reform, and the economic restructuring that results from it, may provide the keys to the economic development of a South Africa where the fruits of labor will be more equitably shared.

Hermann Giliomee

22. Apartheid, Verligtheid, and Liberalism

Apartheid developed in the postwar years as a radical rejection of liberal demands. When the first apartheid measures were introduced in the late 1940s and early 1950s the National party (NP) used racist arguments to justify white supremacy. From the mid-1950s on, growing numbers of the Afrikaner Nationalist intelligentsia began to distance themselves from overt racism. Their commitment to Western values and the Christian creed demanded that apartheid somehow be accommodated to these values and beliefs. They sought to do this without sacrificing Afrikaner political control, a search for the impossible that became ever more urgent as high economic growth and rising black resistance forced the NP to begin the dismantling of apartheid.

The policy of traditional or classic apartheid after 1948 did not constitute a clean break with the past, but rather an elaboration or intensification of the policy of segregation, followed since the inception of the Union of South Africa in 1910. Like apartheid, segregation contained a blend of racism and "cultural idealism" (or cultural pluralism).[1] Under the Smuts government (1939–1948) the racial element was still predominant in a policy characterized by rigid controls

1. For an excellent discussion of these themes, see John David Shingler, "Education and Political Order in South Africa, 1902–1961" (unpublished doctoral thesis, Yale University, 1973).

and severe discrimination against blacks. There was, however, an increasing emphasis on cultural idealism, for which Smuts himself took credit. This strand insisted on the maintenance of the indigenous social structure of Africans as semiautonomous entities under white supervision.[2] D. F. Malan, the first NP prime minister, was at pains to stress that apartheid did not mean a rejection of cultural idealism. He remarked in 1948: "Apartheid is not the caricature which is so often made of it. On the contrary, it means for the non-whites the development of a greater degree of autonomy and of self-respect together with the provision of greater opportunities for autonomous development according to their nature and capacity."[3] (Translated).

Within his own circles, Smuts came under increasing attack from English-speaking liberals. They demanded the abandonment of white supremacy in favor of a policy of political participation and equality for blacks. In the social field they wanted government to accept that the process of racial integration, particularly in the cities, was irreversible. In the field of education they mocked cultural idealism as either wishful thinking or reactionary because it wanted to preserve an indigenous African culture on the point of collapse. In its place they held up a vision of a society based on a common loyalty of South African citizens, a shared political identity, a lingua franca (English), and a common Christian faith. In English-language universities and the South African Institute of Race Relations liberals demanded an educational policy designed to create such an order.[4]

For Afrikaner Nationalists of the postwar era there could be no compromise with these liberal demands. The NP depicted the 1948 election as a stark choice between liberalism and apartheid. A policy statement on the eve of the election presented the options:

> On the one hand there is the policy of equalisation which propagates equal rights for all civilized and developed people, regardless of race or colour within the same structures and the gradual granting of the vote to non-whites in proportion to their capacity to avail themselves of democratic rights. On the other hand we have the policy of apartheid which has grown out of the experience of the settled white population and is based on the principles of justice and fairness. Its object is the maintenance and protection of the white population as a pure white race.[5] (Translated).

Apartheid was thus proposed as a radical alternative to the principal

2. Ibid., pp. 15–17.
3. S. W. Pienaar, ed., *Glo in u Volk: Dr. D. F. Malan, as Redenaar, 1908–1954* (Cape Town: Tafelberg, 1964), p. 243.
4. Shingler, "Education and Political Order," pp. 233–41.
5. *Die Transvaler,* 29 and 30 March 1948.

demands of liberalism. While the liberal position implied equal political rights and social justice, the Nationalists demanded the preservation of white political power and of white interests and privilege. To some extent, though, the Nationalists reckoned seriously with liberal values, at least insofar as they attempted to escape the charge that they were mere racists. Nationalist intellectuals in the 1950s made considerable rhetorical efforts to give greater content to the notions of cultural idealism. They urged that more resources be spent on the social and economic uplift of the black groups or communities and that these groups be given increasing opportunities to administer themselves in their segregated townships or "homelands." In doing this the Nationalists drew not only on the ideology of segregation, which was largely British-inspired, but also on the Dutch Reformed Church (DRC) experience in mission work and on the writings of educationists and anthropologists in the neo-Calvinist or Christian National tradition.

In the view of the apartheid ideologues, their policy offered a better formula than that of liberals for dealing with the explosive forces of South African society. Blacks and whites living together in integrated residential areas and competing in a common system for power, jobs, and access to amenities and services would, in the Nationalist mind, inevitably lead to escalating conflict. The greater the number of competitive points of contact, the greater the friction. Hence, the apartheid formula: reduce the points of contact by increasing separation. Nationalists conceded that apartheid was an affront to the black middle class, which demanded freedom and equality in a common society. However, they insisted that liberal efforts to promote the black cause did not amount to much more than "skimming off the cream," which would benefit only the black elite. In contrast, they argued, apartheid would yield benefits to far greater numbers by providing mass education and by giving blacks, on an apartheid basis, access to political office, civil-service and professional jobs, and business opportunities. Nationalists argued that blacks would not have enjoyed these opportunities in open competition with better-educated whites and that apartheid actually offered them a better deal than liberalism.

Behind these sentiments lay the deep desire of Nationalists to see their rule as legitimate, that is, as a form of government that operated not only in their own but also in black interests. This is the context of a remark by John Vorster, who paid a brief holiday visit to Rio de Janeiro before he became prime minister in 1966. Asked what he thought of Brazilian society, he responded: "There the black man does not have a chance." In 1971 he would reiterate this view when he declared: "The chances and opportunities which exist today for blacks were created and made possible as a result of the policy of separate development."[6]

The "idealistic" versions of apartheid should not simply be accepted at their own valuation. In fact, during the 1950s two conceptions of apartheid competed with each other in the ranks of Nationalists. On the one hand there were farmers and businessmen who advocated "practical apartheid" based on a high economic growth rate and the increasing but differential incorporation of Africans in the work force. Any threat this posed to white supremacy was to be countered by denying Africans political and economic rights. On the other hand, many members of the intelligentsia insisted on "idealistic" apartheid. They rejected a growing economic dependence on African labor as a lethal threat to white survival. Yet, because they considered the denial of political and economic rights to Africans immoral if the economy was to become ever more dependent on their labor, they argued that the African homelands had to be developed as meaningful political and economic alternatives for Africans which would justify sending increasing numbers back to their "homes."[7]

The spearhead of this second conception of apartheid was the Stellenbosch-based South African Bureau of Racial Affairs (SABRA), which was established in 1949 primarily to give apartheid an intellectual basis. Its crowning achievement was the research that leading members contributed to the Tomlinson Commission. In 1956 the commission proposed a considerable increase of expenditure on the uplift of the homelands.[8]

The SABRA intellectuals had mixed success. Malan told them in the early 1950s that their proposals for a drastic form of territorial separation were impractical. Hendrik Verwoerd, minister of Native affairs from 1950 to 1958, was hostile to the Tomlinson proposals. He consistently refused to provide the funds or create the conditions that would make possible the economic regeneration of the homelands. However, some time after he became prime minister in 1958, he switched his position from supporting undiluted white supremacy to that of separate development more similar to the SABRA stand on black political rights. This called for the homelands to be granted a growing measure of self-government, and perhaps even independence in the mid- to long-term future. That these "states" had little hope of ever attaining economic

6. O. Geyser, ed., *B. J. Vorster: Select Speeches* (Bloemfontein: Institute for Contemporary History, 1977), p. 160.

7. Deborah Posel, "The Meaning of Apartheid before 1948: Conflicting Interests and Blueprints within the Afrikaner Nationalist Alliance," unpublished seminar paper, 7 March 1986.

8. Union of South Africa, *Report of the Commission for the Socio-Economic Development of the Native Areas within the Union of South Africa* (U.G. 61-1966).

self-sufficiency hardly concerned Verwoerd. If pressed on the issue, he would merely refer to the example of Britain, which was leading its three poverty-stricken protectorates, Basutoland, Swaziland, and Bechuanaland, to independence.

This switch did not really satisfy the quest of many Nationalist intellectuals for an ethical base for apartheid. During the late 1950s prominent churchmen, editors, academics, and professional people expressed their concern, usually in private, about the lack of an acceptable justification, theological or secular, of apartheid. An American observer, Edwin Munger, reported that there were increasing criticisms in the DRC in Transvaal and the Cape Province of the government's racial policy. At the end of 1960, delegations from these two churches attended the Cottesloe conference organized by the World Council of Churches and there they expressed their conviction that urban Africans had the right to own land and to participate in the government. They also supported a resolution that there could be no objection to mixed marriages or to direct representation of colored people in Parliament. Verwoerd, however, mobilized opposition against these resolutions, and within a short time all the Afrikaans churches renounced them.[9]

The Verwoerd-inspired clamp-down greatly compounded the dilemma of the Nationalist intellectuals who wanted to justify apartheid in terms of some universal scheme. They rejected liberalism because of its implications for Afrikaner nationalism: political abdication, social integration, and what N. J. Rhoodie called "Africanization at the biogenetic level."[10] However, with their Christian value system, they remained troubled by a principled rejection of liberalism on racist grounds.

The crisis of Nationalist conscience became particularly acute at the time of Cottesloe, but as far back as 1946 N. P. van Wyk Louw, the leading Afrikaner poet and a greatly respected intellectual, had been grappling with this issue. Louw was one of the first Nationalist intellectuals to realize that cultural idealism was an insufficient defense of apartheid. Decolonization of the postwar world made many in the West and in the new states suspect that any special concern with indigenous cultures was simply a pretext for perpetuating white supremacy. Louw believed that apartheid had to be based on the principle of political nationalism and that it had to be demonstrated that such a policy was not necessarily in conflict with the kind of liberal nationalism acceptable to, and indeed practiced by, the nations of Western Europe. In this sense Louw was the forerunner of the "idealist wing" of the National party,

9. A. H. Lückhoff, *Cottesloe* (Cape Town: Tafelberg, 1978).

10. N. J. Rhoodie, *Apartheid and Racial Partnership in Southern Africa* (Pretoria: Academica, 1969), p. 128.

which in the past four decades has chiefly been concerned with arguing that apartheid in its more progressive guise could be squared with the more moderate elements of Western liberalism. In the late 1960s the so-called "Cape Nats" would pick up this banner, and in the 1970s it was the turn of the *verligtes,* the "enlightened ones."

In an essay published in 1946, Louw called Alfred Hoernlé one of the most "brilliant" and "worthy" representatives of South African liberalism and spoke of his "incomparable lucidity."[11] He also used a passage from Hoernlé as a prefatory quotation in his collection of essays *Liberale Nasionalisme* (1958). The quote read: "There is no spiritual bridge between the dominant and the dominated other than the bridge built by those who, loving liberty for itself, will not be content until it is enjoyed, not only by themselves, but by all those to whom it is now denied."[12] In the same book Hoernlé had argued that, unlike segregation based on white supremacy, "total separation" could in principle be squared with liberal ideals:

> There is segregation as an instrument of domination; segregation which joins the segregated in the same social and political structure with the dominant white group, but subjects them to the denial of important rights and keeps them at a social distance implying inferiority. . . . Total separation envisages an organisation of the warring sections into genuinely separate self-contained, self-governing societies, each in principle homogeneous within itself, which can then cooperate on a footing of mutual recognition of one another's independence.[13]

Louw did not reject liberalism as such, but argued, along with Hoernlé, that European liberalism had its roots in countries with a homogeneous racial or ethnic composition. Louw challenged liberal thinkers to devise a policy for the future of South Africa that would be true to the great liberal principles of Europe without entailing injustice in the "multinational" South African state. Louw pointed out that the liberal demand for freedom, equal justice, and equal opportunities for blacks would mean that whites would be reduced to an impotent minority among a mass of blacks, making the Afrikaner "as helpless as a Jew was in Germany."

For Louw, then, the South Africa drama was a classic tragedy of two "rights" in conflict with each other. He rejected a solution which called for the abandonment of either liberalism or nationalism. Despite the "polar tensions" between these two principles, they "belong with each

11. N. P. van Wyk Louw, *Liberale Nasionalisme* (1958) reprinted in *Versamelde Prosa* 1 (Cape Town: Tafelberg, 1986), pp. 502–6.

12. R. F. A. Hoernlé, *South African Native Policy and the Liberal Spirit* (Johannesburg: Witwatersrand University Press, 1945), p. 186.

13. Ibid., pp. 168–69.

other and constitute the texture of South African history." The "stalemate" of black and white nationalism could be resolved in one of two ways: either through the "ploughing under" of the less numerous groups or by "separate development" of the different groups. In another essay also written in 1946 on the subject of nationalism, Louw developed his line of thought somewhat further. He stated:

> For Nationalism to be based on a true political principle it has to be true for everyone. Accordingly, the recognition of the nationalist principle for the Afrikaner logically has to imply the recognition of all other national groups in South Africa. Hence, we should not speak of ourselves as the nation (*volk*) of South Africa, but as one of the *volke* of South Africa."[14] (Translated).

It is not difficult to see that this scheme of thought could lead to the full-blown separate-development ideology, which held that liberal principles of freedom and equal justice were accommodated by the policy of multinationalism based on separate homelands for Africans and "separate freedoms" for whites and blacks.

Louw's essays in 1946 were one of the first publications by Nationalist thinkers to use the key concepts of "separate development" and "multinationalism," euphemisms for apartheid that would become very popular in the 1960s. It took some time before they percolated through to a wider audience. By the beginning of the 1960s, Nationalist opinion-makers who favored a more "liberal" interpretation of apartheid, such as Piet Cillie, editor of *Die Burger,* and Willem van Heerden, editor of *Dagbreek,* began to press for a relaxation of some of the crudest apartheid practices. In their view, only "grand apartheid," which safeguarded white survival, was important, but not "petty apartheid" which pandered to white prejudices. Measures such as banning mixed audiences at concerts merely irritated people and achieved nothing. What Cillie and others were saying was that some of the minor outworks of Afrikaner political power could be safely dismantled.[15]

It was Cillie and a *Burger* colleague, Schalk Pienaar, who developed the ideological scheme of "grand apartheid" along very similar lines as those proposed earlier by Louw and the SABRA thinkers. Although termed "Cape liberal Nationalists" or Cape Nats, Cillie and Pienaar, like their successors, the *verligtes* of the 1970s, were not liberals in the true sense of the word. They were above all Afrikaner Nationalists whose concern was continued Afrikaner rule. There is in their thinking no shift to individual rights and in particular to freedom of association as the basis for political participation. For them the basis of all political activity remained the "ethnic" groups as the government defined them.

14. Louw, *Liberale Nasionalisme,* pp. 502–6.
15. See *Die Burger,* 12 December 1959 and 9 January 1960 (Dawie column).

What distinguished them was their insistence on the ''idealistic'' element of apartheid, that the black ''ethnic'' groups be given greater opportunities to administer themselves. They also demanded a greater normalization of social relations and an end to crude and offensive social apartheid.

The culmination of thinking by the Cape liberal Nationalists found expression in the *Burger*'s ''Dawie'' column and a subsequent essay by Cillie. A Dawie column in 1964, significantly entitled ''The Idea of Separate Freedom,'' stated:

> It is exciting to be present at the birth of an irresistible idea. Or perhaps we should talk about the decisive evolution of an idea. I mean the principle of separate freedoms which has developed out of the apartheid idea once it was recognised that in principle no artificial limits could be set for ''Bantu-selfgovernment'' in the homelands . . . For increasing numbers of young people separate freedoms is the burning idea they have sought in their desire to transform South Africa into a better land for all its peoples . . . I have heard it compared with the principle of equality in the American constitution, which, once accepted, started a process with its own momentum which has ploughed through American history.''[16] (Translated).

In another article, entitled ''Terug na ons Geloof in Vryheid'' (''Back to our belief in freedom''), Cillie asked how it came about that the Afrikaner nationalists, the first anticolonialists of Africa, were now in the dock, charged with being colonialists and oppressors themselves. He argued that old-fashioned colonialism not only became ''impractical'' in the modern world and made coexistence with others impossible; it also made it impossible for Afrikaners to live with themselves under such a system because it was against their own best principles and insights. Cillie, like Louw, rejected the application of a liberal model of decolonization to the various peoples sharing freedom in one country. For white South Africans to integrate the black majority would, in Cillie's view, not mean a broadening of democracy but ''creeping and irrevocable conquest, the sort of thing that invokes a mortal struggle.'' It is for this reason that ''militant liberalism which does not shrink back from black majority rule has for Nationalists the appearance of treason.'' Cillie's own solution was for the whites to become less dependent on black labor in ''our own national territory.'' This territory ''must be defined clearly'' so that there would be a territory for the non-African nations under no circumstances to be subjected to African domination, while on the other hand there would be the homelands of the African nations where they could enjoy their own, free existence. For coloreds

16. *Die Burger,* 6 June 1964 (Dawie column).

and Indians a "political link-up with white nationhood" was envisaged which did not amount to permanent subordination.[17]

By the mid-1960s the principal role of these "progressive" Nationalists was to give full expression to the "positive" or "idealistic" elements in apartheid. Verwoerd himself had slapped down the Cottesloe proposals; he had engineered a purge of the "liberal" academics in SABRA and rejected Cillie's pleas for direct representation of coloreds in Parliament. His acceptance of the possibility of independence for the African homelands was done grudgingly, as a quid pro quo for terminating all representation of Africans by whites in Parliament, and as a sop to world pressure.[18]

Yet Verwoerd managed to hold up to Afrikaner Nationalists a highly persuasive ideological vision of apartheid as a consistent and ethical solution to South Africa's problems. He recast liberal values in nationalist terms and imposed this definition on South Africa, projected not as one country but as a region comprised of "national states." Liberty was defined as national self-determination and equality as full statehood and rights as something attainable for people in their respective "homelands."[19] By 1964 Verwoerd was saying that "we are also following a policy of liberating nations." And: "We will not allow ourselves to be dictated to by world opinion but we take into account that there is a striving for freedom and self-determination by all nations."[20] Verwoerd and his successor, Vorster, claimed confidently that, in the latter's words, "the policy of separate development can be tested by any unprejudiced person against the requirements of Christianity and morality, and it will be found to meet all these requirements."[21] The terminology of the "progressive" or "liberal" Nationalists had conquered the National party, or rather the party had conquered the terminology.

The gulf between ideology and political reality had, however, become ever wider as a result of some structural shifts in society that manifested themselves from 1960 on. Perhaps the most important political fact in

17. Piet Cillie, "Terug na ons Geloof in Vryheid," *Standpunte* 49 (1964) reprinted in Louis Louw, ed., *Dawie* (Cape Town: Tafelberg, 1965), pp. 285–90.

18. For a full discussion, see Deon Geldenhuys, *South Africa's Black Homelands* (Johannesburg: South African Institute of Race Relations, 1981); Hermann Giliomee, "The Changing Political Functions of the Homelands," in Hermann Giliomee and Lawrence Schlemmer, eds., *Up Against the Fences: Poverty, Passes and Privilege in South Africa* (Cape Town: David Philip, 1985), pp. 39–56.

19. See A. N. Pelzer, ed. *Verwoerd Speaks* (Johannesburg: Afrikaanse Pers, 1963). The best academic analysis of apartheid is still A. James Gregor, *Contemporary Radical Ideologies* (New York: Random House, 1968), pp. 221–76.

20. Rhoodie, *Apartheid and Racial Partnership*, pp. 124–25.

21. Vorster, *Select Speeches*, p. 90.

South African history is that from 1700 to the 1950s the proportion of whites to the overall population of South Africa was always sufficient to man all the strategic positions in the political, economic, and administrative system of the country. Whites owned almost all the land, did all the skilled and most of the semiskilled jobs in the mines and factories, and staffed the top and medium-level positions in the civil service, army, and police. Unlike Brazil, South Africa never needed to produce a relatively free and more privileged mulatto class to occupy the intermediate positions in the economy and to form a bridge between the poor and the rich, and between blacks and whites. By 1960, however, a vital change began to make itself felt. Between 1910 and 1960 whites constituted 20 percent of the total population, but from that year the white demographic base started to shrink. By 1985 the proportion of whites to the total population had fallen to 15 percent, and it is projected to shrink to 11 percent by 2020. An acute shortage of white manpower developed in both the public and private sectors.

The 1950s and 1960s saw the apartheid state greatly increasing the number of whites employed to staff the apartheid bureaucracies and to implement the myriad of apartheid laws. By the mid-1970s these bureaucracies had come up against their own limits. The state had overreached itself in its own spending and administrative capacities, and there were simply not enough whites available to staff the top and medium levels of both the private and public sectors. The mammoth Department of Bantu Administration and Development found itself more and more incapable of stemming the flow of Africans to the cities. Increasingly the government wanted blacks—or at least the most "developed" section of them—to take over the administration of their own communities, to implement influx control, and to supplement the thinly stretched white police and defense forces. As President Botha expressed it somewhat crudely in his authorized biography:

> I realise that there are today tens of thousands and hundreds of thousands of brown people who are in all respects better than the weakest [*swakste*] whites. This is one of the burning questions of our population. We must give these people a say [*"inspraak"*], a greater share in the land—in the administration of the country, as civil servants, and in many other positions which you cannot fill with your weak whites. . . . If we don't do this we will cause our own downfall.[22] (Translated)

A similar development occurred in the private sector. After the rapid economic growth of the 1960s, white workers were unable to meet the need for skilled labor. Between 1971 and 1977 whites contributed only a quarter of the increase in fully employed skilled blue-collar workers

22. Dirk and Johanna de Villiers, *PW* (Cape Town: Tafelberg, 1984), p. 89.

(15,600 out of 65,700). This skilled-labor shortage, accentuated by strikes by black workers, in particular by the extensive Durban strikes of 1973, forced the government to embark on a series of labor reforms in the 1970s. It removed the restrictions on the training of blacks and on collective bargaining by introducing works committees and, after these proved to be failures, accepted independent black unions in the statutory industrial relations system. In the wake of the Wiehahn Report (1979), the government attempted to bring blacks into a common industrial relations system by way of carefully controlled, segregated African unions which excluded migrants. However, black resistance forced government to accept racially integrated unions, including those with a strong component of migrant labor.

The result of these developments is a major change in the racial profile of the labor market. By the beginning of the 1980s whites still filled more than 90 percent of all the top administrative and management jobs, but the percentage of whites in medium-level manpower had dropped from 82 percent in 1965 to 65 percent in 1981.[23] The entry into medium-level positions has been spearheaded by colored and Indian workers, but the advance of Africans has also been significant.

Table 1: *African Occupational Advancement*

	Africans as a Proportion of All Employees in Higher-Level Occupations	
Sector	1970	1980
Professional, higher-level technical, and related workers	21%	29%
Administrative, managerial, and clerical workers	18%	27%

Source: L. Schlemmer in D. van Vuuren et al., *Change in South Africa* (Durban: Butterworth, 1983), p. 276.

These changes also altered the class composition of the black communities. If white-collar occupations are taken as a rough indication of middle-class status, the colored and Indian middle class increased considerably in the 1970s. Between 1970 and 1980 the middle class within the colored community grew from 12 percent to 19 percent and that in the Indian community from 38 percent to 48 percent. In the

23. S. S. Terblanche and J. J. Jacobs, *Struktuurverandering in die middelvlakmannekrag* (Pretoria: HSRC, 1983), pp. 17–22.

African case, the proportion increased from a mere 5 percent to 8 percent.[24]

Blacks moving onto the more strategic levels of the economy and reaching middle-class status have inexorably affected the white/black power balance. They forced the government to abandon its attempt to use Africans, as far as possible, as migrant laborers and to "denationalize" most Africans by declaring them citizens of independent homelands. The elaborate migrant system of the apartheid state was constructed in the 1950s when the economy was still largely built upon mining and agriculture. However, the three and a half decades since the end of World War II saw the growing predominance of the manufacturing sector, which increasingly demanded a productive work force settled on a family basis in the cities. Ultimately this need began to prevail over the policy that limited African family accommodation in the cities and insisted that Africans live in the cities only on a temporary basis. The lobbying by big business for reforms that would stabilize the African urban labor force, together with the concerted Progressive Federal party attacks in Parliament, remained a constant pressure upon government. But it has been the series of black urban revolts since 1976 that have been decisive in compelling the government to accept the African claim to be treated as permanent residents with political rights.

Table 2: *Contribution of Sectors to the National Economy (GDP) at Constant 1974 Prices by Kind of Economic Activity*
(Percentage Distribution)

Year	Agriculture, Forestry, Fishing	Mining, Quarrying	Manufacturing	Commerce, Catering	Government	General, Other
1950	14.5	15.1	16.5	11.3	11.2	31.4
1960	11.9	17.8	19.1	10.7	10.8	29.5
1970	8.3	18.3	21.2	12.2	9.5	30.5
1980	8.5	11.5	25.6	12.1	9.9	32.4

Sources: S. B. Greenberg, *Race and State in Capitalist Development* (New Haven: Yale University Press, 1980), p. 426; *South African Statistics*, 1982, 21.8.

To meet the expected growing demand for skilled labor, the government since the early 1970s has massively expanded black, and particularly African, education. The results can be seen in Table 3.

The system of apartheid was introduced in the 1950s when the bulk of the African population was illiterate or barely literate and performed unskilled work. For the apartheid state it was relatively easy to deny

24. This is based on the research and projections of Jan Sadie and Jill Nattrass.

Table 3: *African Enrollment in Higher Education Since 1960*

Year	Secondary School	Highest School Standard (Grade)	University Students
1960	54,598	717	1,871
1965	66,568	1,606	1,880
1970	122,489	2,938	4,578
1975	318,568	9,009	7,845
1980	577,584	31,071	10,564

Source: C. Bundy, "Schools and Revolution," *New Society,* 10 January 1986.

such a population political rights and to deflect their aspirations to distant "homelands." The African population of the mid-1980s is much better educated and trained—and much more radicalized politically. Surveys have consistently shown that the higher the level of education of African children, the more acute their political discontent and the more pressing their political and status demands.

Economic and demographic shifts and the rapid expansion of black secondary education were the major forces that undermined classic apartheid. Of secondary importance, but not insignificant, were the changing class composition of the Afrikaners and the effect of world pressure on the apartheid system. Both contributed to the growing legitimacy crisis of apartheid. When the apartheid policy was implemented in the 1950s the majority of Afrikaners were insecure blue-collar workers or marginal farmers dependent on the state to maintain their living standards and social segregation. By the mid-1970s, however, at least 70 percent of the Afrikaners belonged to a relatively secure middle class (Table 4). For this middle class the crude racism and discrimination of old-style apartheid, the forced removals of blacks, and all the other coercive acts were becoming increasingly difficult to reconcile with their professed norms and values. This middle class insisted on a less obnoxious form of apartheid.

Table 4: *Percentage of Afrikaners in Broad Categories of Occupation, 1936–1977*

Category	1936	1946	1960	1970	1977
Agricultural occupations	41.2	30.3	16.0	9.7	8.1
"Blue collar" and other manual	31.3	40.7	40.5	32.4	26.7
"White collar"	27.5	29.0	43.5	57.9	65.2
	100.0	100.0	100.0	100.0	100.0

Source: J. Sadie cited in H. Giliomee and H. Adam, *Afrikanermag: Opkoms and Toekoms* (Stellenbosch: UUB, 1981), p. 130.

The first important legislative retreat from apartheid occurred in 1972 when some of the constraints on black labor were relaxed. It is no coincidence that the first significant moves occurred in the economic field. As Merle Lipton remarks, when the upper-class Nationalists were forced to choose between their ethnic preferences and their class interests, they opted for their class interests as long as this choice did not compromise the group's security and power.[25]

Business interests pressed for labor reforms, and in general the more affluent sections of Afrikaner society were prepared to accept modifications of social apartheid that would permit integrated sport and cultural activities and social intercourse between white and black in international hotels, restaurants, and at conferences. Supporters of this position became known as *verligtes* ("enlightened ones"). Their spokesmen were newspaper editors, academics, businessmen, some clergy, and a few politicians. Against them in the National party were ranged the *verkramptes* (literally "cramped-up"), headed by some politicians and intellectuals, but drawing their support from marginal farmers, lower-level civil servants, and workers. From the late 1960s on, a split in the Nationalist alliance widened; it became particularly pronounced in 1982 when eighteen members of the National party caucus broke away to form the Conservative party.

Verligtes have rarely enjoyed a decisive political say in the NP. However, they were important as opinion-formers and image-builders who presented apartheid policy in a more liberal guise or clothed it in universal academic jargon with particular emphasis on the concepts of pluralism and consociationalism. *Verligtes* served several functions: preparing the ground for reform within the Afrikaner community, preventing an erosion of Afrikaner support to the liberal-leaning Progressive Federal party, attracting electoral support from English-speaking whites, and persuading Western opinion-makers that structural change was under way. Most of them believed that they followed the only viable strategy of promoting reform from within the ranks of the Afrikaner community, a strategy which above all called for *loyal* opposition. The main objective of the *verligtes* was to reformulate the apartheid ideology within the party without forcing a split.

The terms *verlig* and *verkramp* had been coined in 1967 by Willem de Klerk (an academic who went on to become a newspaper editor) with the intention of presenting both positions as unacceptable extremes. However, *verlig* soon became a banner behind which the Cape Town–based *Nasionale Pers* newspapers rallied. In 1972 de Klerk restated his

25. Merle Lipton, *Capitalism and Apartheid: South Africa, 1910–1964* (Aldershot: Wildwood House, 1986), pp. 374–75.

position. Accepting the positive connotation of *verligtheid*, he argued that it stood for "equality in diversity." "Diversity" in fact meant the four statutory apartheid groups which the state defined and imposed: white, colored, Asian, and black. Noting the world's call for equal rights, de Klerk declared: "We reject integration but the alternative is not perpetual discrimination." In such a context, "equality in diversity" meant to be responsive to the demand for the "national development of all peoples up to the point of full independence," equal opportunities within a framework of diversity, participation of coloreds and Indians in political and economic activities in the "white" area, and an emphasis on interaction and communication at various levels.[26]

Whereas *verkramptes* unequivocally championed white supremacy and called for the fullest measure of apartheid, *verligtes* and also some mainstream nationalists such as Gerrit Viljoen, who served both as rector of the Randse Afrikaanse University and chairman of the Afrikaner Broederbond, increasingly began to think of apartheid as a pliable instrument of Afrikaner nationalism, but not its master. Viljoen stated in 1972: "Apartheid is an 'open' solution for the problem of relations between peoples. It is not dogmatic or final, not a good in itself, but a method, a process—not a final answer."[27]

Because the maintenance of Afrikaner nationalist control over South Africa was a nonnegotiable goal of *verligtes*, they did not seek compromise of that control. And as the apartheid system, built on the four statutory groups, conceals and fosters Afrikaner rule, they did not propose the abolition of its substance. As Schalk Pienaar wrote in 1974: "The plural South African political dispensation which has been developed by the NP is basic. But within that framework there will be in terms of Nationalist policy an acceptance by people of each other."[28]

The Soweto uprising of 1976 destroyed the *verligte* illusion of apartheid as a potentially just solution. It imparted a greater urgency to *verligte* pleas for a basic change in white attitudes toward blacks. Most prominent was the work of the Stellenbosch philosophy professor Willie Esterhuyse, whose book *Afskeid van Apartheid* (Farewell to Apartheid) demanded a basic change in white attitudes toward blacks. In his plea for reform of institutionalized racial discrimination, Esterhuyse suggested a "dramatic dismantling of symbols" to give new hope to blacks. These symbols were above all the racial sex laws, the Population Registration Act

26. Willem de Klerk, "The Concepts *'Verkramp'* and *'Verlig,'* " in N. J. Rhoodie, ed., *South African Dialogue* (Johannesburg: McGraw-Hill, 1972), pp. 520–31. See also his views a decade later in *Politieke Gesprek* (Johannesburg: Perskor, 1980).

27. Gerrit Viljoen, *Ideaal en Werklikheid: Rekenskap deur 'n Afrikaner* (Cape Town: Tafelberg, 1978), p. 85.

28. Schalk Pienaar, *Tien Jaar Politieke Kommentaar* (Cape Town: Tafelberg, 1975), p. 99.

(which defined the four statutory groups), and the Group Areas Act (which segregated residential areas).[29] Yet in *Afskeid van Apartheid* Esterhuyse was still ambiguous as to whether some of the main apartheid laws had to be abolished or whether they simply had to be "softened." (In subsequent books Esterhuyse took a clearer reformist stand.)

The same ambiguity is to be found in the thinking of Willem de Klerk. In a book published in 1984 he boldly declared that the old peremptory political style of Afrikaners was giving way to dialogue, negotiation, co-decision-making, and compromise. At the same time, however, he insisted upon the Afrikaners' right to retain the leadership role. De Klerk also called for the removal of ethnicity as a compulsory ethnic structure "except where group interests are decisive." In practice this meant that whites had the right to retain their own residential areas and schools but that "grey areas" had to be created where some whites and blacks could live together.[30]

Thus, although from 1979 *verligtes* were calling apartheid dead or bidding it farewell, they provided no alternative to its cornerstones of prescribed group membership and decisive control by the white group. In 1982 matters came to a head in a bitter press altercation between *verligtes* and some Afrikaner intellectuals outside the National party framework, sometimes labeled *oorbeligtes* (literally "overexposed"), who had become increasingly critical of the *verligte* strategy. A member of the latter group, André du Toit, published a comprehensive critique of the *verligte* position. A provocative formulation of the *oorbeligte* critique occurred in a speech by John Degenaar, another Stellenbosch philosophy professor, who argued that unless *verligtes* were prepared to take a public stand against the basic tenets of National party policy, they were a stumbling block to change because they created the impression of reform but were only prepared to allow the kind of change that did not upset Afrikaner control.[31]

In reply, the *verligtes* reiterated their credo that the only social base for reform was the NP, which had to be in control of South Africa in order to bring about an orderly transformation of society in which there will be increasingly less discrimination and a more equitable distribution

29. W. F. Esterhuyse, *Afskeid van Apartheid* (Cape Town: Tafelberg, 1979), p. 76.

30. Willem de Klerk, *Die Tweede Revolusie* (Johannesburg: Jonathan Ball, 1984).

31. I should declare a bias as one of the small group of *oorbeligtes* engaged in this polemic against the *verligtes*. For a perceptive account of the debate between *verligtes* and their antagonists, the so-called *oorbeligtes*, see Helen Zille, "The Civil War that sprang forth from The John," *Frontline*, November 1982, pp. 34–36. The fullest critique of the *verligte* position is that developed by André du Toit, "Facing up to the Future," *Social Dynamics* 7 (1981):1–27. A good condensation of Degenaar's views is found in his *Voortbestaan in Geregtigheid* (Cape Town: Tafelberg, 1980). I elaborate on some of the points in this chapter in my *Parting of the Ways: South African Politics, 1976–1982* (Cape Town: David Philip, 1982).

of wealth. To this the *oorbeligtes* responded by saying that the National party, as an ethnic party, could not be expected to introduce any reforms that would weaken its hold on power, and that the only realistic reform strategy was to build up a genuinely reformist party. This meant that the *verligtes* had to break away from the National party in order to help start a realignment of political forces. This vehement debate, largely in the correspondence columns of *Die Burger,* the Cape Town Nationalist newspaper, drew considerable attention, but in the end these polemical exchanges produced more heat than light, with neither grouping prepared to concede ground on the crucial differences setting them apart.

During the late 1970s another ideological grouping arose in Afrikaner ranks, a market-oriented liberalism of which the main exponents have been Jan Lombard, an influential Pretoria professor of economics and government economic adviser, and Johan van Zyl, an ex-professor of economics and Executive Director of the Federated Chamber of Industries. The neo-liberals were (initially at least) nationalists, but their main concern became safeguarding the capitalist system and effective group rights (not racially defined) rather than the defense of Afrikaner political hegemony. The approach of the neo-liberals both in content and process differs considerably from that of the *verligtes* with respect to promoting reform. While *verligtes* want the state to establish political structures and transfer some wealth from the rich to the poor, the neo-liberals, echoing similar views gaining ground in the United States and Britain, reject such a strategy of reform from above. For them the main needs were to narrow the scope of state intrusions in the economy and in civil society, to devolve powers to the regions as part of a genuine thrust toward federation, and to deregulate a range of economic and social functions from monetary controls and job color bars to personal intimacy.[32] The neo-liberals thus want to give freer rein to market forces, which would lead to social progress through a new emphasis on individual rights, decentralized power, and freedom of association.[33] Their strategy is to influence not only government but also business as a significant social force in the ruling group which could propose to government an alternative sociopolitical system. Neo-liberals like Lombard and van Zyl are Northern-based and enjoy close links with the business community. Central to their thinking is their belief that the

32. This is a major theme in a forthcoming book by Stanley Greenberg, *Legitimating the Illegitimate* (Berkeley: University of California Press).

33. The seminal work of the neo-liberals is J. A. Lombard, *Freedom, Welfare and Order: Thoughts on the Principles of Political Co-operation in the Economy of Southern Africa* (Pretoria: Bureau of Economic Research, 1978). For van Zyl's thinking, see *Post-Apartheid South Africa: The protection of minority and group rights* (Pretoria: FCI, 1986).

dramatic structural changes in the economy and demographic composition of the country, especially in the years ahead, demand a fundamentally new strategy on the part of government to achieve stability and political legitimacy.

The Wiehahn Commission, which investigated a new system of industrial relations, was deadlocked between those who wanted to specify racial and political requirements for trade union membership, and the market-oriented liberals who advocated freedom of association granting all workers the same rights and permitting them to join any trade union across color lines. The former viewpoint prevailed in the commission, but as a result of worker resistance the government was soon compelled to accept the principle of freedom of association.

In the 1980s the Lombards and van Zyls took up the struggle to introduce the same principle in the political system. The main thrust of their political writings has been the insistence that the reform process be based on individual rights and freedom of association (as manifested in a free market system) rather than, as *verligtes* would have it, on the good intentions of government to meet popular needs. The main strands of their thinking are: (1) Individual rights must be entrenched. (2) People with common interests must be allowed to incorporate in groups—in the same way as business corporations are established under a Companies' Act—with the right to associate politically on various levels as long as they do not infringe the rights of all other individuals and groups. (3) In contrast to the *verligtes,* who advocate reform from above, the neo-liberal approach favors building a new order from below. Normalized relations based on free association must be introduced on the interpersonal and local-government levels and expanded in phases to ultimately reach the central government level.

Lombard's thinking can hardly be called radical, even in the South African context. Certainly the first stages of his reform process are quite conservative, even to the point of accepting the three ethnic chambers of Parliament. However, in contrast to the *verligtes,* he suggests an approach that could break down the exclusive white (Afrikaner) minority control. In January 1986 the Lombard–van Zyl thinking found concrete expression in a business charter issued by the Federated Chamber of Industries, of which van Zyl is chief executive. The charter committed itself to a wide range of rights and principles, including freedom of thought, equal educational opportunities, freedom of movement, freedom of association, freedom of peaceful assembly, separation of state powers, supremacy of the law, freedom of the press, and free formation of political parties.

The Botha government has been influenced to some extent by both the *verligtes* and the market-oriented liberals. *Verligtes* have, principally, provided the ideology for the new phase of apartheid which I call reform-apartheid, while the market-oriented liberals have provided a new mode of thinking about industrial relations and the justification for withdrawing state subsidies in transport, housing, and other fields. Botha's style of reform-apartheid is influenced most strongly by technocratic imperatives on the one hand, and by the large bureaucracy it has built up on the other, particularly the Department of Constitutional Development, headed by Chris Heunis, which is setting up a whole new edifice, of "own affairs" and "general affairs" structures. The essential feature of reform-apartheid is the government's attempt to present its rule as in the interests of all South Africa's peoples. It projects the structures it has set up as vehicles for "common decision-making" and "broadening democracy." But while government has a clear desire to give all groups a "say" in government (in Afrikaans the untranslatable term *inspraak* is used), the government equally has no inclination to abandon its power to have the final say. In fact, despite the government's protestations, power has been further centralized in the central government's hands and executive accountability has been even further diminished. As the constitution of 1983 provides, the Indian and colored houses have no effective veto in the tricameral Parliament. Moreover, the government's restructuring of the second and third tiers of government has brought a further concentration of power in Pretoria's hands.

There is thus a distinct double-edged quality in the constitutional dimension of reform-apartheid. On the one hand, there is a new willingness of NP leaders to agree that wealth, opportunities, and even decision-making will have to be shared among all South Africa's peoples. On the other hand, there is the Afrikaner government's firm conviction that only continued Afrikaner rule can ensure progress along that road. Or to put it differently, the government accepts economic growth, training, job creation, and stable food prices as primary goals but always premised on the maintenance of firm control by a fairly unified Afrikaner ethnic group as the stable political center of South Africa. The Botha government, indeed, considers an Afrikaner nationalist leadership as the only one that can enjoy the trust of the Afrikaners. In its view, only a government enjoying majority Afrikaner support can successfully orchestrate all the technocratic skills and abilities that serve the material welfare of everyone in the country. To improve efficiency in its managerial style of government, the Botha cabinet increasingly wants "inputs" from black elites on all levels of government, without relinquishing its grip on any of the political levers. This is the background to a private statement by a prominent business leader: "We Afrikaners must try to find the secret of sharing power without losing control." This view is increasingly being challenged by the black subordinate population and, to a lesser extent, by organized business in its enlightened self-interest.

It has always been the main objective of the Cape liberal Nationalists and *verligtes* to persuade the Western world that the "idealistic" element of apartheid belongs to the mainstream of Western political thought and practice. At the same time, they have tried to persuade their Afrikaner constituency that this feature of apartheid would not undermine Afrikaner rule but would in fact stabilize it. In the early 1970s Van Zyl Slabbert argued that *verligtheid* is an attempt by academics, professionals, and journalists to reconcile their professional values with their commitment to Afrikaner nationalism.[34] In the late 1970s and early 1980s there was an entire industry of academics trying to square the apartheid policy and the government's constitutional proposals with accepted liberal concepts such as pluralism, consociationalism, and federalism. In contrast, market-oriented liberals such as Lombard have taken the individualistic principles of Western thinkers such as Adam Smith, Milton Friedman, and Frederick von Hayek and have tried to apply them to the South African situation.

The Botha government has seized upon every concept, phrase, and sentiment in academic thinking that could give its policies and practices a liberal appearance. However, as far as political representation is concerned, both *verligte* academics and government insist that the debate can only be about "continued democratisation and the extension of political participation to all South Africa's population groups."[35] These "groups" are still the four apartheid groups. We find no real shift to the classic liberal notion of individual political rights. In general, the government's whole approach toward political rights is still profoundly illiberal. Recently I listened for an entire morning to a top civil servant's exposition of what he called the "dramatic reform package" of the 1986 session of Parliament. He argued that a "radically transformed" political framework has been created that recognizes a common citizenship and grants freedom of movement to all people. "From now on," he said, "the entire emphasis will be on *people* for whom *institutions* must be established to provide for their *needs*." Not once was the term "rights" used. In his view, addressing the needs of people in the fields of housing, health, and education quite clearly supersedes the liberal demand for

34. F. Van Zyl Slabbert, "Afrikaner Nationalism, White Politics and Political Change in South Africa," in Leonard Thompson and Jeffrey Butler, eds., *Change in Contemporary South Africa* (Berkeley: University of California Press, 1975), pp. 3–19.

35. Willie Esterhuyse, "Verligtheid: The Road Ahead," *Sunday Times*, 2 December 1984.

political rights. In South Africa, he seemed to say, needs are far more important than rights.

While the neo-liberal Afrikaners, in their formulation of principles and rights, have come ever closer to mainstream Western liberalism, the position of the *verligtes* and technocrats is more ambiguous. They increasingly talk about rights, but this is negated by their continued rejection of or lack of support for one of the most fundamental liberal rights, freedom of association. A clearer resemblance may be to the political thinking and praxis of Eastern European regimes, which have abandoned the democratic premise of socialism in favor of a bureaucratic oligarchy that sets up what a recent book calls a "dictatorship over needs." This justifies political repression by claiming for the oligarchy an indispensable role in addressing social needs. In opposition to the governments of Eastern Europe stand those whose objective is socialism as radicalized democracy, not a dictatorship of any kind.[36] In South Africa all the makings of a "dictatorship over needs" are present. The only effective democratic counter to this will be a liberalism that emphasizes both individual rights and social needs in a coherent program that could appeal to people across class and racial divides.

36. For the Eastern European debate, see Ferenc Feher, Agnes Heller, and Gyorgy Markus, *Dictatorship over Needs* (Oxford: Basil Blackwell, 1983).

Lawrence Schlemmer

23. Prospects for a Liberal Society in South Africa

What are the prospects for a South African order based on the liberal values of individual freedom, protected rights, increasing equity, and social justice? This question can be analyzed from a variety of perspectives. In this chapter I concentrate neither on the political culture nor on the balance of power among political factions but on the social structures of the society which determine the prospects of liberalism. Human rights are not only promoted by a public culture, demanded by politicians, or supported by a legal system or constitution. They are also a product of a total social, political, and economic order. This explains why democracy and human rights have been such poor exports and are likely to remain imperfectly realized in many societies.

It is perhaps easiest to define liberalism by what it is not. It opposes those who would impose any system or set of values on a society and institutionalize intolerance of alternative values and interests; and it rejects the assumption that any single doctrine or party organization can claim to know what will assure the greatest good for society. Liberals believe that the greatest good is achieved by the maximum possible freedom of individual choice, but they do not thereby necessarily oppose the use of state power for the public good. They can claim to be less rigid than others in their social doctrine, and are less likely than nationalists, conservatives, or radicals to seek to exclude other viewpoints and party doctrines from the arena of politics. A liberal one-party government, a liberal military dictatorship, or even a liberal oligarchy are thus contradictions in terms. Critics of liberalism, in consequence, almost inevitably attack liberals for excessive tolerance or weakness, or find liberal policies subtle, perhaps disguised, forms of elitism or discrimination.

In this paper, liberalism is defined as *formal* tolerance and respect for the rights and freedoms of those of differing persuasions. A liberal society is what is frequently referred to as an "open" society. Liberal governments exist either because historical processes and social permutations make a system of institutional tolerance possible, or because various checks and constraints limit the powers of government. It is this aspect of liberalism that is the subject of the analysis which follows.[1]

Democracy and civil liberty tend to emerge when the potential for conflict between groups or strata is low enough so that social order can be maintained with minimal use of force and without the suppression of individual or group interests. Hence democratic responsiveness and civil liberties arise out of an interplay of particular social forces and structures, which can be loosely grouped as social, economic, and political. A liberal democratic society would have the following characteristics:

(1) *Cross-cutting divisions and overlapping memberships.* Where status or cultural groups have several uniform and consistent interests that coincide with one another, a spirit of total opposition is encouraged. An example would be a society where race is "correlated" with income and educational differences. Where material interests consistently coincide with cultural, racial, or status identity, it is hard to accommodate conflicts constructively within a wider unity. On the other hand, where two groups have some interests in common, their opposing interests do not engender comprehensive conflict. Where individuals belong to several organized or unorganized groups with diverse interests and outlooks, their attitudes will tend to moderate as a result of cross-pressures, producing the tolerance and balance necessary for an open society.

(2) *Variety and complexity of interest groups in a dynamic balance.* Civil liberty and the exercise of political freedom is impossible in a society in which particular interest groups perceive themselves to be wholly at odds with opposing interests. Where there is no or little prospect of coalitions of interest, or where there is a lack of variety and complexity

1. This analysis is based on conclusions drawn *inter alia* from Rolf Dahrendorf, *Society and Democracy in Germany* (London: Weidenfeld and Nicholson, 1968); Talcott Parsons, *The System of Modern Societies* (Englewood Cliffs, N.J.: Prentice-Hall, 1971); W. K. Jordan, *The Development of Religious Toleration in England* (Cambridge: Harvard University Press, 3 vols., 1932); Karl de Schweinitz, *Industrialisation and Democracy* (Glencoe: The Free Press, 1964); and H. H. Gerth and C. Wright Mills, *From Max Weber* (London: Routledge & Kegan Paul, 1970).

of interests, it is difficult for any particular group to form alliances. One group will thus protect and maximize its share of power with an intensity that undermines tolerance for the opportunities of others.

(3) *Opportunities for individual economic, occupational, and social mobility.* Citizens must have the opportunity to practice occupations or engage in ventures relatively unfettered by discriminatory legislation and stifling bureaucracy; social advancement must be based substantially on individual achievement, influenced as little as possible by group affiliations. Where such individualism is effective, social differentiation results within a group, which limits the development of compact majorities. (See 8 below).

(4) *A high degree of voluntary organization in society.* Numerous clubs, associations, chambers, guilds, and fraternities provide forums for the articulation of community needs separate from government bureaucracies controlled by elites. They thus place a web of influence between communities and the authorities and, through lobbying processes, provide influential information to government on community needs.

(5) *Positive expectations of social progress, relatively high quality of life, and an absence of a strong sense of deprivation.* These features tend to reduce the level of interest in politics and the intensity of political aspirations, which in turn promote moderate, conciliatory attitudes and discourage extremism.

The economic context is clearly of critical importance, affecting all the conditions outlined above, and especially (3) and (5), so an almost binding precondition is: (6) *Economic growth outstripping population growth.* An adequate growth in per capita incomes is essential, a development most often fostered by a growing free-market economy without excessive monopolies or state intervention.

Most established democratic societies have been relatively successful in overcoming what is often referred to as the "hump" of development. As economic development begins to occur, mortality rates fall and population increases relatively rapidly. With new opportunities for higher wages, expectations also rise rapidly. If, however, population growth outstrips employment opportunity and if expectations exceed the capacity for wage increases, critical discontents arise that may force increasingly authoritarian controls upon the system.

If the economy is successful in staying ahead of population growth and popular expectations, an evolution toward more liberal policies is facilitated. Radical theorists might argue, however, that if the workers assume control of the economy the authoritarian consequences of slow per capita growth can be avoided. It is difficult to concede this point, since in most cases new "worker states" have taken similar measures to those of authoritarian capitalist states; i.e., to curtail the influence of trade unions and to impose coercive discipline on the unemployed or underemployed.

When the economy can sustain strong per capita income growth, and particularly where the organization of the economy is on free-market principles, a number of conditions foster a liberalization of social controls.[2] First, the urgency of wants is reduced, lessening the need for coercive discipline. Second, an expanding economic pie means that concessions to one interest group need not necessarily involve a diminution of rewards to another. Conflicting interests can be accommodated and need not threaten the basic order in the economic system. Third, successful wage bargaining strengthens independent trade unions as important voluntary organizations to countervail the power of major employers and the state. Fourth, successful wage bargaining also helps to establish ground rules for conflict resolution and negotiation in the society as a whole. The *process* of negotiation brings contending parties closer to each other's points of view and helps to establish the general value of *compromise.*

The establishment of a process of negotiation and the consequent valuing of compromise in economic activities have important consequences in encouraging a politics of accommodation. Because the market is impersonal, it receives less focused hostility than the state. Where the state controls and administers welfare benefits, housing, and services it can very readily become a focus of discontent and instability. In an expanding, varied economy in which workers can sell their labor to the highest bidder, they are not forced to mobilize collectively as their only means of redress. They can move around, exercising choice to seek improved benefits, thus reducing the level of concerted opposition. Similar processes affect entrepreneurs who in a free-enterprise system tend to promote an ideology resistant to centralized state control and social engineering, one that indirectly promotes social liberty. An independent private sector also introduces a pole of influence relatively separate from that of the state, hence fostering a balance of power in society. A free-enterprise system can also protect trade unions from state control. Even though capitalists may not be sympathetic to trade unions, the free-enterprise, noncentrally planned system facilitates the independence of capital and labor alike, hence promoting the balance of influence necessary in a democracy.

Our third group of processes can be roughly characterized as political: (7) *Common basic goals and a relative absence of primordial or intensely felt*

2. Some of these conditions are set out in de Schweinitz, *Industrialisation and Democracy.*

group loyalties. Where groups are associated with primary loyalties based on descent, kinship, or strongly held ethnic feeling in opposition to broader national loyalties, democracy becomes particularly problematic. The concept of a "loyal opposition"—loyal to the nation but opposed to the policies of the governing party—is basic to most Western democracies. In deeply divided societies, however, such a fundamental loyalty of parties cannot be readily assumed. Nor, often, can one assume a fundamental acceptance of the basic economic or political system. If in an established capitalist society a *major* opposition party has a program to nationalize *all* industry and institute a one-party state, the governing party's commitment to democratic norms could easily weaken, as it attempted to prevent an opposition victory at the polls. Widely divergent ideologies in a society, held by substantial proportions of the population, seldom coexist with democracy and freedom.

(8) *Absence of "compact" majorities.* Where one segment of a society constitutes a clear majority, smaller segments will resist a system of open political competition for the obvious reason that they fear being perpetually excluded from a share in power. In a democracy, all significant political groups having the capacity to seize power and overturn the democratic rules must be able to contemplate a loss of power at the polls without seeing it as intolerable or irrevocable. Socioeconomic development must have proceeded to a point where it introduces social differentiation into what would otherwise be a permanent demographic majority.

(9) *Plurality of authority and status.* Decentralization and hence plurality of government, the existence of independent authority, particularly in the courts, and constitutional arrangements for arbitration such as an upper house of review further strengthen checks and balances in a society.

(10) *Broadly based political organizations and parties.* Such parties have to reconcile different interests and consequently usually have a tendency toward moderation. Political organizations founded on single-stranded loyalties or interests, on the other hand, tend to produce relatively intense opposition and inclinations to extremism, which in turn undermine the mutual respect among politicians necessary in democracies.

The preceding propositions suggest that nonviolent developments toward democracy can occur only if the aspirations of all groups are accommodated and channeled within a framework of institutional political bargaining. Attitudes, interests, and ideologies of excluded sections of the population will remain divergent from those of the center if no mechanisms exist to conciliate and accommodate them. Their leaders could not be expected to adhere to the institutionalized rules of the political game, and in such conditions multiparty democratic systems become unworkable. Freedom and order are incompatible if the basis of the order is not acceptable to all significant groups.

The presence of ethnic identities, communal loyalties, or regional differences in a society will obviously make a number of the above conditions for democracy difficult to achieve. In such cases the emergence or maintenance of democratic stability requires additional processes and institutions, prominent among them strong, legitimate, group-based leadership willing to form political coalitions with leaders of other groups and to establish political bridges between contending groups or regions.[3] This is the only viable substitute for the integrative processes in more homogeneous democracies. Groups in a heterogeneous society must recognize each other's right to exist and must respect each other's collective commitments to group identity and self-determination.

South Africa has a number of features that powerfully militate against the establishment of democratic institutions. Because of a long history of social segregation and institutional separation, the different races have few political and social interests in common, although overlapping and shared interests are found in the economic sphere. Even where blacks have been able to achieve the same life-style, occupations, educational levels, and material possessions as whites, residential segregation and separate education have prevented them from identifying with whites and adopting common interest and values with them. Upwardly mobile black people in South Africa do not undergo the normal process of identification with middle-class urban values and life-styles. Because of social segregation and formal racial classification, material progress among blacks leads to what is termed "status inconsistency"—a conflict between superior economic status and inferior racial status. Hence potentially middle-class blacks become more sensitive to their racial status as they come closer to white life-styles, and many are radicalized by this perception and identify more self-consciously with the black majority. Moreover, the impression whites have of a potentially compact black majority is strengthened by this process.

South Africa also faces a serious problem in accommodating the aspirations of the burgeoning population of black secondary-school graduates. If the average growth of gross domestic product stays below 5 percent per year, black unemployment tends to increase, most markedly among youth. Hence a substantial and probably growing segment of South Africa's population, and the one with the greatest ability to generate social turmoil, is not being integrated into the institutional

3. See Arend Lijphart, *Power-Sharing in South Africa* (Berkeley: University of California Press, Institute of International Studies, Policy Papers in International Affairs, No. 24, 1985).

structure of society. Almost no commonalities of interest between this group and the established society exist.

In most cases race and ethnic status are strongly correlated with economic and educational inequality, mutually reinforcing these group differences and encouraging group stereotypes. Until recently, employment practices and remuneration patterns have been able to capitalize on the lower social status and lack of political influence of blacks. Hence sharp cleavages and conflict in the workplace intensify group polarization. Since the workplace is the one setting where blacks and whites meet directly, the perceptions and conflicts generated in industrial relations powerfully reinforce the consciousness of an inevitability of conflict between black and white in the society at large.

Whites widely believe that Africans (or Africans, coloreds, and Asians) would form a compact or substantially unified and permanent majority in any system of open political participation. Thus they fear the prospect of "mass politics" in an open democracy, reasoning that once they have lost power, they will be totally excluded forever from active participation or a share in government. The adoption by several black or open parties of the rhetoric of "liberation," and more recently revolutionary "transformation," suggest a total elimination of white political influence which reinforces these fears. Those fears are hardly of recent origin. Whites have long had a collective consciousness of being potentially, perhaps actually, an embattled minority in a hostile continent. Afrikaner ethnic identity, forged in a history of pioneer conflicts with other groups, white and black, gives added strength and focus to the collective consciousness of a segment of the dominant minority. Hence whites, with the exception of the middle-class intelligentsia, have a marked sense of a basic incompatibility between their interests and values and those of blacks. Even reformist whites have difficulty anticipating a nonracial consensus on basic values.

That consensus has not been furthered by South Africa's recent economic history. The South African economy has not yet passed over the development "hump" referred to above. Sustained high levels of growth, and increases in black wages and incomes at rates exceeding those of whites, in the late seventies and early eighties gave many observers the impression that increasing black well-being would defuse political tensions. However, the depth of the current recession, increasing capital intensity in production, less optimistic forecasts of medium-term economic growth by official planners (estimated medium-term average gross domestic product growth is now around 3 percent), and the manifestly depressing effects on the economy of political instability and the disinvestment campaign all suggest that black incomes will not increase as rapidly as before and that unemployment will expand. After a period of fast growth which raised expectations, South Africa now appears to be facing too sluggish a growth rate to reduce the scope of discontent.

Furthermore, although in the past the state had established the precedent of supplying subsidized housing, transport, and a variety of other services, under pressure of chronic inflation it has now reduced spending. Government-supplied services will, in consequence, be reduced before either business or community organizations are adequately geared to supply housing and other services in a free-market context. As in all systems in which a less than affluent state administers the lives and welfare of poorer people, the government has become the focus of sharp discontent and welfare protest. Thus the structure of the economy almost guarantees a widespread rejection of the free-market system in the short to medium term. The new emphasis of the government on self-help housing and assistance to small businesses may act as a corrective in due course. Unless the economy grows more rapidly, however, a mounting crisis of discontent will stimulate unrest and violence, thus delaying the emergence of a broad underlying acceptance of that economic system which will facilitate liberalization. The destruction and looting of businesses by unemployed youth and younger adults in the unrest of the mid-1980s clearly typifies the problem.

Enormous difficulties thus lie ahead in establishing minimum consensus on overall socioeconomic goals and a sustained process of democratization. However, certain positive signs do exist. Despite its structural problems, a basically strong and fairly self-sufficient economy has developed in South Africa with a proven capacity in the past to generate increasing welfare, although not full employment. There is also considerable communication between the races through newspapers, some of which have considerable readership in all groups, and among opinion leaders in the religious, educational, academic, and business spheres. Presumably, harmonious relations persist between the races in public places, in commerce, and, despite episodes of sharp industrial conflict, in normal employment situations. Moreover, large numbers of the (older) unemployed blacks have learned to generate their own opportunities in a variety of informal sector pursuits and small businesses. An independent black trade union movement, despite the economic difficulties and its occasional radical rhetoric, is establishing norms of negotiation and compromise in industry that serve as a model to the rest of society. Finally, a tradition of social protest and an active commitment to social justice have developed among most mainline churches, the universities, and in several important voluntary organizations.

Despite all the positive signs, the dominant white communities are still firmly resistant to changes that would affect their life-styles. Indeed, the present anxieties and stresses are making many whites more resistant to change, a tendency seen, for example, in increasingly active right-wing movements. It is highly unlikely that the present government, while it remains in control of security resources, will abdicate unless voted out of power by whites in favor of a party committed to majority rule, and this outcome is unlikely. In the medium term, the best prospects for democratization lie in a governing coalition between a white party and one or more other parties either black or nonracial. One is looking in the short to medium term at prospects for "power-sharing" rather than at a fully open democratic process. The medium-term future can perhaps be seen as a fairly limited period of transition to a more conventional democracy in the Western mode, offering minorities the reassurance of a power base while the society is developing toward complete democracy.

There are certain minimum requirements for relative stability and for setting the society on a trajectory toward a growth in prosperity and an acceptably open democracy.

(1) *The participation of all South Africans in central decision-making.* This need not be on the so-called Westminster system or the one-person-one-vote franchise in a unitary state. Such a system would not be remotely acceptable to most whites, and unalleviated demands for it would most likely produce a political stalemate or a white backlash. However, general representation in a central legislature is obviously necessary. Not only is such representation an essential ingredient of any liberal democracy, but anything less would lack legitimacy among blacks and in international opinion.

(2) *A devolution of substantial powers to decentralized regional governments.* Bringing government and administration closer to the people is desirable in its own right, but there are other benefits. South Africa's regions are varied in the readiness of whites to accept power-sharing. A variety of surveys and polls, particularly by Market and Opinion Surveys (Pty) Ltd., have shown that in the metropolitan areas of Johannesburg, Durban-Pietermaritzburg, the Cape Peninsula, and possibly the eastern Cape, majorities or near majorities of white voters are willing to endorse power-sharing with blacks as long as adequate protection of minority interests is provided. The Natal-KwaZulu area and the other metropolitan areas mentioned above, which include the country's major black townships, could be identified as areas in which early power-sharing in empowered regional governments could take place.

(3) *Minority safeguards in the central and regional legislative bodies.* A range of different constitutional arrangements to protect minority interests can be considered. While protection for minorities is needed in

the short term to induce whites to negotiate power-sharing, they are essential components of a liberal democracy and would benefit all South Africans in the long term. Safeguards might possibly include provisions like: minority veto rights; disproportional representation on an area or constituency basis (a racial basis of representation would generate conflict between groups and is politically a nonstarter among blacks); an upper house of review, in which minority interests are substantially represented; the testing of the constitution by an independent judiciary; or entrenched clauses in the constitution, requiring two-thirds or larger majorities to effect fundamental changes in the constitution.

(4) Just as the frustration of blacks out of power now calls for more than protection from oppressive controls, the fears of whites perhaps call for more than formal, negative safeguards. The transition period seems to call for a *"grand coalition" at the executive level.* This means a cabinet, and perhaps in addition some form of federal council or upper chamber, in which all major parties, some of which will inevitably represent ethnic groups, are able to participate actively, if not on the basis of parity, at least in some other form of balance acceptable to minorities. The representation in the executive might have to be backed by appropriate representation in the civil service, including the police and army.

(5) As important as minority and majority rights may be, it is equally important that *cross-cutting ties, interests, and patterns of identification between racial and ethnic groups* begin to occur. This requires above all the *desegregation of facilities and of residential areas.* Despite the manifest determination among many whites to resist the integration of schools and suburban areas, pressure must be mounted to achieve promptly the flexibility of local options and the establishment of substantial areas of open urban housing with integration of public facilities. Desegregation could then spread on a voluntary basis. If desegregation can begin in areas in which whites and other minorities are most tolerant of social reform, the devolution of powers to regional authorities and other safeguards for minorities will not be seen as occurring within a purely racial framework, as are virtually all the recent reforms of the present government.

(6) *Serious promotion and upgrading of the informal sector in the black areas, so that it can begin to provide housing, social services, and rudimentary amenities.* This is one of the only ways in which the quality of life in these areas can be upgraded without high government spending, which carries with it the danger of restimulating inflation and constraining economic recovery because of increased expenditure on an unproductive bureaucracy. The promotion of small businesses in the black communities, operating with no unnecessary constraints, will also serve to

promote individualism and independence of spirit, which are requirements for successful democracies. A vital precondition, however, is the deregulation of the economy to a point far beyond present goals. The small-business sector should be virtually freed of all licensing and other requirements except for essential health regulations.

(7) *Facilitating the increased growth of successful black leadership at the local level, within a framework of voluntary associations.* Leadership and voluntary organization is not something that can be artificially stimulated with any guarantee of success. Leadership in the black communities is so deeply polarized and voluntary organization so narrowly focused or attenuated, however, that large lacunae exist in many parts of the country. Often the leadership and organization is either passive and compliant or militant and destructive, both consequences of repressive security action. The situation requires a continuum of organizations competing for support in the communities. A network of voluntary organizations would discourage demagogy and extremism and provide mediation in times of crisis and conflict. It would also constitute a pool of talent from which effective democratic leaders would be drawn.

South Africa needs tough, resilient, and far-sighted black leaders drawn from organized constituencies such as political parties or large voluntary organizations that employ elective procedures. Leaders of this type are able to negotiate and compromise because they can take offers and options back to their constituencies for debate. On the other hand, symbolic leaders or spokesmen leaders, of which South Africa has a fair share, find it difficult to negotiate and compromise because they cannot gain ratification of their decisions from an organized following; having built their reputations on strong rhetoric, they have to continue it.

The private sector, liberal political parties, and voluntary organizations have a role to play in training community organizers assisting fledgling community organizations. While the present government remains in power, they can also mediate on behalf of community organizations when conflicts with the authorities arise, thus helping to protect, in however limited a way, community leadership from security action which in the past has destroyed much potentially constructive leadership. Community organizations and their leaders must be allowed independence and must be free from manipulation, both by government and liberal organizations. In particular, blacks must be left alone to choose their own leaders and not have the boundaries of community organizations dictated to them by outsiders.

(8) *The protection of human rights.* This issue is exceedingly problematic in a society in which the scope of inequality stimulates large numbers of people to contemplate open insurrection. In a period of transition

toward a more open society, the high expectations of those committed to an unqualified democracy in the short run will be actively opposed to what they will see as incomplete or gradualist reforms limiting their own bargaining strength. In such a context the rights of individuals may be difficult to protect even with a justiciable bill of rights. A great deal of repressive legislation and practice will probably continue, as almost invariably happens with even major changes of regimes. Thus a review of security legislation is urgently needed, and consideration should be given to establishing a special tribunal of prominent people from all communities, as well as professional experts.

(9) *Reform in education.* It is generally assumed that democracies require voters with evaluative and critical minds. The system of education imposed by the South African government on blacks, with its well-known emphasis on rote learning and its enormous problems in attaining minimum standards of quality, certainly does not contribute to the development of the kind of independent thought our future society will need. This is also true, perhaps to lesser degrees, of white, colored, and Indian education.

Educational reform is urgent. In any castelike society in which categories of people are ascribed an inferior social status, education becomes a critically important pathway to self-worth and dignity. This is a basic reason why there is such an intense demand for a single department of education in South Africa. As long as educational systems are racially separated, education cannot claim to impart *universal* symbols of worth to blacks. Segregated education will also remain a focus of highly politicized discontent and unrest. Apart from the enormous technical problems that have to be overcome, such as shortages of qualified teachers, staff, and equipment, a single department of education with the supreme symbolic reassurance of universal claims to worth and dignity is completely unavoidable as a basis for political development in our society.

(10) *Economic growth.* Without growth of gross domestic product approaching 5 percent or more, sustained as an average until the turn of the century, political reform and progress toward human rights will be significantly impeded. Under conditions of slow growth a white government, or white representatives in a multiracial government, will be powerfully constrained by the possibility of negative reactions from the white electorate, which will tend to resist any major redistribution of state expenditure toward blacks. Equally, under conditions of slow growth, it will obviously be much more difficult to reduce blacks' sense of deprivation. The tempo of black advancement in industry will be slowed down and the growth of a black middle class impeded. A sluggish economy will delay the emergence of the social preconditions

for the kind of natural checks, balances, and overlaps between political interest groups that are essential for the functioning of a democracy.

Organizations demanding change must therefore act as a lobby to encourage government policies that promote economic growth. This is not the place for a technical exposition of ways in which to promote growth, nor is the author qualified to give such an exposition. Among the many possible recommendations, however, one especially salient for liberalization is that the black private sector be equipped to participate in large-scale provision of infrastructure and housing in urban and periurban areas. The housing backlog is probably now in excess of 700,000 units.[4] Utmost flexibility of standards must be accepted and low-interest loans must be given on a large scale for the upgrading of shacks and the building of core houses and owner-builder homes in "site and service" schemes, in which local authorities provide building sites and lay on services. In the creation of infrastructure, black labor contractors should be used to attain the greatest possible labor intensity and creation of jobs. Such a program would stimulate independent black entrepreneurship, meet basic community needs, and stimulate job creation and economic growth—all at the same time.

All the steps suggested above will take some time. However, given the enormous and dangerous pressures on the South African economy and government, both from within the country and abroad, any undue time lag could cause serious damage to South Africa's capacity for change toward a more open, liberal society. The South African government must therefore take certain immediate steps to help restore faith in the reform process in South Africa and rebuild economic confidence. Commencement of visible negotiations between the government and significant and credible black leaders, and the unbanning of political organizations will be essential first steps. Negotiations will not be problem-free, and may be protracted, but as an interim step while a new constitutional order is being negotiated, the government could offer membership in the cabinet to the black leadership groups that establish themselves as negotiating partners. Leadership so incorporated into the daily business of government could play a valuable role in facilitating the process of constitutional negotiation. Nothing less than a set of moves with such keynote symbolic significance could establish the credibility which the reform process in South Africa needs to succeed.

Open democracies on the Western model are by no means the final answer to problems of human development. However, no alternative

4. See *Vaderland* editorial, 21 August 1986, for housing backlogs in the common area. If homeland urban areas are added, the total backlog would be well over 700,000.

system presently appears to offer a superior combination of general quality of life, freedom of expression, and protection from state oppression or bureaucratic constraints. Notwithstanding the "democratic centralist" rhetoric of socialist or one-party states, no alternative systems thus far have produced more widespread equality of access to effective power. The Western democratic system offers the one great advantage of a relative absence of a formalized concentration of power in a single institution—the state. This "pluralistic" principle of power is the goal toward which South Africa should strive. Pluralistic democracy at least provides opportunity for people at large to mobilize against inequality and constraints.

The challenge of working for democratic reform in South Africa is not exactly the same as working for what is termed "majority rule." A full democracy implies majority rule in one form or another, but majority rule is not necessarily a democracy, as we know from experience on every continent. Sir Arthur Lewis long ago reminded us in the context of West Africa that majority rule can operate on the principle of exclusion: "To exclude the losing groups from participation in decision-making clearly violates the primary meaning of democracy."[5] Majority rule is fully consonant with liberal democratic principles only where major parties or coalitions of parties are likely to be sufficiently balanced in strength to alternate in government. The way in which change occurs will be fundamental in ensuring the emergence of democratic forms in our society.

Liberalism in South Africa has been sustained substantially by values rooted in the social experiences of Europe and the United States, values drawn into South African political culture through external standards of reference which intellectuals, mainly English-speaking, have doggedly maintained. We must recognize that South African liberalism, however strongly we affirm the desirability of its goals, understandably appears to many as a neocolonial political culture, an ongoing means of sustaining European, South African white, and external dominance. The Cape liberal tradition was an import, and though it had a period of considerable influence before 1910, it withered during the emergence and consolidation of the modern South African state with its massive burden of intergroup tensions, and is held by some to have been merely an elaborate system of limited co-option.

If South African liberals are to promote the processes which will yield a democratic outcome, they will need a more indigenous social theory of liberalism than they have had so far. Without a rigorous liberal theory, fully applicable to South African conditions, liberals will remain vul-

5. Sir Arthur Lewis, *Politics in West Africa* (London: Allen & Unwin, 1965), pp. 64–65.

nerable to attack from the hitherto far more systematic white nationalists on the one hand and the revisionist or materialist intelligentsia on the other.

The work on democracy in plural societies or consociational democracy provides many of the building blocks for a South African liberal theory, but some of the prescriptions require elaboration and criticism in the light of a detailed examination of South Africa's political problems.[6] One example will suffice. Prominent in the proposals of the consociationalists is the idea of a political cartel or negotiated settlement between leaders of all segments in society. These segments are normally assumed to be ethnic. In South Africa, however, institutionalized ethnicity has been promoted mainly by white conservatives. How are black nonracial democrats or liberal whites to be mobilized and articulated into a negotiated resolution of intergroup conflict? This is where categories of relevance other than ethnic groups have to be identified in a South African context. Trade unions and employer organizations and possibly even professional associations have to be considered as political instruments in a democratically geared resolution of conflict to counterbalance the powerful ethnic or majoritarian mobilization on either side of the liberal position.

These and other problems of political development have to be intensively considered in developing a resilient theory of liberal change for South Africa. This essay is an attempt to encourage this process.

6. Lijphart, *Power-Sharing*, pp. 83–117.

F. Van Zyl Slabbert

24. Incremental Change or Revolution?

There is no reason why incremental change and revolution cannot contribute to one another. A preference for the one is no guarantee of the prevention of the other; to become prescriptive on the abstract merits of incremental change without relating them to the present processes of change going on in South Africa is a pointless exercise.

How one uses the word "change" in political discussion in South Africa has become a political litmus test for ideological preference, moral rectitude, and one's possible position of privilege and state of grace in postapartheid South Africa. A distinction must be drawn between planned and unplanned change: the first refers to deliberate attempts on the part of individuals, organizations, or movements to bring about or prevent a certain state of affairs in South Africa; the second to changes that cannot be ascribed to any individual, organization, or movement, but nevertheless impinge on and create the context within which attempts at planned changes take place. Examples of the latter are population increase and migration, unemployment, agricultural and mineral prices, droughts and floods, and so on. Anyone who is confident about the outcome of planned change irrespective of the impact of unplanned changes is blessed with an extraordinary degree of faith and trust in luck.

It is precisely this faith and dependence on luck which underpins revolutionaries' confident commitment to planned change, and it is exactly these qualities which are far less prevalent in the timid designs of incrementalists. Incrementalists appear to be overwhelmed by the complex interrelations of factors involved in any successful attempt at planned change and particularly by lack of control over them in such a social experiment. Revolutionaries—left and right—are driven by their conviction that a number of strategic factors hold the key to success; their entire plan is geared to getting control over them. Incrementalists thrive in a liberal democratic environment where there is a multiparty political system, checks and balances against the abuse of power, and a free flow of information. In such a society, academics with competing points of view, as well as professional experts, can bombard policy planners with as much information as possible, almost compelling them to take into account "all relevant facts" before embarking on a program of change. Politicians invariably opt for the (s)lowest common denominator so as not to alienate constituencies. In such an environment, the revolutionary invariably comes across as being silly, immature, and marginal.

However, in a repressive, nondemocratic environment, left or right, the roles are reversed and the revolutionary comes into his own. The incrementalist becomes the defender wittingly or unwittingly of "the system," "regime," or oppressors. The revolutionary has no difficulty in ridiculing the incrementalist's cautious prescriptions for change when viewed in the light of the enormity of present injustice and oppressions and the need for radical "total" change. The incrementalist may be correct about the desirability of caution but politically irrelevant; the revolutionary appears highly relevant precisely because he has thrown caution to the wind.

I think liberals in South Africa are going to have to prevent incrementalism from becoming an albatross around their necks in today's increasingly repressive and undemocratic society. Incrementalism as an approach to planned change above all presupposes power to influence such change, or at least the influence to affect those who have such power. If liberals have neither, their insistence on incrementalism simply becomes a futile bleating that clouds their whole position. Surely one is not a liberal only because one believes in incremental change. To insist on this in the South African context is to emasculate the contribution liberal thinking can make in the struggle against domination and repression. Moreover, it forces the liberal into a futile defense of incremental change whenever challenged by the revolutionary alternative. I say futile because if those who govern are determined to maintain their dominance and extend oppression, there is no way that anyone can explain with any degree of plausibility to oppressed people how to get rid of their oppression incrementally.

To concede that planned incremental change appears not to be possible in a particular period is not to abandon its validity in all circumstances nor to succumb to the inevitability of the revolutionary alternative. Liberals have to judge whether or not a planned policy change originating from government would promote liberal principles and values. What do liberals do if the planned incremental change extends totalitarian control? Do they choose to influence the totalitarianism of the regime they know because they wish to avoid the totalitarianism of the revolutionary they fear?

Nothing is easier than dichotomizing complex situations and forcing either/or choices on people. South African society is caught up in a process of polarization that has developed increased momentum over the last three or four years. As is inevitable in such a process, issues become focused and choices crystallize. Not that they have not been there before, but now there is a greater urgency to make choices which appear to be irreversible. This is so because once certain choices have been made they almost automatically involve one in broader, more general, processes of change. One has much less control over these broader processes than over one's initial choice, so what starts off as a fairly straightforward, even morally unambiguous, decision very soon involves one in issues and problems that become very complex. However, despite the complexity of the issues and because of the polarization in which they arise, people often expect simple yes or no answers to solving them. Consider the following: "Do you oppose apartheid laws or support them?" "Do you oppose compulsory racial/ethnic group membership or support it?" These are simple questions and it is not difficult to answer them. But what about: "Are you helping to maintain or to dismantle apartheid?" or "Are you strenghtening those who oppose or those who maintain apartheid?"

These more difficult questions cannot be resolved by academic discussion. In a broad sense there is a choice between the "struggle for freedom" and opposition to that struggle, between "liberation" and "oppression," or between "stability" and "freedom." These choices are being starkly posed in recent disputes in South Africa, and though they lack academic neatness, they are politically real. One comes across them in talking to militant township children, church leaders, community organizers, politically aware businesspeople, and Afrikaner student leaders. The fact that across such a spectrum this distinction has been given the status of conventional wisdom does not give it absolute moral or logical authority, but it is nevertheless increasingly the choice that is being presented to organizations, political parties, and movements. It is the natural inclination of the academic to qualify, reformulate, and complicate choices of this kind, and this is right and proper. But this is a luxury denied the politician. To the extent that a liberal wishes to be a politician, he or she is going to have to make an overt political choice.

On the one side "stability," on the other, "freedom"; on the one side repression, on the other, liberation. The government has appropriated "stability," together with its own interpretations of concepts such as "negotiation," "reform," "constitutional change," and "consensus," and has effectively debased them as instruments of incremental change by linking them to repression. The "struggle" has appropriated "freedom," together with "people's power," "liberation," "justice," "equality," "boycotts," and "sanctions," and has very effectively inflated them as instruments of revolutionary change. The traditional liberal political response would be to say: "I like this on that side and this on the other and dislike the following in both" and then proceed to present a coherent and rational alternative position to a potential constituency. Unfortunately, there is no such coherent and rational constituency of any significance available in our present polarized situation. The primary question now that liberals are forced to face is: "Where do you stand in the struggle? For freedom or stability?" They may refuse to choose by calling a plague on the irrationality of both houses and hover around in a fit of sullen irrelevancy. If they do, the struggle for freedom will become the exclusive preserve of the revolutionary, and the maintenance of stability the preserve of increasing repression.

Why has this choice become so urgent from the liberal position? Why now? Traditionally the role that presented itself has been that of mediator, negotiator, conciliator: to work for a society in which the *freedom* of the individual was the basic source of *stability* in society, and to show that the confrontation between *stability* and *freedom* was a basic contradiction that could be resolved by rational people of goodwill. To understand why this position is no longer credible or possible in South Africa, one has to understand some of the developments that have taken place over the last three years.

The new constitution approved in the 1983 referendum among white voters finally destroyed the possibility that fundamental change could occur constitutionally in any conventional sense of the word. The constitution's exclusion of blacks from the new tricameral Parliament, its entrenchment of key apartheid laws, and its creation of a powerful executive president precipitated a process of mass political mobilization against it which has not abated. The constitution was seen as a crude attempt at co-optive domination—which it is—and any attempt at cooperation with or acceptance of it was stigmatized as collaboration by the excluded Africans and by most coloreds and Asians.

I experienced this first hand as leader of the Progressive Federal party (PFP)[1] when I argued the case for participation on a "give it a chance" basis. That party explored "selling itself" in the other two chambers (so-called colored and Indian), only to meet with determined rejection by the communities involved and by most extraparliamentary organizations which opposed the implementation of the constitution. The PFP tried to create a coalition between extraparliamentary forces and itself in order to apply pressure on the government. This was the idea behind the National Convention Movement. Apart from the participation of Inkatha in the venture, which was cited by some organizations as an objection to participation, the PFP involvement in the tricameral Parliament was the other principal objection.

Up until the implementation of the new constitution, the PFP sought a "balance of power" position in white politics in which it could force the government to choose between "doing a deal" with the PFP or with the parties of the ultra right wing. In order to achieve this leverage, a minimum of 25 percent of white electoral support was necessary. The 1983 referendum showed how fickle "soft" support for the PFP was when there was a desertion from its ranks to the government's "yes-vote." The loss of support was from 21 percent of the white electorate in the 1981 election to 16.5 percent in the constitutional referendum of November 1983. Apart from praying for some kind of miracle whereby "left-wing" government MPs do a deal with the PFP, and assuming a compliant and cooperative security structure (a huge assumption), it is not clear what other possible strategies for constitutional leverage are left for a parliamentary opposition working for a liberal democracy.

Ironically, one of the few times the PFP has gained in credibility since 1983 was when some of its members actively identified with those in "the struggle," suffered with them, and took up their causes. I say ironically because such identification usually took place at the cost of electoral support and therefore of strengthening a constitutional base. Molly Blackburn, a provincial representative of the PFP in the Eastern Cape, was adopted by blacks as "the mother of the people" for fearlessly championing their cause. Others in the PFP representation in Parliament have begun to do the same, thus continuing the protesting role made famous by Helen Suzman over thirty-five years. To use Parliament as a forum for protesting against apartheid and as an institutional base to intervene on behalf of those who are persecuted and abused is a

1. The PFP is not the Liberal or even *a* liberal party. It certainly inherited some aspects of South African political liberalism, but its history is far too diverse and complicated simply to depict it as a pure liberal party. It is nevertheless committed to the creation of a liberal democracy in South Africa, and as such is the closest example of a conventional liberal political party in the current situation.

legitimate and defensible strategy. But this role should not be confused with that of presenting Parliament as an effective instrument for constitutional change. Obviously, to use Parliament as a forum for protest and a forum for change need not be mutually exclusive. In "normal" parliamentary politics they are usually complementary. But in the South African context we find that the more authoritarian the political system becomes, the more relevant Parliament as a forum for protest may be but the less relevant as a forum for conventional constitutional change. There is little cheer in promoting Parliament as the only forum for protest simply because all other forums have been ruthlessly suppressed.

Whether Parliament is, or becomes, a forum for change does not only depend on a liberal opposition, but particularly on what government does and how it relates to Parliament. As far as government itself is concerned, the following was its contribution to the destruction of constitutionalism since 1983:

First, the executive presidency immediately began to function more independently from Parliament and in close association with the security apparatus. It is not quite correct to say that the state Security Council is the real inner cabinet, but its function and structure creates the organizational base from which a small group of key individuals can meet regularly and make fundamental decisions of policy. Shifts in regional and domestic policy are decided in this way and not in the conventional cabinet-to-caucus-to-Parliament manner. It was quite apparent to me that more than once in Parliament the National party caucus heard of key policy shifts no sooner than the opposition. Thus one of the important consequences of tricameral politics is the creation of an executive/security presidency which operates increasingly independently of Parliament. This is the effective government of the moment.

Second, the government has no compunction in lying, misleading, or withholding vital information from Parliament. More and more, Parliament has become a constitutional laundry machine for the legislative designs of the executive. Nothing shows up this contemptuous attitude more clearly than the passage in June 1986 of two security bills that had been rejected by the colored and the Indian houses and were thereafter made into law with the assistance of the president's council, which has a built-in Nationalist majority and can be invoked to break deadlocks when there is disagreement among the three houses. While the government waited for this legislative process to run its course, it declared a state of emergency in order to achieve what Parliament had temporarily frustrated.

Third, the government decided to use the South African Defence Force on a more or less permanent basis in the suppression of unrest in the black communities. "Bringing the troops from the border to the townships" was a crucial shift that militarized an already polarized situation. The fact that most of the unrest was due to key aspects of apartheid policy and was a reaction to tricameral politics stripped the South African Defence Force of any neutral "shield" function. Its role became almost irretrievably politicized. Whatever the official protestations to the contrary, the South African Defence Force was seen by the vast majority as partisan in the conflict. The kind of "stability" it was assisting the police to maintain was seen as a threat to the "freedom" of those involved in the struggle and not a precondition for achieving it. Once this happens, constitutionalism becomes even further discredited. These actions by government were in response to, and had been precipitated by, certain actions in extraparliamentary politics. The period 1983–1986 saw a mass mobilization of opposition to government that is unique in the country's history.

Being mobilized is not the same as being organized, and the struggle for the latter is still going on, but the extent of deliberate rejection of government policy and what it stands for is wider and deeper than ever before. The African National Congress is seen as the flagship of the struggle, but it does not represent a tightly knit, rigid approach and it accommodates a diversity of points of view and strategies. Within the boundaries of the struggle there are competing theories on revolution, the class struggle, decolonization, violence, sanctions, free enterprise, and degrees of socialism. But a common culture of resistance is beginning to take shape within which a clearer definition of what it means to belong to the struggle is developing. Once more those in the resistance movement pose questions of stark simplicity: "Are you prepared to identify with the struggle?" "Are you prepared to sacrifice and suffer for the struggle?" "Are you prepared to help communities that are victimized?" "Are you prepared to protest against or resist those who oppose the struggle?"

These questions are seemingly empty of ideological content. When one digs behind them, certain ground rules and demands become clear: no collaboration with those who govern; no participation in government-created constitutional structures; unbanning of banned organizations; release of political prisoners; an unqualified commitment to a nonracial democracy.

Thus the polarization is almost complete, those concerned with *stability* showing scant respect for constitutionalism and those concerned with *freedom* matching their unconcern. It is not a climate in which mediation and incrementalism thrives, and that is why liberals face problems of choice and of redefinition of their role. This dilemma will deepen as government itself has to reckon with diminishing options.

One of them is becoming increasingly obvious and bears some consideration.

What does the government do when its official policy collapses? It experiences increasing internal dissent and external isolation; there is a flight of capital and economic decline. If the government is determined to maintain its position of control and relative dominance, it settles for siege, a massive extension of coercive control. This must form the basic infrastructure of whatever stability the government wishes to maintain under such circumstances. But simple repression is not a durable solution from the government's point of view. It is well aware of the domestic and international costs, although the decision to settle for siege is a clear indication that for the time being the government prefers to downplay the relevance of the external factor. The government cannot even tentatively explore a possible democratic solution, because if its intentions were sincere such a solution would lead inexorably to its own demise. The only strategy apart from continuing brutal repression must be co-optive domination.

Co-optive domination means an extension of the philosophy of the tricameral system whereby statutorily designated categories of people previously excluded from the center of power and decision-making are included (co-opted) to assist in the administration of the state machinery without effectively threatening the position of dominance of the white minority. In fact, ever since the implementation of the tricameral system, the search has been on for a different and effective co-optive strategy for blacks. As one government spokesman said during the 1983 referendum: "We first have to settle the Coloured and Indian problem, then we will look after the blacks."[2] Of course, the homelands policy is a co-optive strategy, but that was co-option *away* from the center, whereas the new focus is on co-option *into* the center of power.

The unfolding of this co-optive strategy is taking place on three levels that are more or less related, but not neatly synchronized with one another. There does not appear to be an evil genius who with Machiavellian cunning is coordinating this strategy on the various levels. The first level is that of ideology. The government has abandoned the homeland policy, accepted black permanence in the urban areas, desegregated aspects of social life, scrapped influx control, acknowledged black trade unions, and so on. The new emphasis is on one citizenship, one constitution, and one united geographic South Africa. It is on this level that most of the confusion has been generated about the pace,

2. This was told to me privately by a government MP when we shared the same platform during the 1983 referendum on the constitution.

direction, and extent of "reform" that the government has promised. The government voices concepts which have more or less accepted meanings in most of the Western world, but their own special meaning in South Africa. This was, I believe, an important reason why the Commonwealth Eminent Persons Group mission aborted. The leaders came in all good faith to help the government achieve its declared goal of getting rid of apartheid and negotiating an alternative, but soon found out that the ideological abandonment of apartheid is not the same as abdicating political control and dominance by the government. Ways and means had to be found to accommodate black South Africans without losing control over the machinery of state.

The second level on which the co-optive strategy revealed itself was the *constitutional* one. At first the government invited black leaders to come and talk. None of significant status came forward. Then it announced the creation of a nonstatutory forum to "discuss a wide range of constitutional issues." Again, no significant response. In the meantime it legislated regional service councils in which black, colored, Indian, and white local authorities could send representatives to "discuss matters of common concern." In 1986 legislation was passed to create a National Statutory Council, with the president himself as chairman, to deliberate on constitutional matters. In the meantime, provincial councils have been scrapped and substituted with a nominated system whereby, at the pleasure of the state president, "even a black can become Administrator." Multiracial provincial executives have been nominated to take over those functions of the former provincial councils which have not been shifted to other constitutional forums. There is also a lot of loose talk about the reorganization of the president's council to include blacks and others into a government of national unity. In many black townships, factionalism and division between different groups have developed. It is difficult to present a clear-cut distinction for all situations, but in squatter communities like Crossroads, for example, fierce conflict developed between the more traditional, less politicized elements as well as beneficiaries of the old system (known as vigilantes or "*Witdoeke*"[3]) on the one hand, and those who protested and opposed the old system and wished to work for a new one (known as the Comrades) on the other. The government's intervention on behalf of the "vigilante" groups in their battles against the "Comrades" is no doubt the first step toward reestablishing some kind of co-optive control on the local government level. It is also the level at which problems of control are most acute.

3. Literally "white cloths," which they wore on their heads or arms for identification during fights.

The third level of co-optive strategy concerns co-optation into the *security* structure. *The White Paper on Defence,* tabled during the 1986 session of Parliament, gave a clear hint that the government was considering extending its drive to blacks to join the army on a volunteer basis. Similarly, the minister of police, Louis le Grange, was quoted in the *Cape Times* of 12 November 1985 as saying that the South African police—its present strength is 60,000—is to be enlarged by an additional 40,000 members, almost doubling its manpower. Granted that comparatively speaking South Africa does not have a large police force, it is quite obvious that such expansion will see more and more blacks entering here as well. A career in the security structure need not be seen as co-optation in the same sense as the other two levels, but in a situation of enduring siege it certainly becomes an integral part of the strategy of co-optive domination.

On all three levels the development of strategy is toward the creation of a multiracial *autocracy* rather than a nonracial *democracy.* A refinement of this strategy over the next few years could very well see, first, a complete liberalization of apartheid laws, except for those that underpin political dominance, thereby deracializing the conflict as much as possible. Second, there could be a progressive suspension of "normal" popular civil government and a creation of more and more nominated/co-opted structures in order to form a "government of national unity" which has to function as a "crisis" government in order to "normalize" and "stabilize" the situation. Third, the government's role as employer will take on increasing importance in a time of declining economic base, and development of security may well become a "growth industry." One can expect a significant degree of affirmative action for blacks in the army and police force. Finally, there could be an appeal, on a propaganda level, for *all* responsible, moderate, and reasonable South Africans to stand together in South Africa's hour of crisis. The argument could be that the choice is between orderly progress toward a democratic South Africa in which the values of Western civilization and free enterprise can be preserved or a socialist dictatorship under Soviet control brought about by a revolutionary destruction of the resources without which South Africans cannot build a new future.

Thus, on the one hand, there could be a *multiracial autocracy* brought about through a strategy of *co-optive domination* in order to maintain *stability* through transition; on the other, a struggle for *freedom* by the masses in order to bring about a *negotiated, nonracial democracy.* What these negotiations will be about, if and when they take place, depends on the duration of the struggle and the level of destruction of human and natural resources. These appear to be the political choices that have crystallized in the process of polarization going on in South Africa at the moment. Where is liberal politics going to position itself? Is it going to choose the "politics of stability" or the "politics of freedom"? Which side is most likely to be influenced toward realizing a liberal democracy in the future?

One thing seems evident. If the choice is for stability, then liberal politics because of its co-option into the establishment will lose all influence in grass-roots extraparliamentary politics. If it is for freedom, it can begin to expect increasing persecution and harassment from the establishment. Whether it chooses freedom or stability, it can expect derision and abuse from the revolutionary—if *freedom,* it will be accused of wanting to dilute, divert, or hijack the revolution; if *stability,* it will be accused of propping up the system of repression and undermining the revolution.

I believe the consequences of the choice should be secondary to the commitment to humane values traditionally associated with liberal movements. If one accepts that part of the liberal political tradition is to oppose the destruction of civil rights and the denial of the dignity of the human being, there is not really much of a choice for liberals. The worst that can be done is to plead the merits of incremental change in an attempt to postpone the decision.

Index